Itsuwaribito・空・

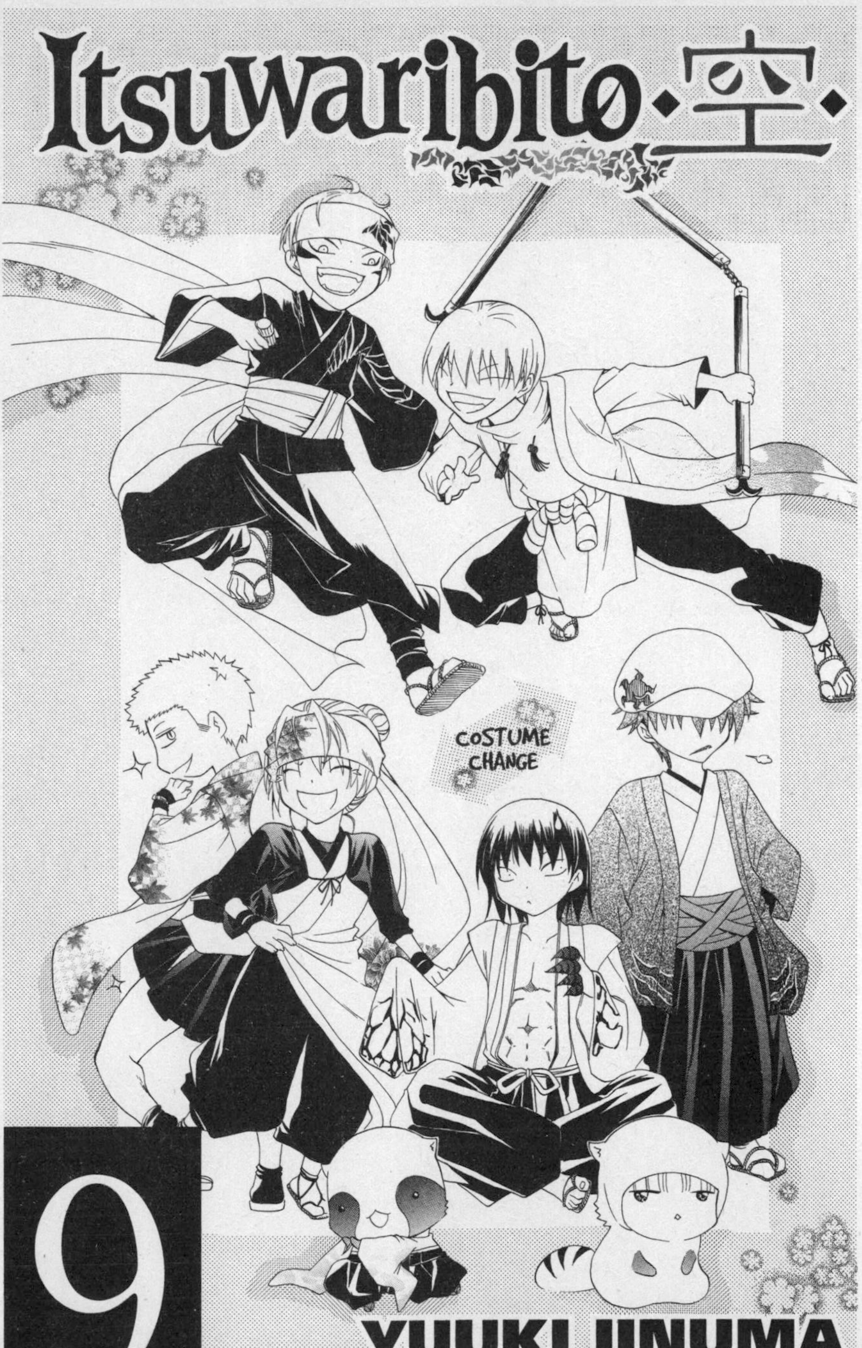
COSTUME
CHANGE

9

YUUKI IINUMA

Contents

Chapter 78 Escape

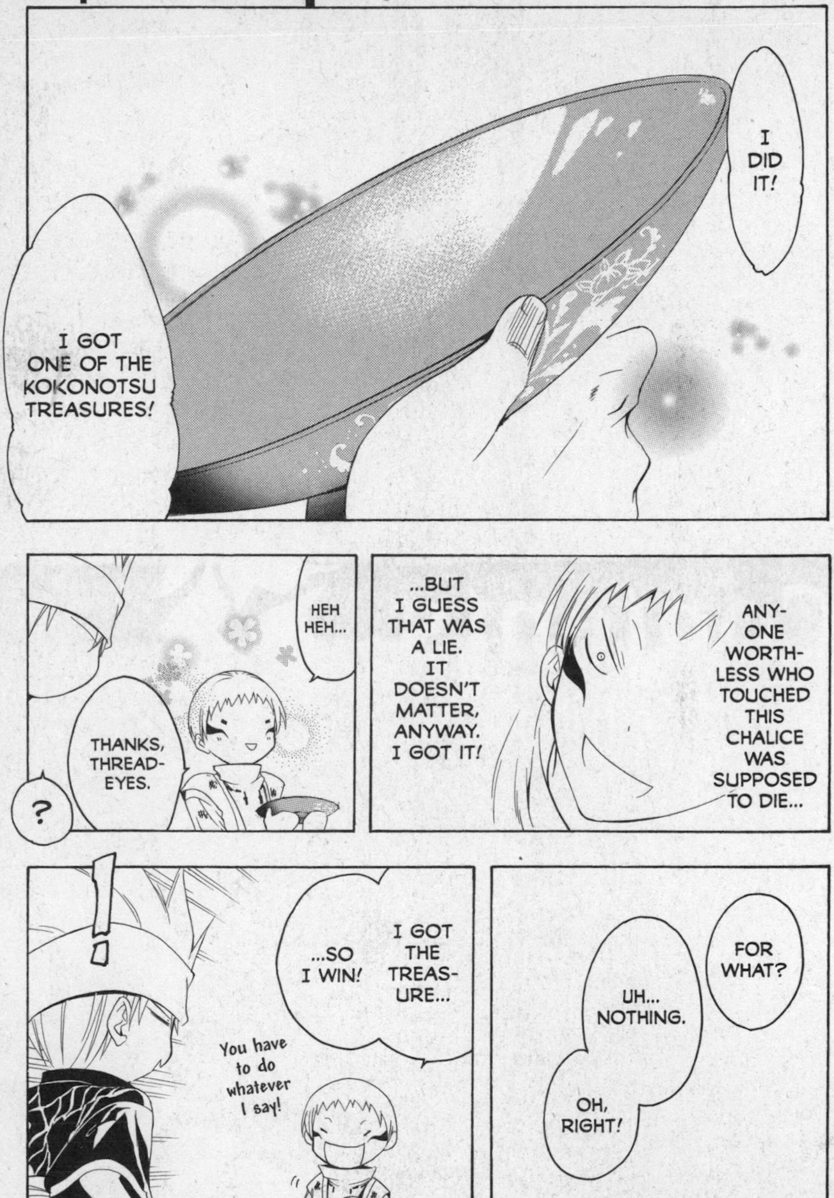
I DID IT!
I GOT ONE OF THE KOKONOTSU TREASURES!
ANYONE WORTHLESS WHO TOUCHED THIS CHALICE WAS SUPPOSED TO DIE...
...BUT I GUESS THAT WAS A LIE. IT DOESN'T MATTER, ANYWAY. I GOT IT!
HEH HEH...
THANKS, THREAD-EYES.
?
FOR WHAT?
UH... NOTHING.
OH, RIGHT!
!
I GOT THE TREASURE...
...SO I WIN!
You have to do whatever I say!

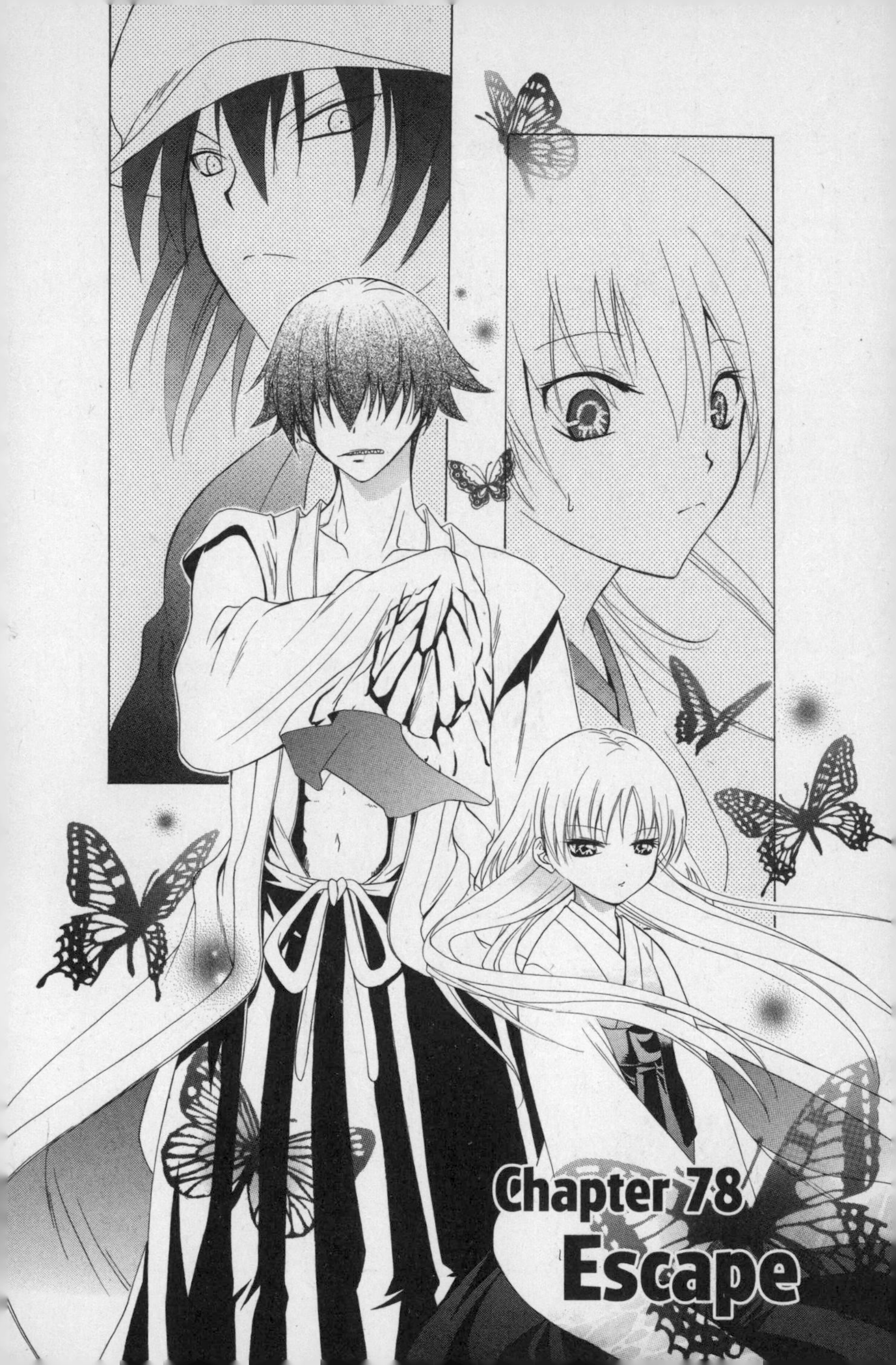
Chapter 78
Escape

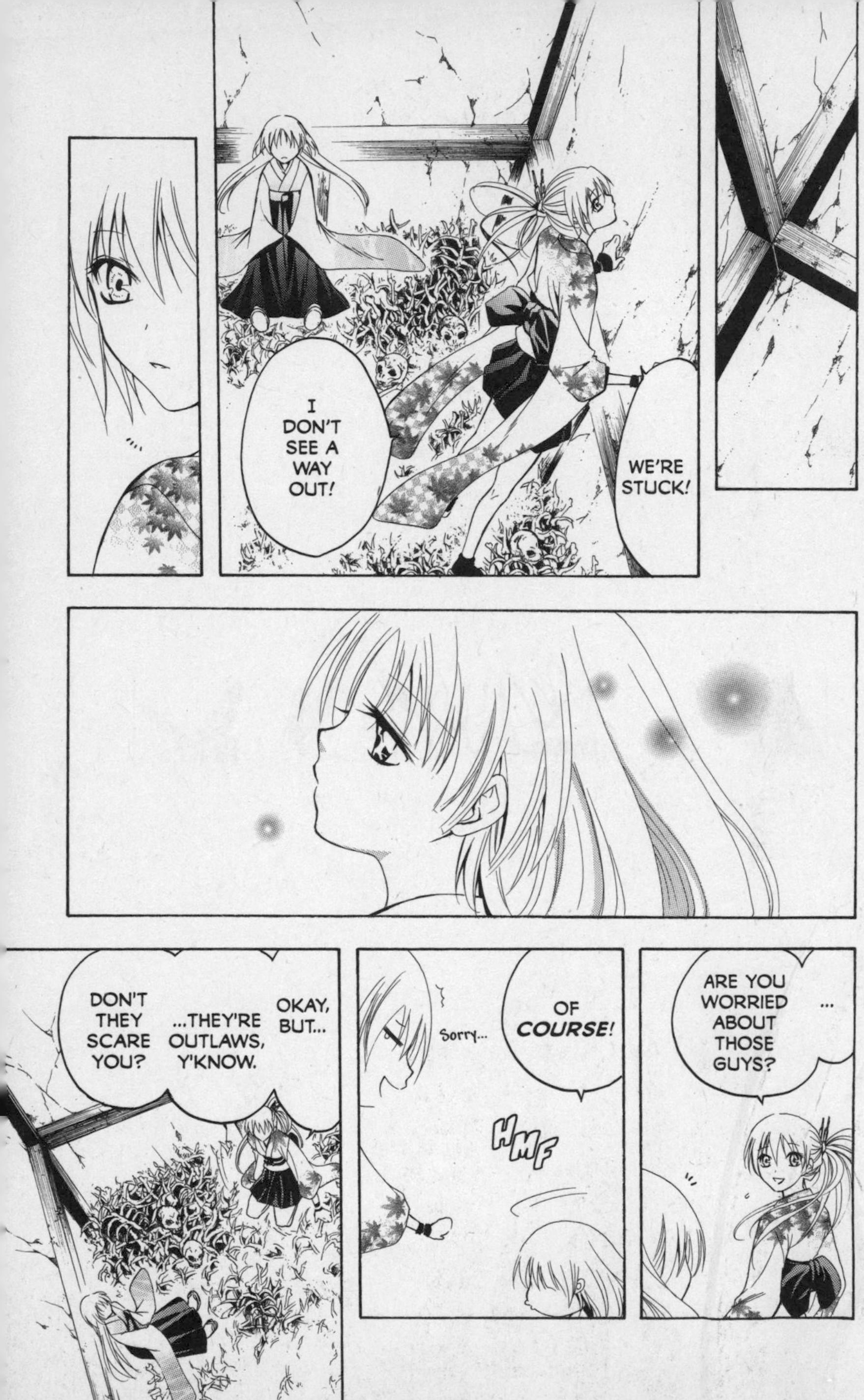
WE'RE STUCK!
I DON'T SEE A WAY OUT!
...
ARE YOU WORRIED ABOUT THOSE GUYS?
OF COURSE!
Sorry...
HMF
OKAY, BUT...
...THEY'RE OUTLAWS, Y'KNOW.
DON'T THEY SCARE YOU?

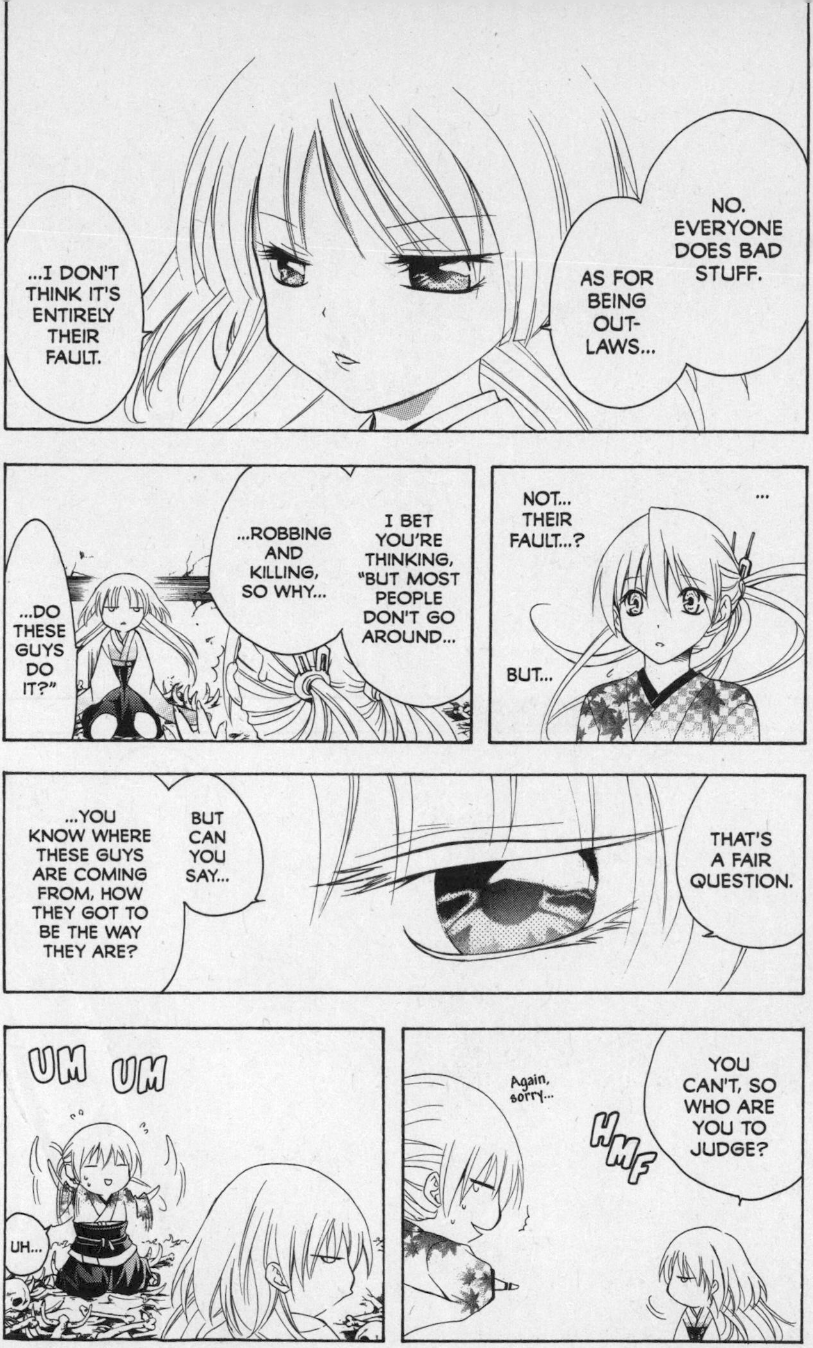
NO. EVERYONE DOES BAD STUFF.
AS FOR BEING OUT-LAWS...
...I DON'T THINK IT'S ENTIRELY THEIR FAULT.
...
NOT... THEIR FAULT...?
BUT...
I BET YOU'RE THINKING, "BUT MOST PEOPLE DON'T GO AROUND...
...ROBBING AND KILLING, SO WHY...
...DO THESE GUYS DO IT?"
THAT'S A FAIR QUESTION.
BUT CAN YOU SAY...
...YOU KNOW WHERE THESE GUYS ARE COMING FROM, HOW THEY GOT TO BE THE WAY THEY ARE?
YOU CAN'T, SO WHO ARE YOU TO JUDGE?
HMF
Again, sorry...
UM
UM
UH...

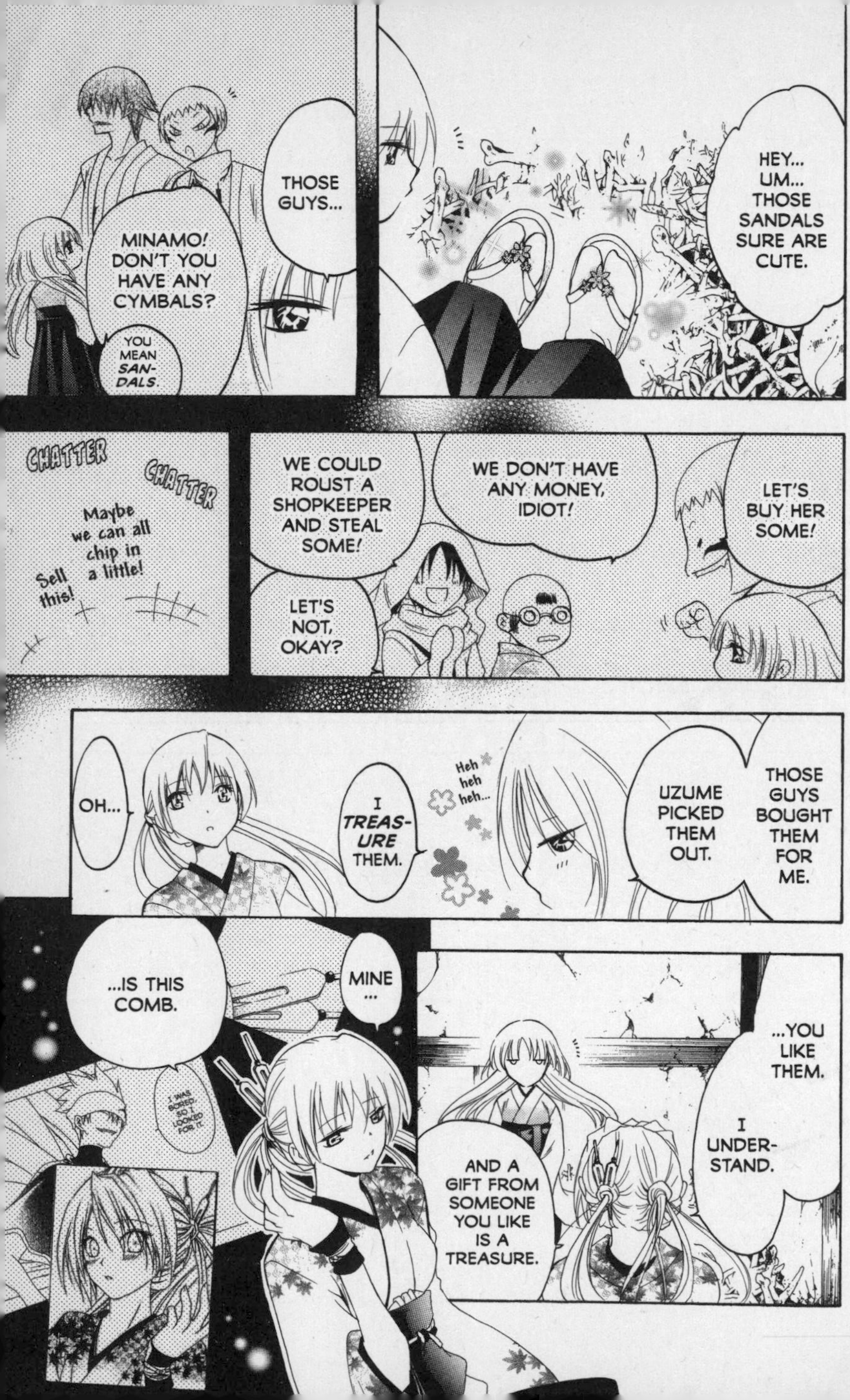
HEY... UM... THOSE SANDALS SURE ARE CUTE.
THOSE GUYS...
MINAMO! DON'T YOU HAVE ANY CYMBALS?
YOU MEAN SANDALS.
LET'S BUY HER SOME!
WE DON'T HAVE ANY MONEY, IDIOT!
WE COULD ROUST A SHOPKEEPER AND STEAL SOME!
LET'S NOT, OKAY?
CHATTER
CHATTER
Maybe we can all chip in a little!
Sell this!
THOSE GUYS BOUGHT THEM FOR ME.
UZUME PICKED THEM OUT.
Heh heh heh...
I TREASURE THEM.
OH...
...YOU LIKE THEM.
I UNDERSTAND.
AND A GIFT FROM SOMEONE YOU LIKE IS A TREASURE.
MINE...
...IS THIS COMB.
I WAS BORED, SO I LOOKED FOR IT.

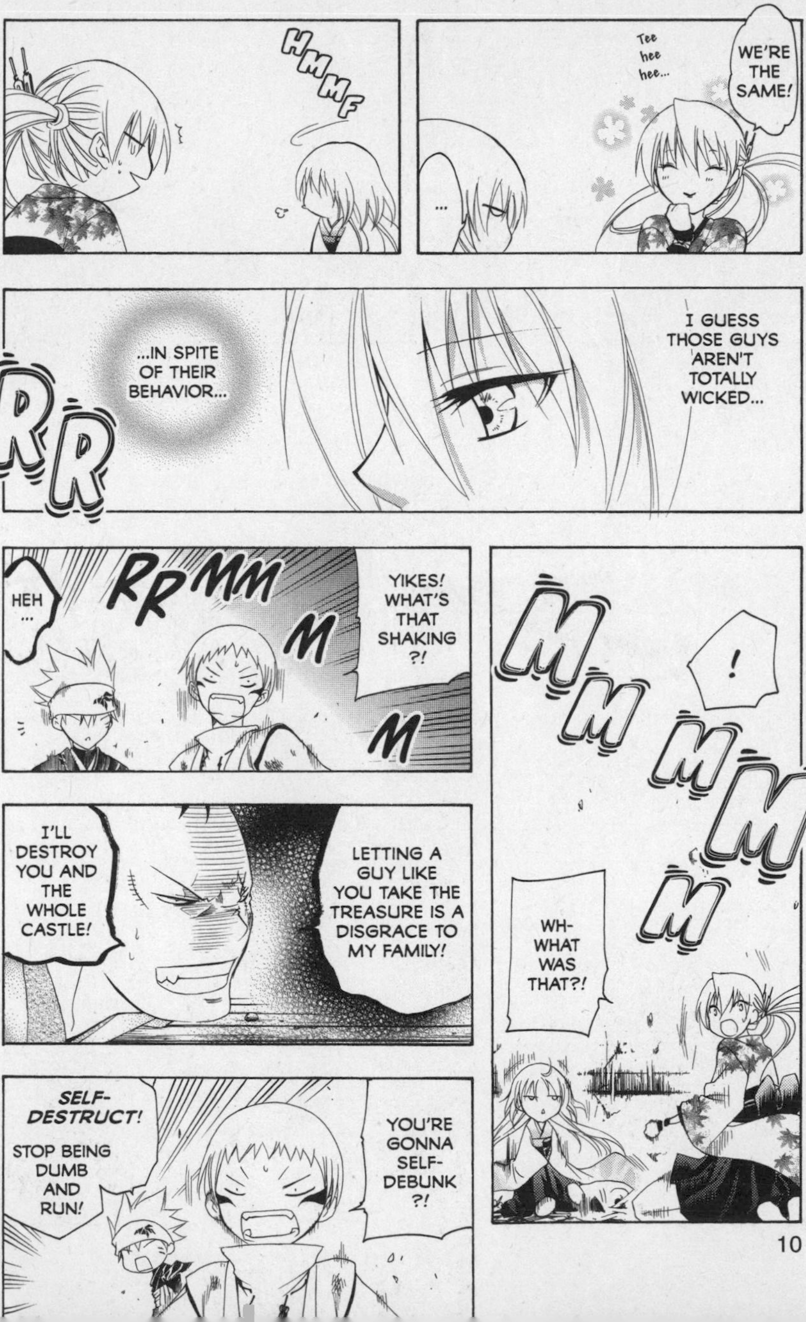
WE'RE THE SAME!
Tee hee hee...
...
HMMF
I GUESS THOSE GUYS AREN'T TOTALLY WICKED...
...IN SPITE OF THEIR BEHAVIOR...
RR
MMMMMM
!
WH-WHAT WAS THAT?!
YIKES! WHAT'S THAT SHAKING?!
HEH...
RRMMMMM
LETTING A GUY LIKE YOU TAKE THE TREASURE IS A DISGRACE TO MY FAMILY!
I'LL DESTROY YOU AND THE WHOLE CASTLE!
YOU'RE GONNA SELF-DEBUNK?!
SELF-DESTRUCT!
STOP BEING DUMB AND RUN!

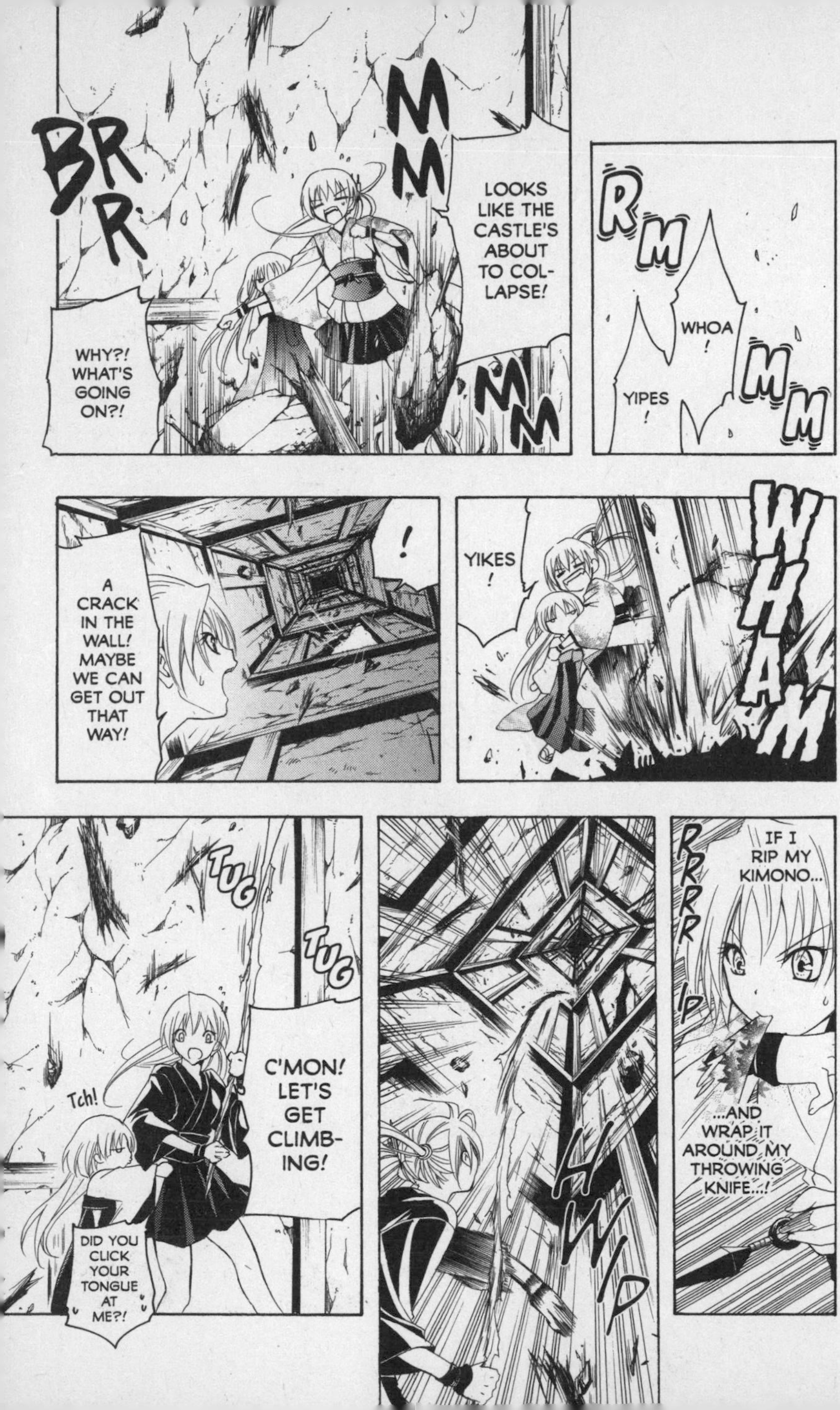
RMMMMM
WHOA!
YIPES!
MMMMM
LOOKS LIKE THE CASTLE'S ABOUT TO COL- LAPSE!
BRRR
MMM
WHY?! WHAT'S GOING ON?!
WHAM
YIKES!
!
A CRACK IN THE WALL! MAYBE WE CAN GET OUT THAT WAY!
RRRRIP
IF I RIP MY KIMONO...
...AND WRAP IT AROUND MY THROWING KNIFE...!
HWIP
TUG
TUG
C'MON! LET'S GET CLIMB- ING!
Tch!
DID YOU CLICK YOUR TONGUE AT ME?!

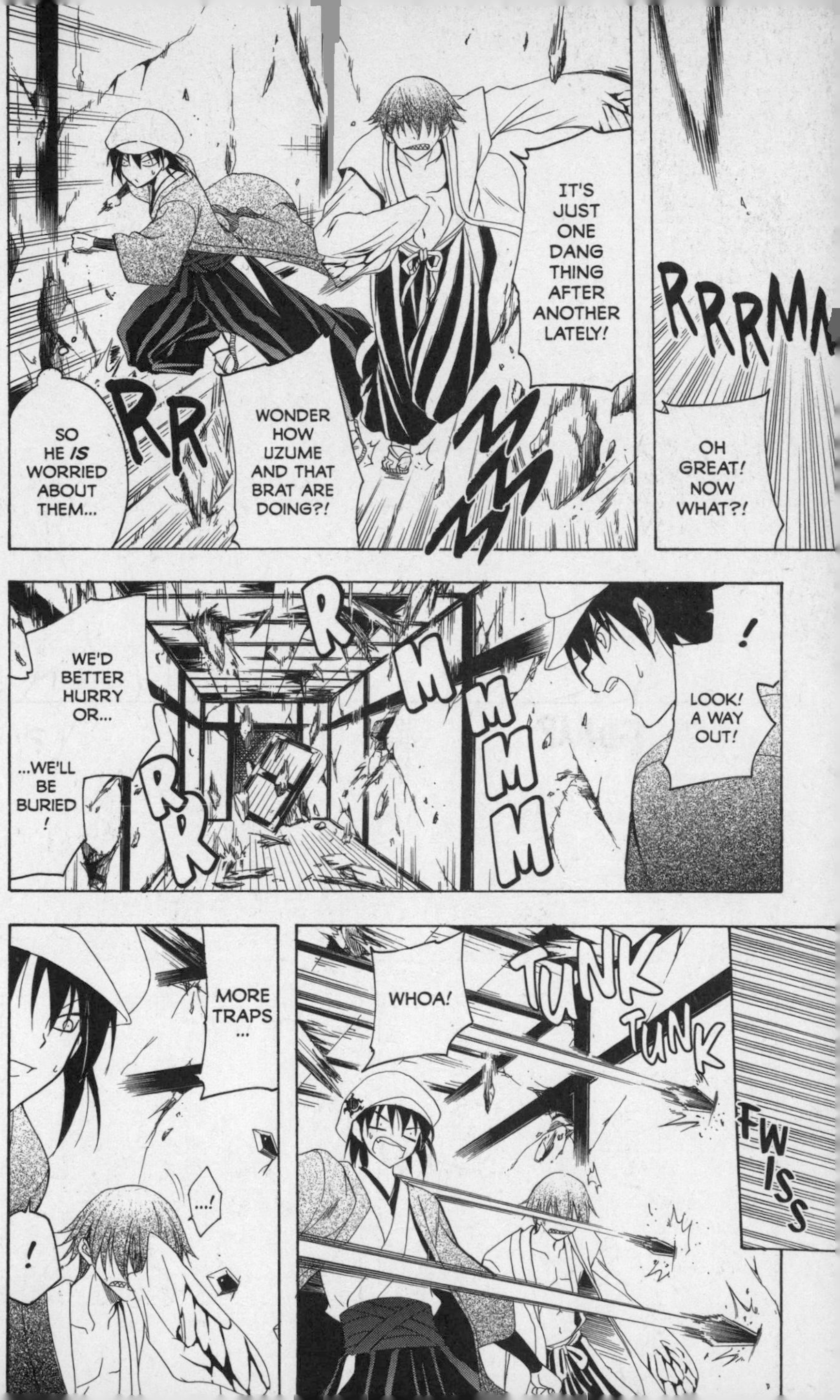
RRRM
OH GREAT! NOW WHAT?!
IT'S JUST ONE DANG THING AFTER ANOTHER LATELY!
WONDER HOW UZUME AND THAT BRAT ARE DOING?!
RR
SO HE *IS* WORRIED ABOUT THEM...
!
LOOK! A WAY OUT!
R
MMMMM
WE'D BETTER HURRY OR...
...WE'LL BE BURIED!
RR
TUNK
TUNK
FWISS
WHOA!
MORE TRAPS...
...!
!

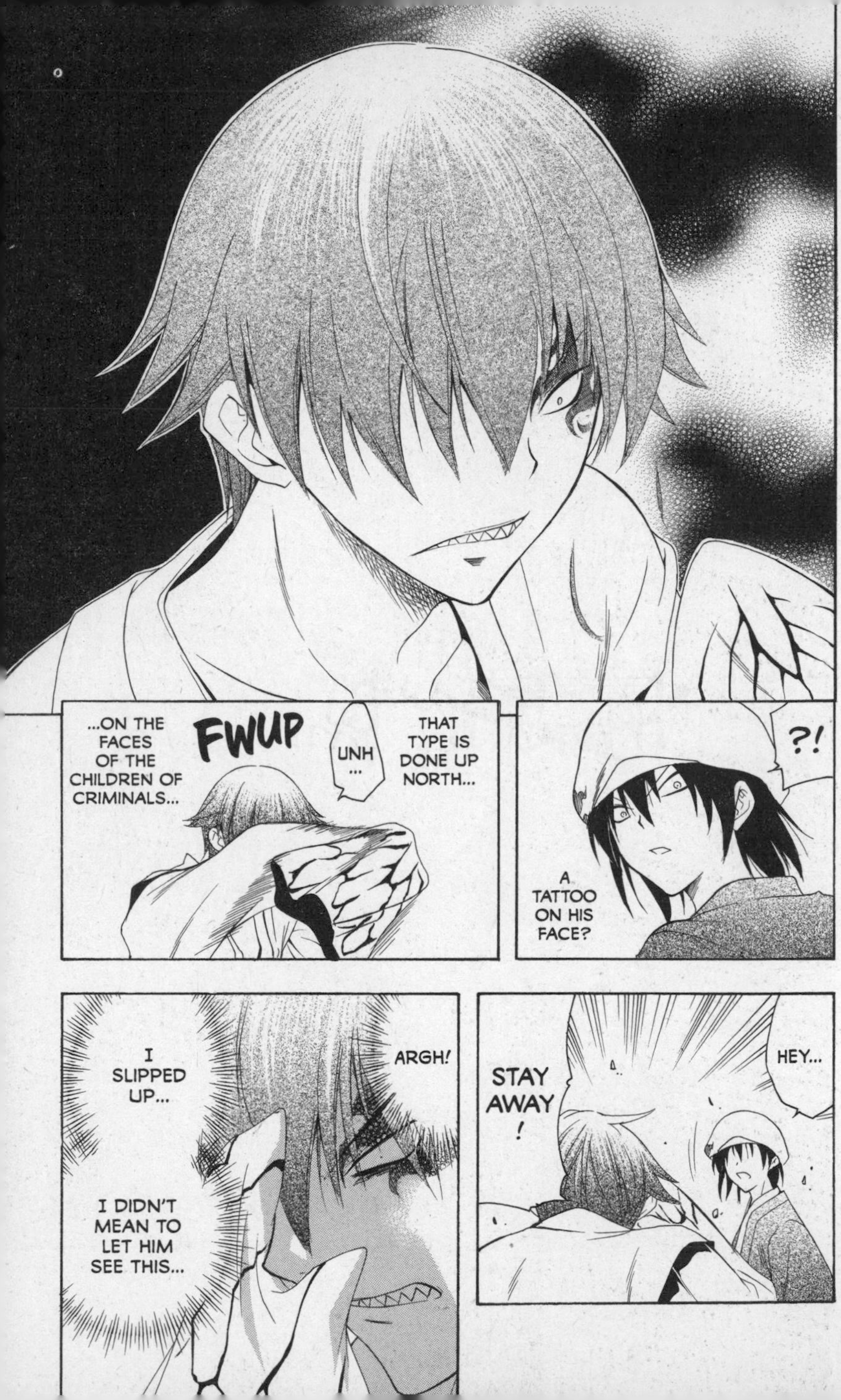
?!
A TATTOO ON HIS FACE?
THAT TYPE IS DONE UP NORTH...
UNH ...
FWUP
...ON THE FACES OF THE CHILDREN OF CRIMINALS...
HEY...
STAY AWAY!
ARGH!
I SLIPPED UP...
I DIDN'T MEAN TO LET HIM SEE THIS...

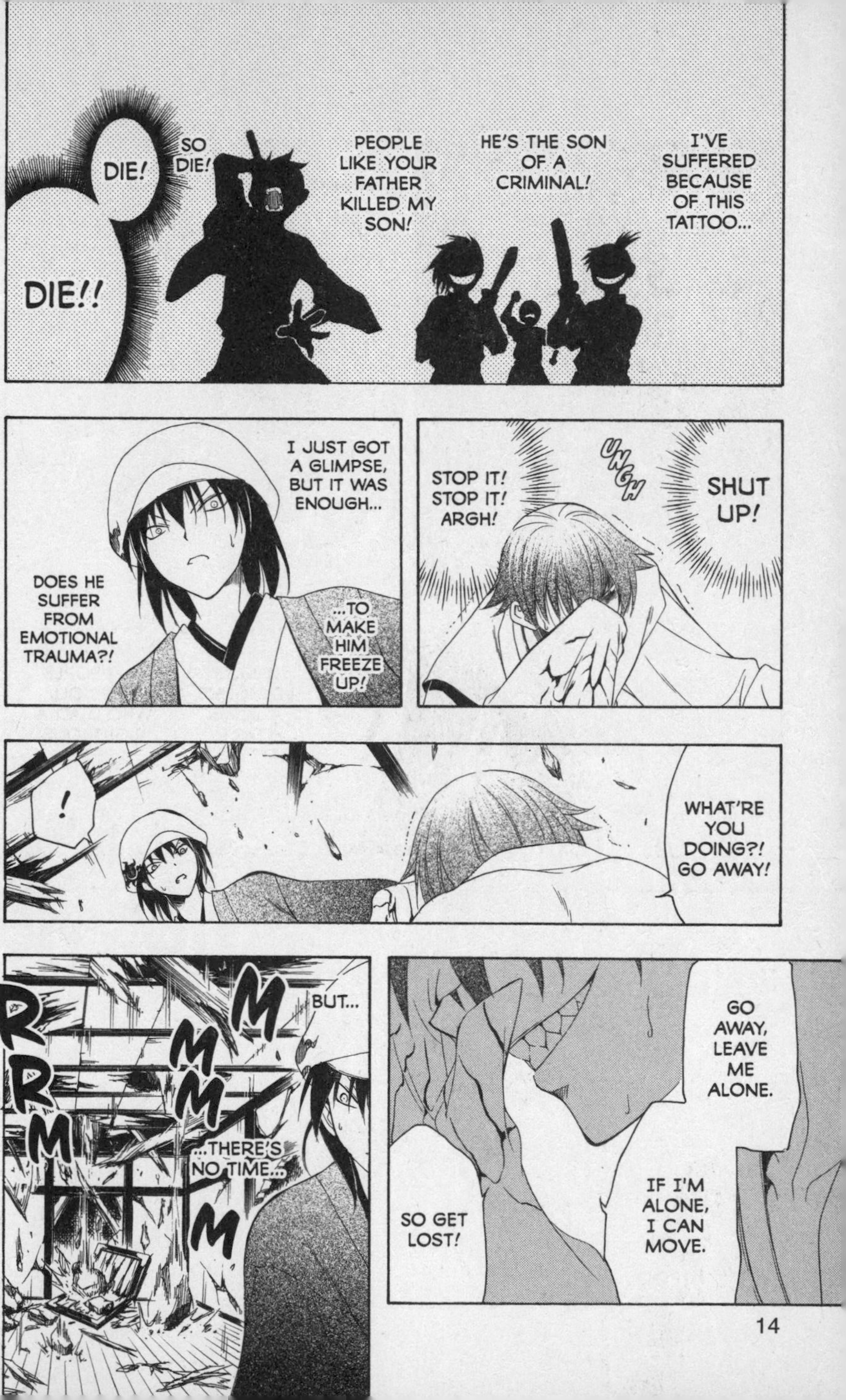
I'VE SUFFERED BECAUSE OF THIS TATTOO...
HE'S THE SON OF A CRIMINAL!
PEOPLE LIKE YOUR FATHER KILLED MY SON!
SO DIE!
DIE!
DIE!!
SHUT UP!
UNGH
STOP IT! STOP IT! ARGH!
I JUST GOT A GLIMPSE, BUT IT WAS ENOUGH...
...TO MAKE HIM FREEZE UP!
DOES HE SUFFER FROM EMOTIONAL TRAUMA?!
WHAT'RE YOU DOING?! GO AWAY!
!
GO AWAY, LEAVE ME ALONE.
IF I'M ALONE, I CAN MOVE.
SO GET LOST!
BUT...
...THERE'S NO TIME...
MMMMMM
RRRM

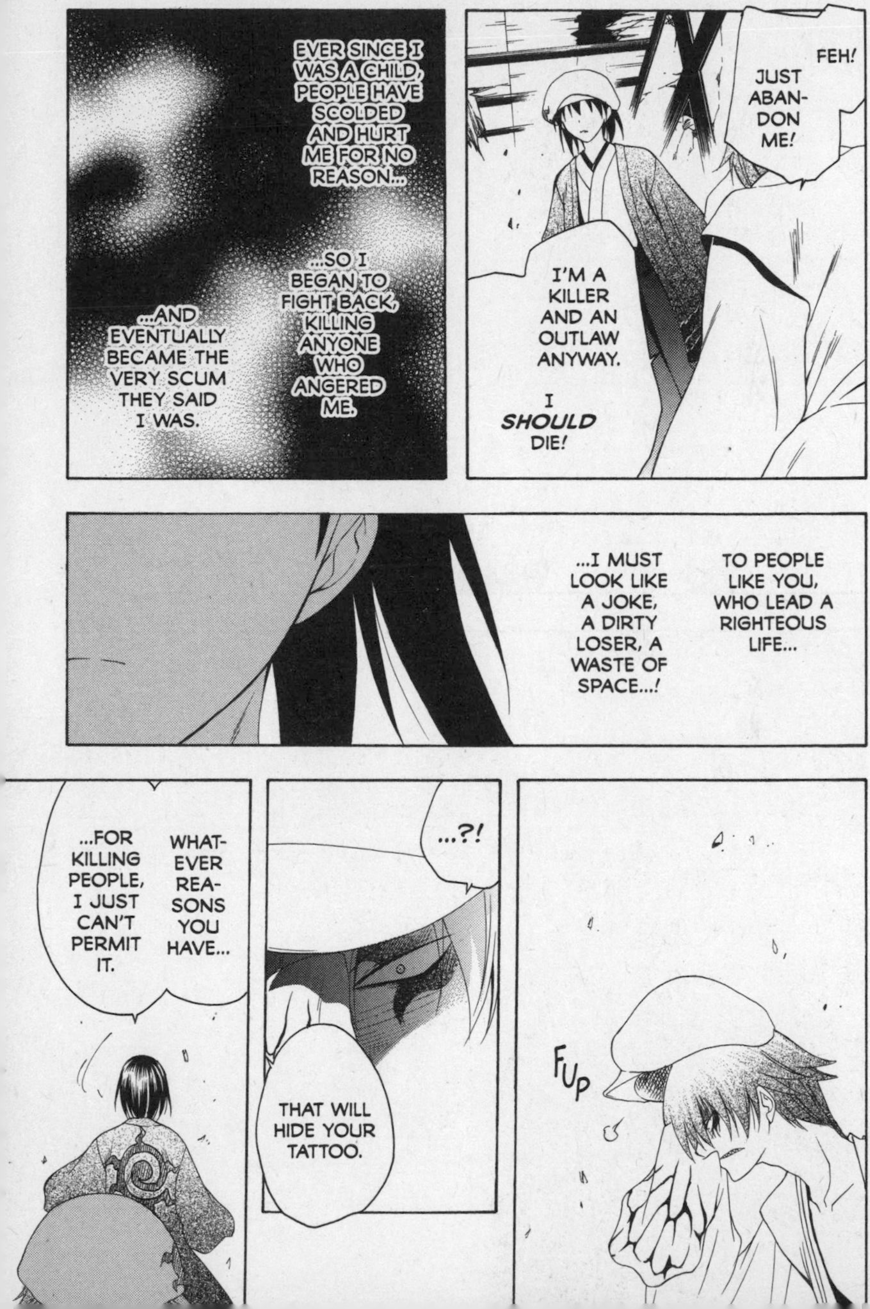
FEH!
JUST ABAN-DON ME!
I'M A KILLER AND AN OUTLAW ANYWAY.
I *SHOULD* DIE!
EVER SINCE I WAS A CHILD, PEOPLE HAVE SCOLDED AND HURT ME FOR NO REASON...
...SO I BEGAN TO FIGHT BACK, KILLING ANYONE WHO ANGERED ME.
...AND EVENTUALLY BECAME THE VERY SCUM THEY SAID I WAS.
TO PEOPLE LIKE YOU, WHO LEAD A RIGHTEOUS LIFE...
...I MUST LOOK LIKE A JOKE, A DIRTY LOSER, A WASTE OF SPACE...!
FUP
...?!
THAT WILL HIDE YOUR TATTOO.
WHAT-EVER REA-SONS YOU HAVE...
...FOR KILLING PEOPLE, I JUST CAN'T PERMIT IT.

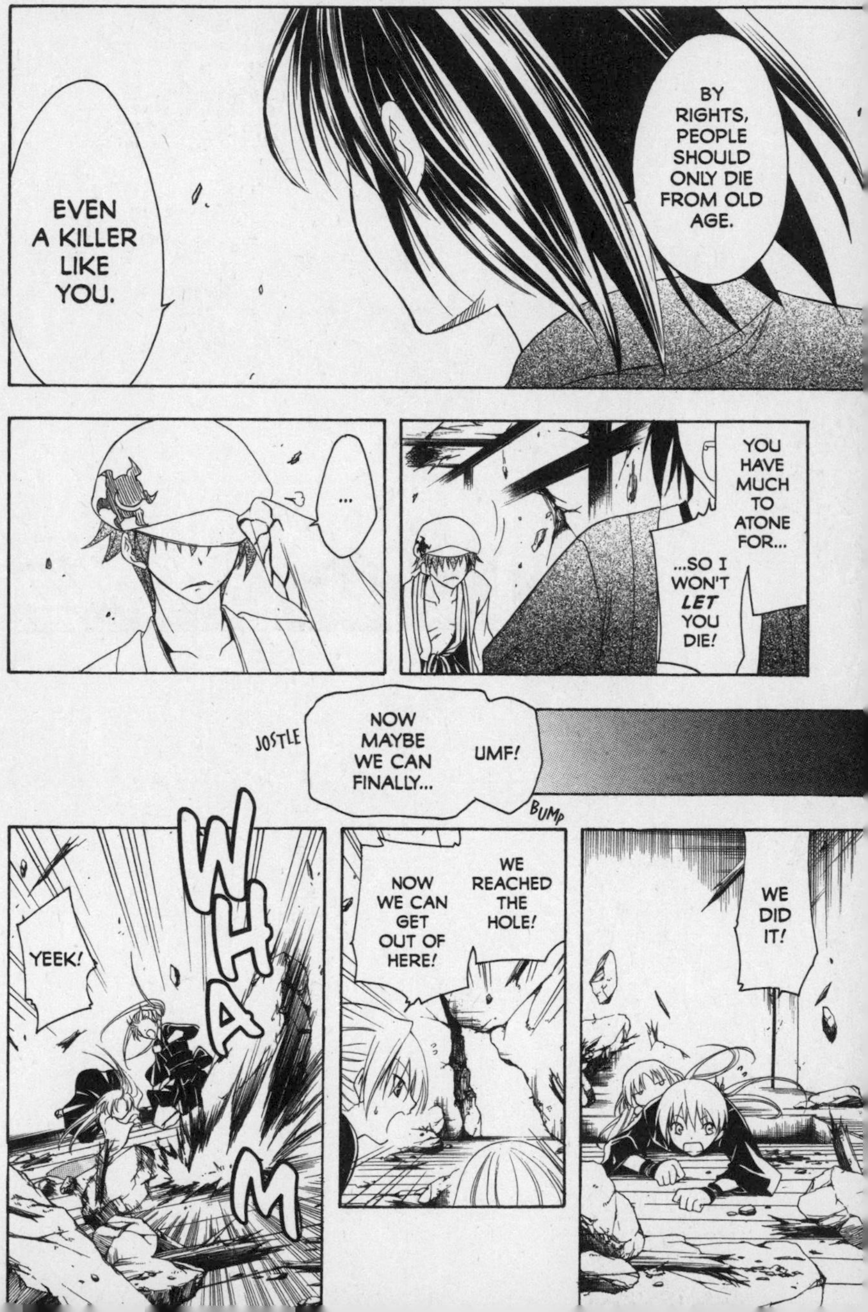
BY RIGHTS, PEOPLE SHOULD ONLY DIE FROM OLD AGE.
EVEN A KILLER LIKE YOU.
YOU HAVE MUCH TO ATONE FOR...
...SO I WON'T *LET* YOU DIE!
...
JOSTLE
NOW MAYBE WE CAN FINALLY...
UMF!
BUMP
WE DID IT!
WE REACHED THE HOLE!
NOW WE CAN GET OUT OF HERE!
YEEK!
WHAM

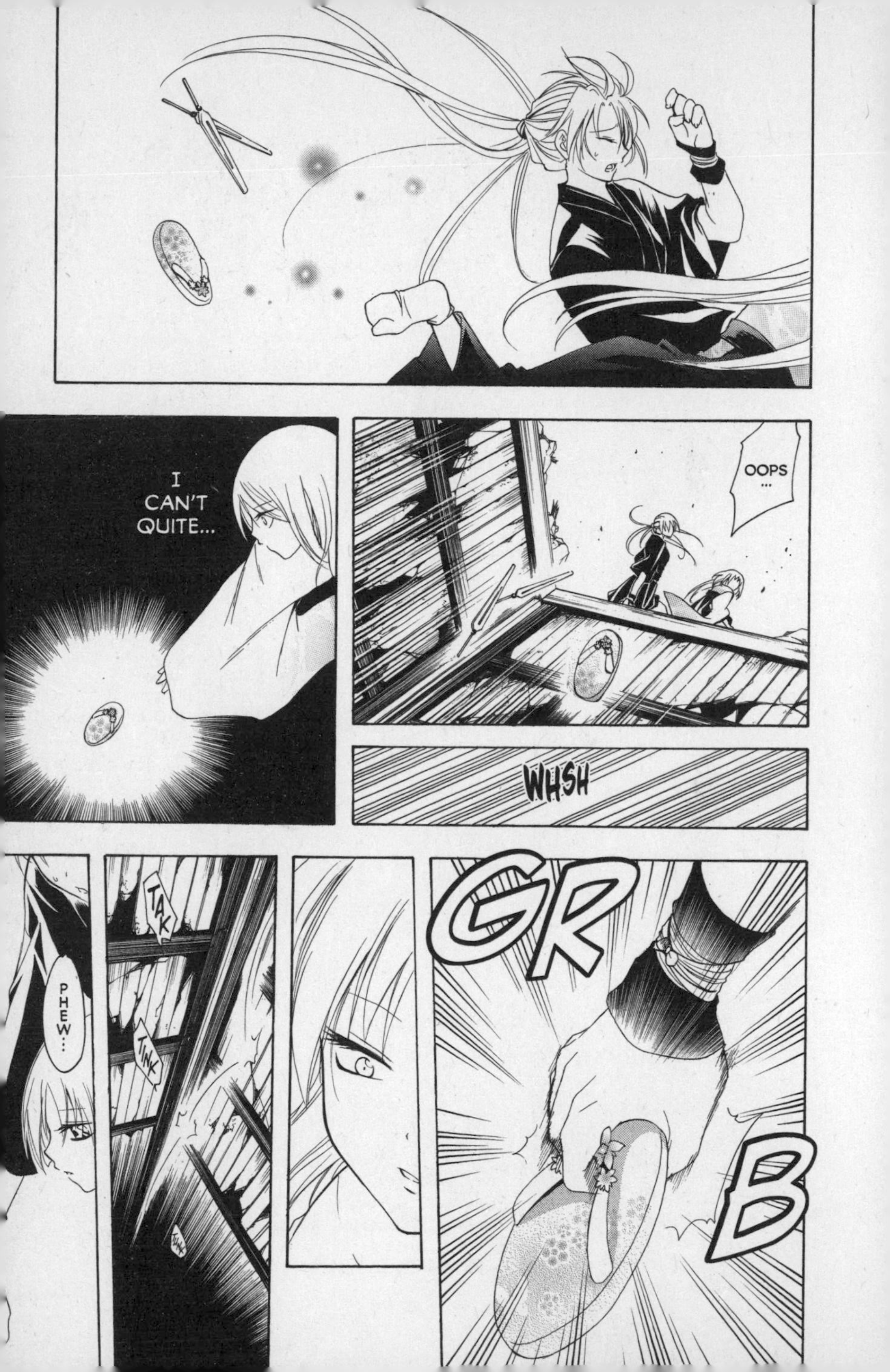
OOPS ...
WHSH
I CAN'T QUITE...
GR
B
TAK
TINK
TINK
PHEW...

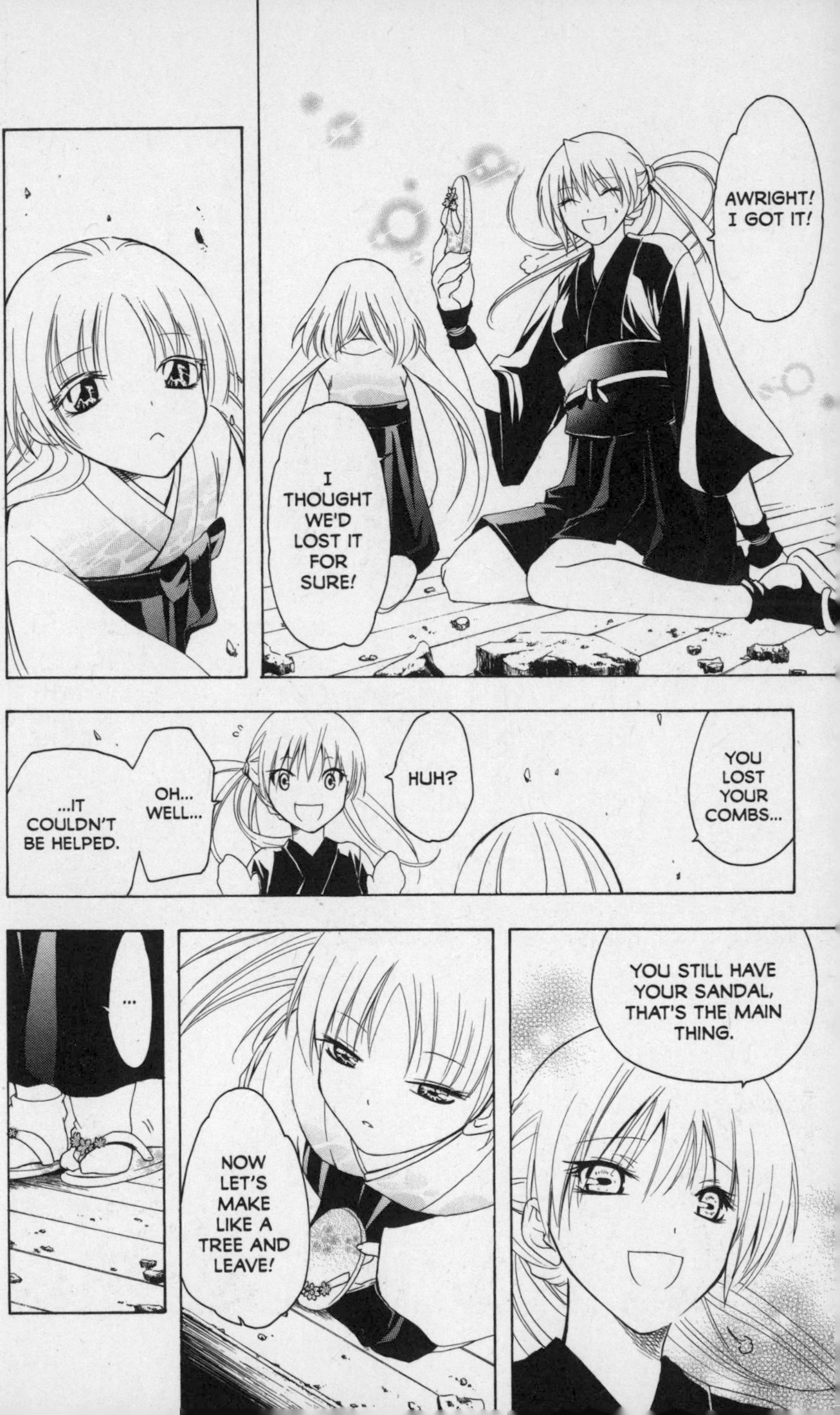
AWRIGHT! I GOT IT!
I THOUGHT WE'D LOST IT FOR SURE!
YOU LOST YOUR COMBS...
HUH?
OH... WELL...
...IT COULDN'T BE HELPED.
YOU STILL HAVE YOUR SANDAL, THAT'S THE MAIN THING.
NOW LET'S MAKE LIKE A TREE AND LEAVE!
...

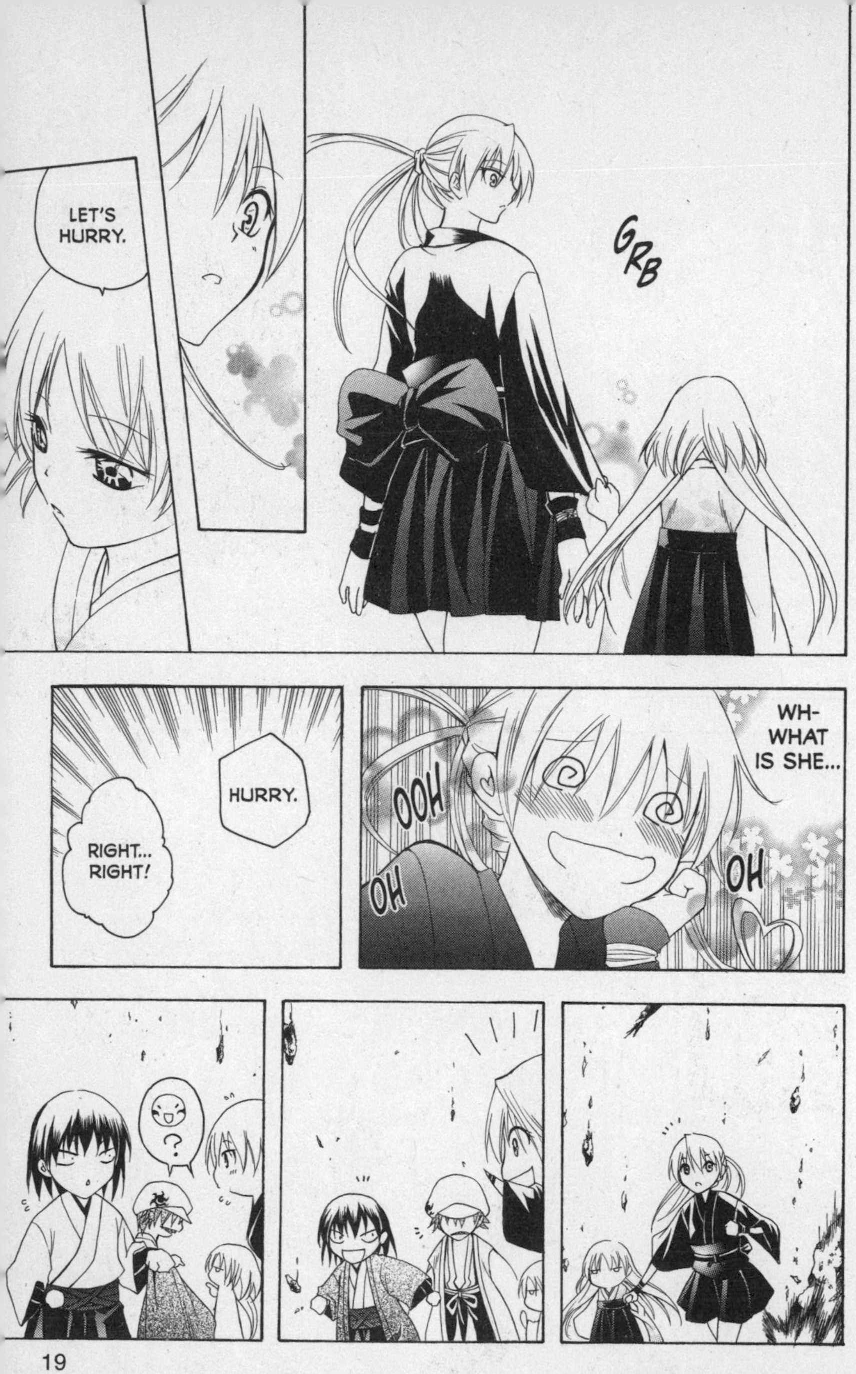
GRB
LET'S HURRY.
WH- WHAT IS SHE...
OOH
OH
OH
HURRY.
RIGHT... RIGHT!
?

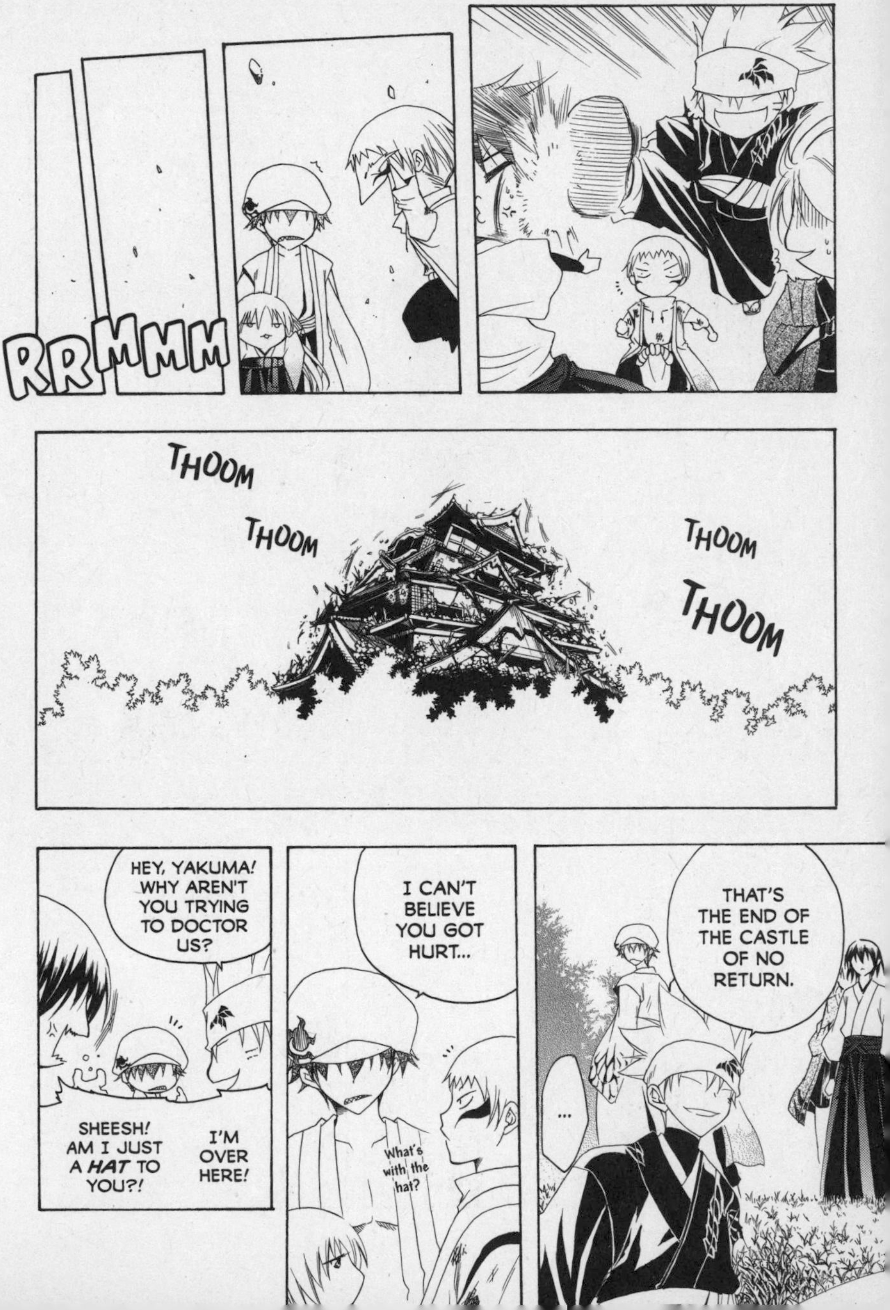
RRMMMM
THOOM
THOOM
THOOM
THOOM
THAT'S THE END OF THE CASTLE OF NO RETURN.
...
I CAN'T BELIEVE YOU GOT HURT...
What's with the hat?
HEY, YAKUMA! WHY AREN'T YOU TRYING TO DOCTOR US?
I'M OVER HERE!
SHEESH! AM I JUST A *HAT* TO YOU?!

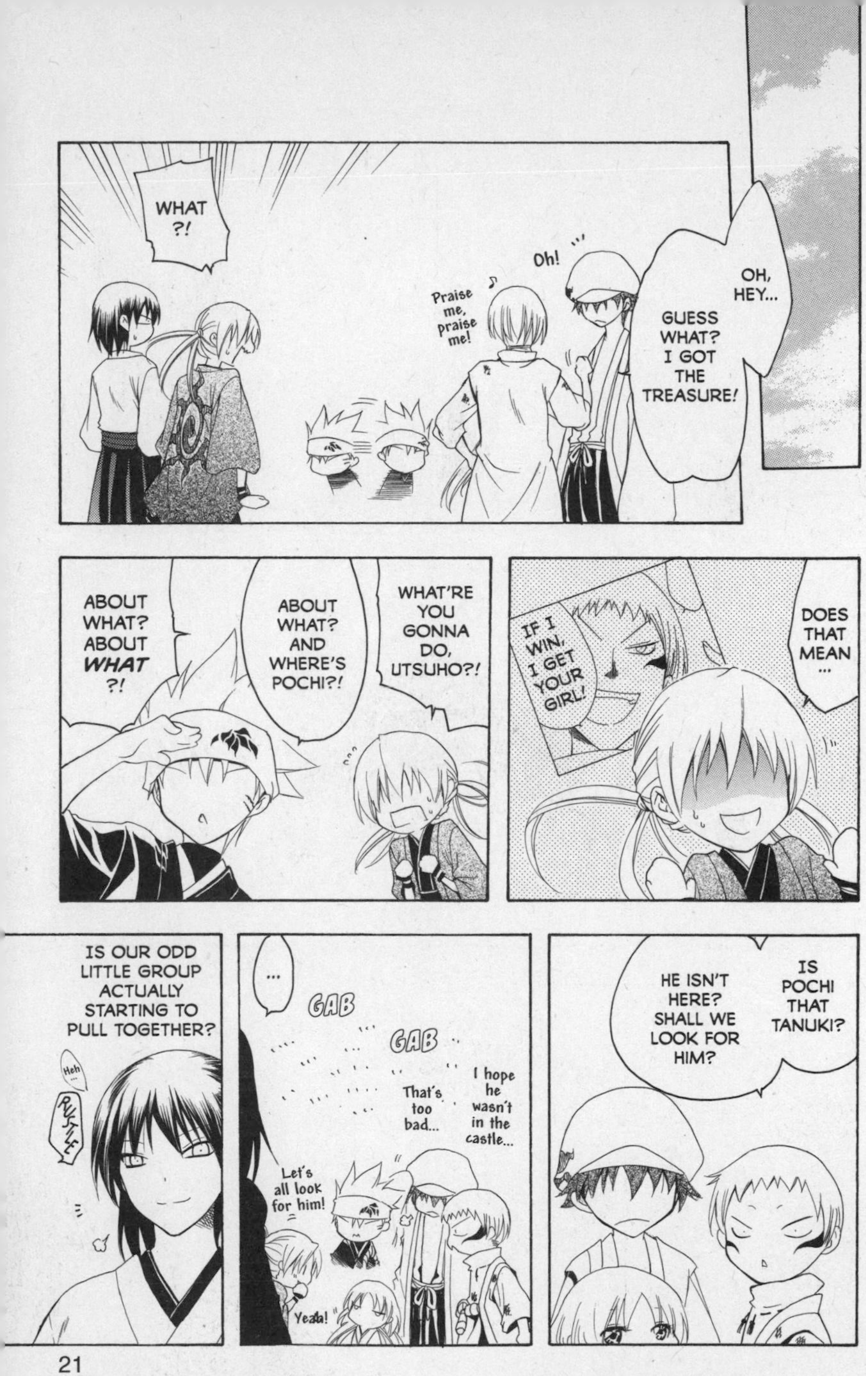
OH, HEY... GUESS WHAT? I GOT THE TREASURE!
Oh!
Praise me, praise me!
WHAT ?!
DOES THAT MEAN ...
IF I WIN, I GET YOUR GIRL!
WHAT'RE YOU GONNA DO, UTSUHO?!
ABOUT WHAT? AND WHERE'S POCHI?!
ABOUT WHAT? ABOUT *WHAT* ?!
IS POCHI THAT TANUKI?
HE ISN'T HERE? SHALL WE LOOK FOR HIM?
...
GAB
GAB
I hope he wasn't in the castle...
That's too bad...
Let's all look for him!
Yeah!
IS OUR ODD LITTLE GROUP ACTUALLY STARTING TO PULL TOGETHER?
Heh ...
RUSTLE

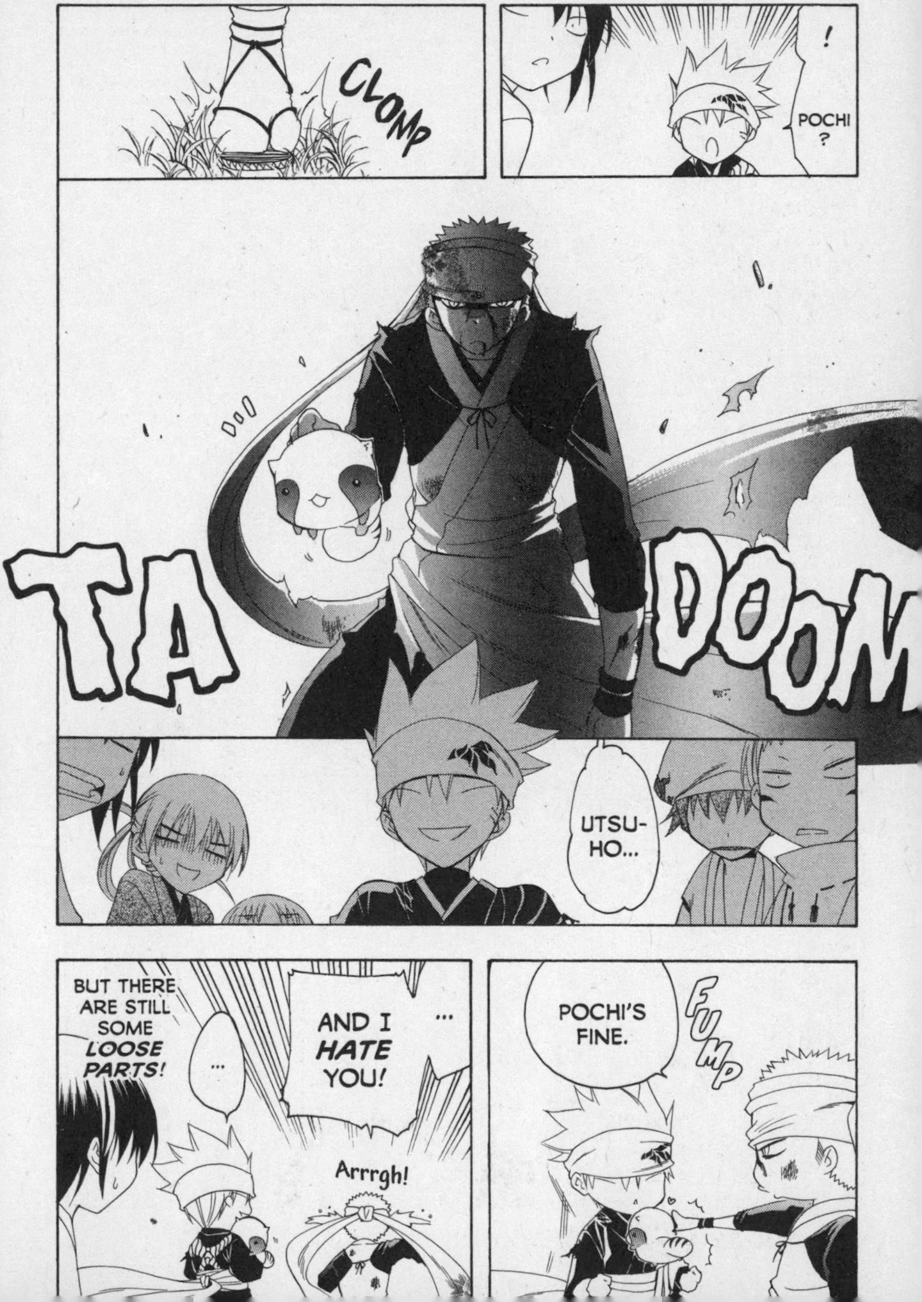
!
POCHI ?
CLOMP
TA DOOM
UTSU- HO...
POCHI'S FINE.
FUMP
...
AND I HATE YOU!
BUT THERE ARE STILL SOME LOOSE PARTS!
...
Arrrgh!

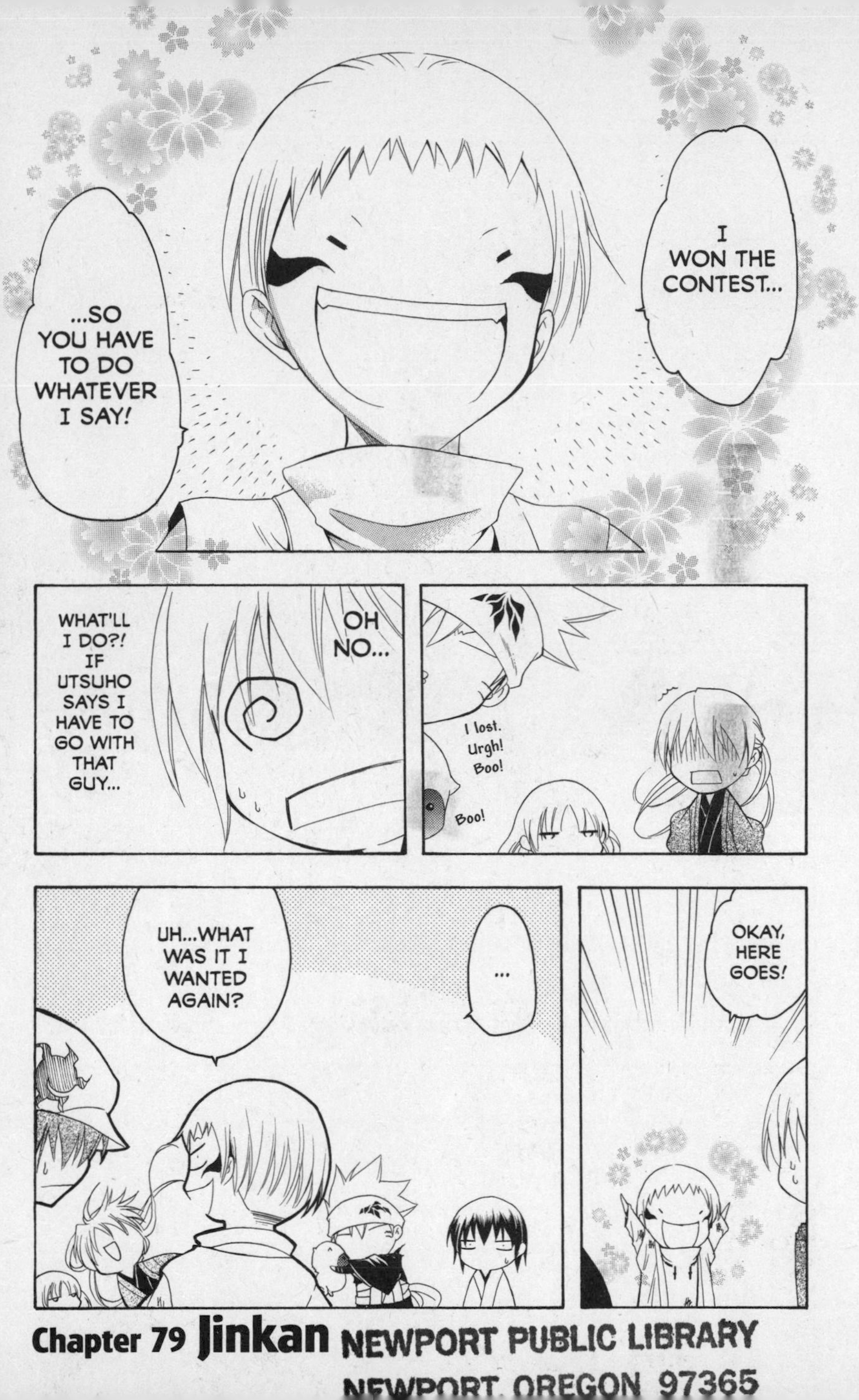
I WON THE CONTEST...
...SO YOU HAVE TO DO WHATEVER I SAY!
I lost.
Urgh!
Boo!
Boo!
OH NO...
WHAT'LL I DO?! IF UTSUHO SAYS I HAVE TO GO WITH THAT GUY...
OKAY, HERE GOES!
...
UH...WHAT WAS IT I WANTED AGAIN?

Chapter 79 Jinkan

Chapter 79
Jinkan

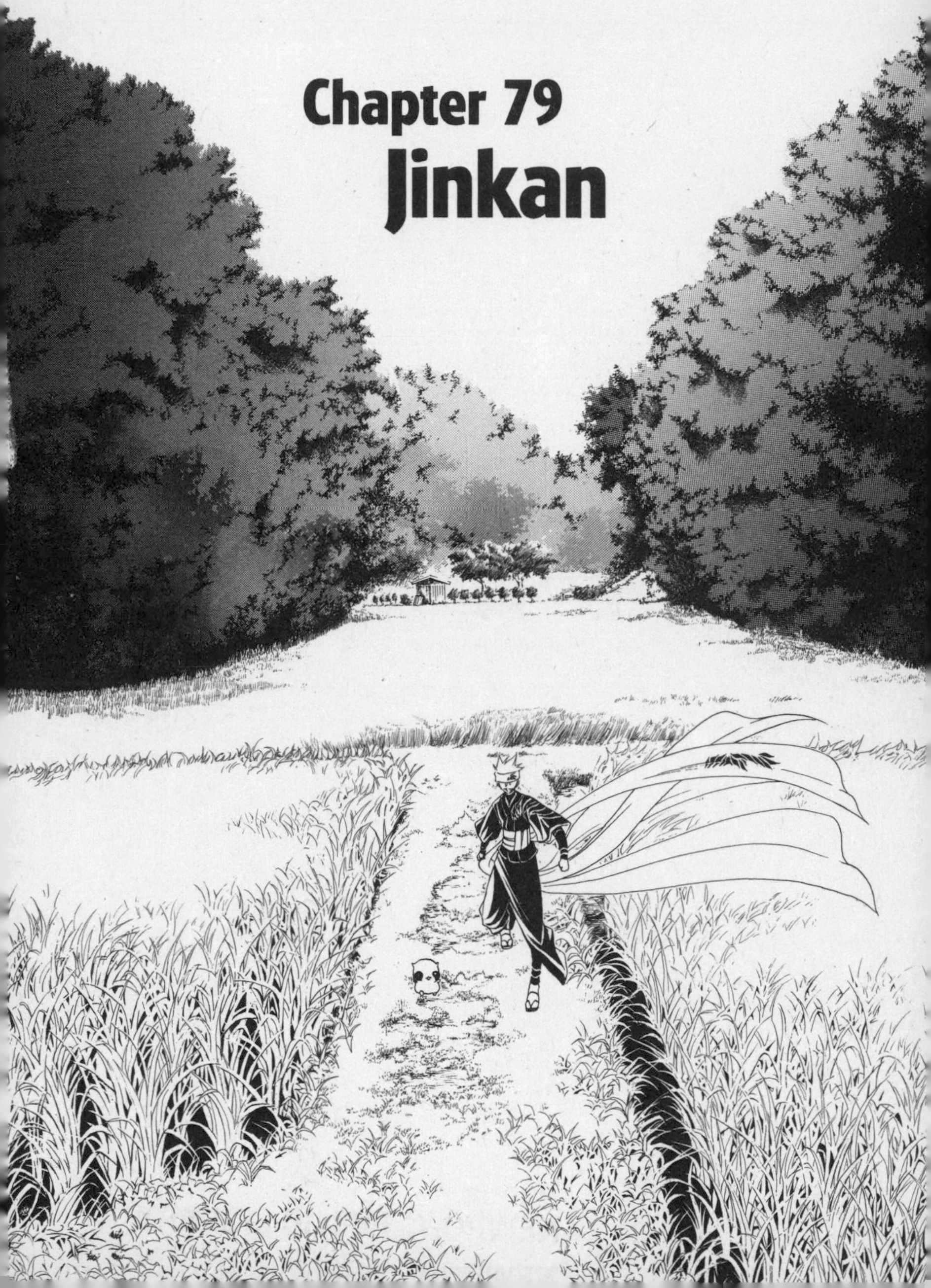

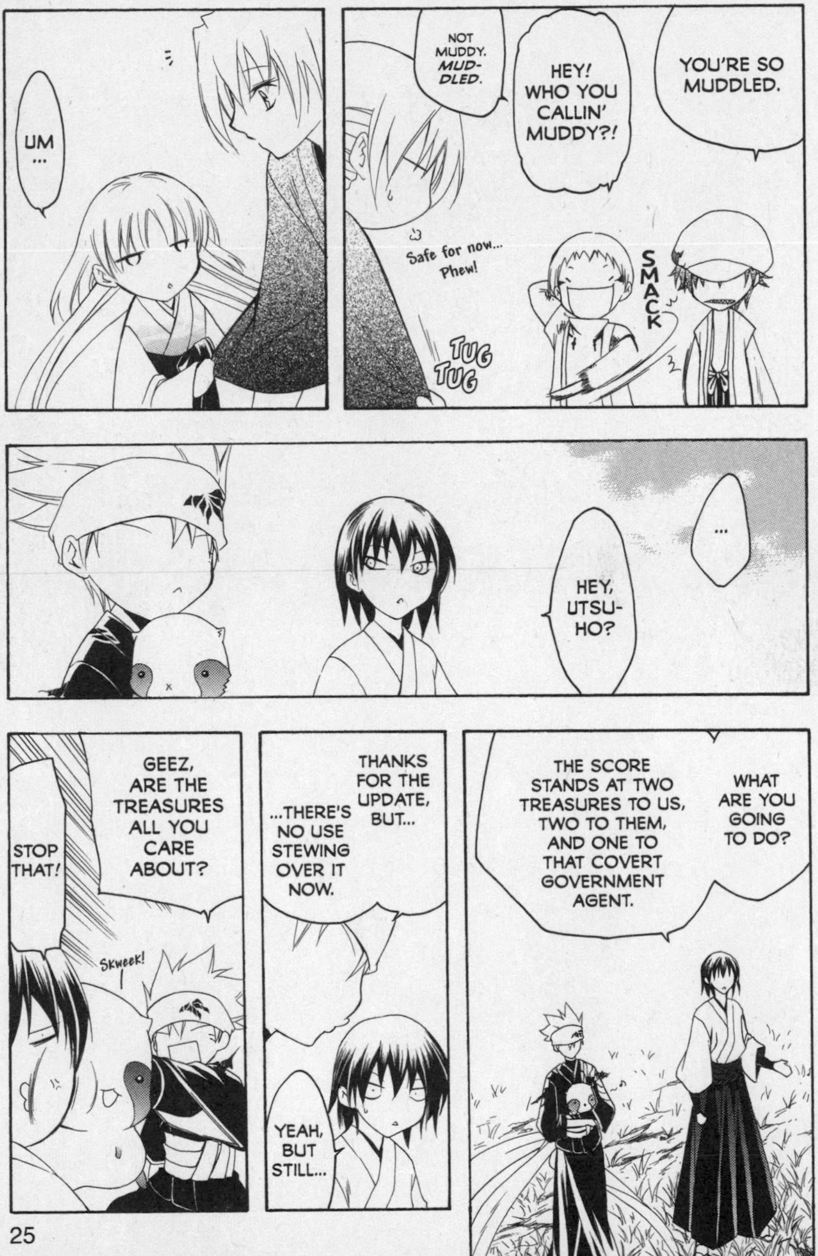

YOU'RE SO MUDDLED.
HEY! WHO YOU CALLIN' MUDDY?!
NOT MUDDY. *MUDDLED.*
SMACK
Safe for now... Phew!
TUG TUG
UM...
...
HEY, UTSUHO?
WHAT ARE YOU GOING TO DO?
THE SCORE STANDS AT TWO TREASURES TO US, TWO TO THEM, AND ONE TO THAT COVERT GOVERNMENT AGENT.
THANKS FOR THE UPDATE, BUT...
...THERE'S NO USE STEWING OVER IT NOW.
YEAH, BUT STILL...
GEEZ, ARE THE TREASURES ALL YOU CARE ABOUT?
STOP THAT!
Skweek!

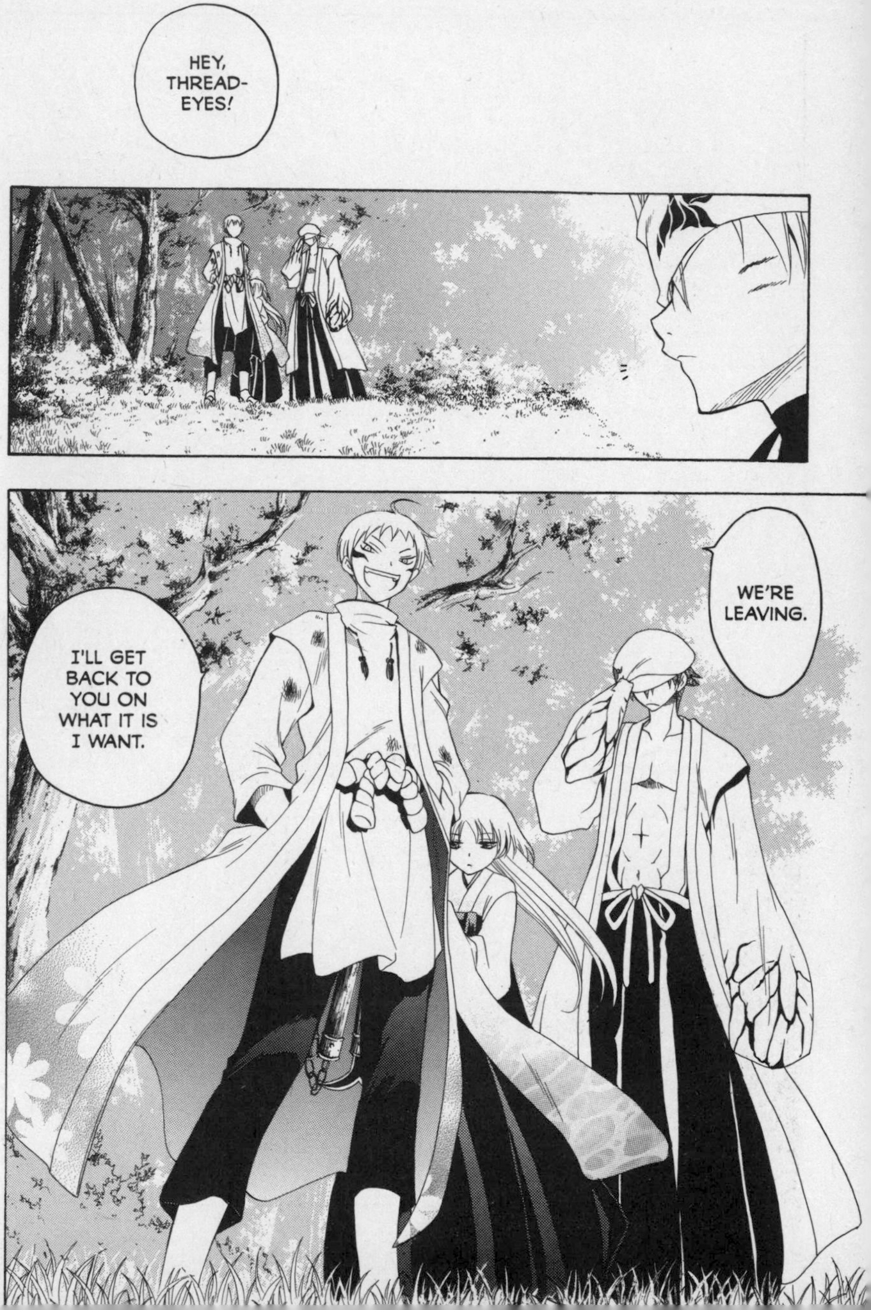
HEY, THREAD-EYES!
WE'RE LEAVING.
I'LL GET BACK TO YOU ON WHAT IT IS I WANT.

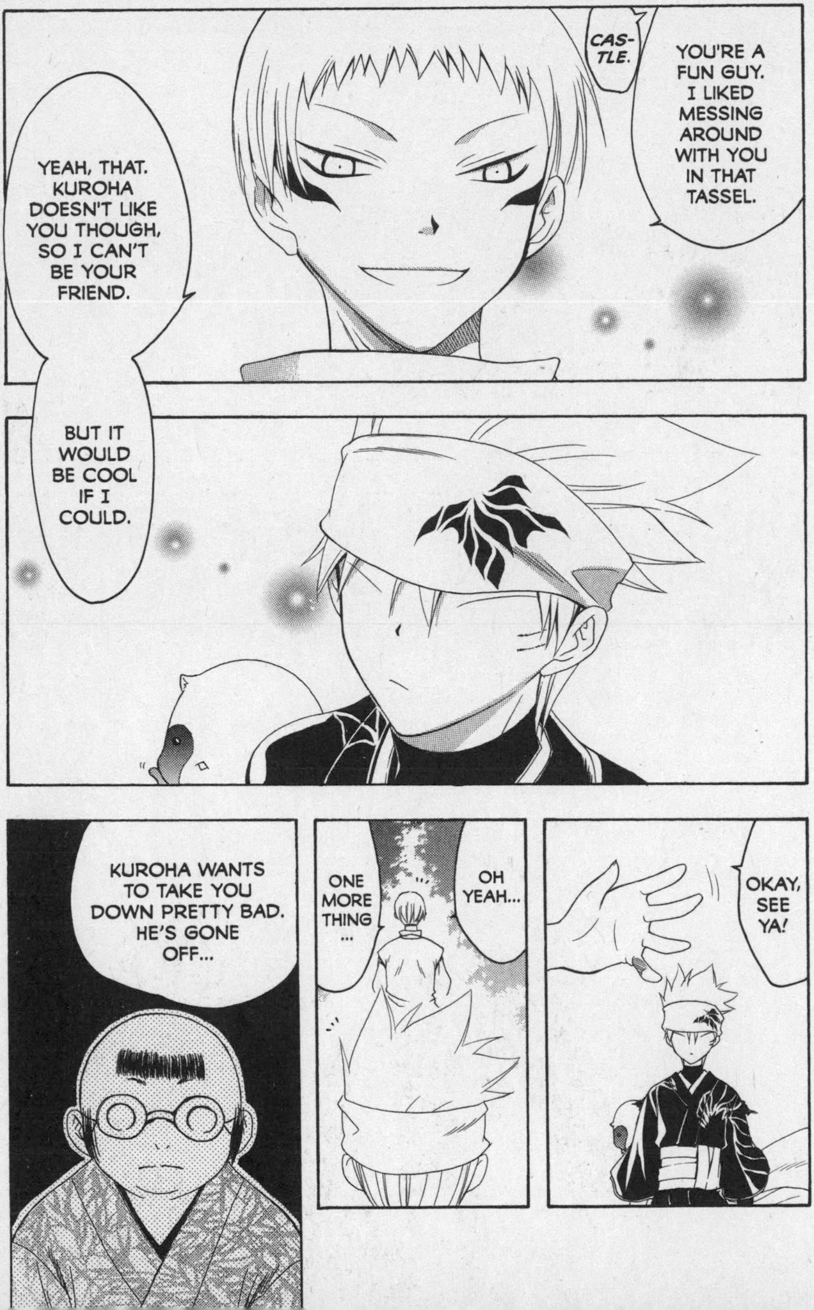
CAS-TLE.
YOU'RE A FUN GUY. I LIKED MESSING AROUND WITH YOU IN THAT TASSEL.
YEAH, THAT. KUROHA DOESN'T LIKE YOU THOUGH, SO I CAN'T BE YOUR FRIEND.
BUT IT WOULD BE COOL IF I COULD.
OKAY, SEE YA!
OH YEAH...
ONE MORE THING...
KUROHA WANTS TO TAKE YOU DOWN PRETTY BAD. HE'S GONE OFF...

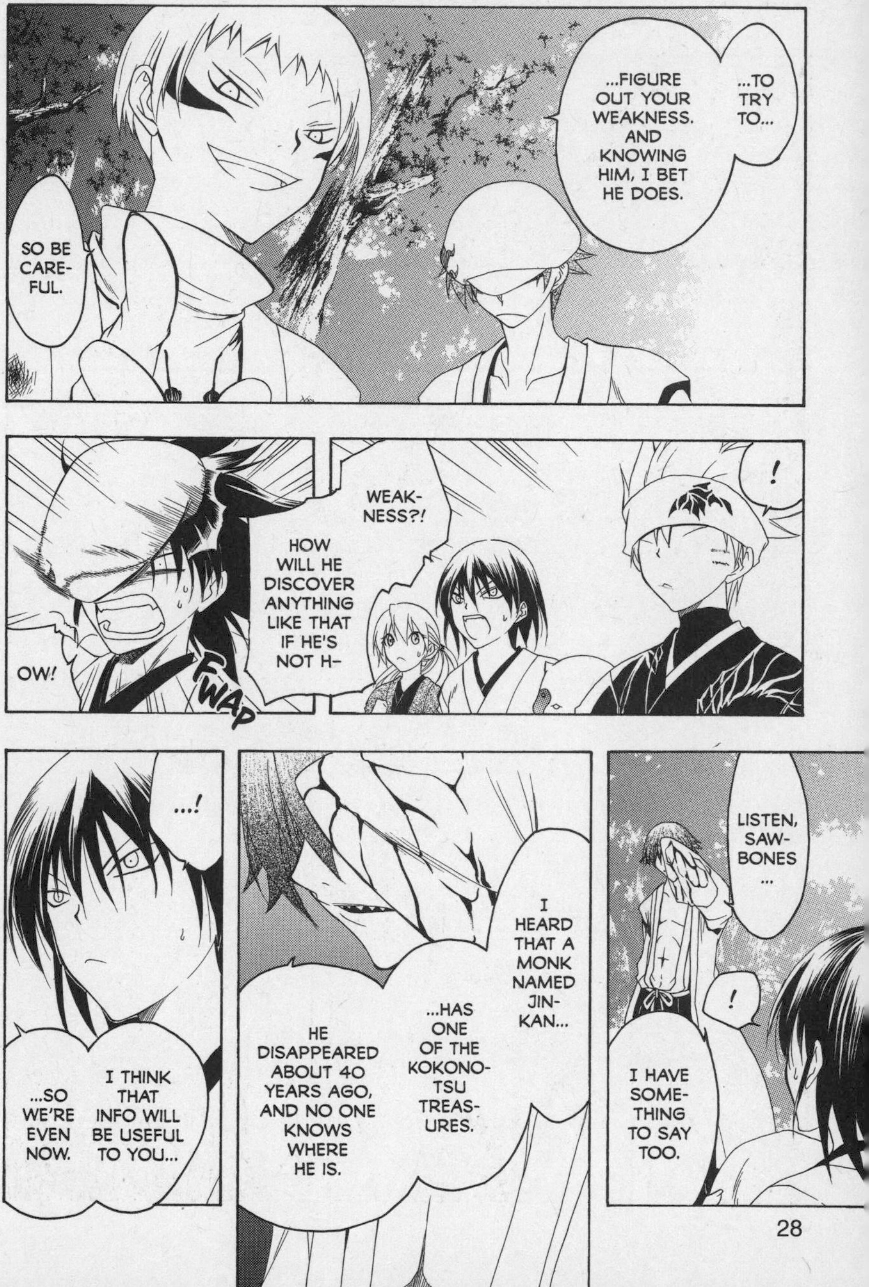

...TO TRY TO...
...FIGURE OUT YOUR WEAKNESS. AND KNOWING HIM, I BET HE DOES.
SO BE CAREFUL.
!
WEAKNESS?!
HOW WILL HE DISCOVER ANYTHING LIKE THAT IF HE'S NOT H-
FWAP
OW!
LISTEN, SAWBONES...
!
I HAVE SOMETHING TO SAY TOO.
I HEARD THAT A MONK NAMED JINKAN...
...HAS ONE OF THE KOKONOTSU TREASURES.
HE DISAPPEARED ABOUT 40 YEARS AGO, AND NO ONE KNOWS WHERE HE IS.
...!
I THINK THAT INFO WILL BE USEFUL TO YOU...
...SO WE'RE EVEN NOW.

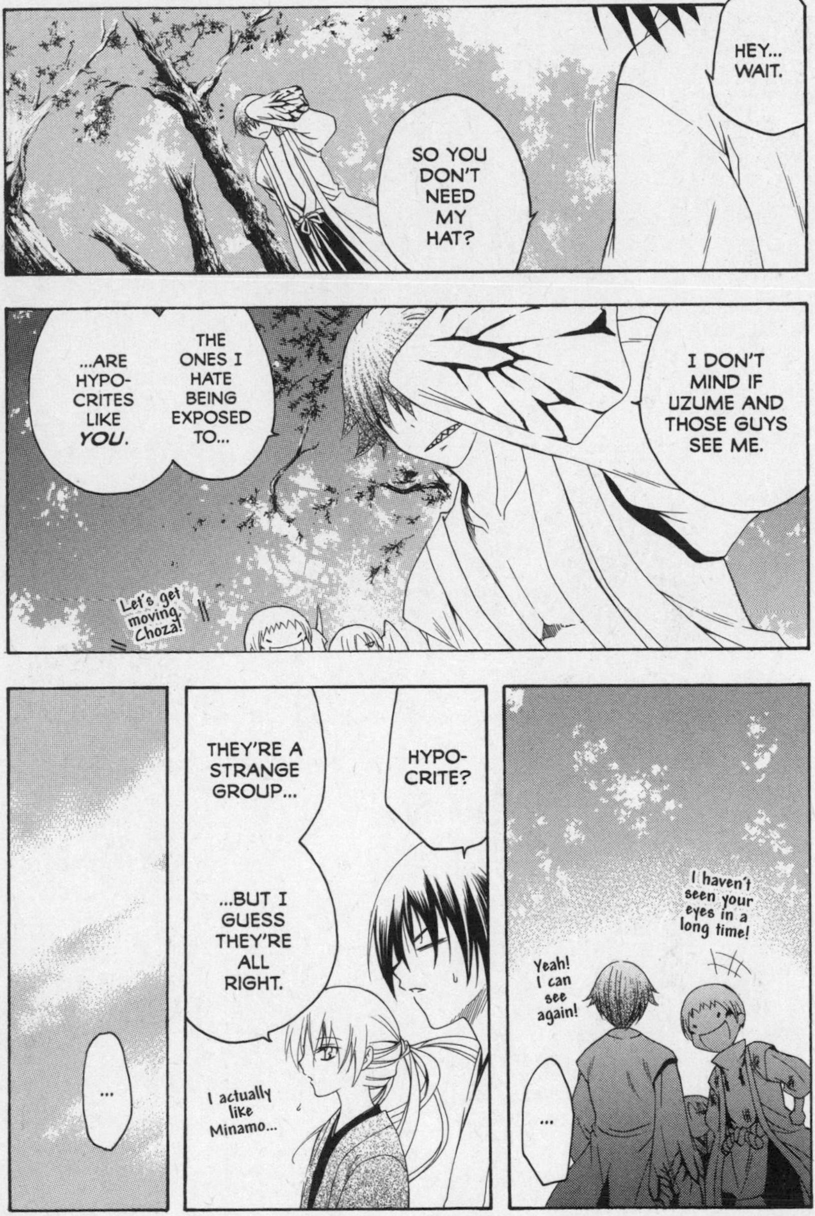
HEY... WAIT.
SO YOU DON'T NEED MY HAT?
I DON'T MIND IF UZUME AND THOSE GUYS SEE ME.
THE ONES I HATE BEING EXPOSED TO...
...ARE HYPOCRITES LIKE *YOU*.
Let's get moving, Choza!
I haven't seen your eyes in a long time!
Yeah! I can see again!
...
HYPOCRITE?
THEY'RE A STRANGE GROUP...
...BUT I GUESS THEY'RE ALL RIGHT.
I actually like Minamo...
...

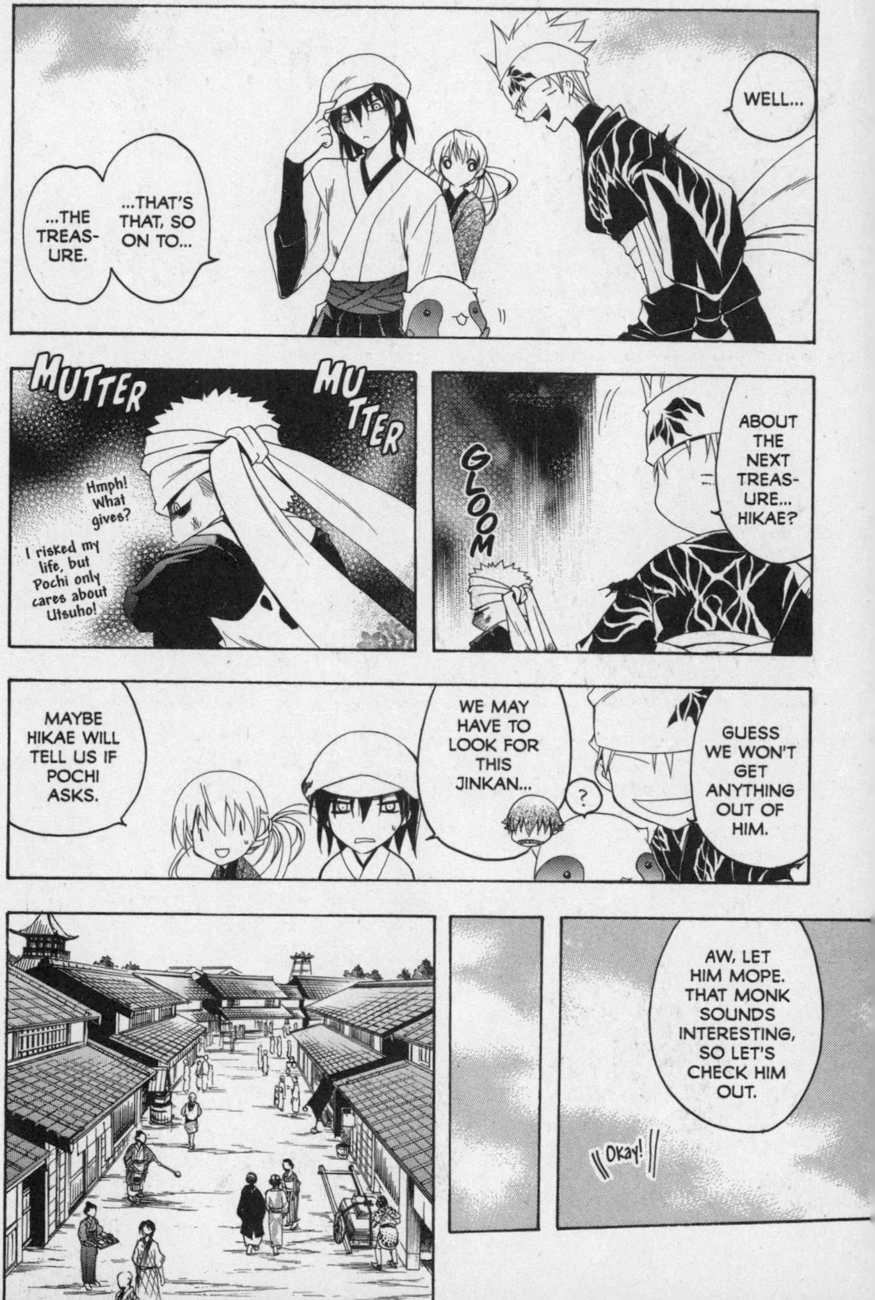
WELL...
...THAT'S THAT, SO ON TO...
...THE TREASURE.
ABOUT THE NEXT TREASURE... HIKAE?
GLOOM
MUTTER
MUTTER
Hmph! What gives?
I risked my life, but Pochi only cares about Utsuho!
GUESS WE WON'T GET ANYTHING OUT OF HIM.
?
WE MAY HAVE TO LOOK FOR THIS JINKAN...
MAYBE HIKAE WILL TELL US IF POCHI ASKS.
AW, LET HIM MOPE. THAT MONK SOUNDS INTERESTING, SO LET'S CHECK HIM OUT.
Okay!

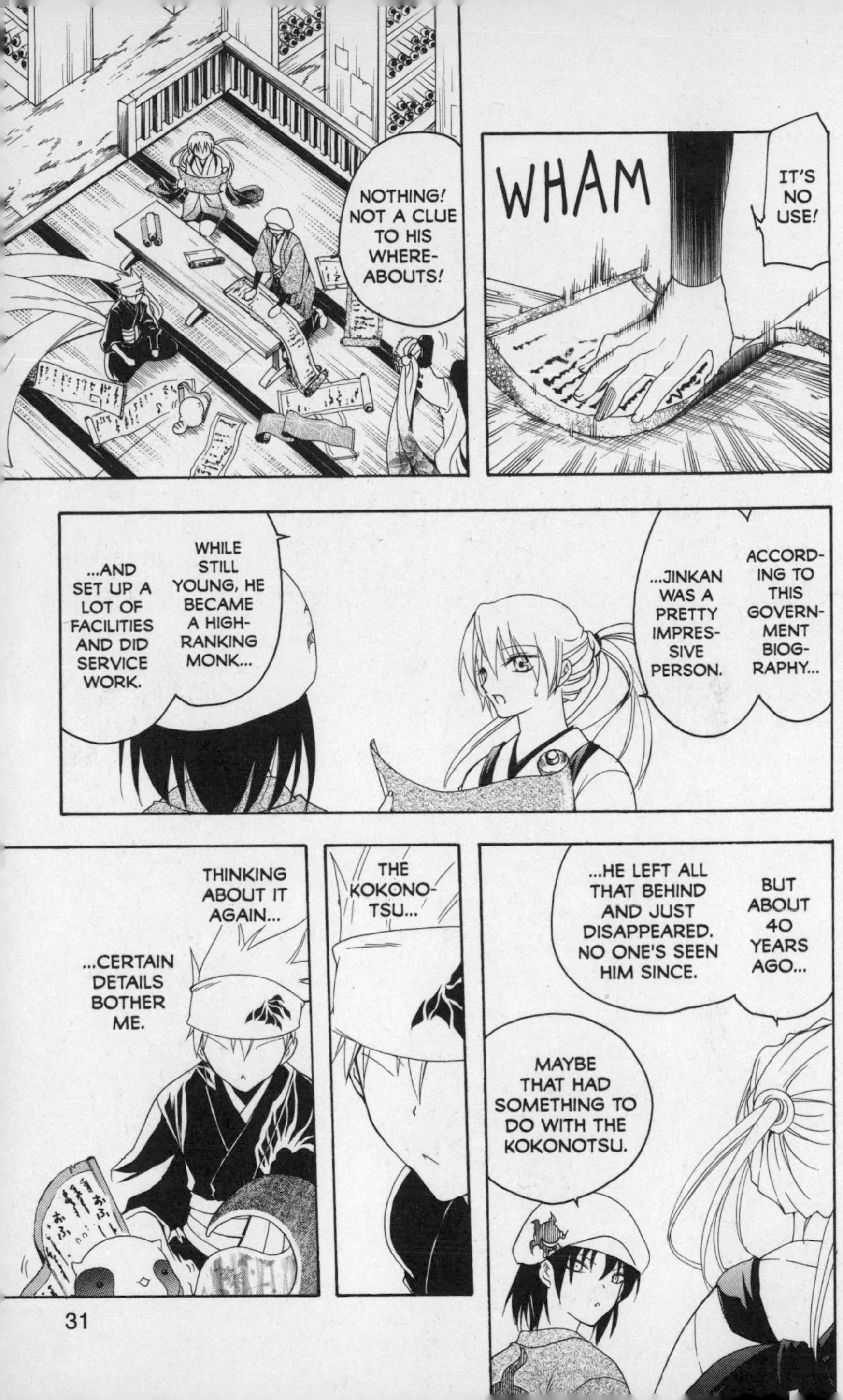
WHAM
IT'S NO USE!
NOTHING! NOT A CLUE TO HIS WHEREABOUTS!
ACCORDING TO THIS GOVERNMENT BIOGRAPHY...
...JINKAN WAS A PRETTY IMPRESSIVE PERSON.
WHILE STILL YOUNG, HE BECAME A HIGH-RANKING MONK...
...AND SET UP A LOT OF FACILITIES AND DID SERVICE WORK.
BUT ABOUT 40 YEARS AGO...
...HE LEFT ALL THAT BEHIND AND JUST DISAPPEARED. NO ONE'S SEEN HIM SINCE.
MAYBE THAT HAD SOMETHING TO DO WITH THE KOKONOTSU.
THE KOKONOTSU...
THINKING ABOUT IT AGAIN...
...CERTAIN DETAILS BOTHER ME.

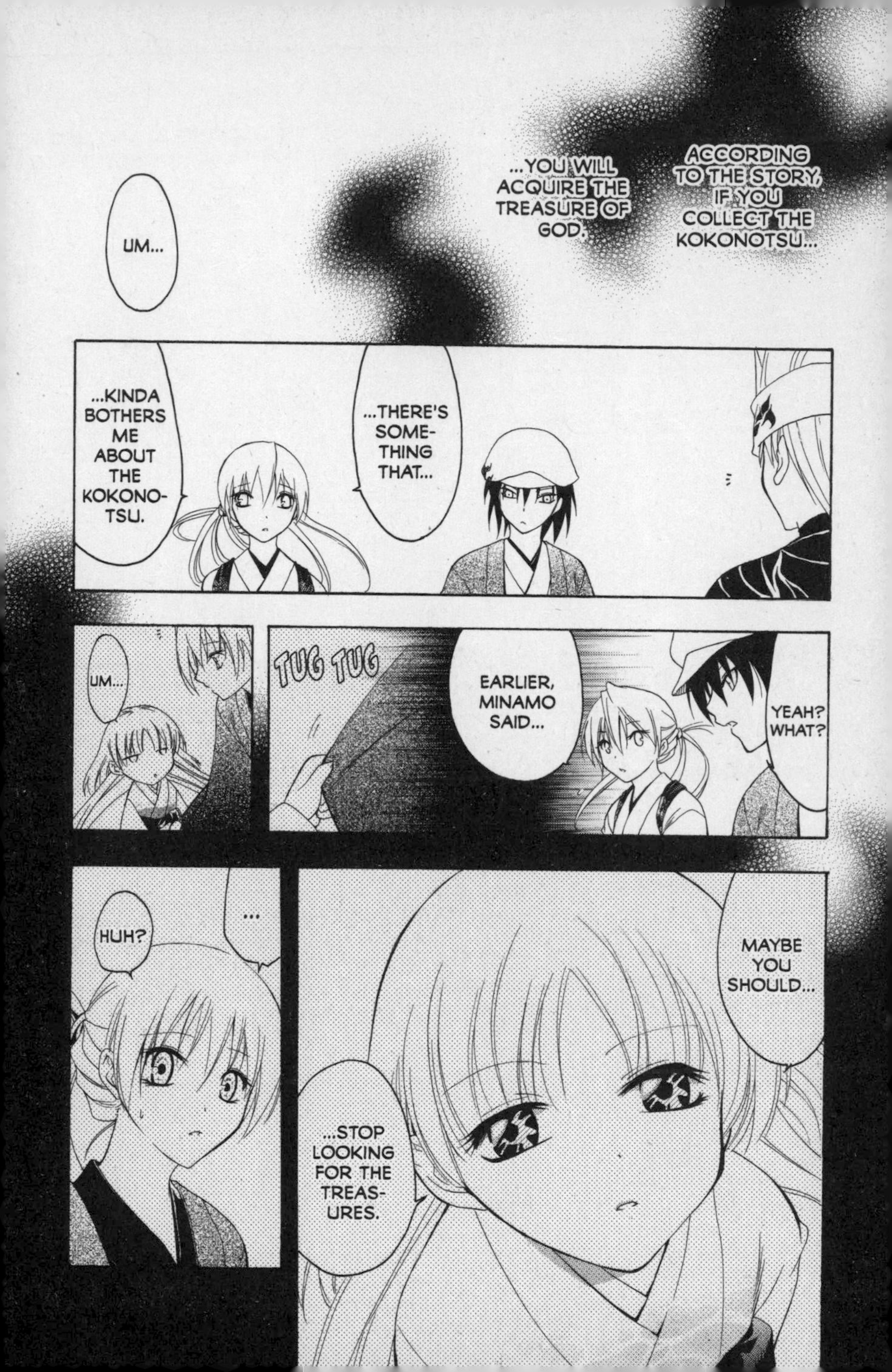
ACCORDING TO THE STORY, IF YOU COLLECT THE KOKONOTSU...
...YOU WILL ACQUIRE THE TREASURE OF GOD.
UM...
...THERE'S SOME-THING THAT...
...KINDA BOTHERS ME ABOUT THE KOKONO-TSU.
YEAH? WHAT?
EARLIER, MINAMO SAID...
TUG TUG
UM...
MAYBE YOU SHOULD...
...STOP LOOKING FOR THE TREAS-URES.
...
HUH?

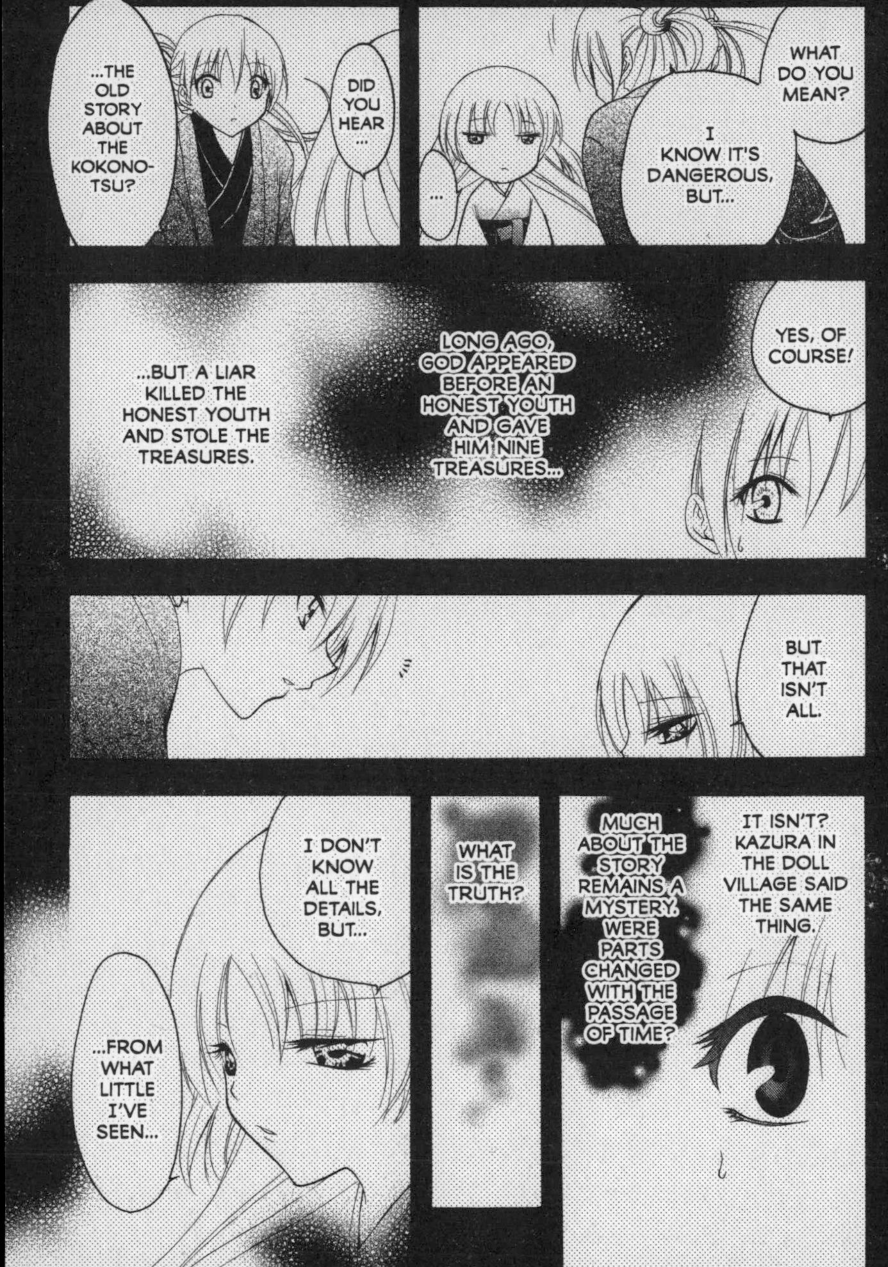
WHAT DO YOU MEAN?
I KNOW IT'S DANGEROUS, BUT...
...
DID YOU HEAR ...
...THE OLD STORY ABOUT THE KOKONO-TSU?
YES, OF COURSE!
LONG AGO, GOD APPEARED BEFORE AN HONEST YOUTH AND GAVE HIM NINE TREASURES...
...BUT A LIAR KILLED THE HONEST YOUTH AND STOLE THE TREASURES.
BUT THAT ISN'T ALL.
IT ISN'T? KAZURA IN THE DOLL VILLAGE SAID THE SAME THING.
MUCH ABOUT THE STORY REMAINS A MYSTERY. WERE PARTS CHANGED WITH THE PASSAGE OF TIME?
WHAT IS THE TRUTH?
I DON'T KNOW ALL THE DETAILS, BUT...
...FROM WHAT LITTLE I'VE SEEN...

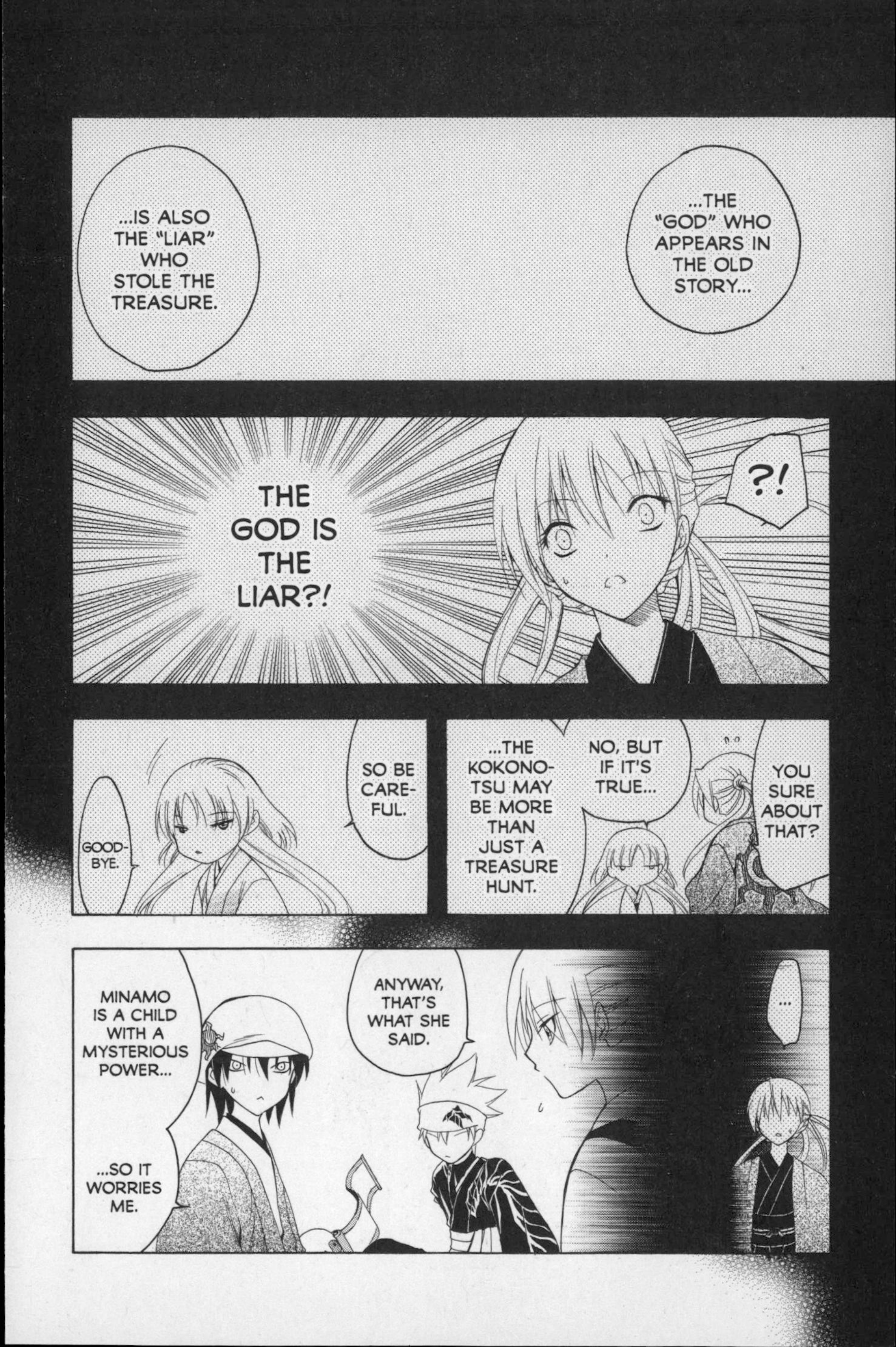
...THE "GOD" WHO APPEARS IN THE OLD STORY...
...IS ALSO THE "LIAR" WHO STOLE THE TREASURE.
?!
THE GOD IS THE LIAR?!
YOU SURE ABOUT THAT?
NO, BUT IF IT'S TRUE...
...THE KOKONOTSU MAY BE MORE THAN JUST A TREASURE HUNT.
SO BE CAREFUL.
GOODBYE.
...
ANYWAY, THAT'S WHAT SHE SAID.
MINAMO IS A CHILD WITH A MYSTERIOUS POWER...
...SO IT WORRIES ME.

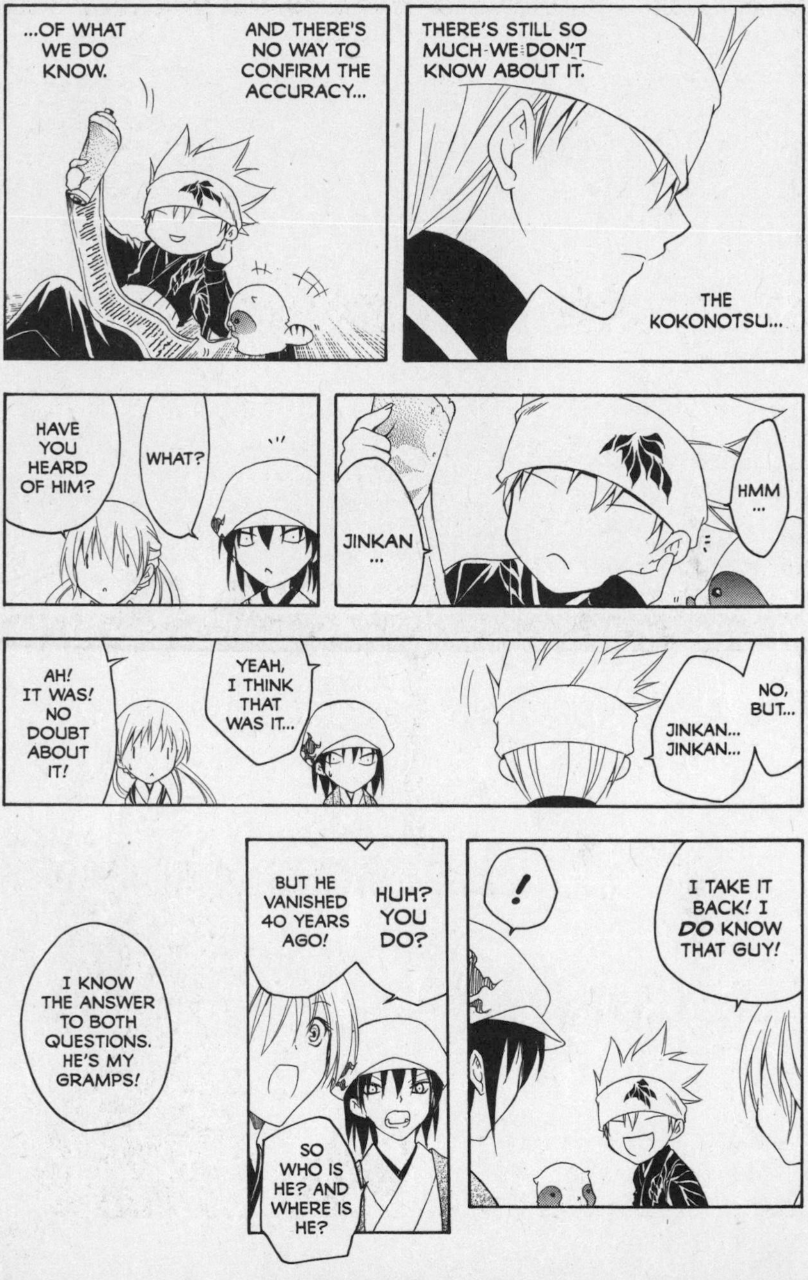
THERE'S STILL SO MUCH WE DON'T KNOW ABOUT IT.
THE KOKONOTSU...
AND THERE'S NO WAY TO CONFIRM THE ACCURACY...
...OF WHAT WE DO KNOW.
HMM ...
JINKAN ...
WHAT?
HAVE YOU HEARD OF HIM?
NO, BUT...
JINKAN... JINKAN...
YEAH, I THINK THAT WAS IT...
AH! IT WAS! NO DOUBT ABOUT IT!
I TAKE IT BACK! I *DO* KNOW THAT GUY!
!
HUH? YOU DO?
BUT HE VANISHED 40 YEARS AGO!
SO WHO IS HE? AND WHERE IS HE?
I KNOW THE ANSWER TO BOTH QUESTIONS. HE'S MY GRAMPS!

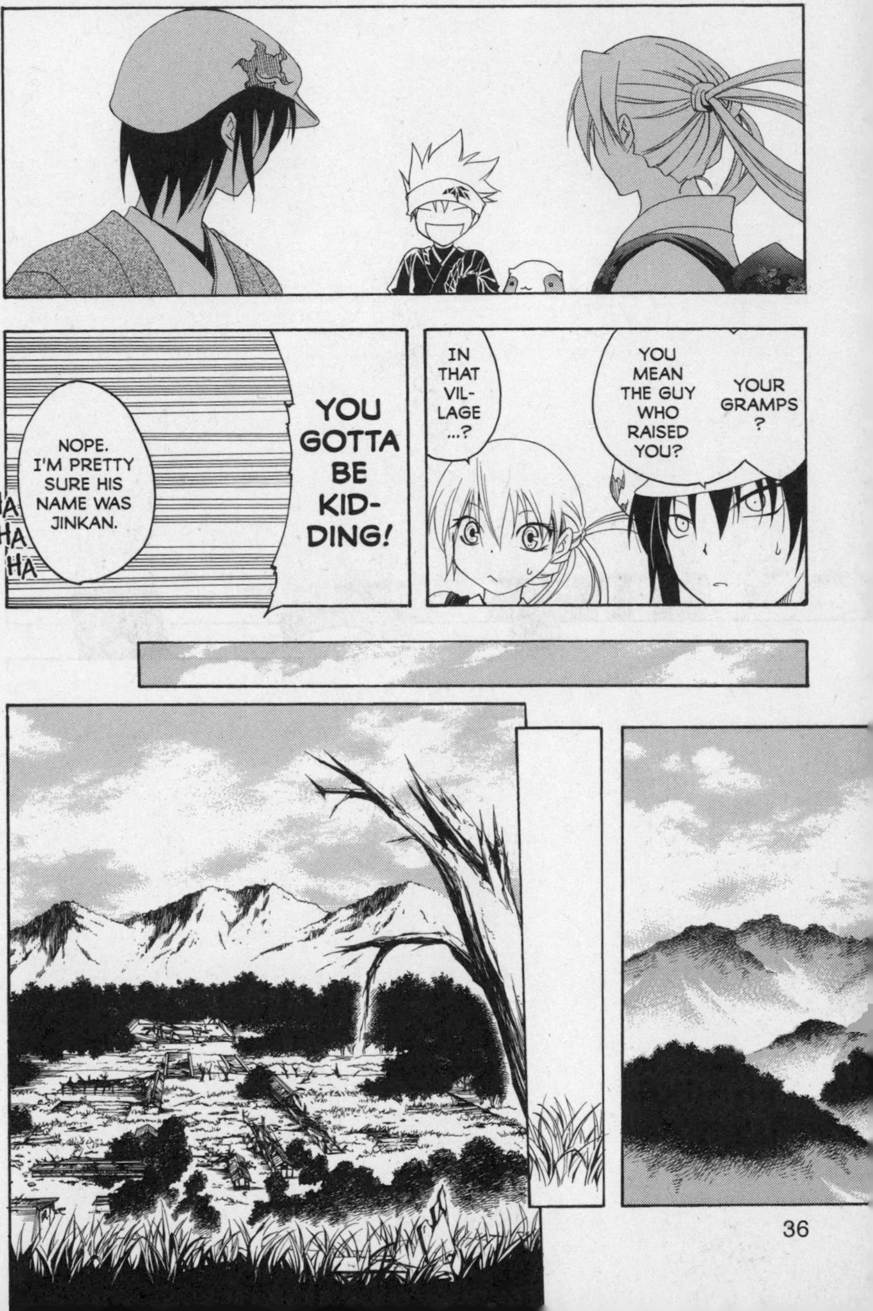
YOUR GRAMPS?
YOU MEAN THE GUY WHO RAISED YOU?
IN THAT VIL-LAGE ...?
YOU GOTTA BE KID-DING!
NOPE. I'M PRETTY SURE HIS NAME WAS JINKAN.
HA HA HA

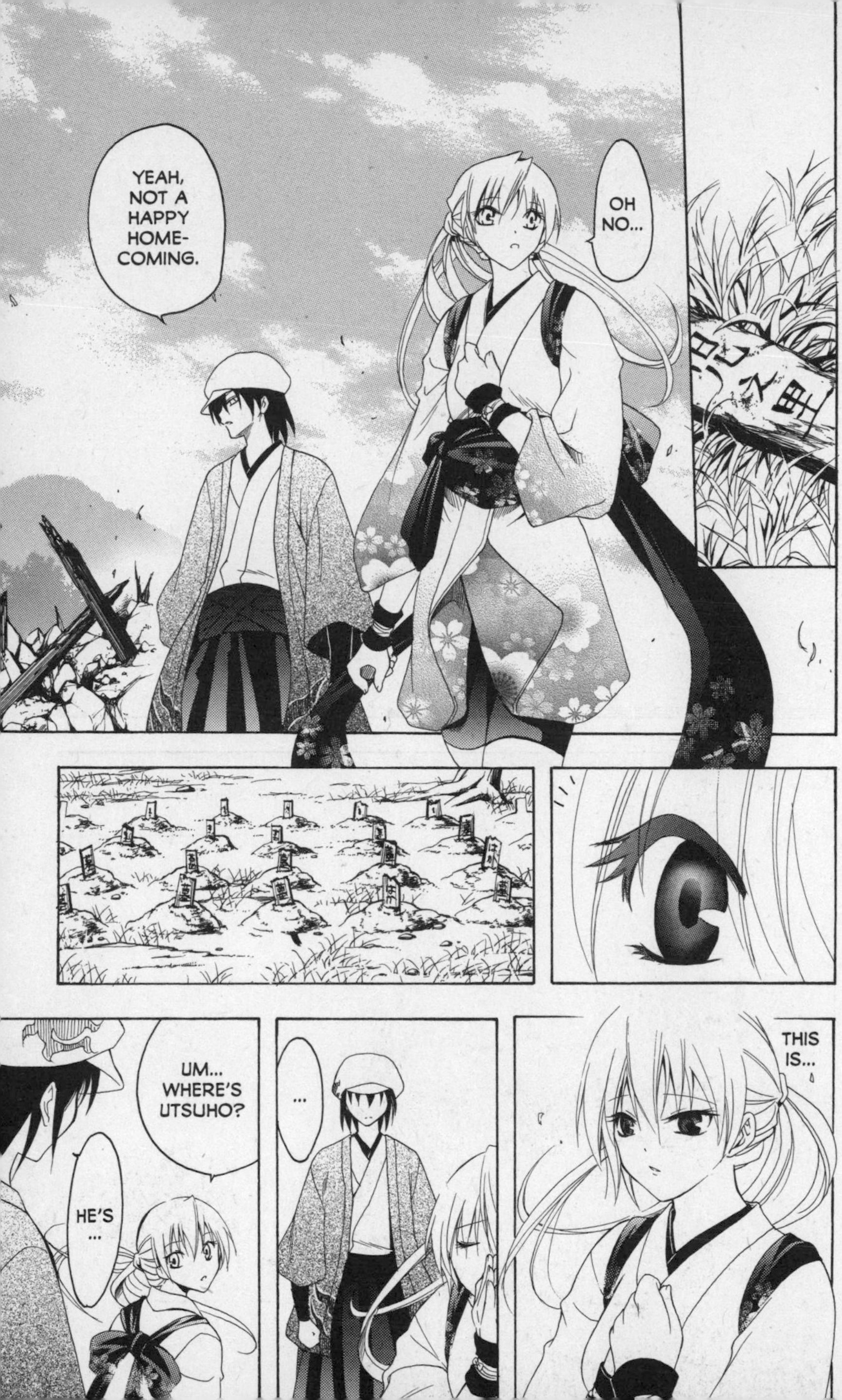
OH NO...
YEAH, NOT A HAPPY HOME-COMING.
THIS IS...
...
UM... WHERE'S UTSUHO?
HE'S ...

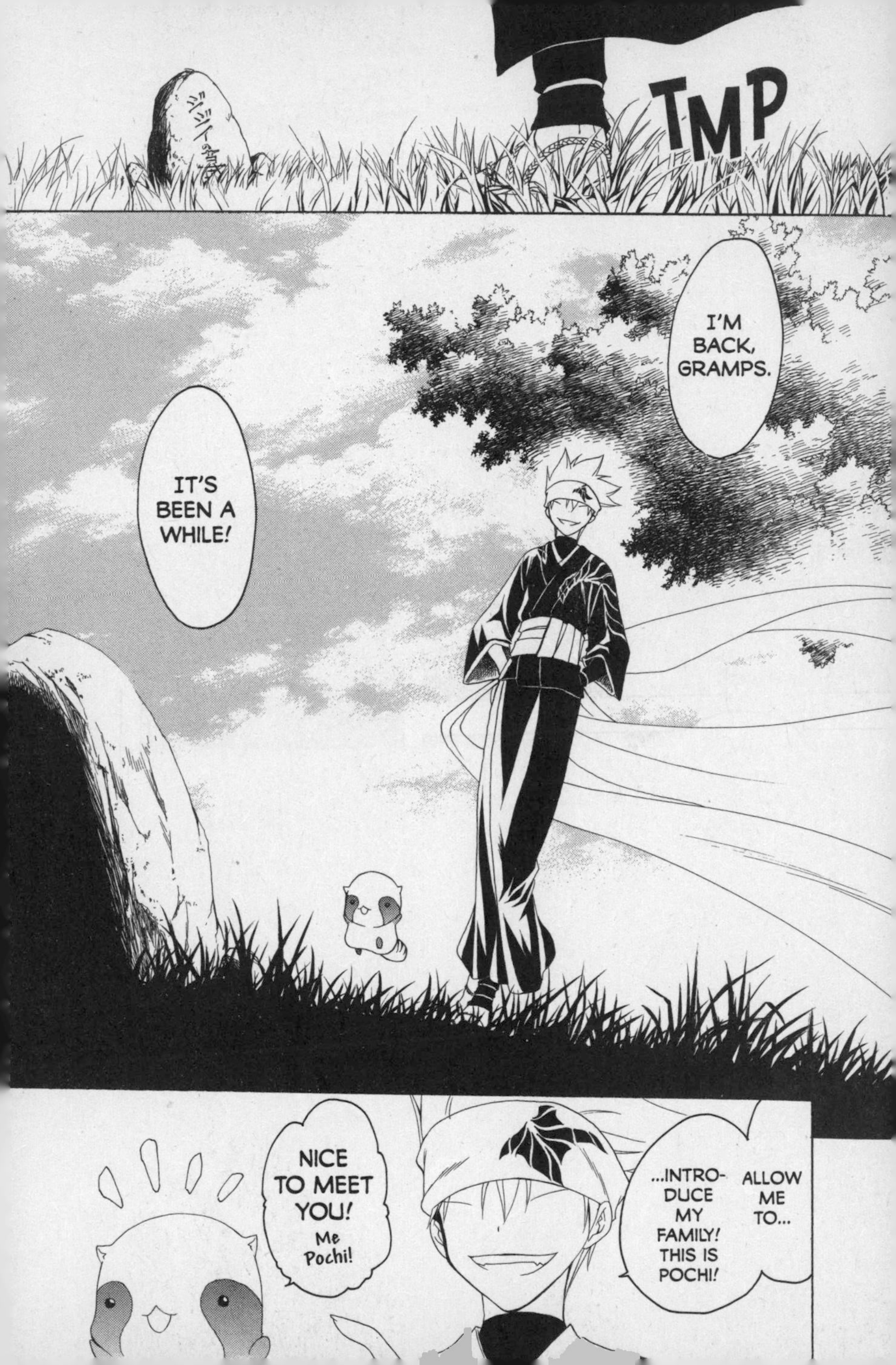
TMP
ジジイの墓
I'M BACK, GRAMPS.
IT'S BEEN A WHILE!
ALLOW ME TO...
...INTRO-DUCE MY FAMILY! THIS IS POCHI!
NICE TO MEET YOU!
Me Pochi!

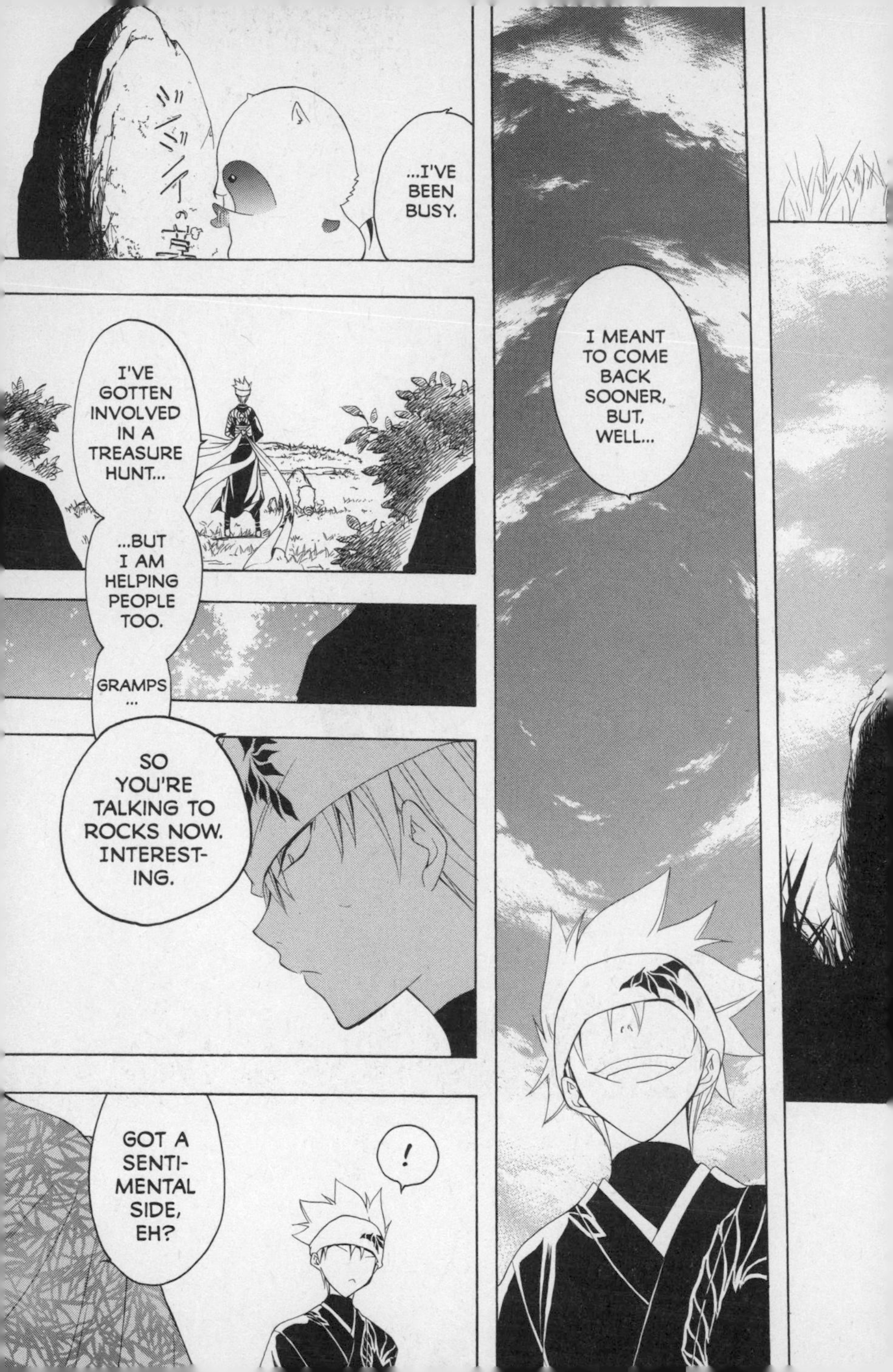
I MEANT TO COME BACK SOONER, BUT, WELL...
...I'VE BEEN BUSY.
I'VE GOTTEN INVOLVED IN A TREASURE HUNT...
...BUT I AM HELPING PEOPLE TOO.
GRAMPS...
SO YOU'RE TALKING TO ROCKS NOW. INTEREST-ING.
!
GOT A SENTI-MENTAL SIDE, EH?

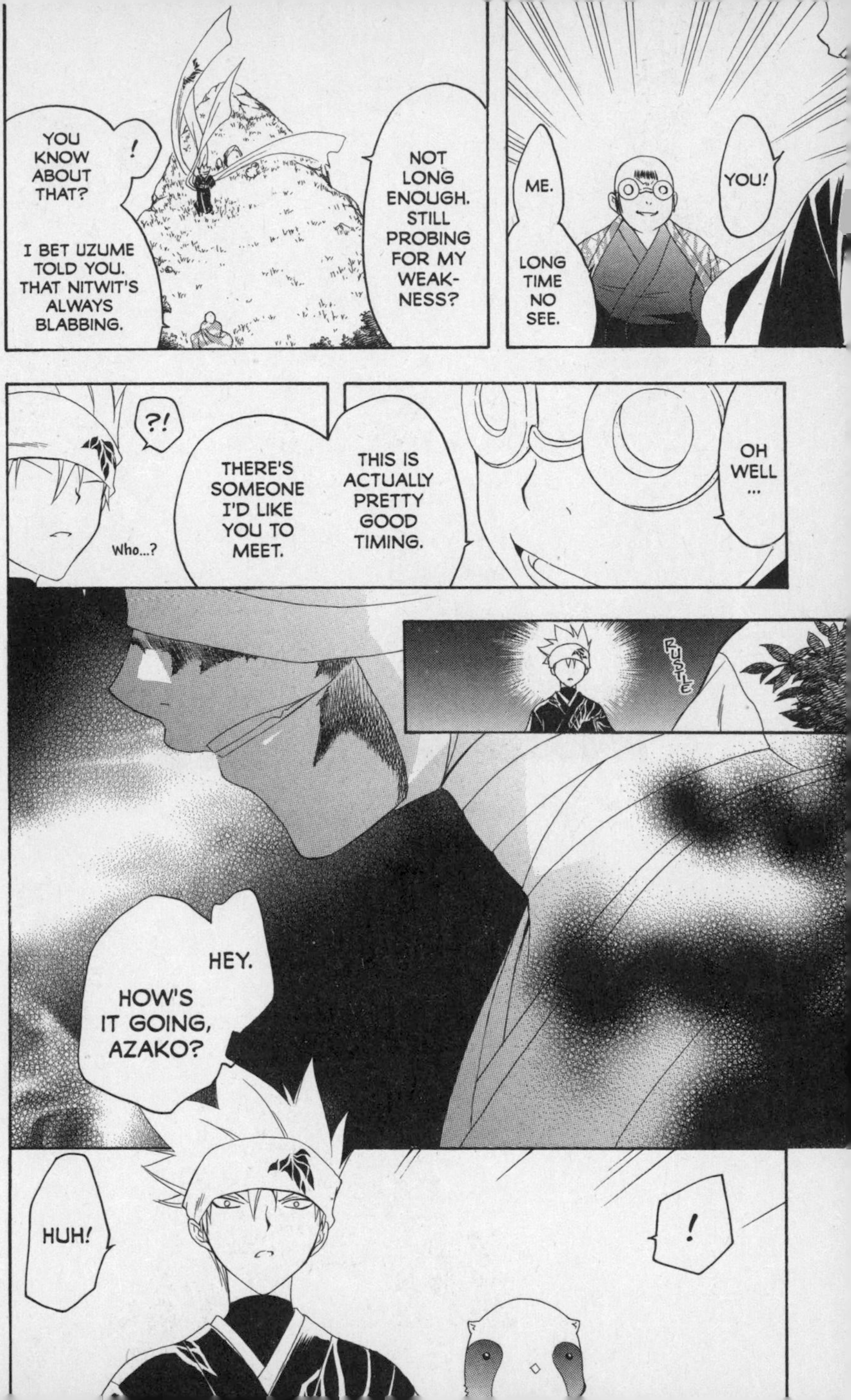
YOU!
ME.
LONG TIME NO SEE.
NOT LONG ENOUGH. STILL PROBING FOR MY WEAK-NESS?
!
YOU KNOW ABOUT THAT?
I BET UZUME TOLD YOU. THAT NITWIT'S ALWAYS BLABBING.
OH WELL ...
THIS IS ACTUALLY PRETTY GOOD TIMING.
THERE'S SOMEONE I'D LIKE YOU TO MEET.
?!
Who...?
RUSTLE
HEY.
HOW'S IT GOING, AZAKO?
!
HUH!

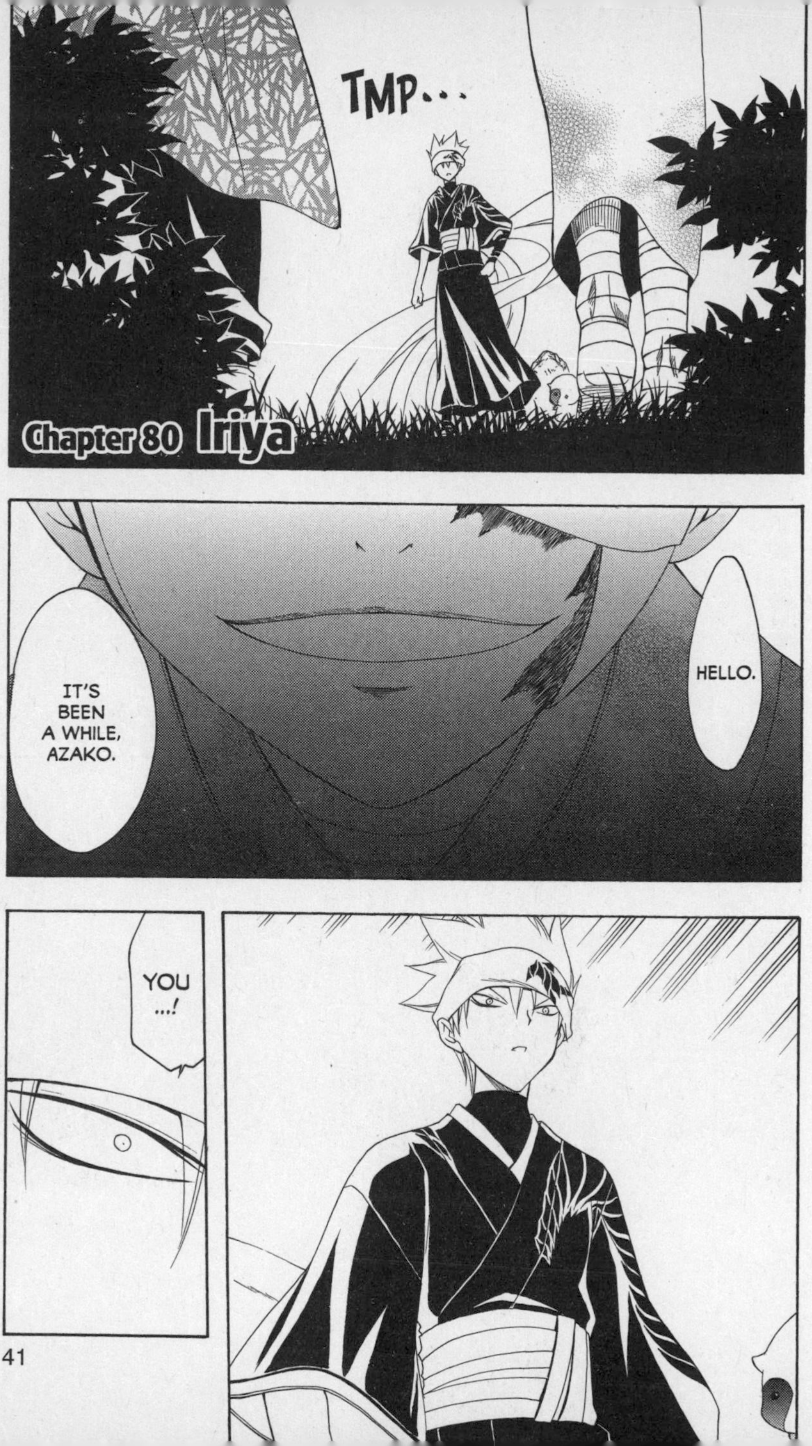
TMP...
Chapter 80 Iriya
HELLO.
IT'S BEEN A WHILE, AZAKO.
YOU ...!

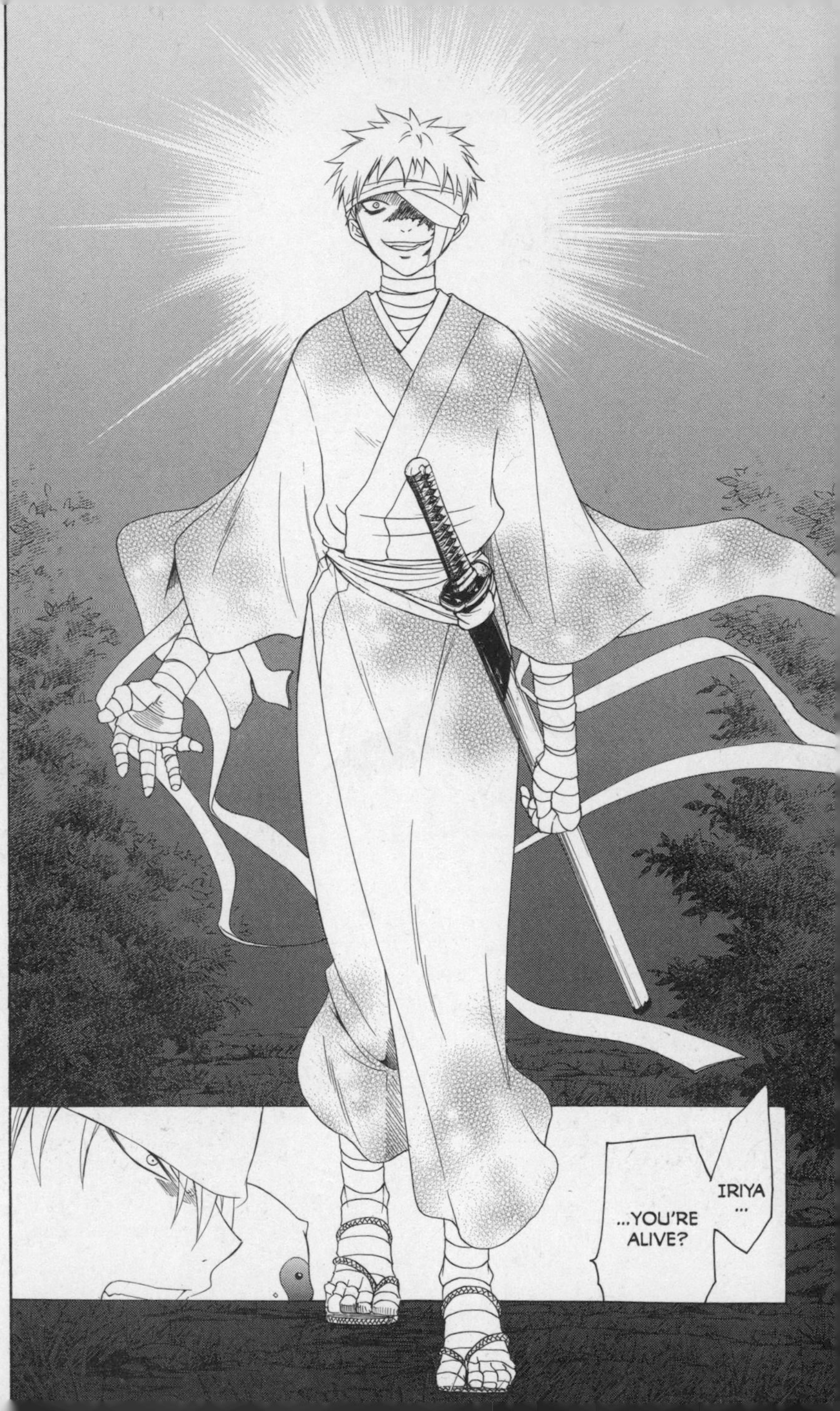
IRIYA ...
...YOU'RE ALIVE?

Chapter 80
Iriya

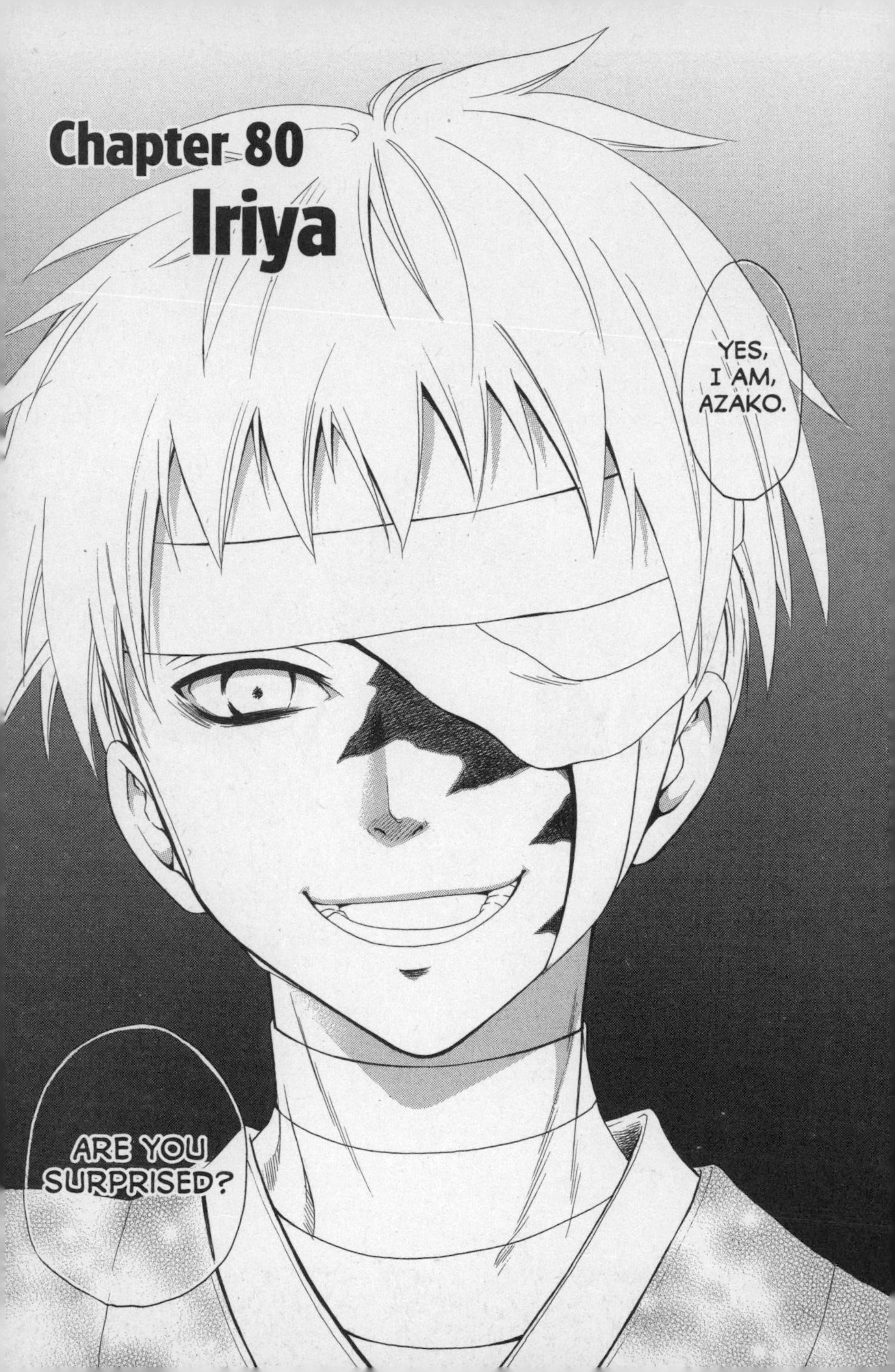
YES, I AM, AZAKO.
ARE YOU SURPRISED?

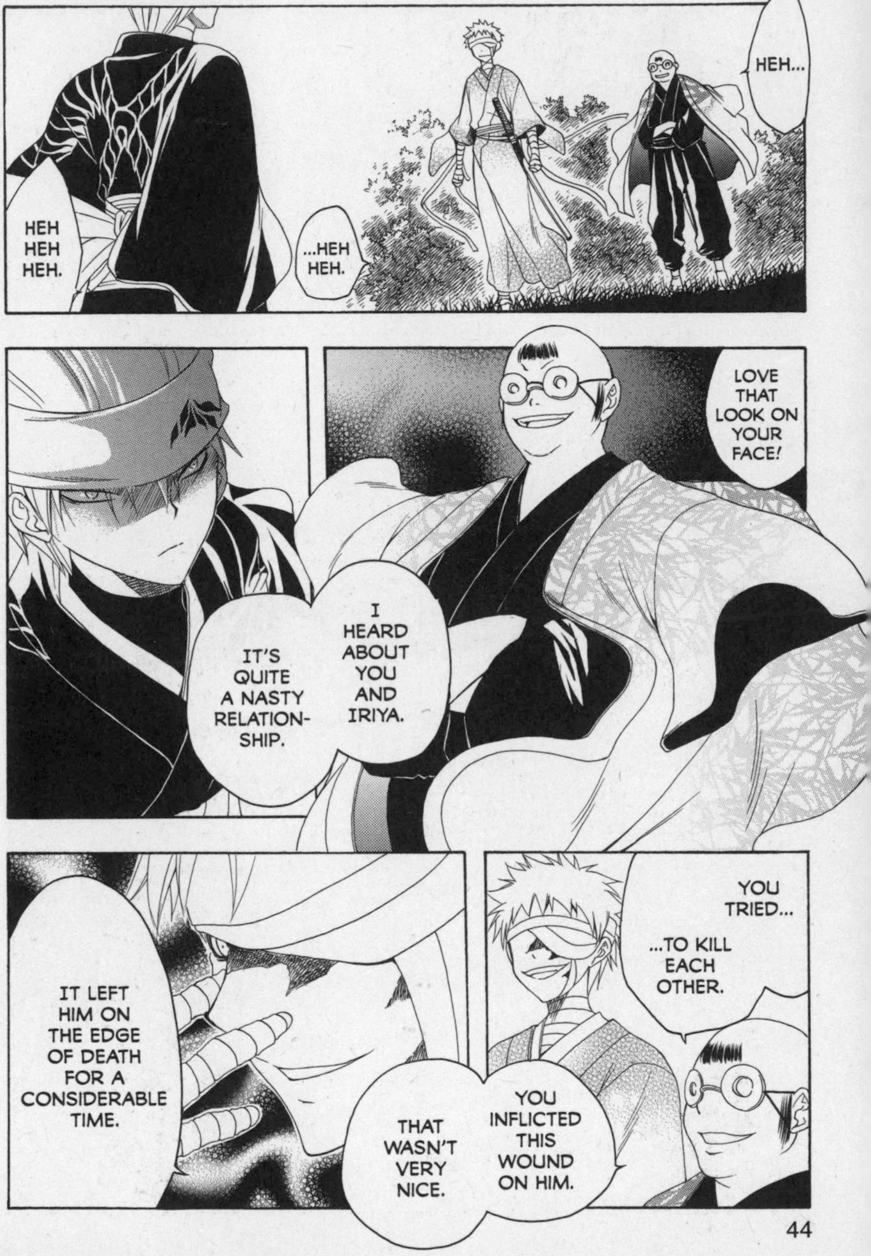
HEH...
...HEH HEH.
HEH HEH HEH.
LOVE THAT LOOK ON YOUR FACE!
I HEARD ABOUT YOU AND IRIYA.
IT'S QUITE A NASTY RELATIONSHIP.
YOU TRIED...
...TO KILL EACH OTHER.
YOU INFLICTED THIS WOUND ON HIM.
THAT WASN'T VERY NICE.
IT LEFT HIM ON THE EDGE OF DEATH FOR A CONSIDERABLE TIME.

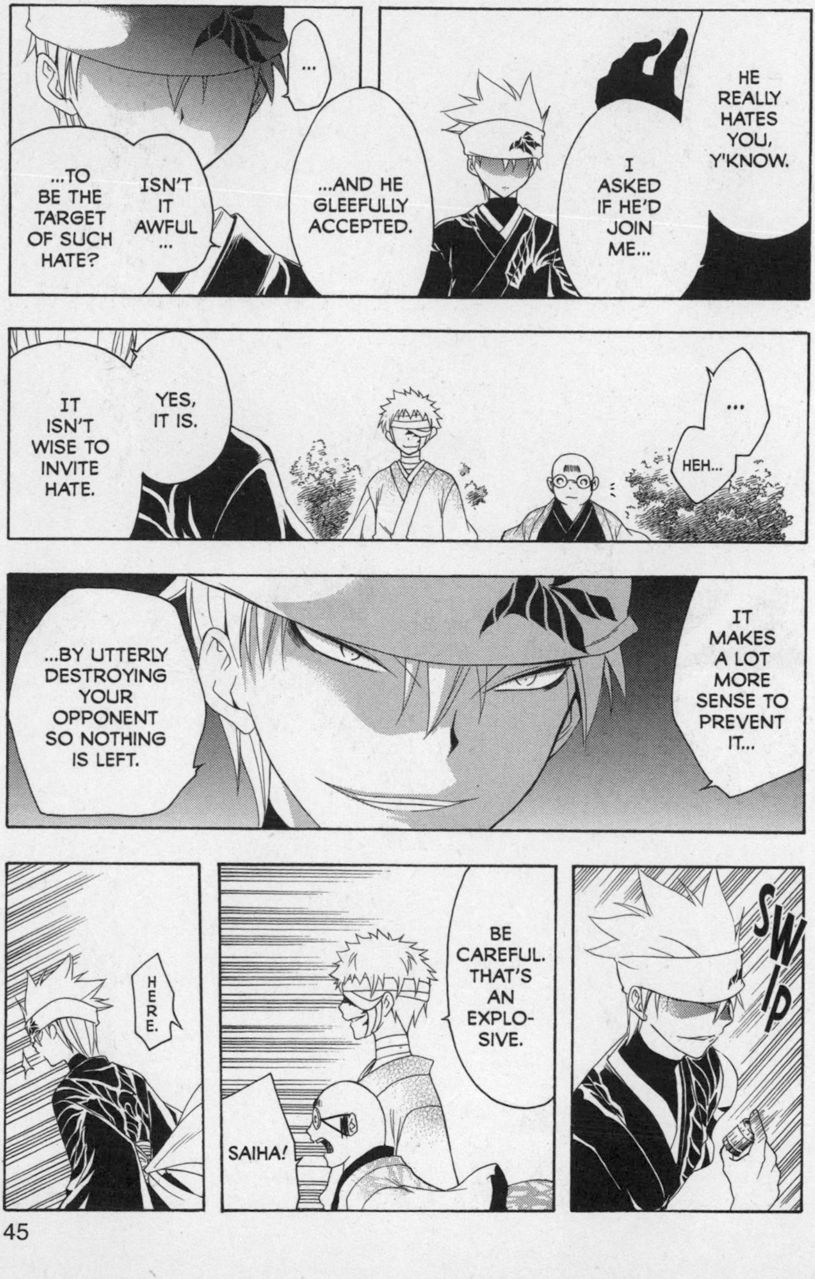
HE REALLY HATES YOU, Y'KNOW.
I ASKED IF HE'D JOIN ME...
...AND HE GLEEFULLY ACCEPTED.
...
ISN'T IT AWFUL...
...TO BE THE TARGET OF SUCH HATE?
...
HEH...
YES, IT IS.
IT ISN'T WISE TO INVITE HATE.
IT MAKES A LOT MORE SENSE TO PREVENT IT...
...BY UTTERLY DESTROYING YOUR OPPONENT SO NOTHING IS LEFT.
SWIP
BE CAREFUL. THAT'S AN EXPLOSIVE.
SAIHA!
HERE.

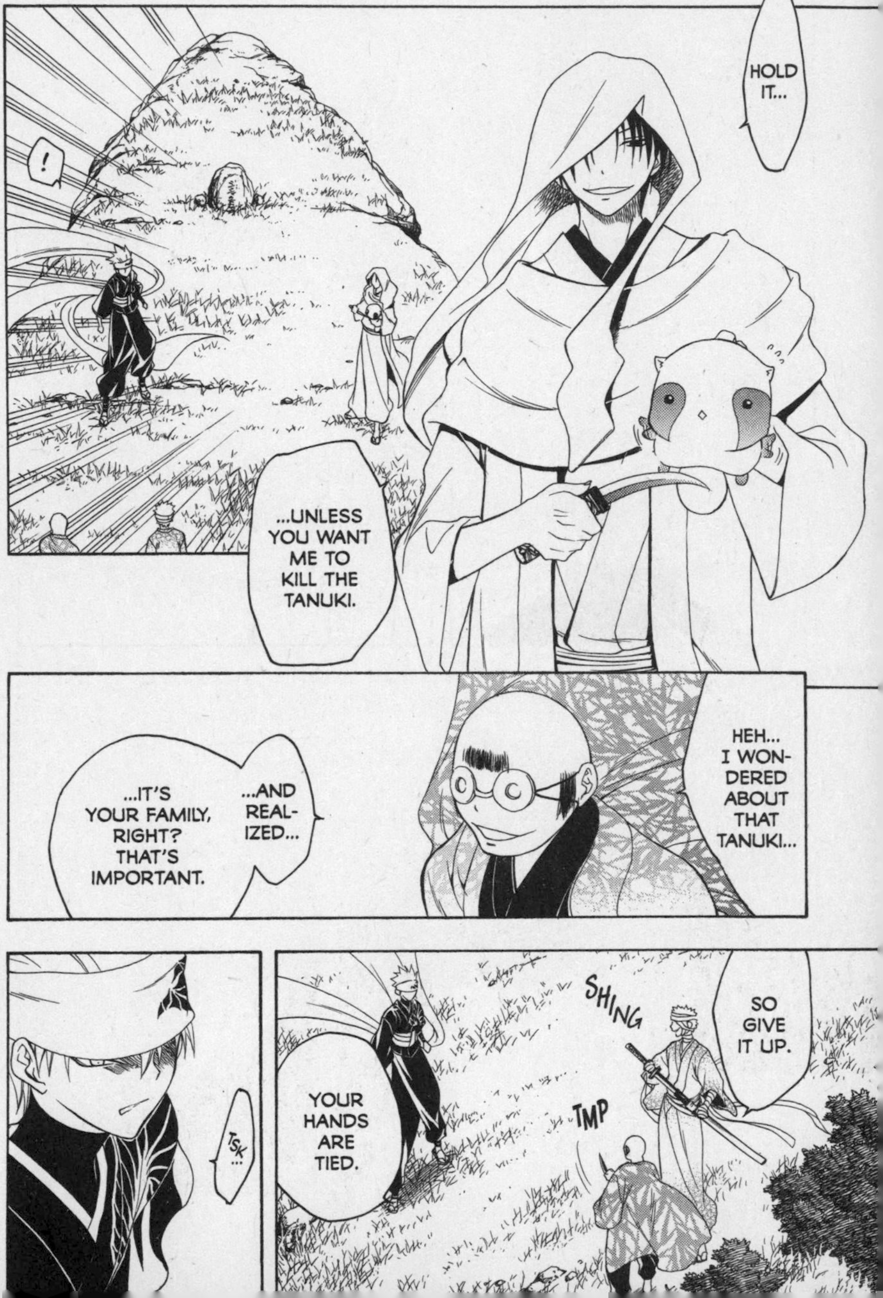
HOLD IT...
...UNLESS YOU WANT ME TO KILL THE TANUKI.
!
HEH... I WONDERED ABOUT THAT TANUKI...
...AND REALIZED...
...IT'S YOUR FAMILY, RIGHT? THAT'S IMPORTANT.
SO GIVE IT UP.
SHING
TMP
YOUR HANDS ARE TIED.
TSK...

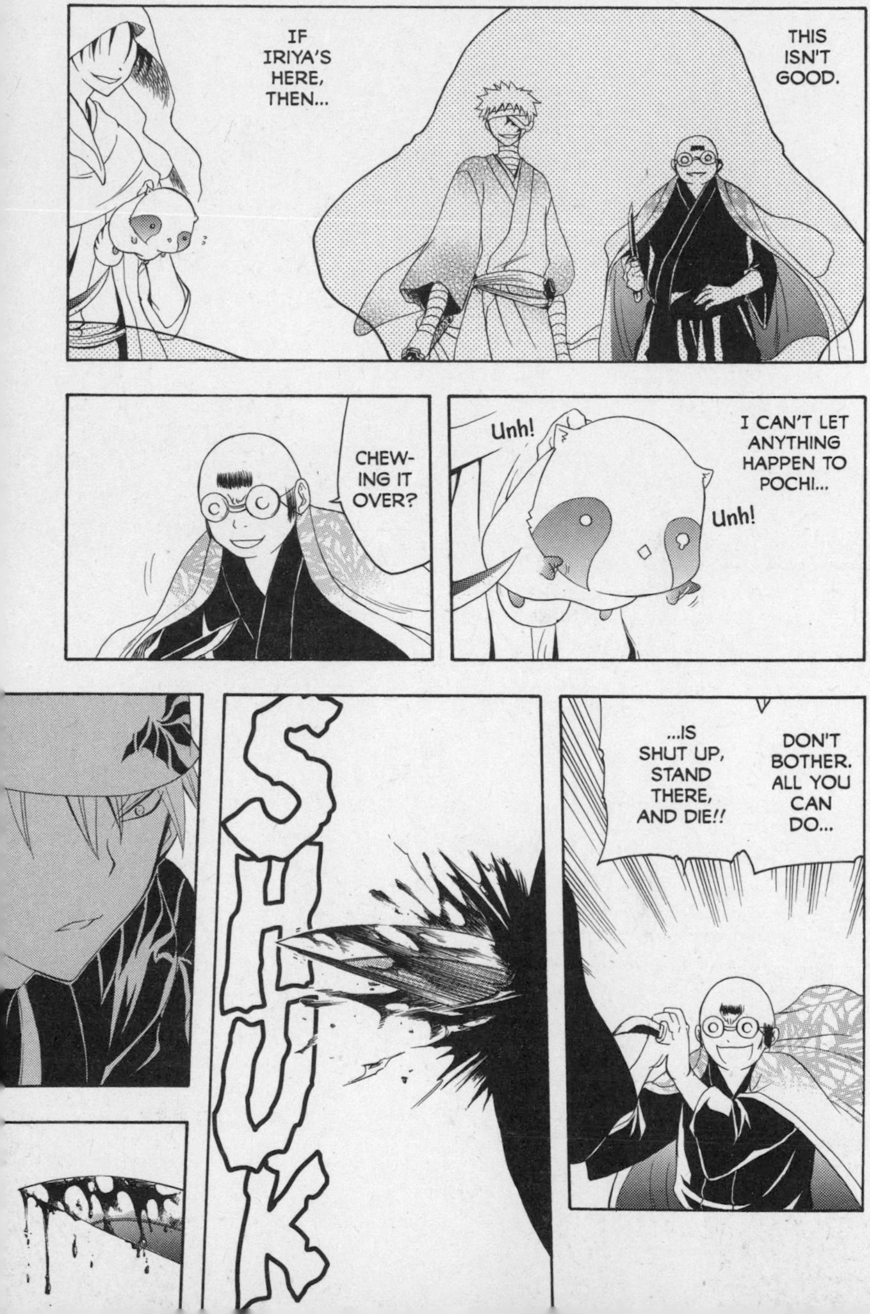
THIS ISN'T GOOD.
IF IRIYA'S HERE, THEN...
I CAN'T LET ANYTHING HAPPEN TO POCHI...
Unh!
Unh!
CHEW-ING IT OVER?
DON'T BOTHER. ALL YOU CAN DO...
...IS SHUT UP, STAND THERE, AND DIE!!
SHUK

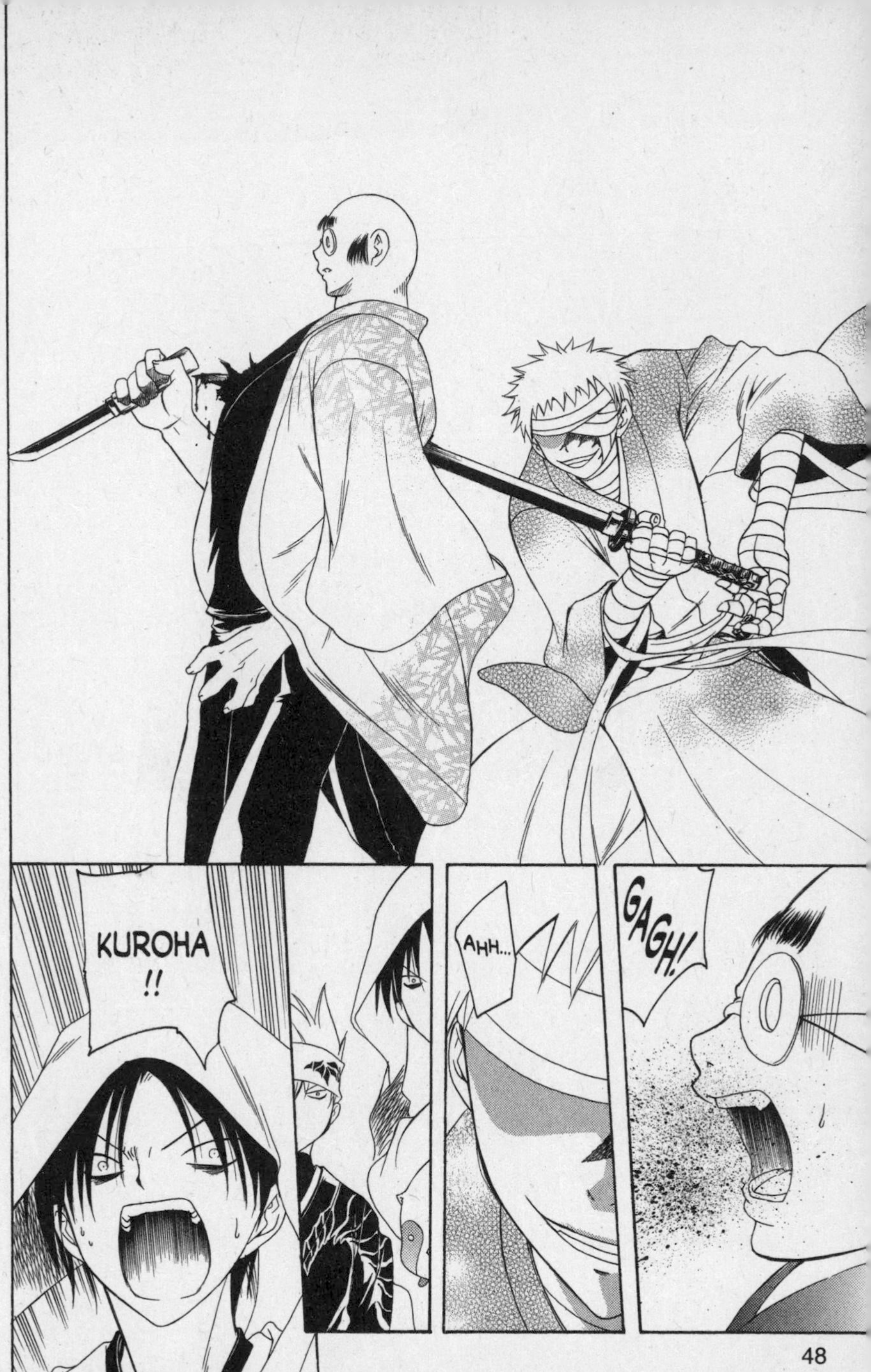
GAGH!
AHH...
KUROHA !!

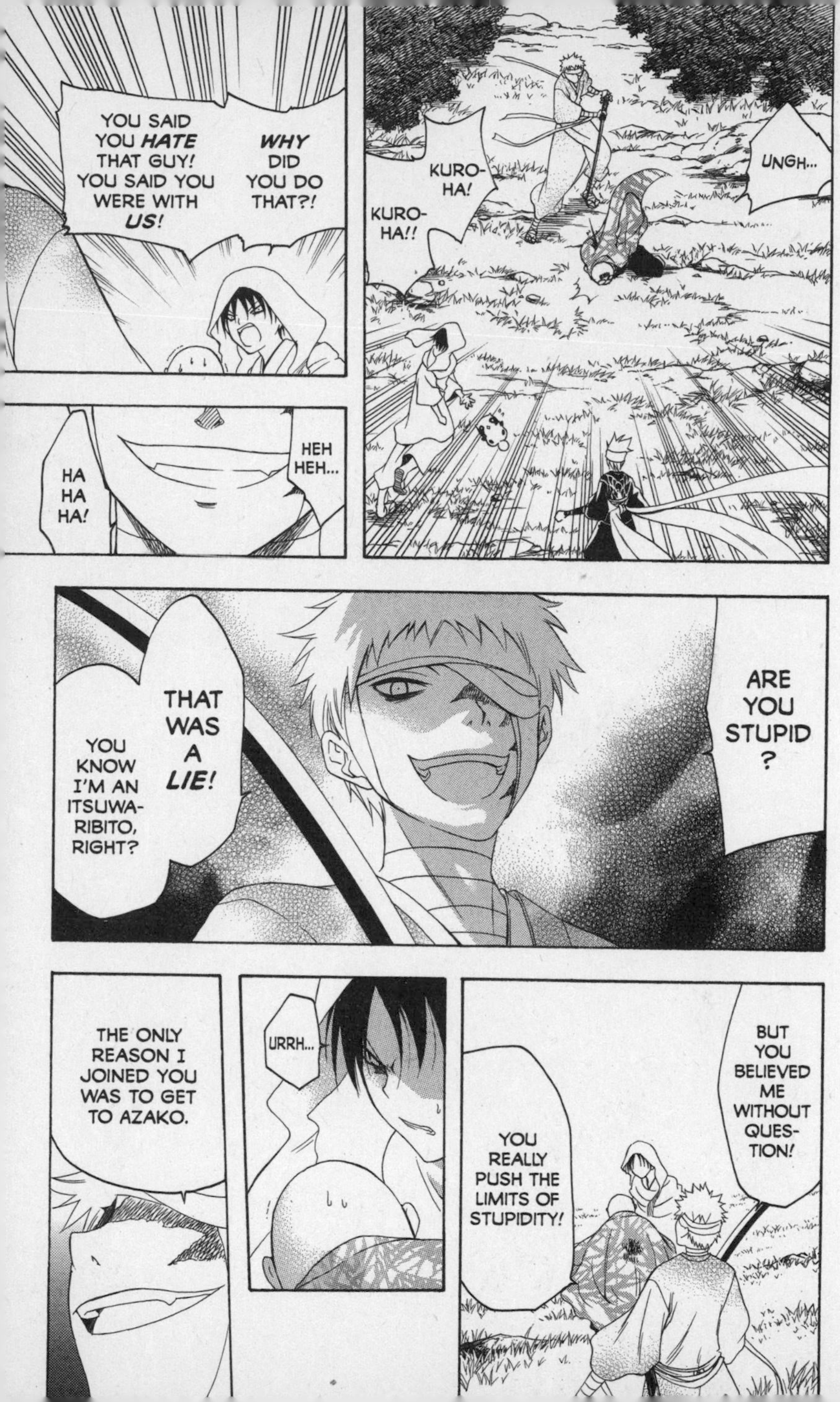
UNGH...
KURO-HA!
KURO-HA!!
WHY DID YOU DO THAT?!
YOU SAID YOU HATE THAT GUY! YOU SAID YOU WERE WITH US!
HEH HEH...
HA HA HA!
ARE YOU STUPID?
THAT WAS A LIE!
YOU KNOW I'M AN ITSUWARIBITO, RIGHT?
BUT YOU BELIEVED ME WITHOUT QUESTION!
YOU REALLY PUSH THE LIMITS OF STUPIDITY!
URRH...
THE ONLY REASON I JOINED YOU WAS TO GET TO AZAKO.

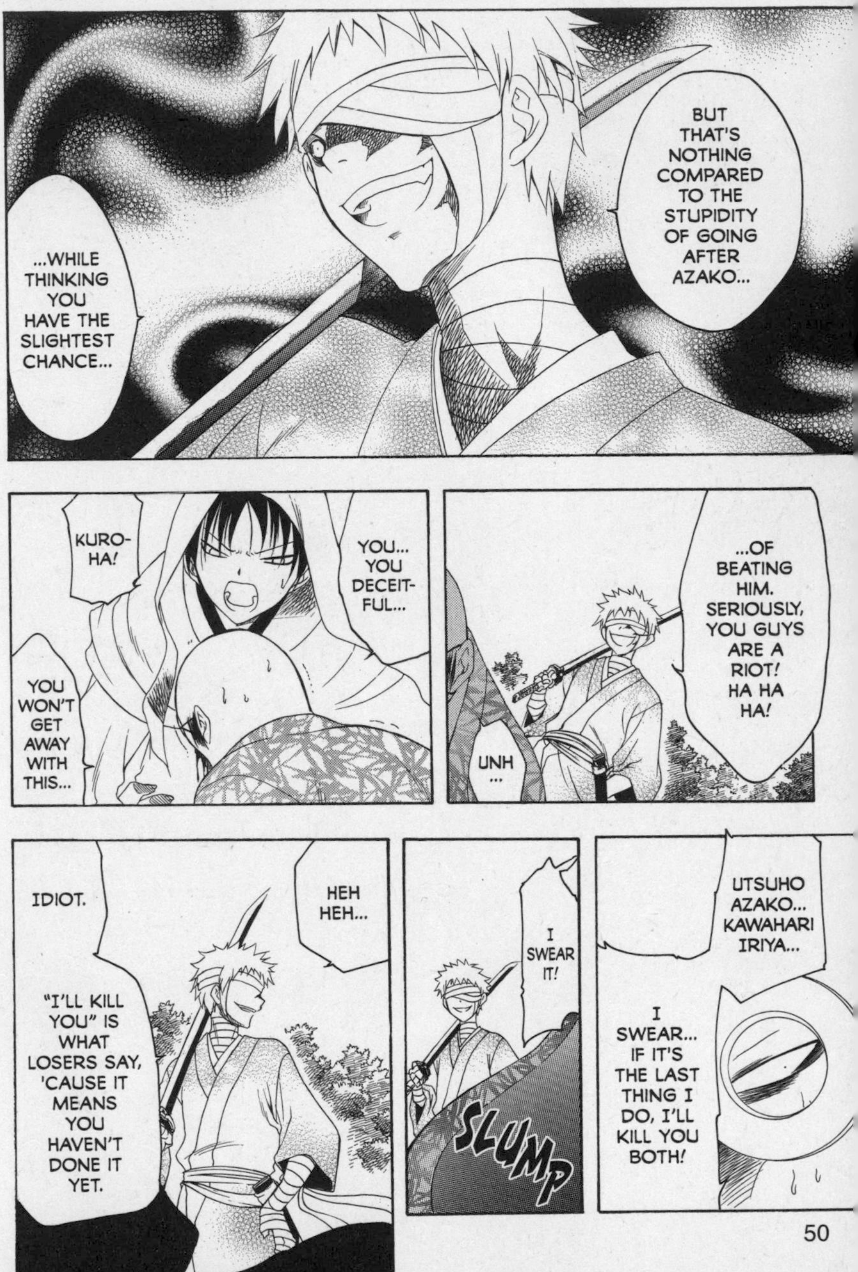
BUT THAT'S NOTHING COMPARED TO THE STUPIDITY OF GOING AFTER AZAKO...
...WHILE THINKING YOU HAVE THE SLIGHTEST CHANCE...
...OF BEATING HIM. SERIOUSLY, YOU GUYS ARE A RIOT! HA HA HA!
UNH...
YOU... YOU DECEIT-FUL...
KURO-HA!
YOU WON'T GET AWAY WITH THIS...
UTSUHO AZAKO... KAWAHARI IRIYA...
I SWEAR... IF IT'S THE LAST THING I DO, I'LL KILL YOU BOTH!
I SWEAR IT!
SLUMP
HEH HEH...
IDIOT.
"I'LL KILL YOU" IS WHAT LOSERS SAY, 'CAUSE IT MEANS YOU HAVEN'T DONE IT YET.

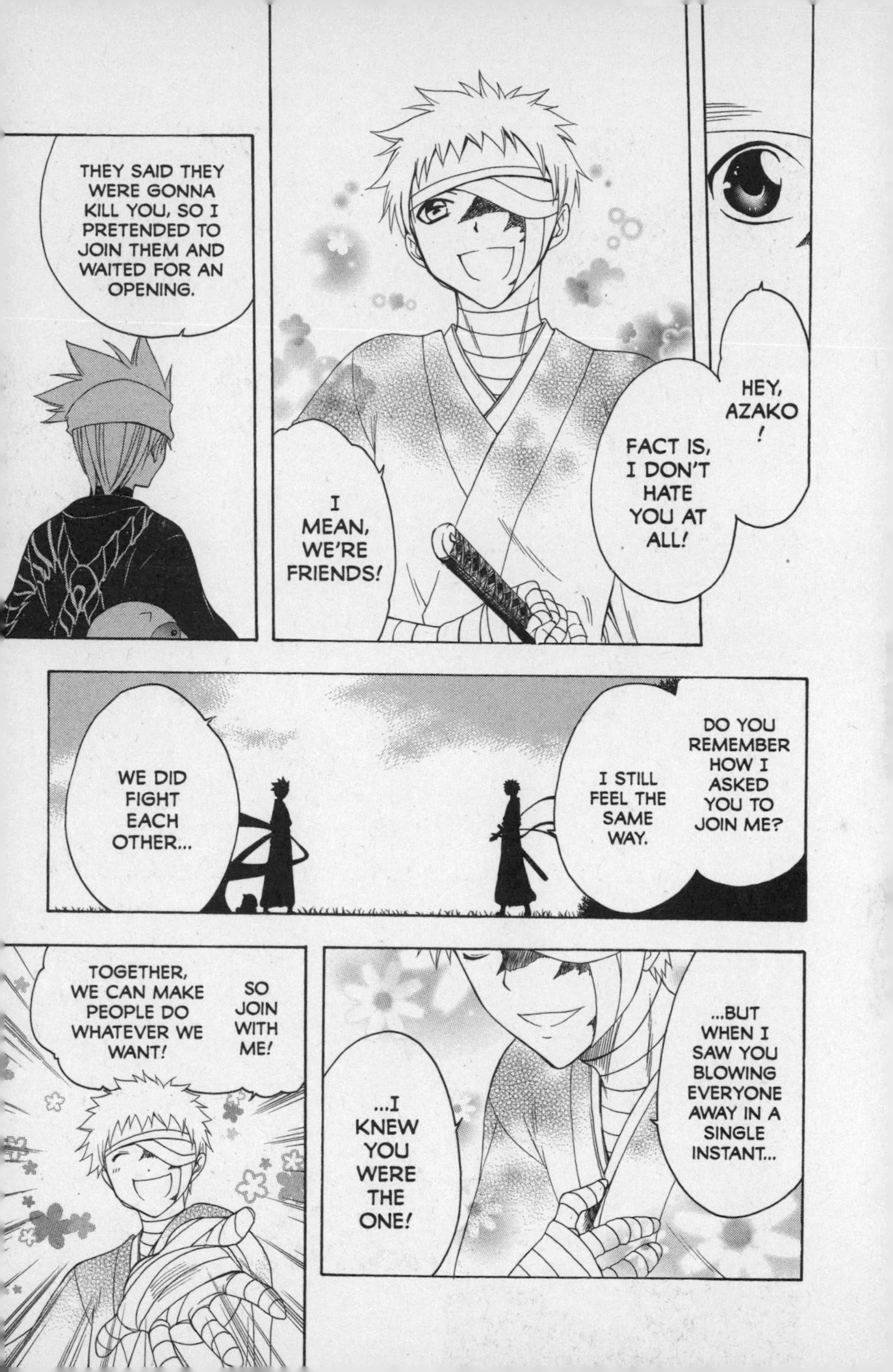
HEY, AZAKO!
FACT IS, I DON'T HATE YOU AT ALL!
I MEAN, WE'RE FRIENDS!
THEY SAID THEY WERE GONNA KILL YOU, SO I PRETENDED TO JOIN THEM AND WAITED FOR AN OPENING.
DO YOU REMEMBER HOW I ASKED YOU TO JOIN ME?
I STILL FEEL THE SAME WAY.
WE DID FIGHT EACH OTHER...
...BUT WHEN I SAW YOU BLOWING EVERYONE AWAY IN A SINGLE INSTANT...
...I KNEW YOU WERE THE ONE!
SO JOIN WITH ME!
TOGETHER, WE CAN MAKE PEOPLE DO WHATEVER WE WANT!

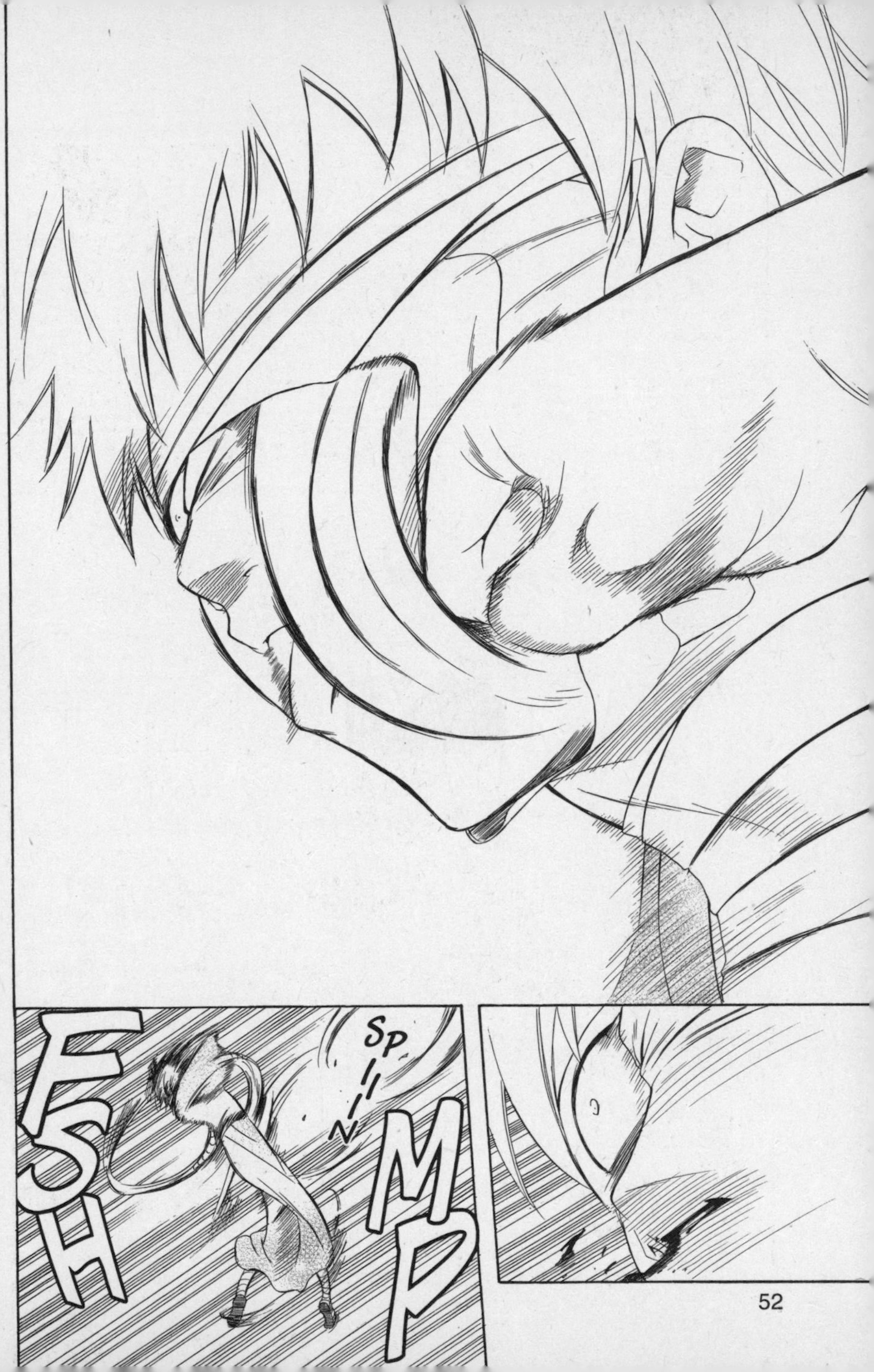
SPIIIN
MP
FSH

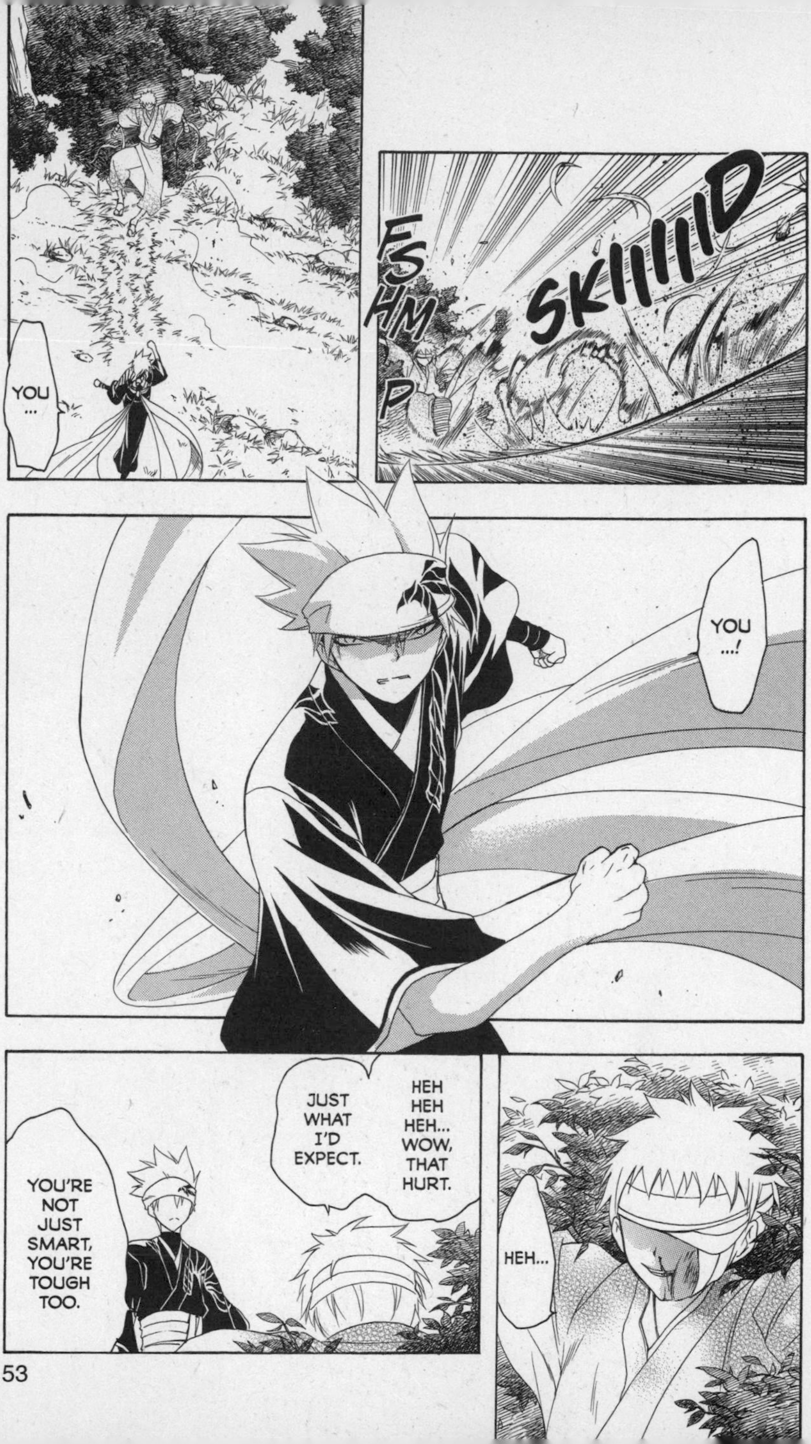
SKIIIIID
FSHMP
YOU ...
YOU ...!
HEH...
HEH HEH HEH... WOW, THAT HURT.
JUST WHAT I'D EXPECT.
YOU'RE NOT JUST SMART, YOU'RE TOUGH TOO.

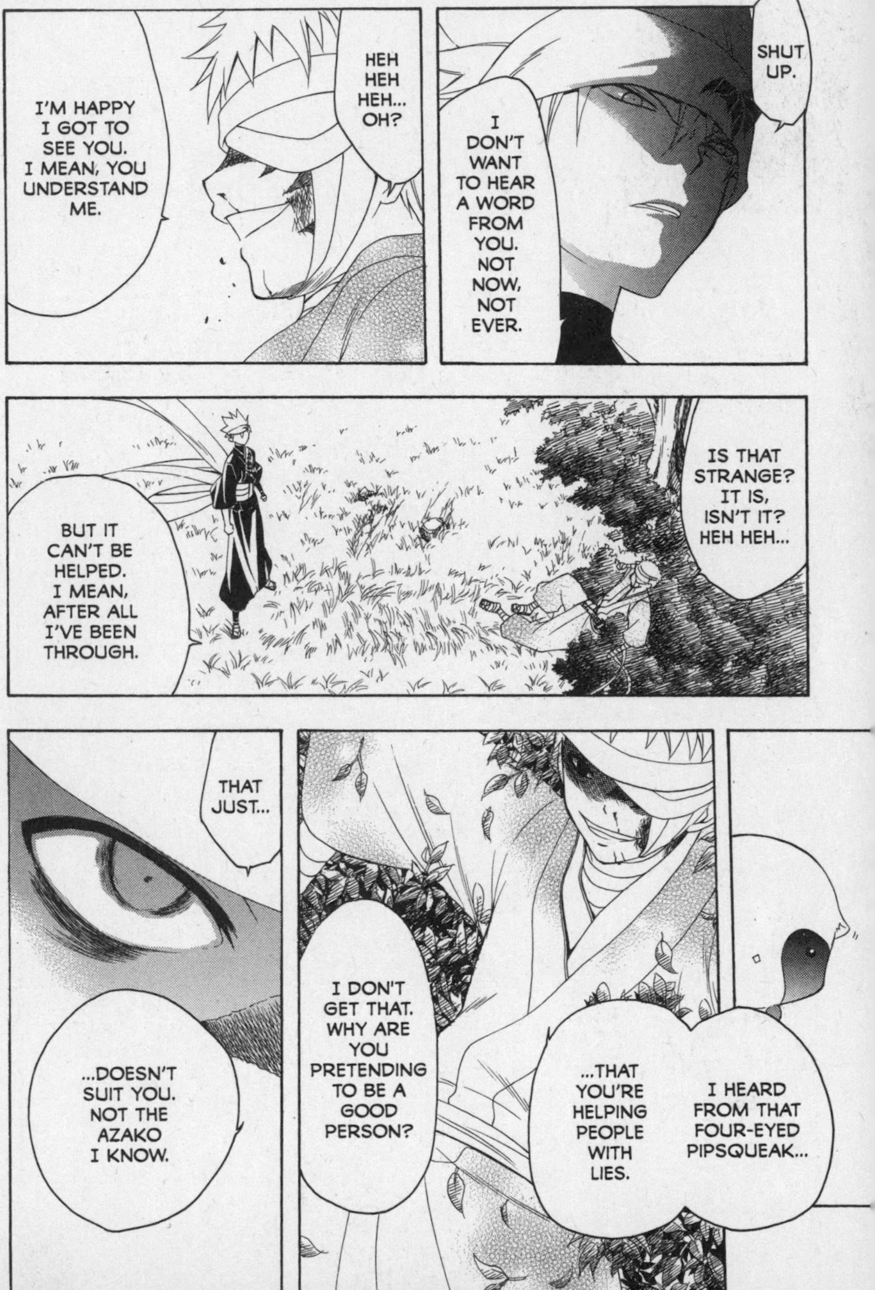
SHUT UP.
I DON'T WANT TO HEAR A WORD FROM YOU. NOT NOW, NOT EVER.
HEH HEH HEH... OH?
I'M HAPPY I GOT TO SEE YOU. I MEAN, YOU UNDERSTAND ME.
IS THAT STRANGE? IT IS, ISN'T IT? HEH HEH...
BUT IT CAN'T BE HELPED. I MEAN, AFTER ALL I'VE BEEN THROUGH.
I HEARD FROM THAT FOUR-EYED PIPSQUEAK...
...THAT YOU'RE HELPING PEOPLE WITH LIES.
I DON'T GET THAT. WHY ARE YOU PRETENDING TO BE A GOOD PERSON?
THAT JUST...
...DOESN'T SUIT YOU. NOT THE AZAKO I KNOW.

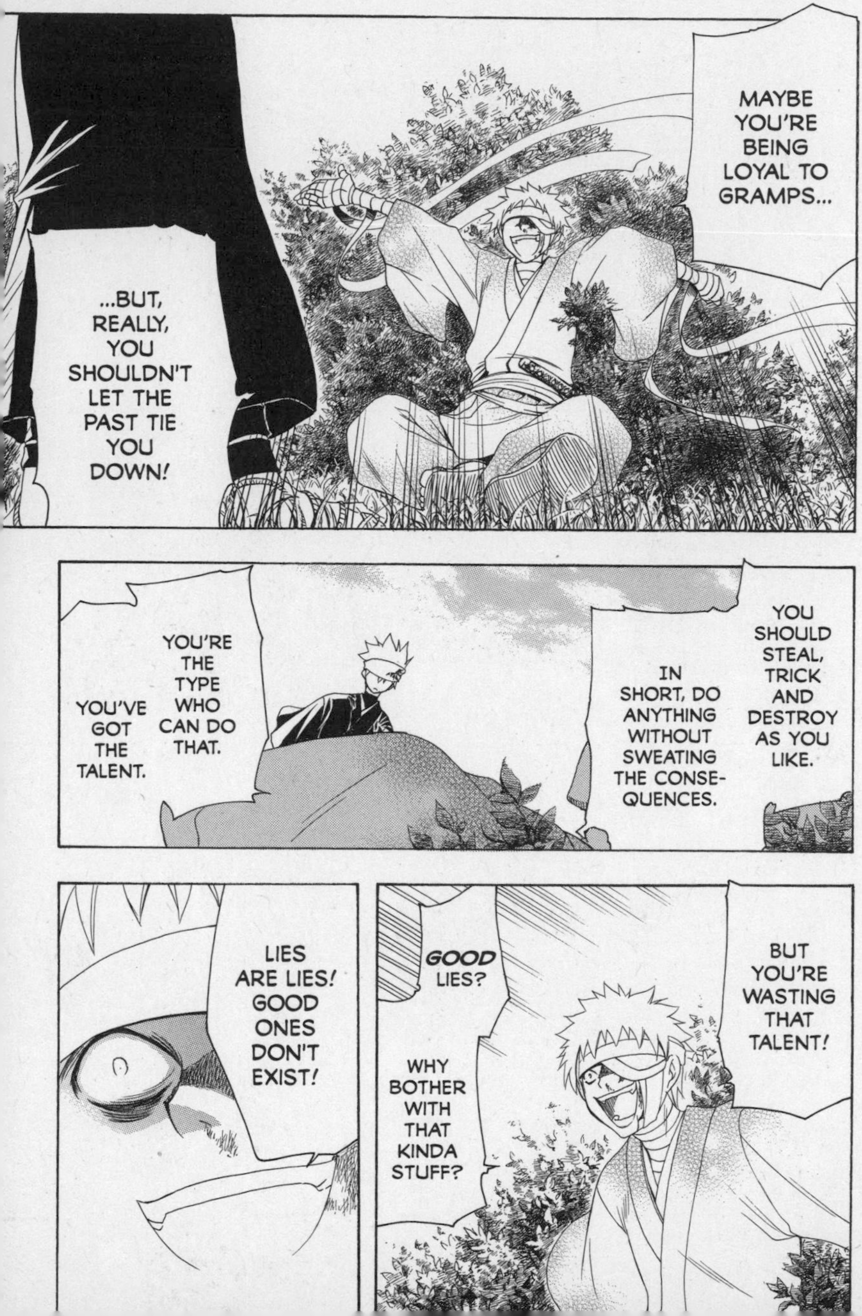
MAYBE YOU'RE BEING LOYAL TO GRAMPS...
...BUT, REALLY, YOU SHOULDN'T LET THE PAST TIE YOU DOWN!
YOU SHOULD STEAL, TRICK AND DESTROY AS YOU LIKE.
IN SHORT, DO ANYTHING WITHOUT SWEATING THE CONSE-QUENCES.
YOU'RE THE TYPE WHO CAN DO THAT.
YOU'VE GOT THE TALENT.
BUT YOU'RE WASTING THAT TALENT!
GOOD LIES?
WHY BOTHER WITH THAT KINDA STUFF?
LIES ARE LIES! GOOD ONES DON'T EXIST!

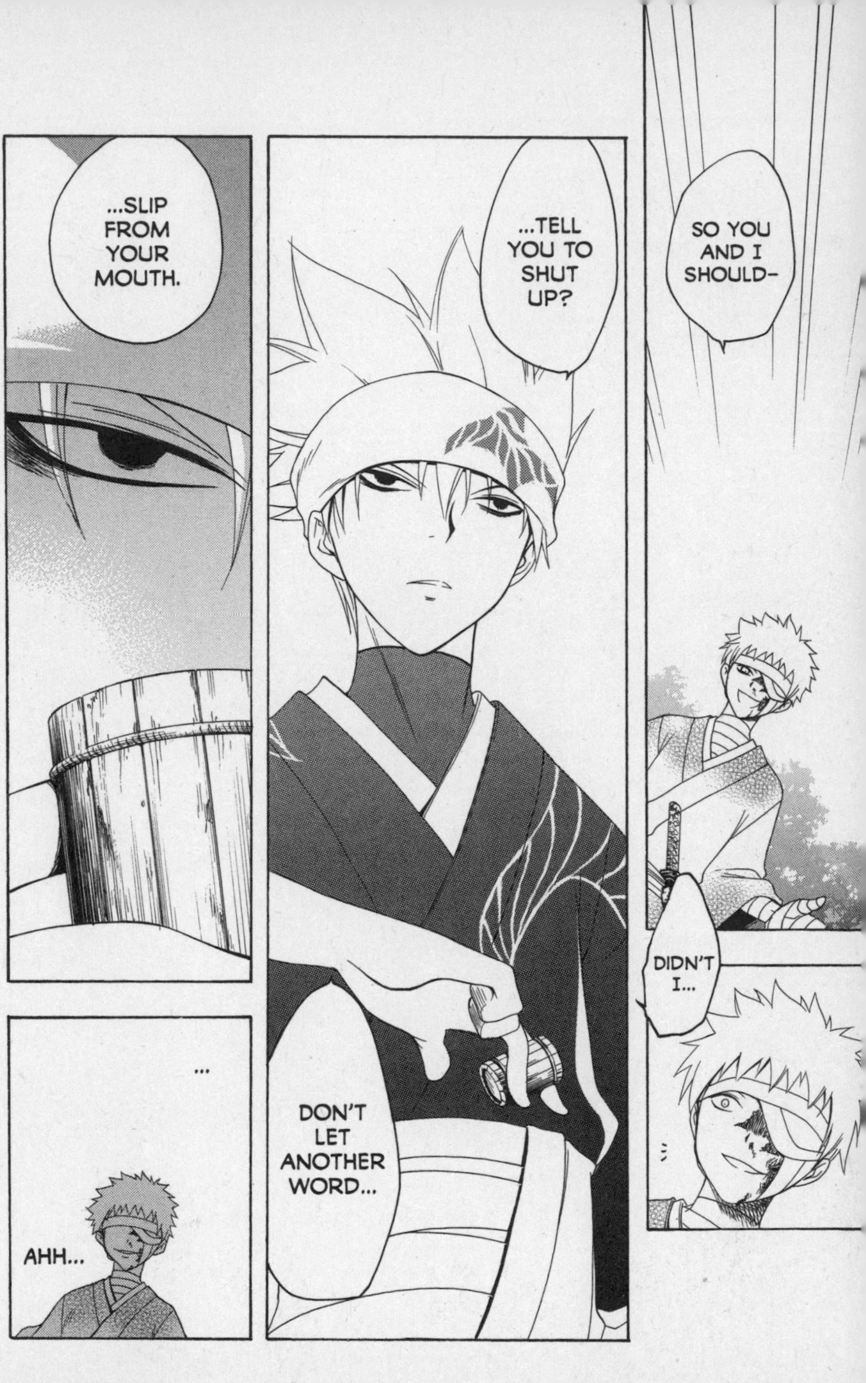
SO YOU AND I SHOULD-
DIDN'T I...
...TELL YOU TO SHUT UP?
DON'T LET ANOTHER WORD...
...SLIP FROM YOUR MOUTH.
...
AHH...

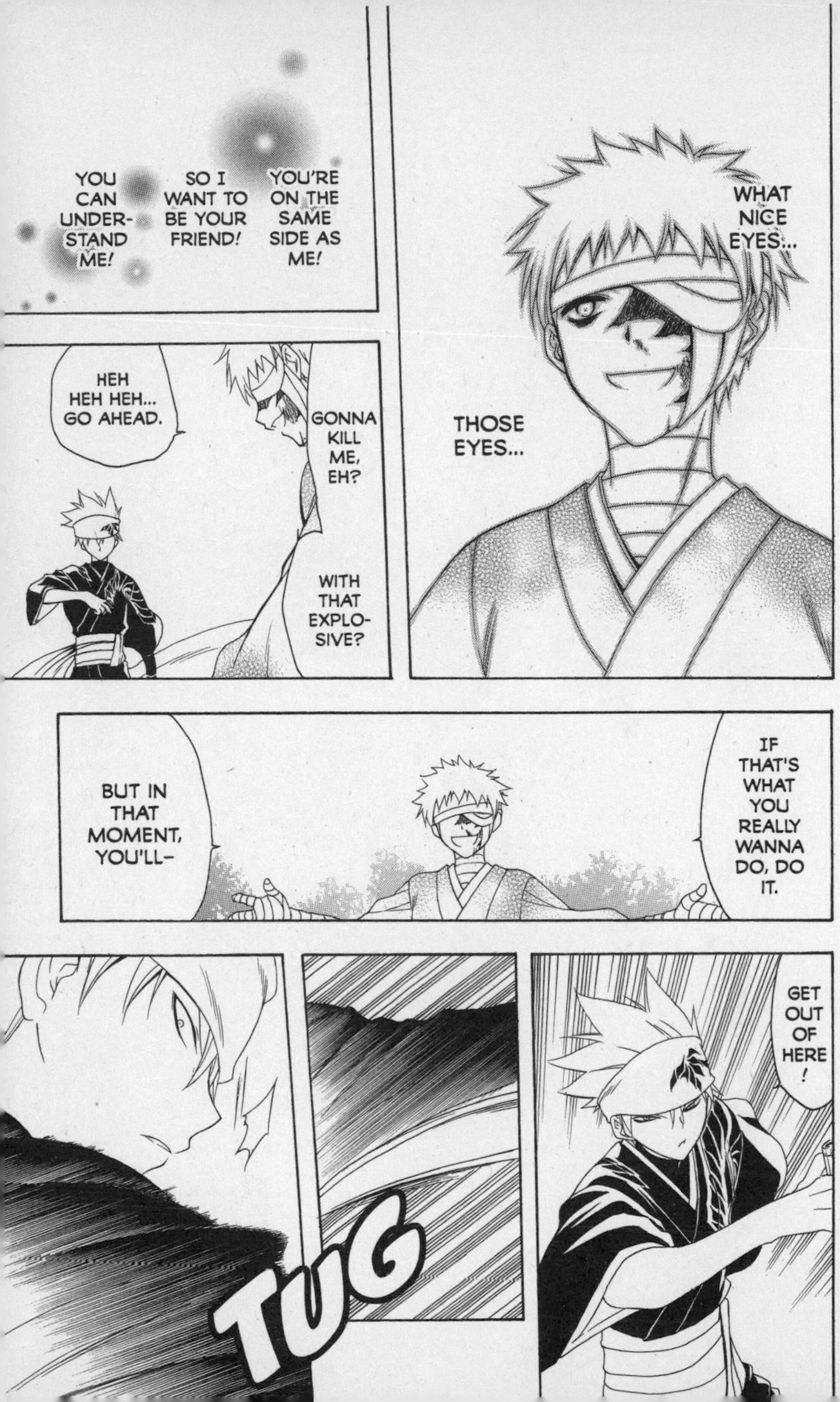
WHAT NICE EYES...
THOSE EYES...
YOU'RE ON THE SAME SIDE AS ME!
SO I WANT TO BE YOUR FRIEND!
YOU CAN UNDER-STAND ME!
GONNA KILL ME, EH?
WITH THAT EXPLO-SIVE?
HEH HEH HEH... GO AHEAD.
IF THAT'S WHAT YOU REALLY WANNA DO, DO IT.
BUT IN THAT MOMENT, YOU'LL–
GET OUT OF HERE!
TUG

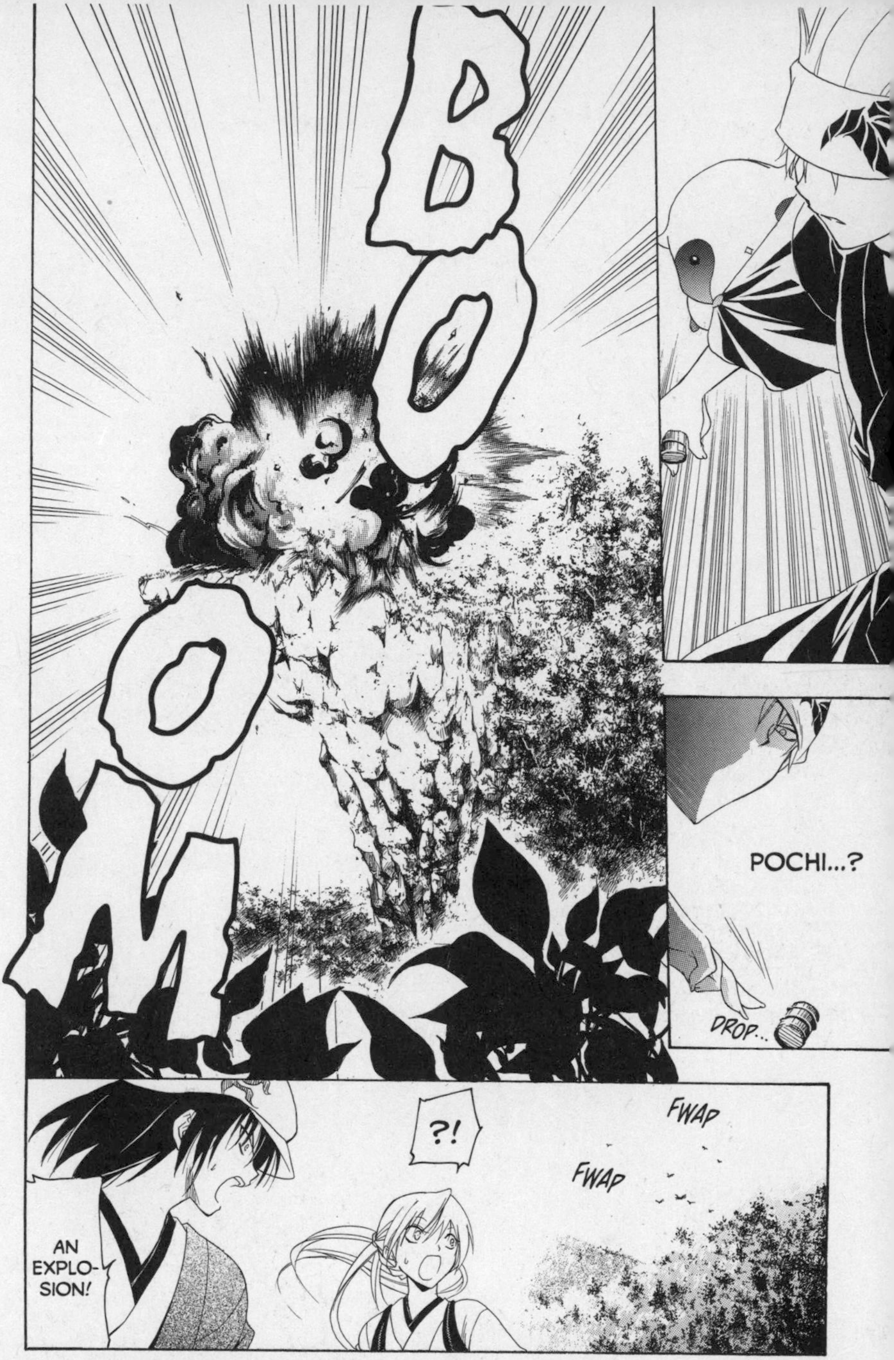
POCHI...?
DROP...
BOOM
?!
FWAP
FWAP
AN EXPLOSION!

Chapter 81 Letter

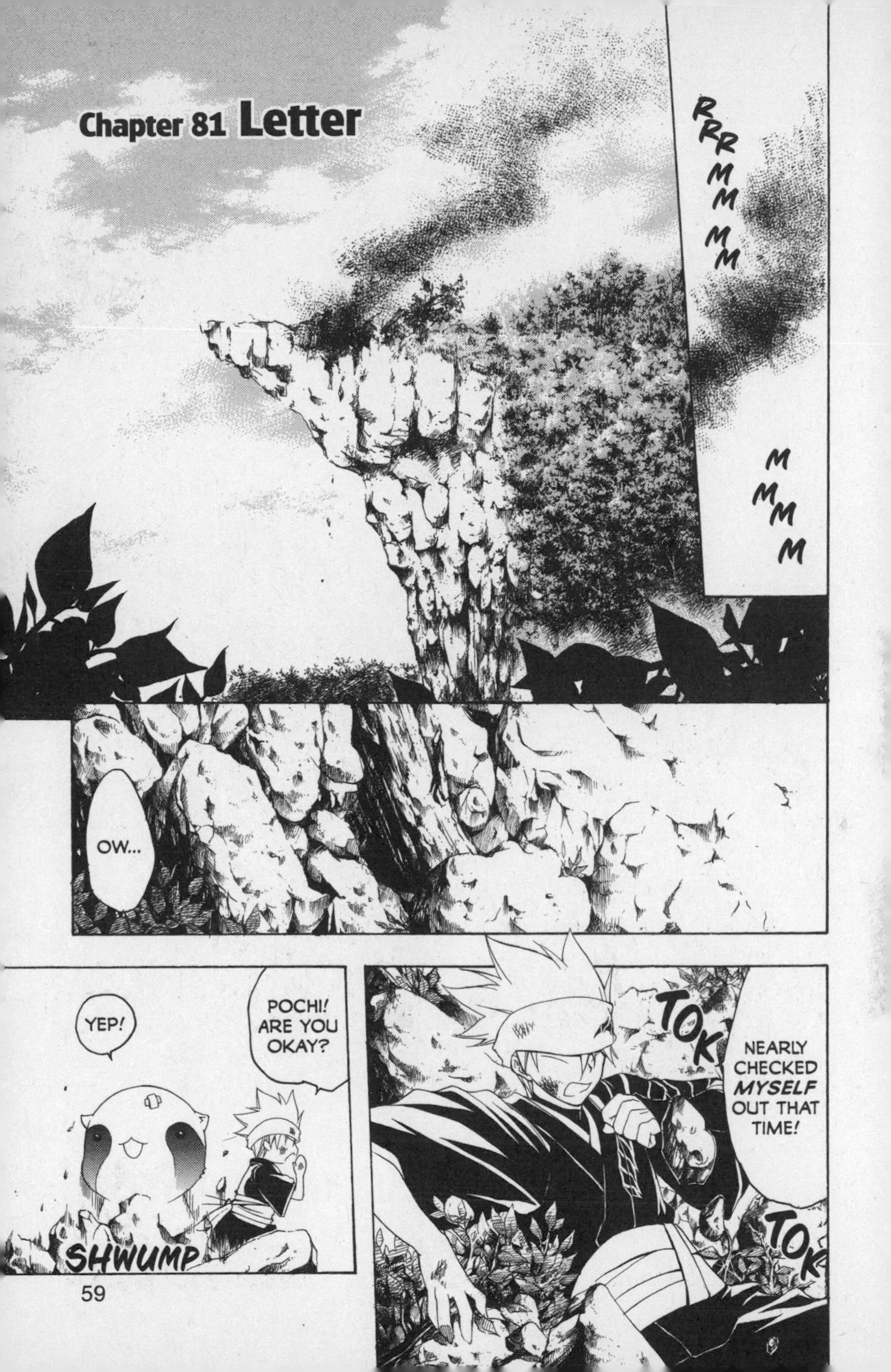
RRRMMMMMM
MMMMM
OW...
TOK
NEARLY CHECKED *MYSELF* OUT THAT TIME!
TOK
POCHI! ARE YOU OKAY?
YEP!
SHWUMP

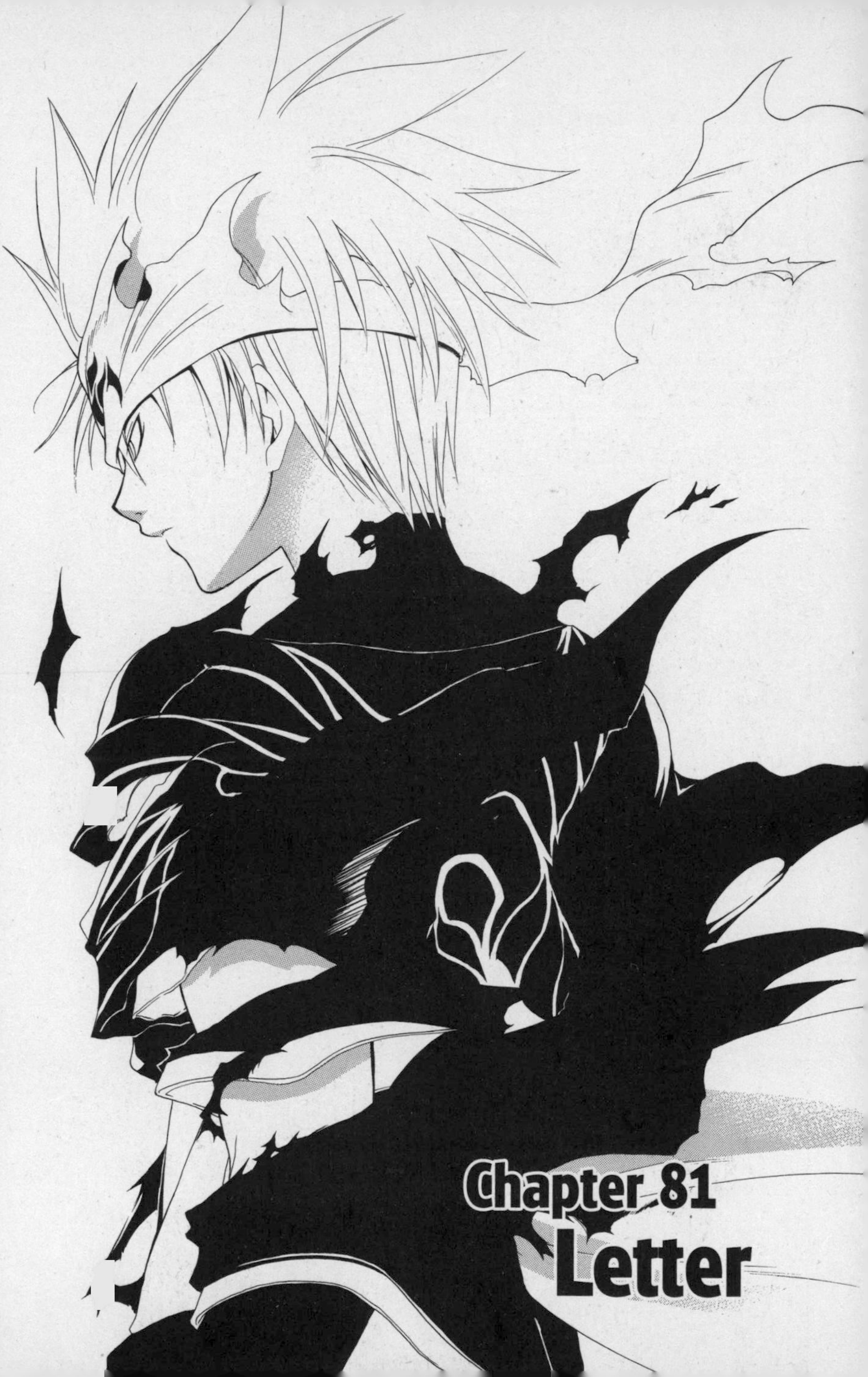
Chapter 81
Letter

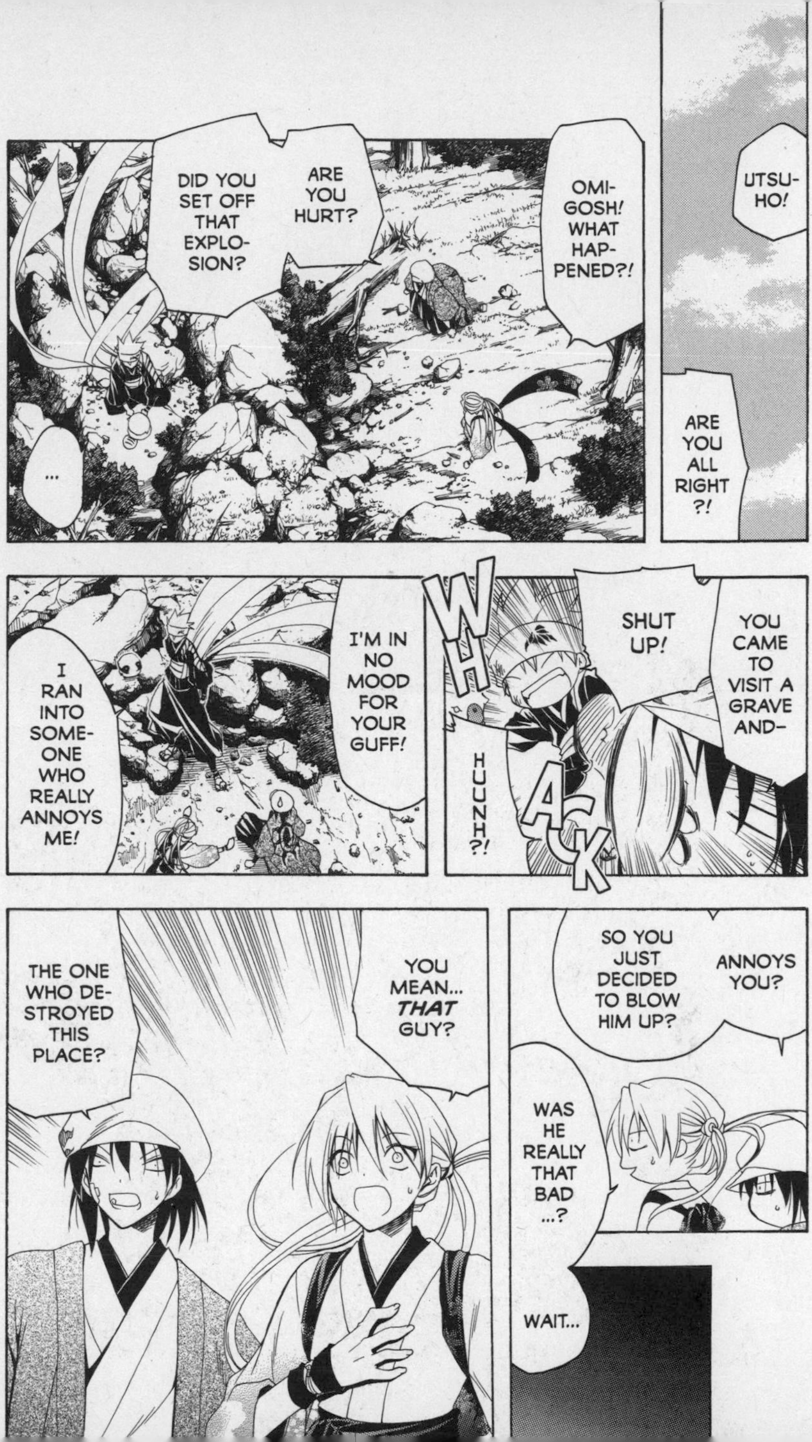

UTSU-HO!
ARE YOU ALL RIGHT?!
OMI-GOSH! WHAT HAP-PENED?!
ARE YOU HURT?
DID YOU SET OFF THAT EXPLO-SION?
...
YOU CAME TO VISIT A GRAVE AND–
SHUT UP!
WHACK
HUUNH?!
I'M IN NO MOOD FOR YOUR GUFF!
I RAN INTO SOME-ONE WHO REALLY ANNOYS ME!
ANNOYS YOU?
SO YOU JUST DECIDED TO BLOW HIM UP?
WAS HE REALLY THAT BAD ...?
WAIT...
YOU MEAN... *THAT* GUY?
THE ONE WHO DE-STROYED THIS PLACE?

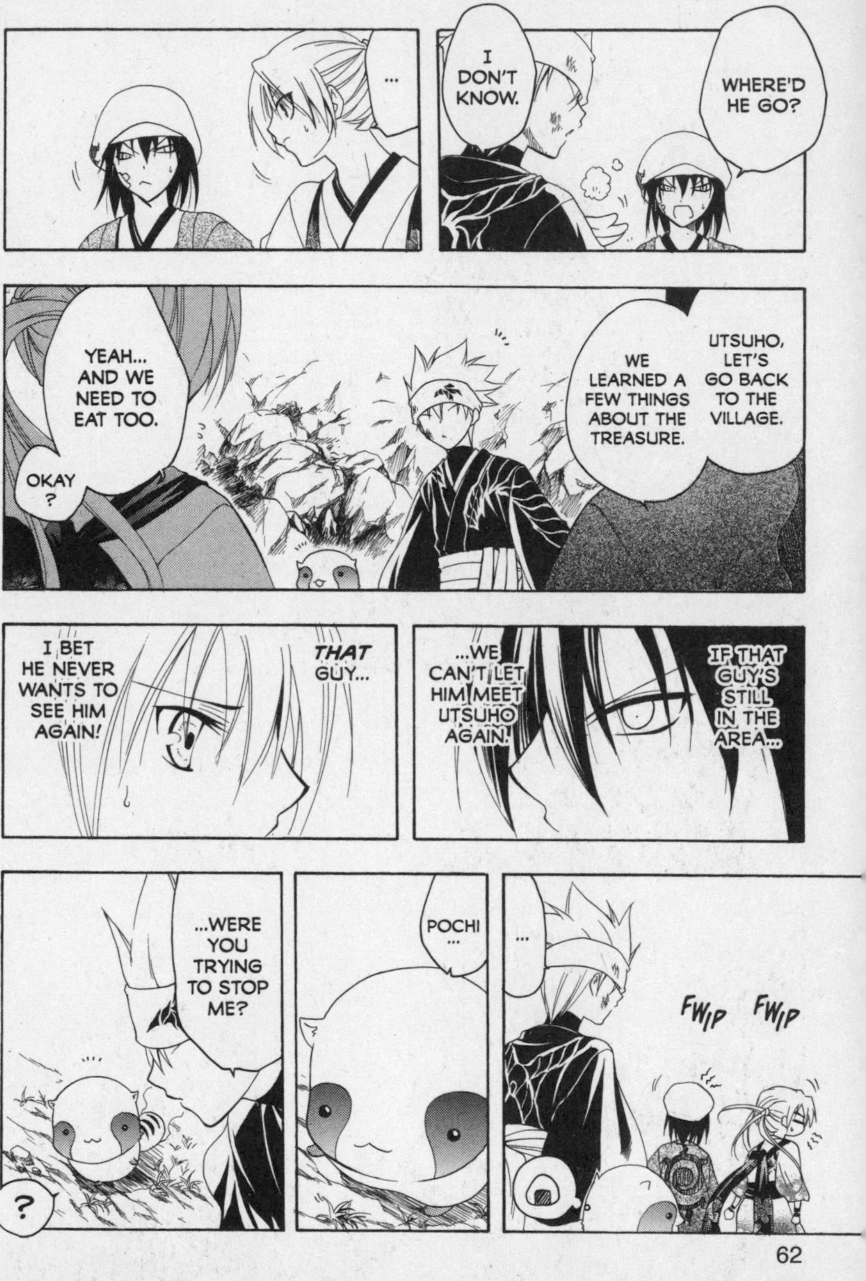
WHERE'D HE GO?
I DON'T KNOW.
...
UTSUHO, LET'S GO BACK TO THE VILLAGE.
WE LEARNED A FEW THINGS ABOUT THE TREASURE.
YEAH... AND WE NEED TO EAT TOO.
OKAY?
IF THAT GUY'S STILL IN THE AREA...
...WE CAN'T LET HIM MEET UTSUHO AGAIN.
THAT GUY...
I BET HE NEVER WANTS TO SEE HIM AGAIN!
FWIP FWIP
...
POCHI...
...WERE YOU TRYING TO STOP ME?
?

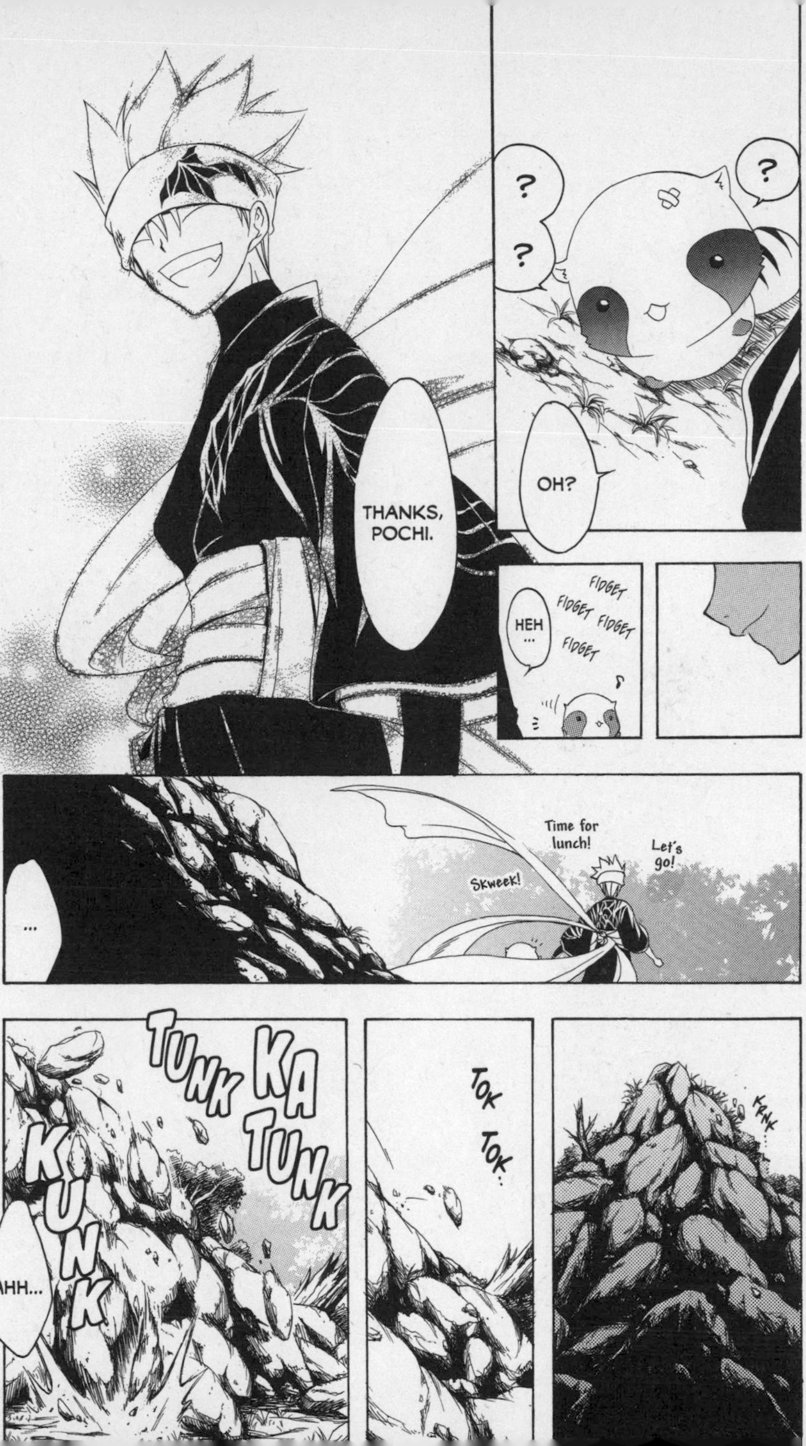
?
?
?
OH?
HEH ...
FIDGET
FIDGET
FIDGET
FIDGET
THANKS, POCHI.
Let's go!
Time for lunch!
Skweek!
...
KRNK...
TOK
TOK..
TUNK
KA
TUNK
KUNK
AHH...

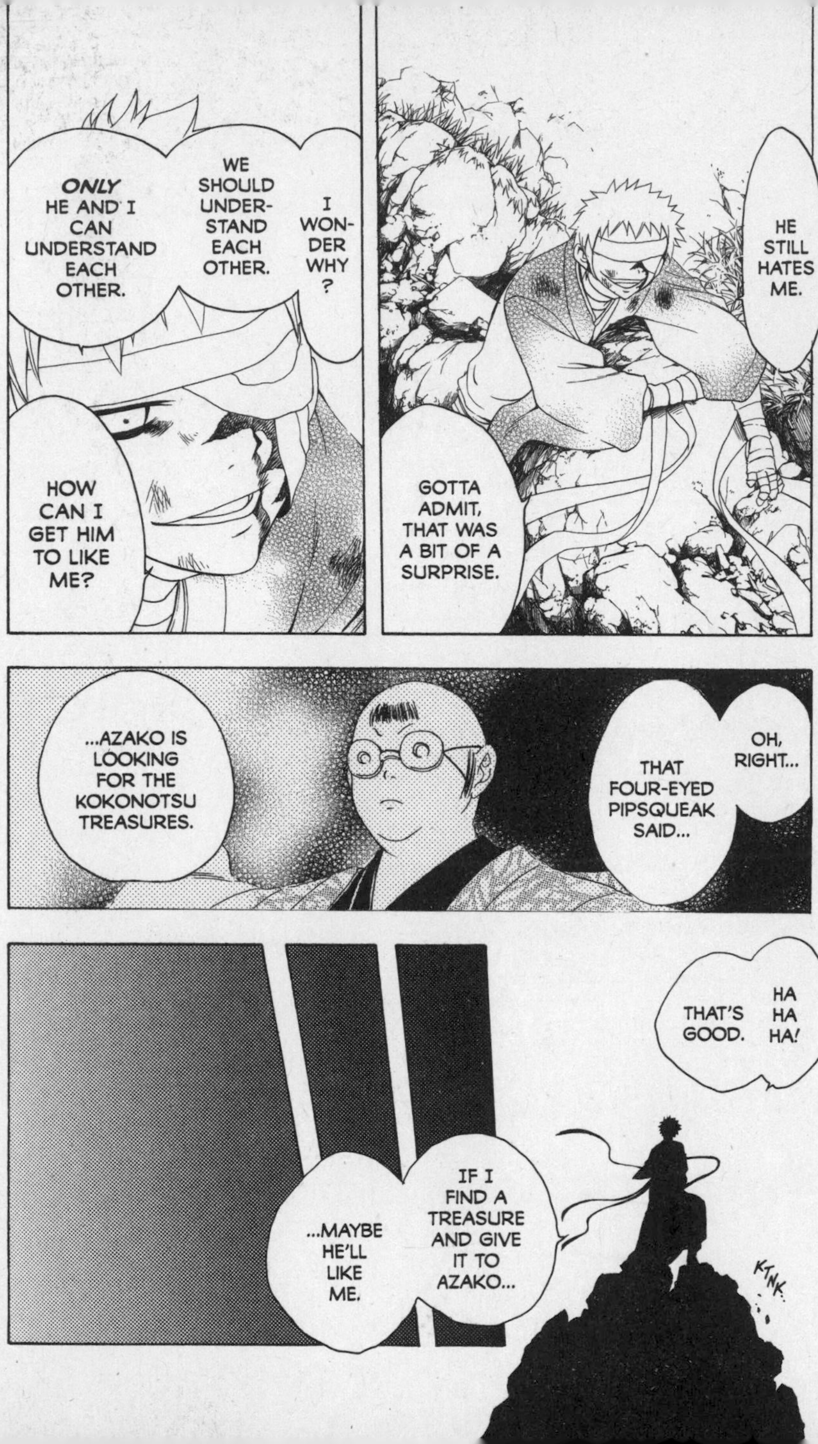
HE STILL HATES ME.
GOTTA ADMIT, THAT WAS A BIT OF A SURPRISE.
I WONDER WHY?
WE SHOULD UNDERSTAND EACH OTHER.
ONLY HE AND I CAN UNDERSTAND EACH OTHER.
HOW CAN I GET HIM TO LIKE ME?
OH, RIGHT...
THAT FOUR-EYED PIPSQUEAK SAID...
...AZAKO IS LOOKING FOR THE KOKONOTSU TREASURES.
HA HA HA!
THAT'S GOOD.
IF I FIND A TREASURE AND GIVE IT TO AZAKO...
...MAYBE HE'LL LIKE ME.
KTNK

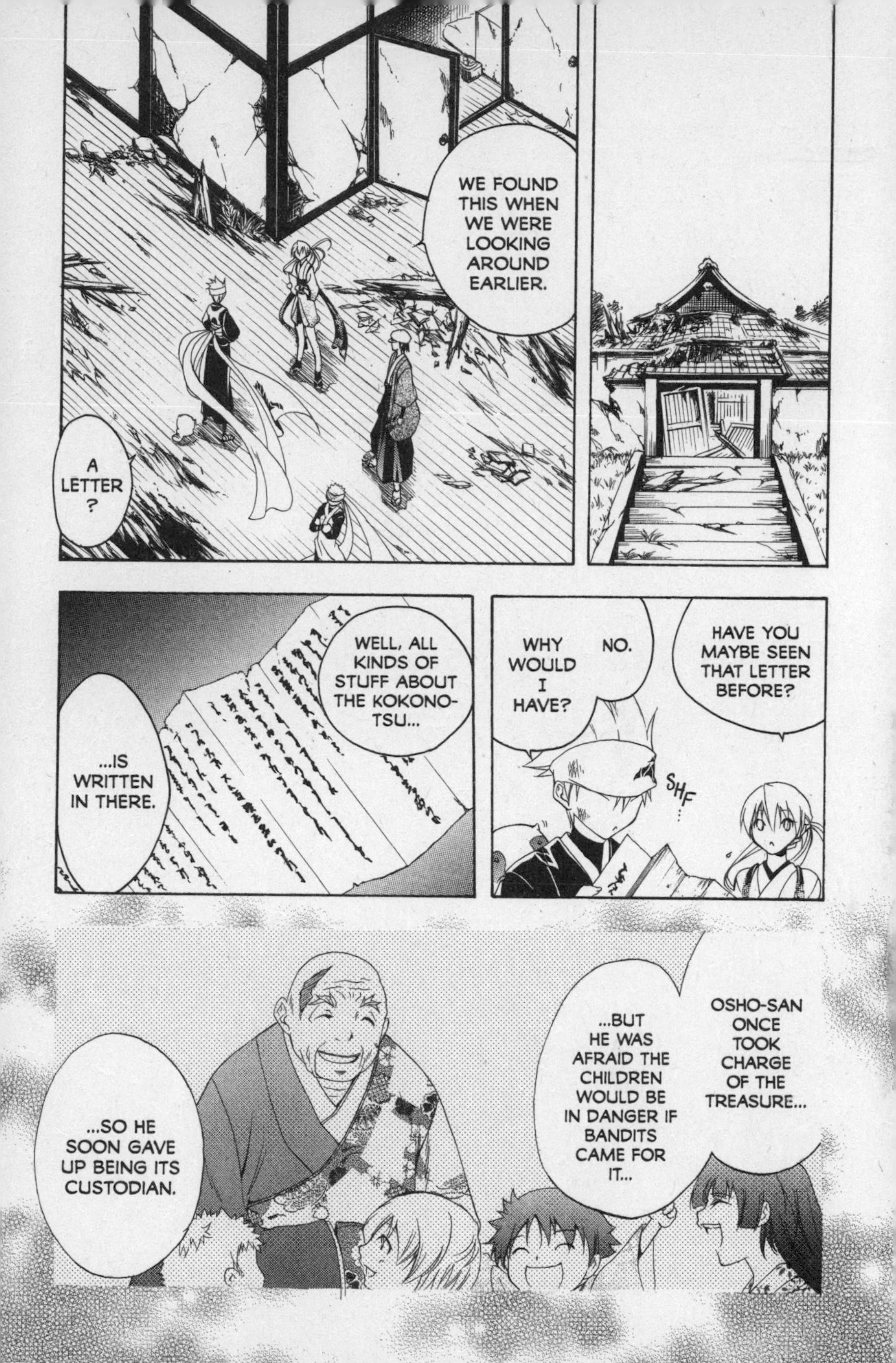
WE FOUND THIS WHEN WE WERE LOOKING AROUND EARLIER.
A LETTER?
HAVE YOU MAYBE SEEN THAT LETTER BEFORE?
NO.
WHY WOULD I HAVE?
SHF...
WELL, ALL KINDS OF STUFF ABOUT THE KOKONO-TSU...
...IS WRITTEN IN THERE.
OSHO-SAN ONCE TOOK CHARGE OF THE TREASURE...
...BUT HE WAS AFRAID THE CHILDREN WOULD BE IN DANGER IF BANDITS CAME FOR IT...
...SO HE SOON GAVE UP BEING ITS CUSTODIAN.

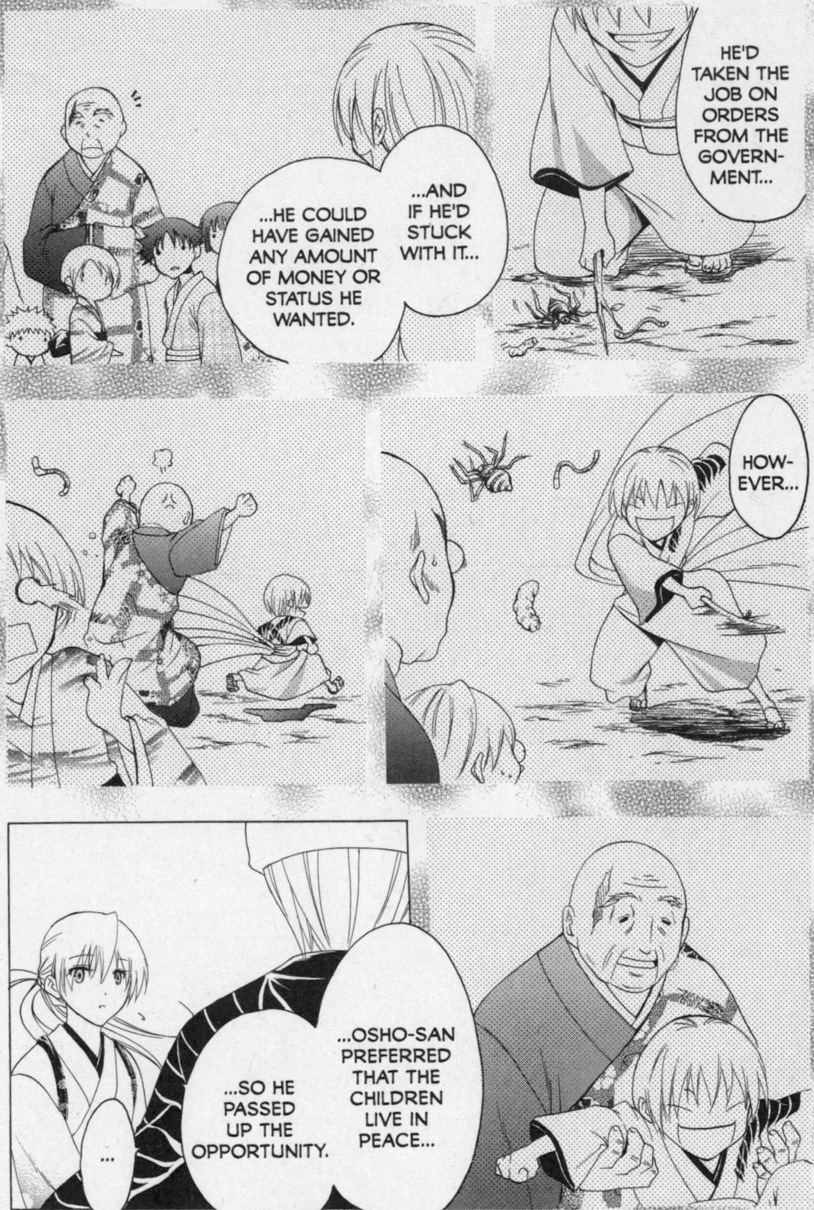
HE'D TAKEN THE JOB ON ORDERS FROM THE GOVERN-MENT...
...AND IF HE'D STUCK WITH IT...
...HE COULD HAVE GAINED ANY AMOUNT OF MONEY OR STATUS HE WANTED.
HOW-EVER...
...OSHO-SAN PREFERRED THAT THE CHILDREN LIVE IN PEACE...
...SO HE PASSED UP THE OPPORTUNITY.
...

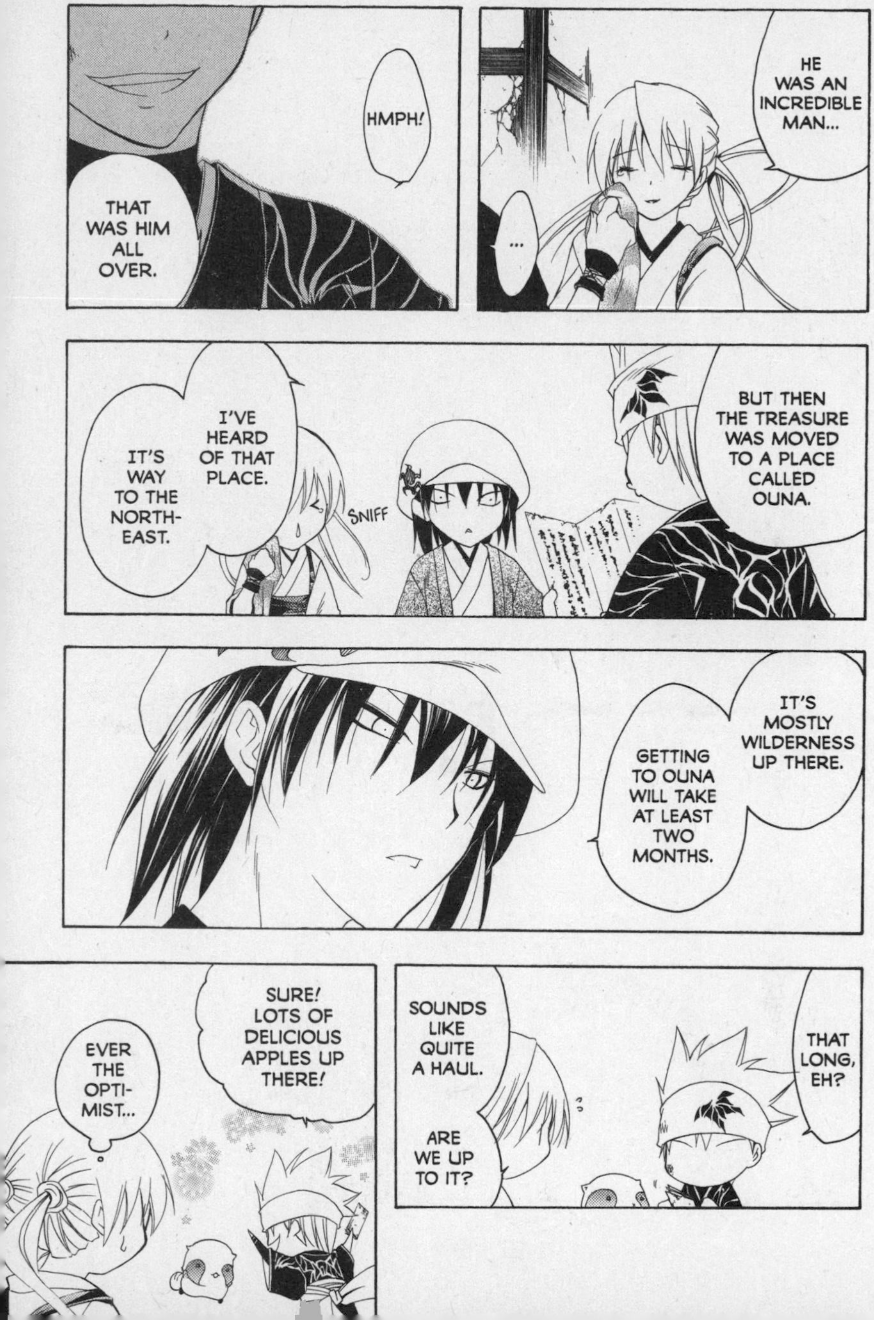
HE WAS AN INCREDIBLE MAN...
...
HMPH!
THAT WAS HIM ALL OVER.
BUT THEN THE TREASURE WAS MOVED TO A PLACE CALLED OUNA.
I'VE HEARD OF THAT PLACE.
IT'S WAY TO THE NORTH-EAST.
SNIFF
IT'S MOSTLY WILDERNESS UP THERE.
GETTING TO OUNA WILL TAKE AT LEAST TWO MONTHS.
THAT LONG, EH?
SOUNDS LIKE QUITE A HAUL.
ARE WE UP TO IT?
SURE! LOTS OF DELICIOUS APPLES UP THERE!
EVER THE OPTIMIST...

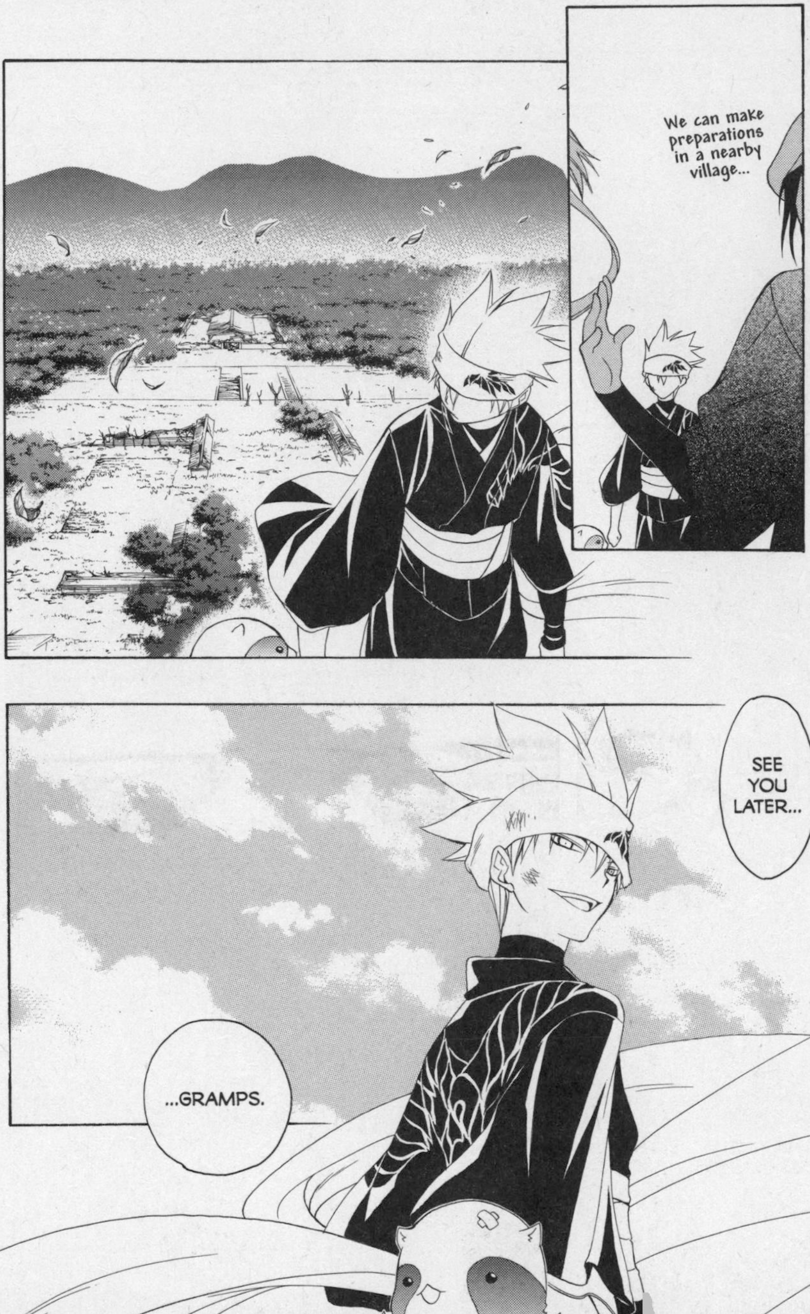
We can make preparations in a nearby village...
SEE YOU LATER...
...GRAMPS.
clap clap

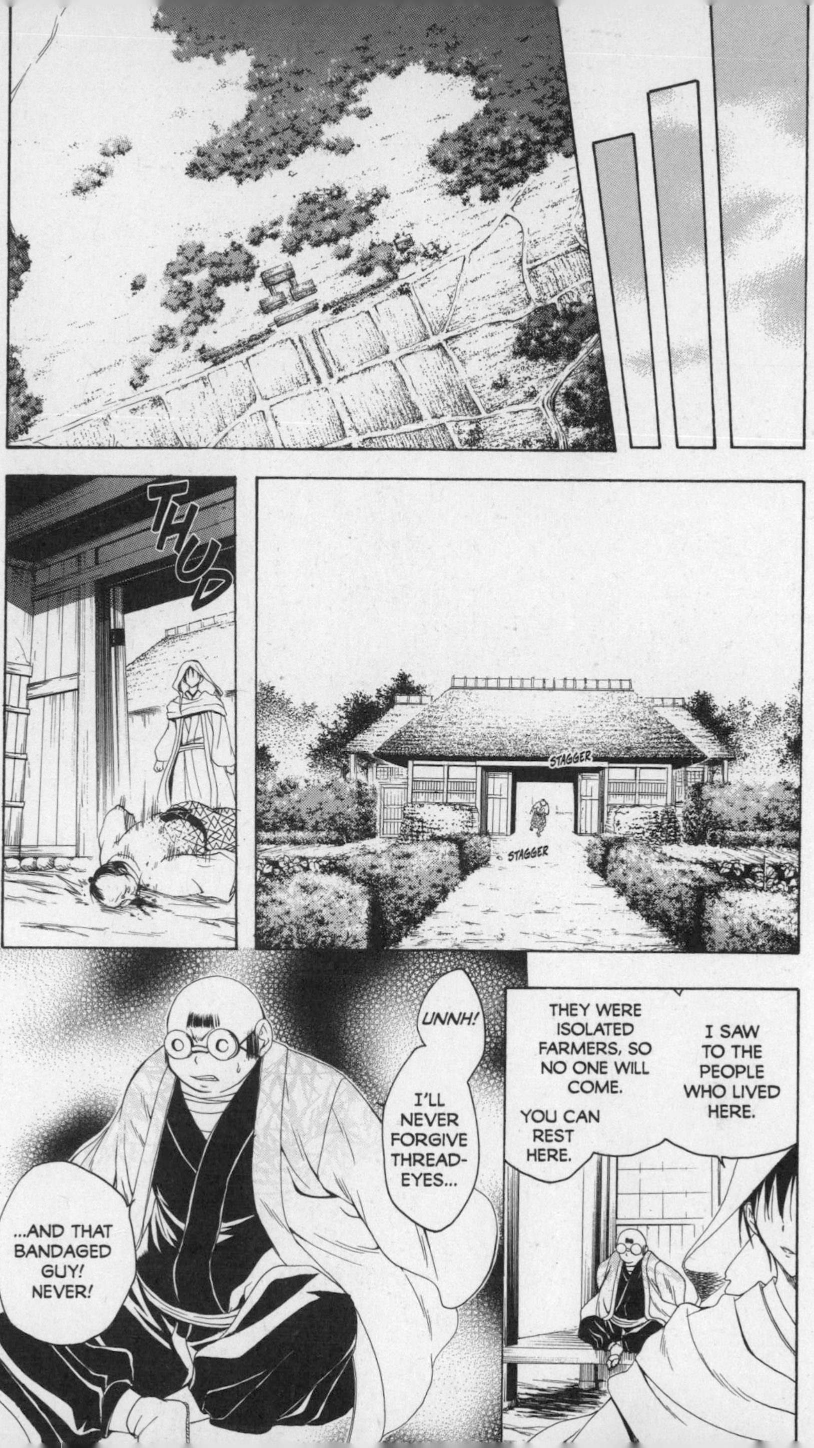
STAGGER
STAGGER
THUD
I SAW TO THE PEOPLE WHO LIVED HERE.
THEY WERE ISOLATED FARMERS, SO NO ONE WILL COME.
YOU CAN REST HERE.
UNNH!
I'LL NEVER FORGIVE THREAD-EYES...
...AND THAT BANDAGED GUY! NEVER!

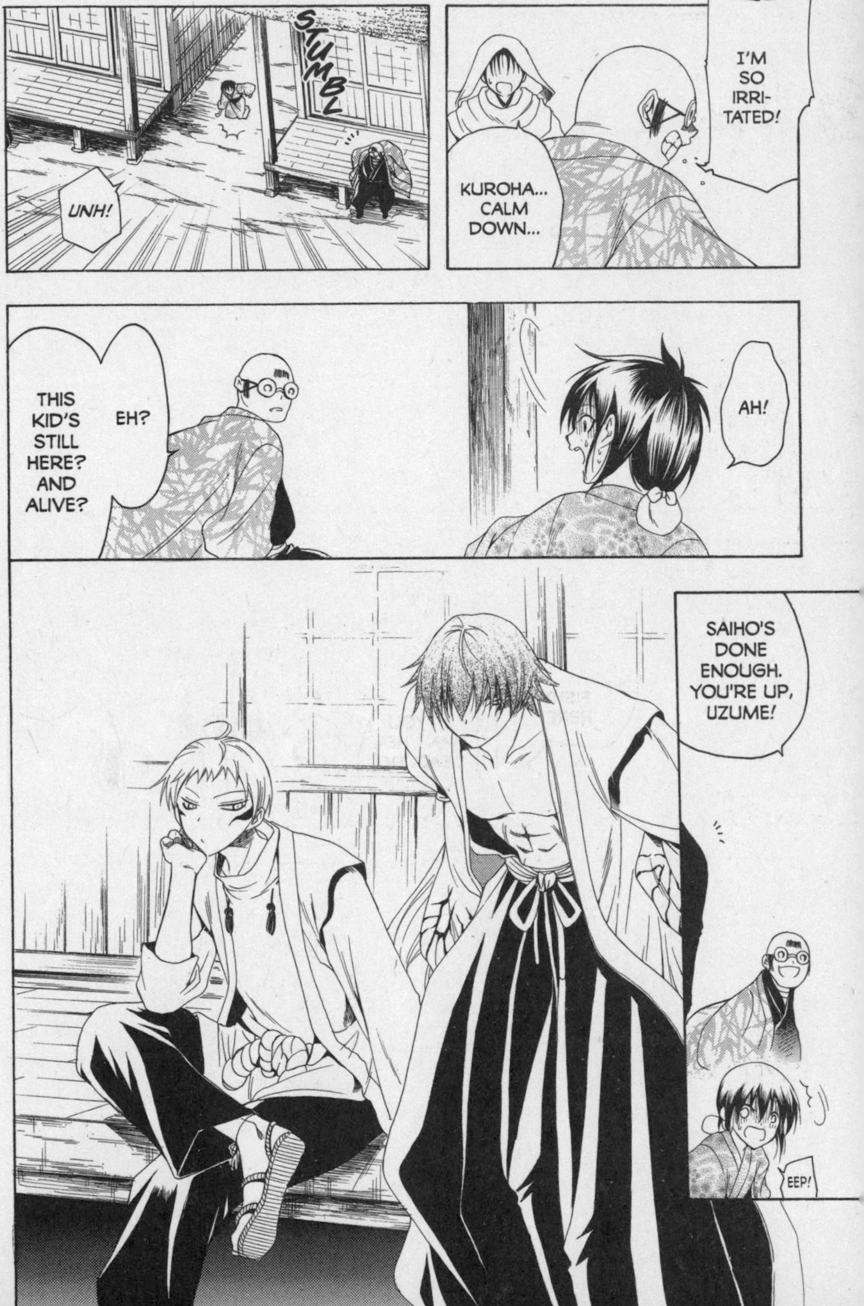
I'M SO IRRITATED!
KUROHA... CALM DOWN...
STUMBL
UNH!
AH!
EH?
THIS KID'S STILL HERE? AND ALIVE?
SAIHO'S DONE ENOUGH. YOU'RE UP, UZUME!
EEP!

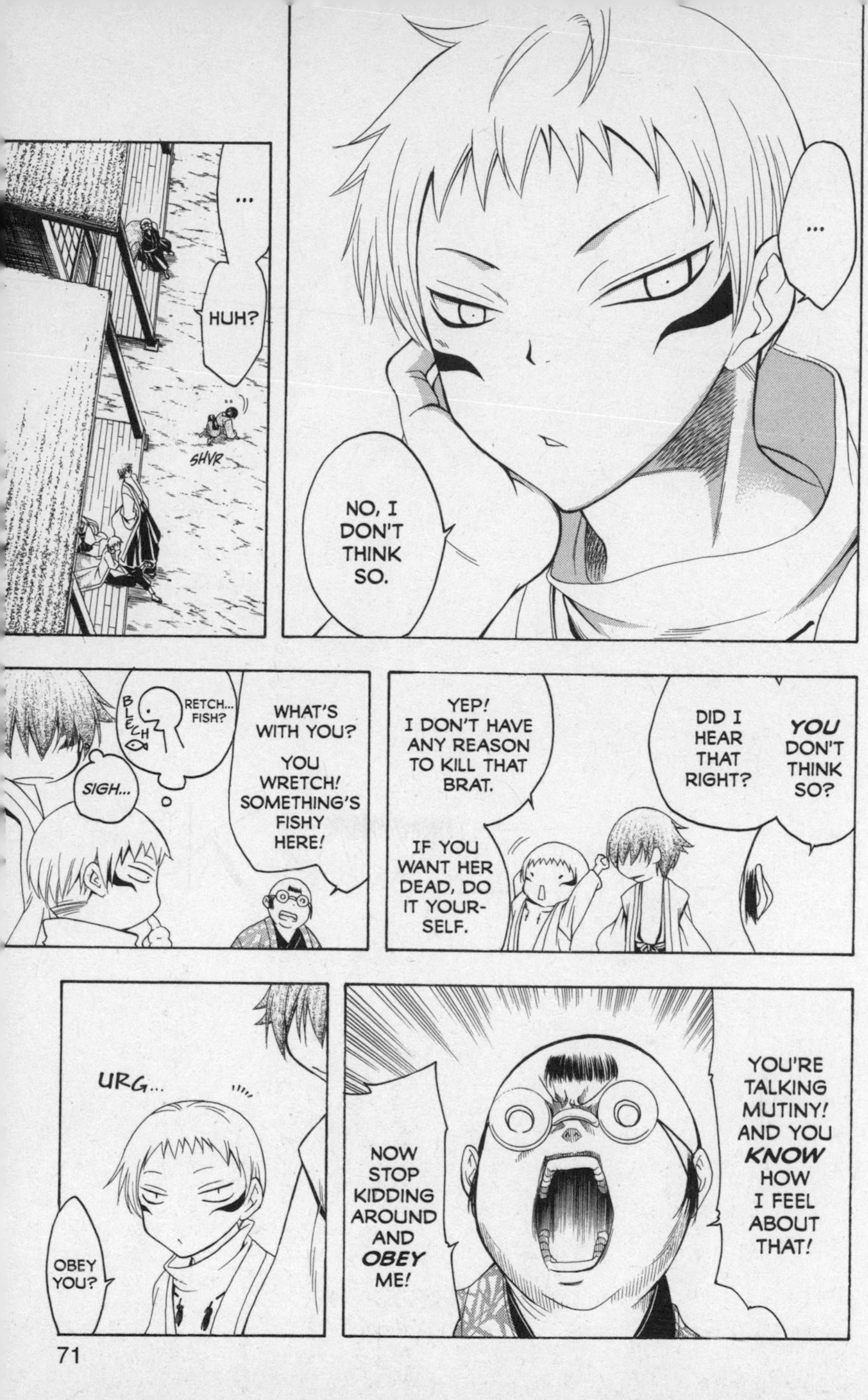
...
NO, I DON'T THINK SO.
...
HUH?
SHVR
YOU DON'T THINK SO?
DID I HEAR THAT RIGHT?
YEP! I DON'T HAVE ANY REASON TO KILL THAT BRAT.
IF YOU WANT HER DEAD, DO IT YOUR-SELF.
WHAT'S WITH YOU?
YOU WRETCH! SOMETHING'S FISHY HERE!
RETCH... FISH?
BLECH
SIGH...
YOU'RE TALKING MUTINY! AND YOU KNOW HOW I FEEL ABOUT THAT!
NOW STOP KIDDING AROUND AND OBEY ME!
URG...
OBEY YOU?

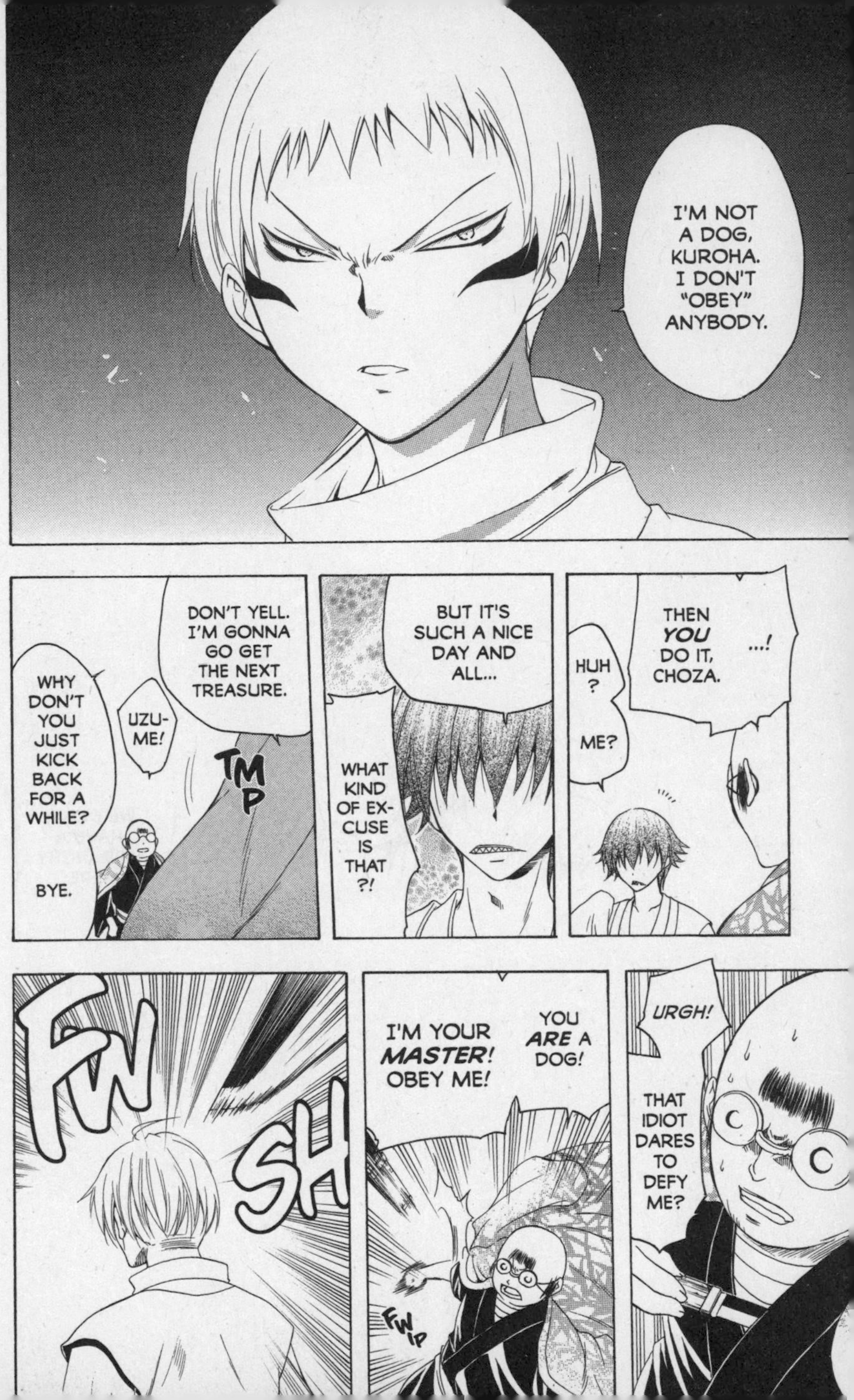

I'M NOT A DOG, KUROHA. I DON'T "OBEY" ANYBODY.
...!
THEN *YOU* DO IT, CHOZA.
HUH? ME?
BUT IT'S SUCH A NICE DAY AND ALL...
WHAT KIND OF EX-CUSE IS THAT?!
DON'T YELL. I'M GONNA GO GET THE NEXT TREASURE.
UZU-ME!
TMP
WHY DON'T YOU JUST KICK BACK FOR A WHILE?
BYE.
URGH!
THAT IDIOT DARES TO DEFY ME?
YOU *ARE* A DOG!
I'M YOUR *MASTER*! OBEY ME!
FWIP
FWSH

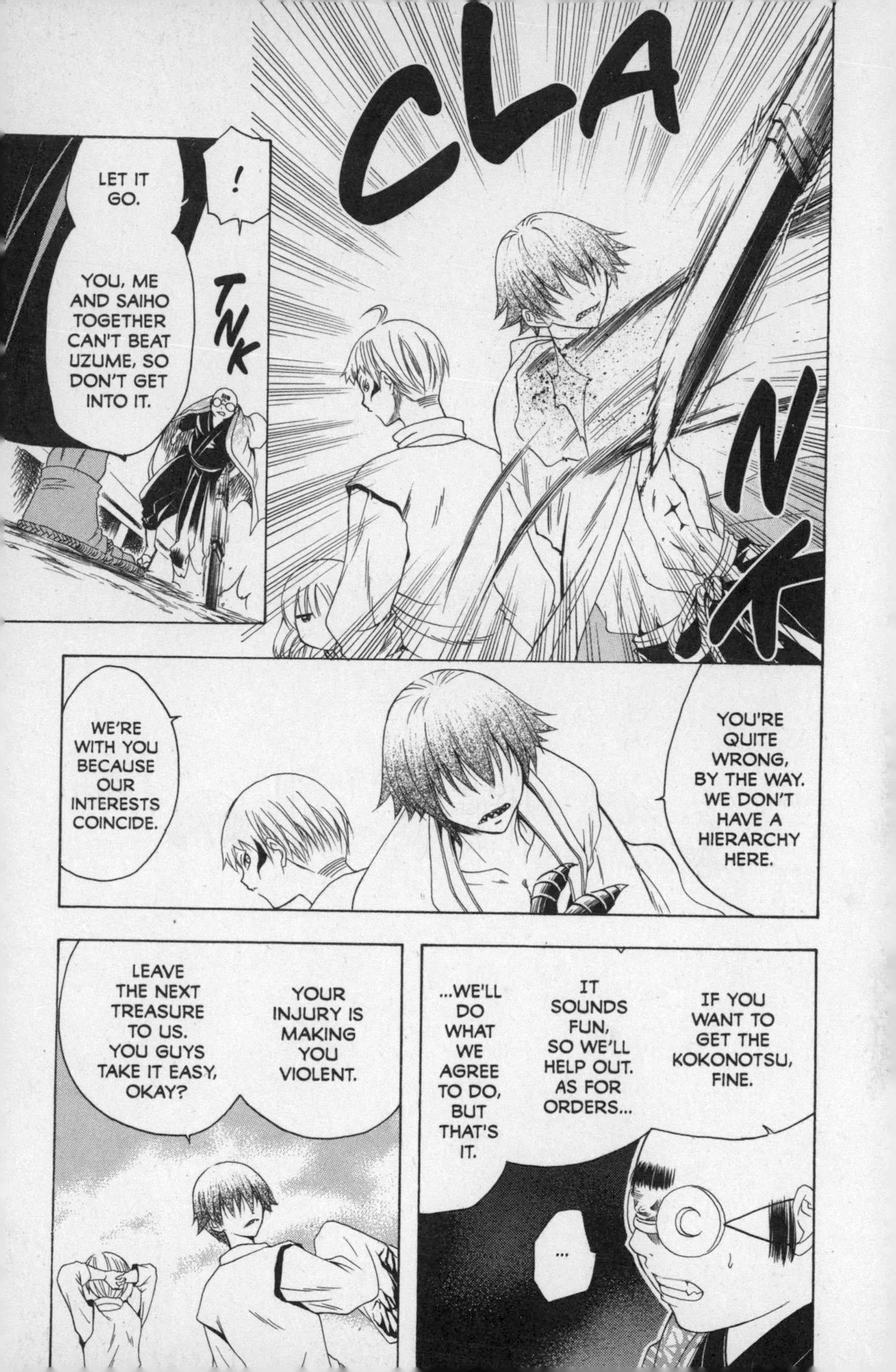
CLANK
!
TNK
LET IT GO.
YOU, ME AND SAIHO TOGETHER CAN'T BEAT UZUME, SO DON'T GET INTO IT.
YOU'RE QUITE WRONG, BY THE WAY. WE DON'T HAVE A HIERARCHY HERE.
WE'RE WITH YOU BECAUSE OUR INTERESTS COINCIDE.
IF YOU WANT TO GET THE KOKONOTSU, FINE.
IT SOUNDS FUN, SO WE'LL HELP OUT. AS FOR ORDERS...
...WE'LL DO WHAT WE AGREE TO DO, BUT THAT'S IT.
...
YOUR INJURY IS MAKING YOU VIOLENT.
LEAVE THE NEXT TREASURE TO US. YOU GUYS TAKE IT EASY, OKAY?

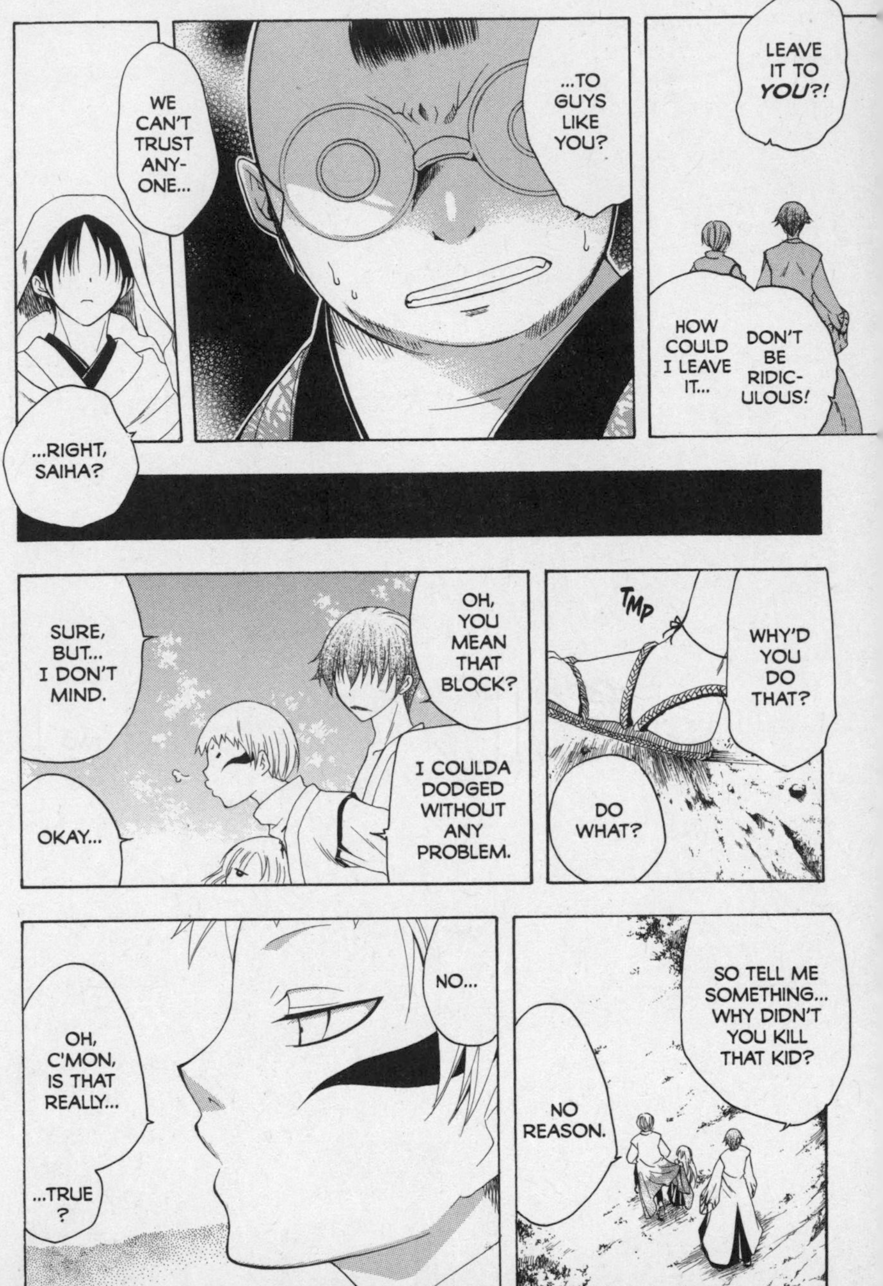
LEAVE IT TO YOU?!
DON'T BE RIDICULOUS!
HOW COULD I LEAVE IT...
...TO GUYS LIKE YOU?
WE CAN'T TRUST ANY-ONE...
...RIGHT, SAIHA?
TMP
WHY'D YOU DO THAT?
DO WHAT?
OH, YOU MEAN THAT BLOCK?
I COULDA DODGED WITHOUT ANY PROBLEM.
SURE, BUT... I DON'T MIND.
OKAY...
SO TELL ME SOMETHING... WHY DIDN'T YOU KILL THAT KID?
NO REASON.
NO...
OH, C'MON, IS THAT REALLY...
...TRUE?

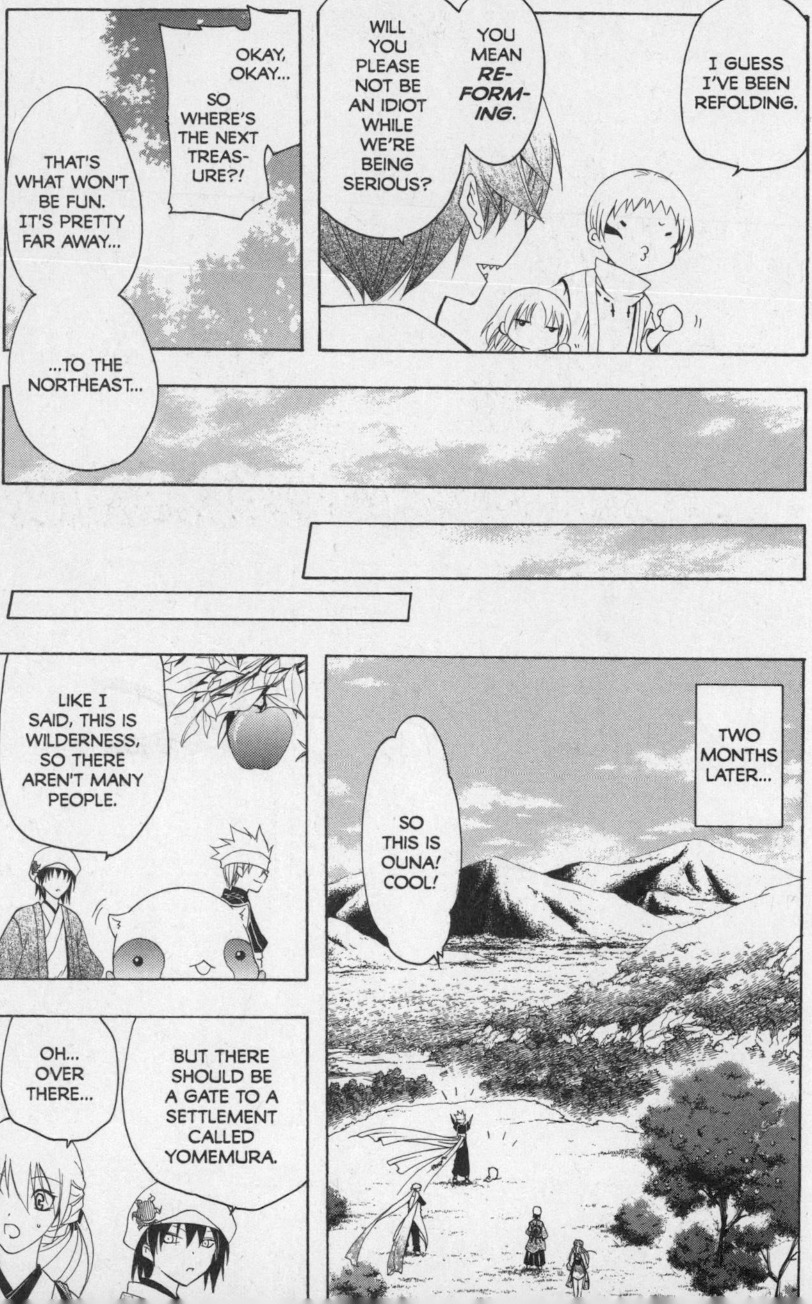
I GUESS I'VE BEEN REFOLDING.
YOU MEAN *RE-FORMING*.
WILL YOU PLEASE NOT BE AN IDIOT WHILE WE'RE BEING SERIOUS?
OKAY, OKAY... SO WHERE'S THE NEXT TREASURE?!
THAT'S WHAT WON'T BE FUN. IT'S PRETTY FAR AWAY...
...TO THE NORTHEAST...
TWO MONTHS LATER...
SO THIS IS OUNA! COOL!
LIKE I SAID, THIS IS WILDERNESS, SO THERE AREN'T MANY PEOPLE.
BUT THERE SHOULD BE A GATE TO A SETTLEMENT CALLED YOMEMURA.
OH... OVER THERE...

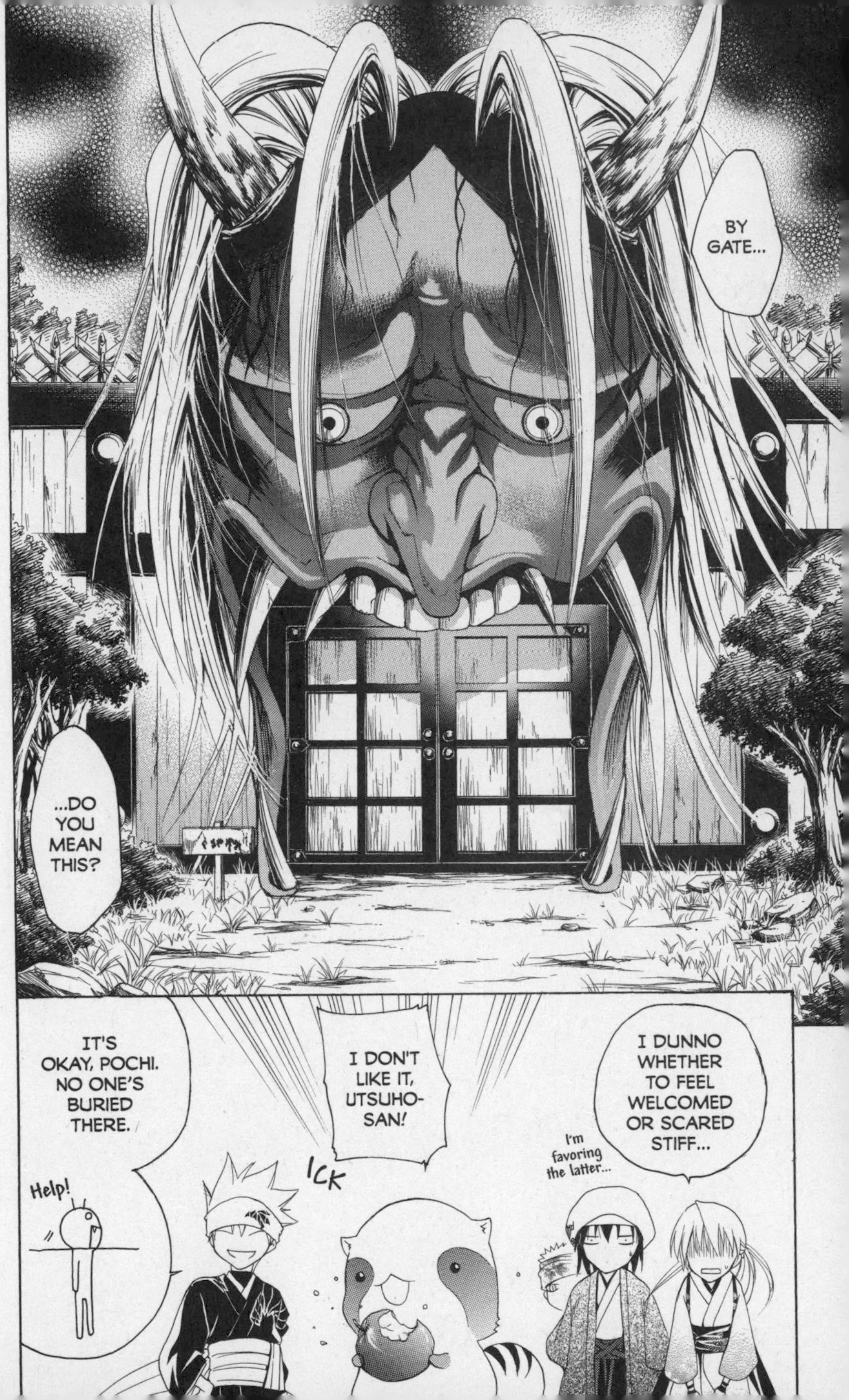
BY GATE...
...DO YOU MEAN THIS?
I DUNNO WHETHER TO FEEL WELCOMED OR SCARED STIFF...
I'm favoring the latter...
I DON'T LIKE IT, UTSUHO-SAN!
ICK
IT'S OKAY, POCHI. NO ONE'S BURIED THERE.
Help!

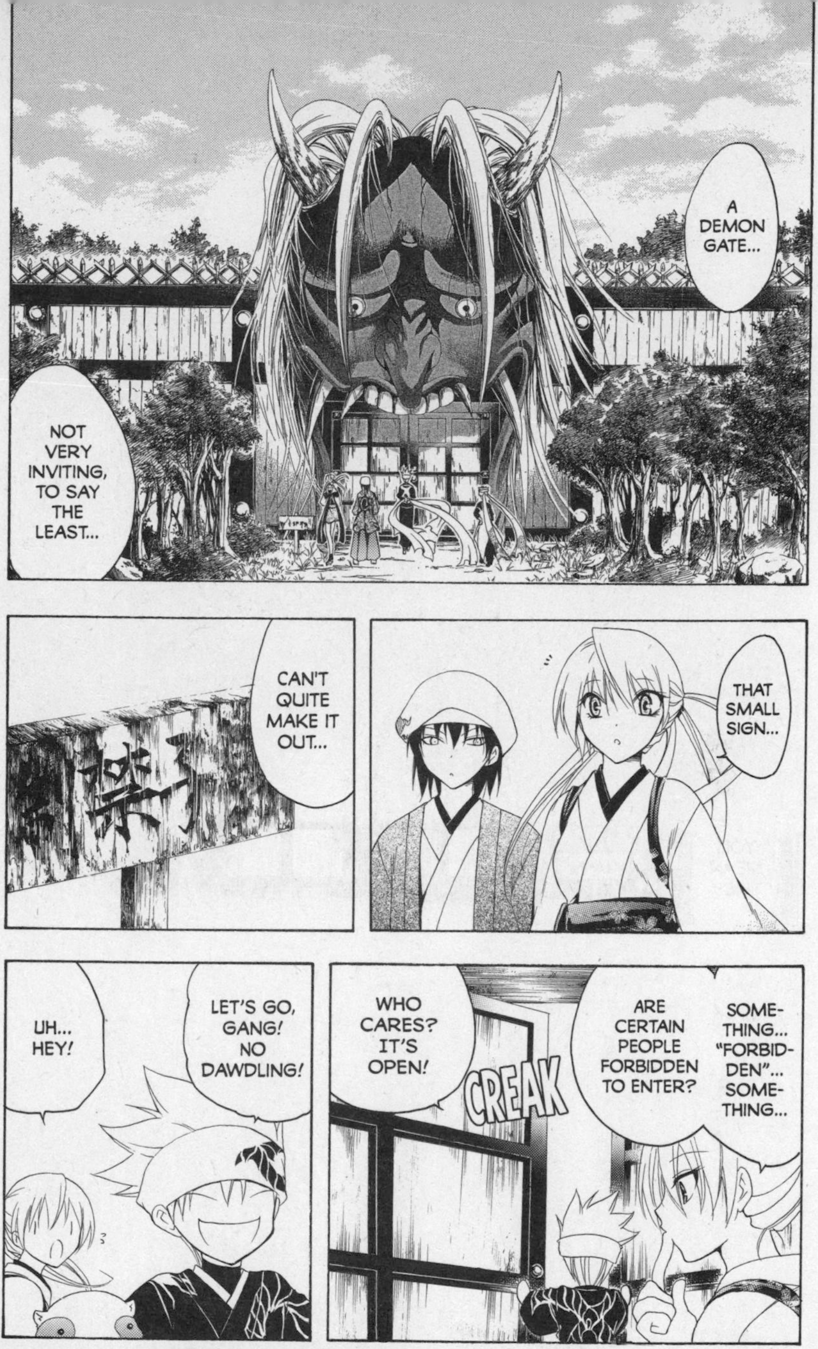
A DEMON GATE...
NOT VERY INVITING, TO SAY THE LEAST...
THAT SMALL SIGN...
CAN'T QUITE MAKE IT OUT...
SOME-THING... "FORBID-DEN"... SOME-THING...
ARE CERTAIN PEOPLE FORBIDDEN TO ENTER?
WHO CARES? IT'S OPEN!
CREAK
LET'S GO, GANG! NO DAWDLING!
UH... HEY!

Chapter 82 Yomemura

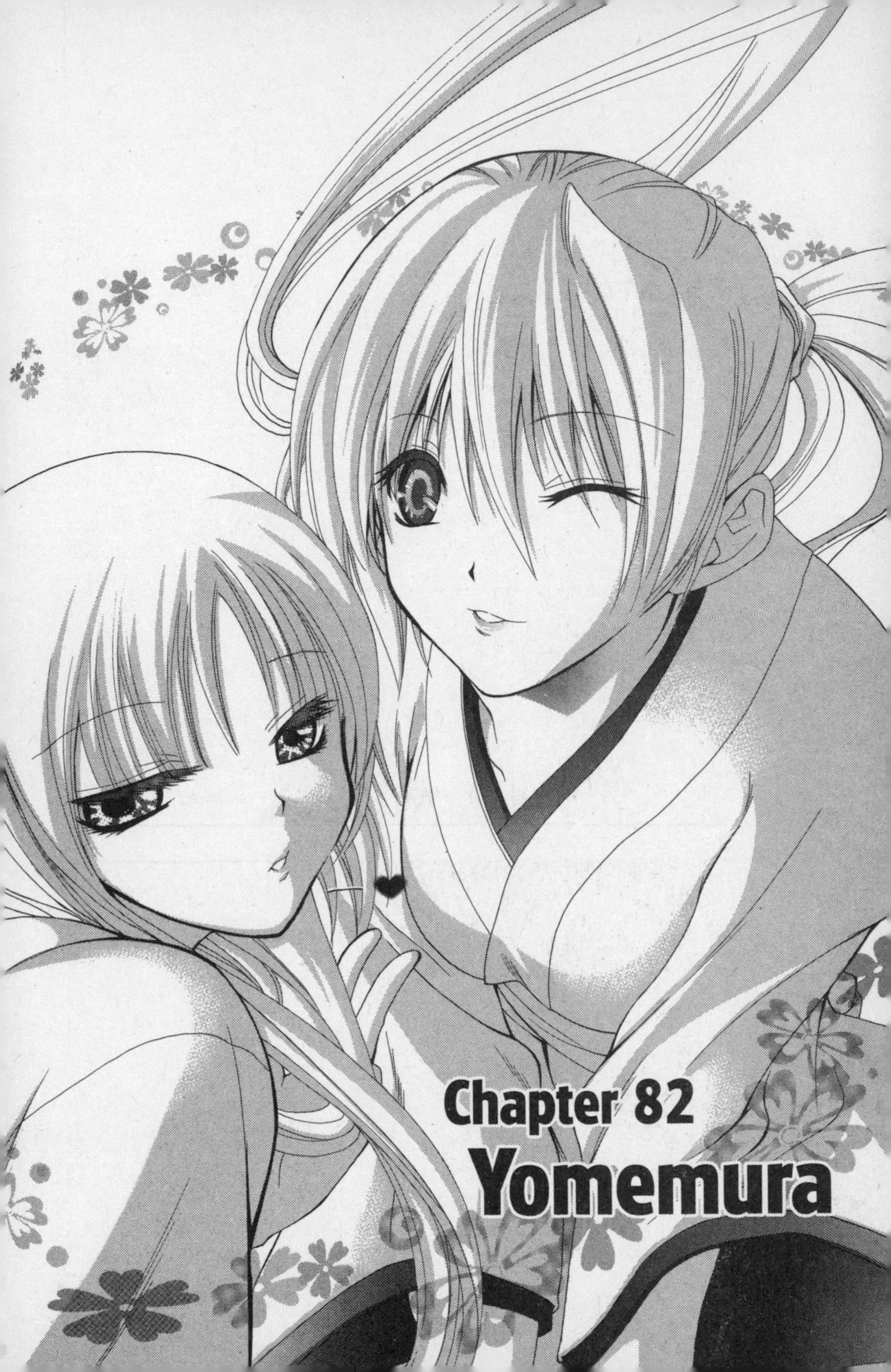
Chapter 82
Yomemura

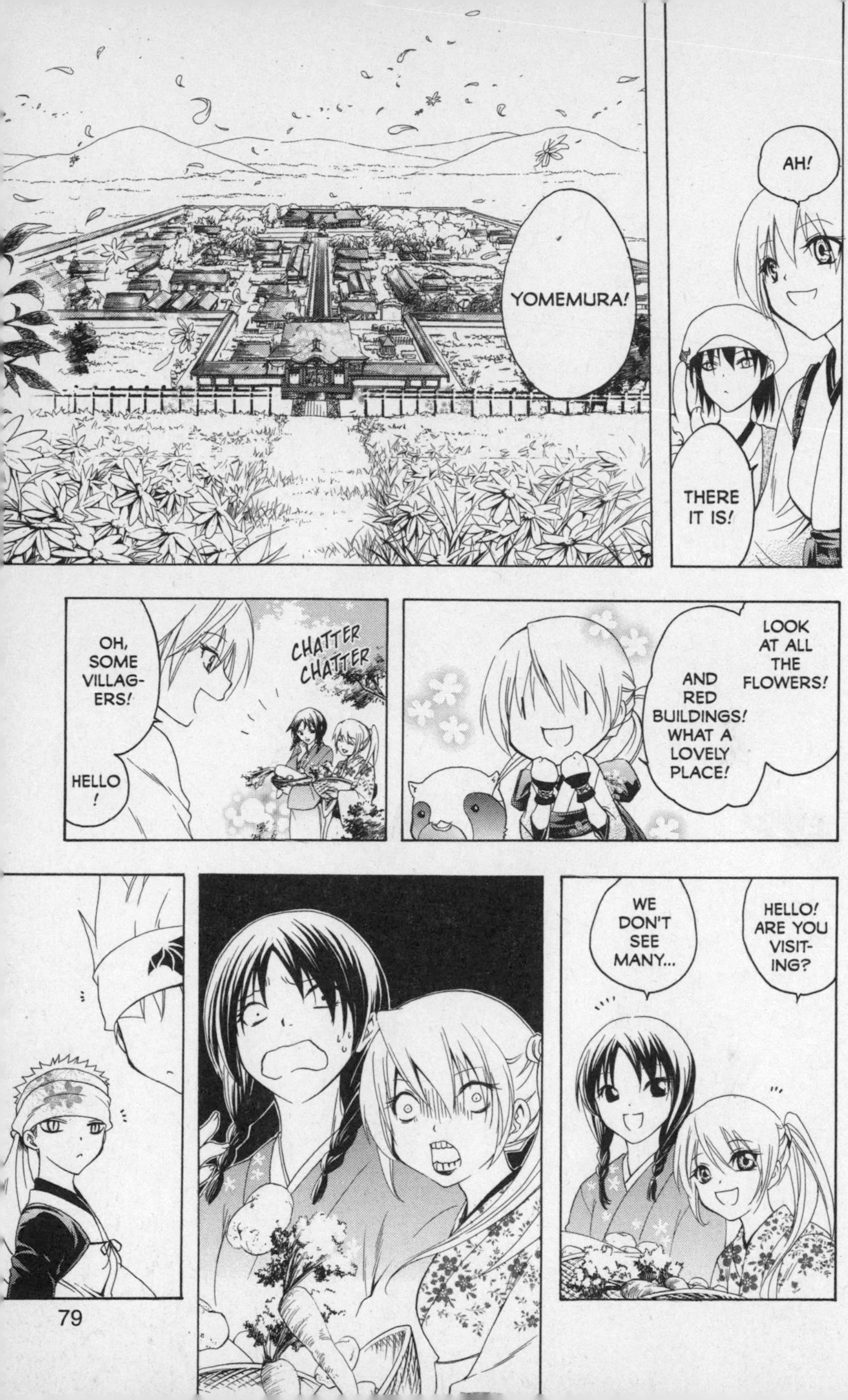
AH!
THERE IT IS!
YOMEMURA!
LOOK AT ALL THE FLOWERS!
AND RED BUILDINGS! WHAT A LOVELY PLACE!
CHATTER CHATTER
OH, SOME VILLAGERS!
HELLO!
HELLO! ARE YOU VISITING?
WE DON'T SEE MANY...

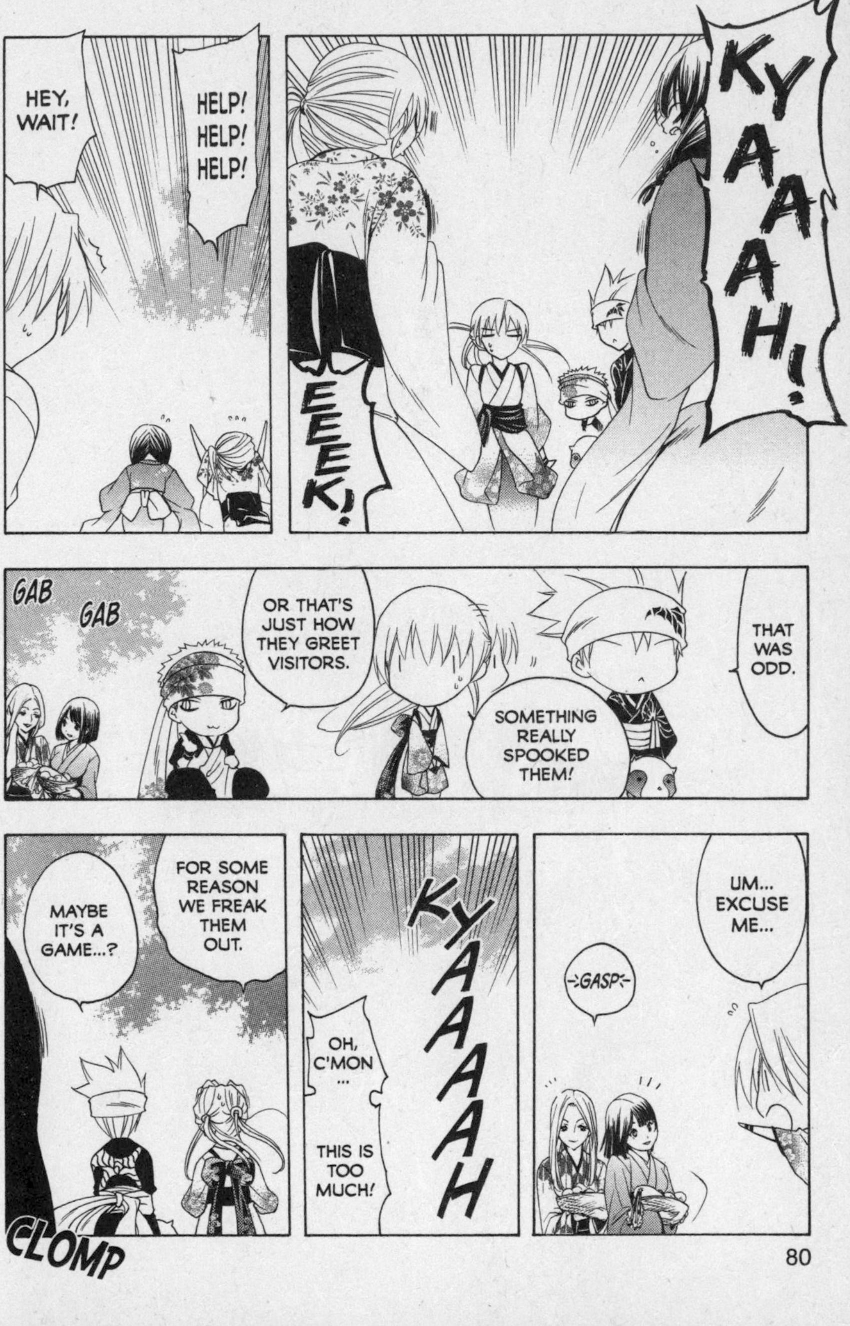
KYAAAH!
EEEEK!
HELP! HELP! HELP!
HEY, WAIT!
THAT WAS ODD.
SOMETHING REALLY SPOOKED THEM!
OR THAT'S JUST HOW THEY GREET VISITORS.
GAB GAB
UM... EXCUSE ME...
GASP
KYAAAAAH
OH, C'MON ...
THIS IS TOO MUCH!
FOR SOME REASON WE FREAK THEM OUT.
MAYBE IT'S A GAME...?
CLOMP

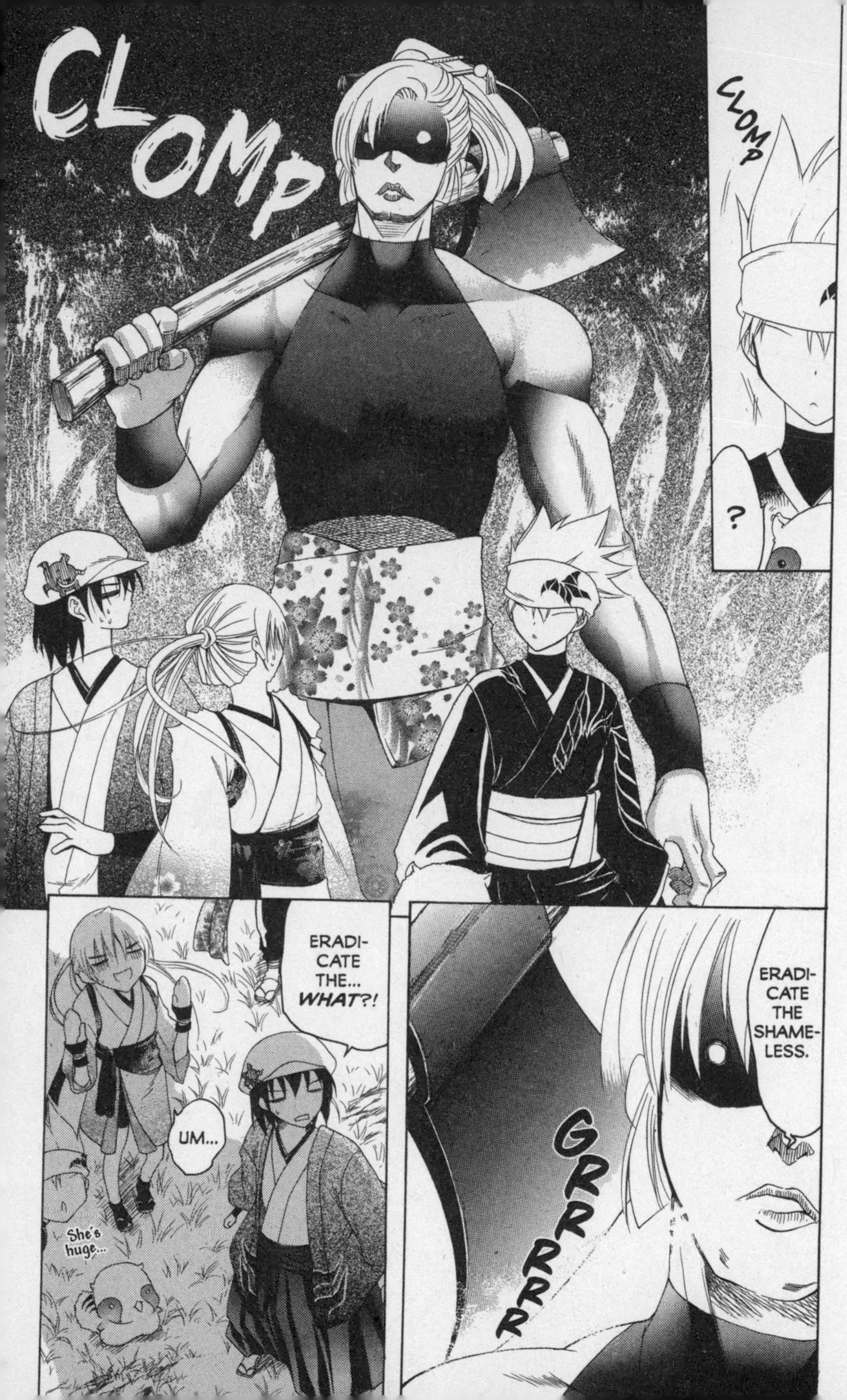
CLOMP
?
CLOMP
ERADI-CATE THE SHAME-LESS.
GRRRRR
ERADI-CATE THE... WHAT?!
UM...
She's huge...

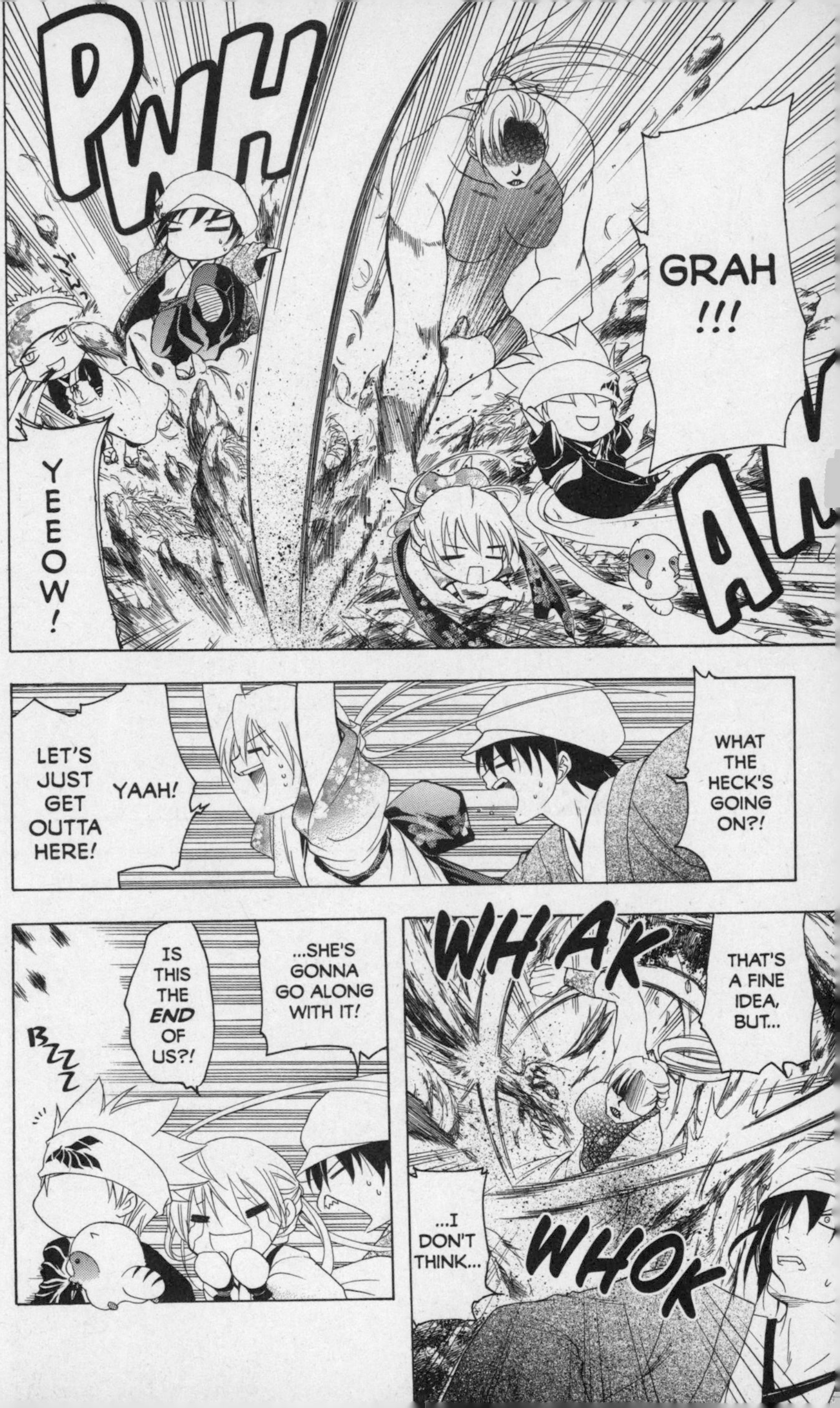
GRAH!!!
PWH
YEEEOW!
WHAT THE HECK'S GOING ON?!
YAAH!
LET'S JUST GET OUTTA HERE!
WHAK
THAT'S A FINE IDEA, BUT...
...I DON'T THINK...
WHOK
...SHE'S GONNA GO ALONG WITH IT!
IS THIS THE *END* OF US?!
BZZZ

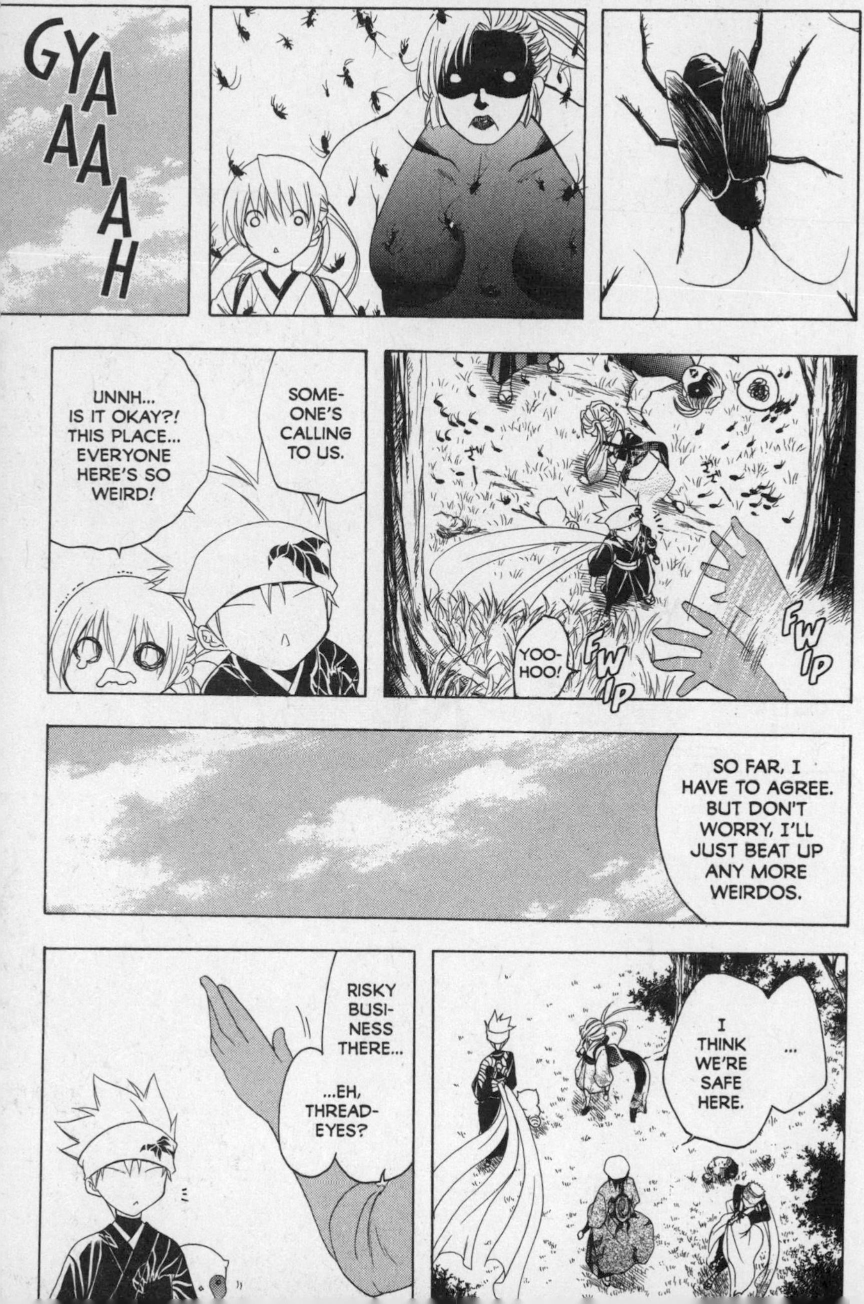
GYAAAAH
FWIP
YOO-HOO!
FWIP
SOME-ONE'S CALLING TO US.
UNNH... IS IT OKAY?! THIS PLACE... EVERYONE HERE'S SO WEIRD!
SO FAR, I HAVE TO AGREE. BUT DON'T WORRY, I'LL JUST BEAT UP ANY MORE WEIRDOS.
...
I THINK WE'RE SAFE HERE.
RISKY BUSINESS THERE...
...EH, THREAD-EYES?

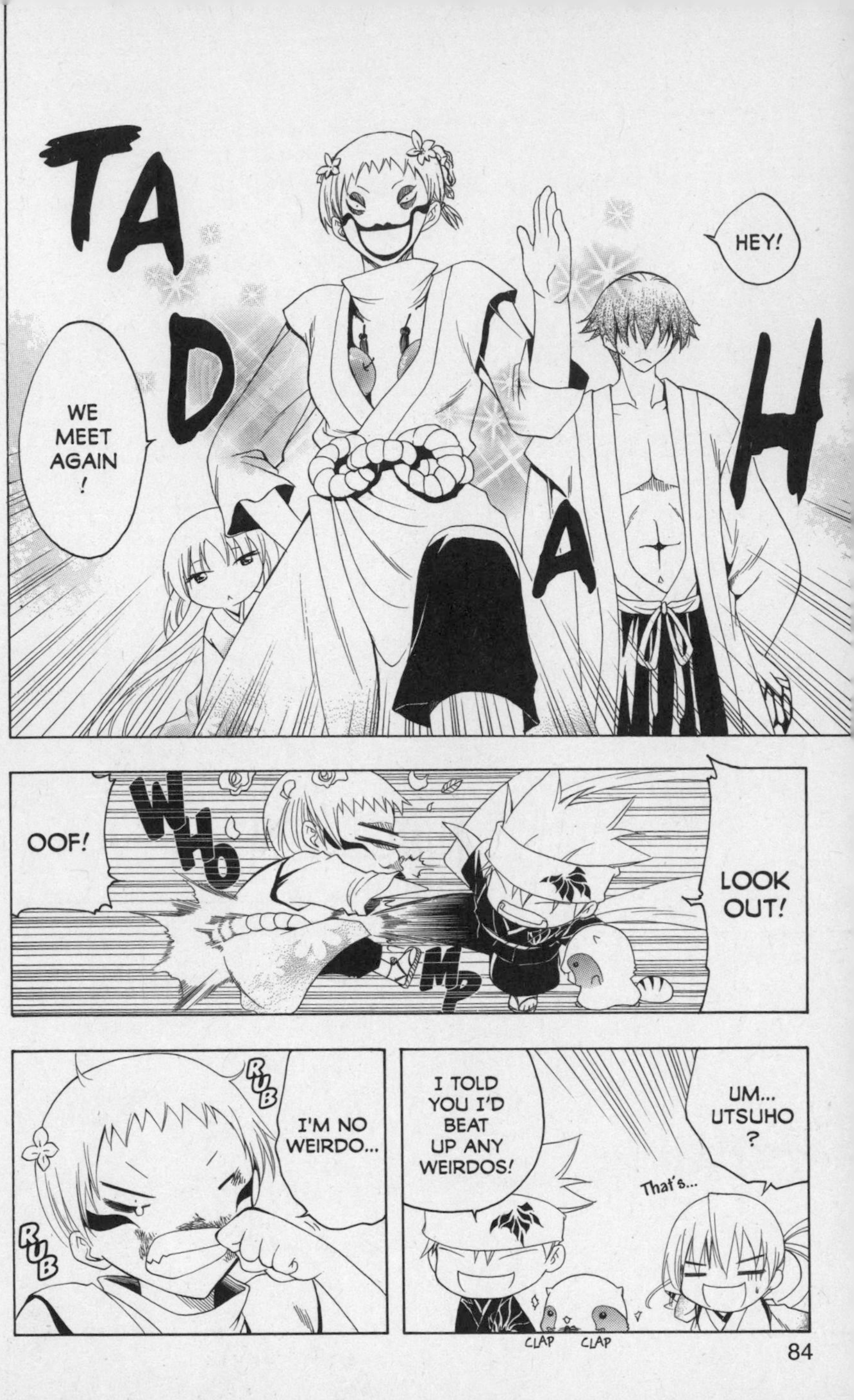
HEY!
TADAH
WE MEET AGAIN!
LOOK OUT!
WHOMP
OOF!
UM... UTSUHO?
That's...
I TOLD YOU I'D BEAT UP ANY WEIRDOS!
CLAP CLAP
RUB
I'M NO WEIRDO...
RUB

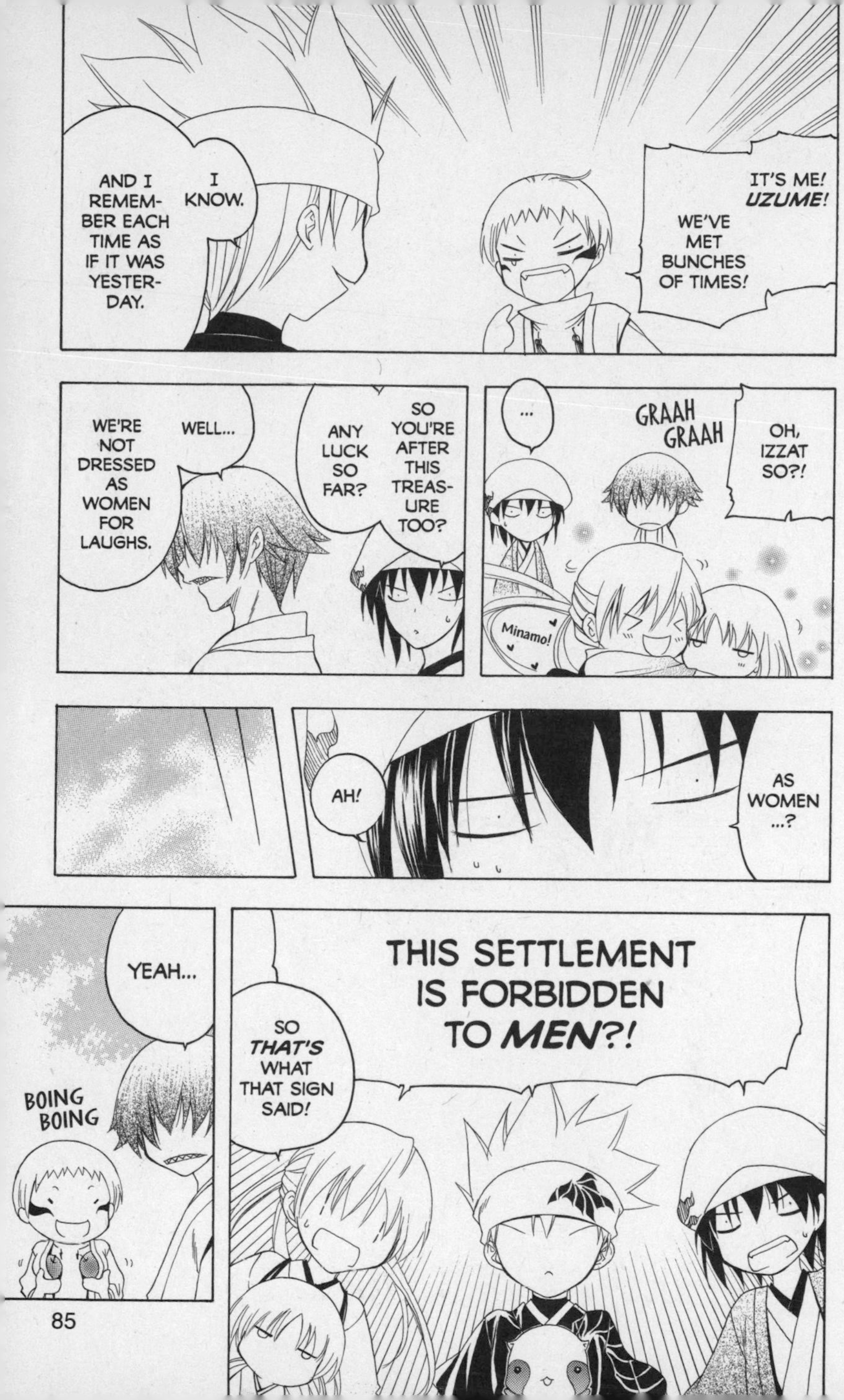
IT'S ME! *UZUME!*
WE'VE MET BUNCHES OF TIMES!
I KNOW.
AND I REMEM- BER EACH TIME AS IF IT WAS YESTER- DAY.
OH, IZZAT SO?!
GRAAH GRAAH
...
Minamo!
SO YOU'RE AFTER THIS TREAS- URE TOO?
ANY LUCK SO FAR?
WELL...
WE'RE NOT DRESSED AS WOMEN FOR LAUGHS.
AS WOMEN ...?
AH!
THIS SETTLEMENT IS FORBIDDEN TO *MEN*?!
SO *THAT'S* WHAT THAT SIGN SAID!
YEAH...
BOING BOING

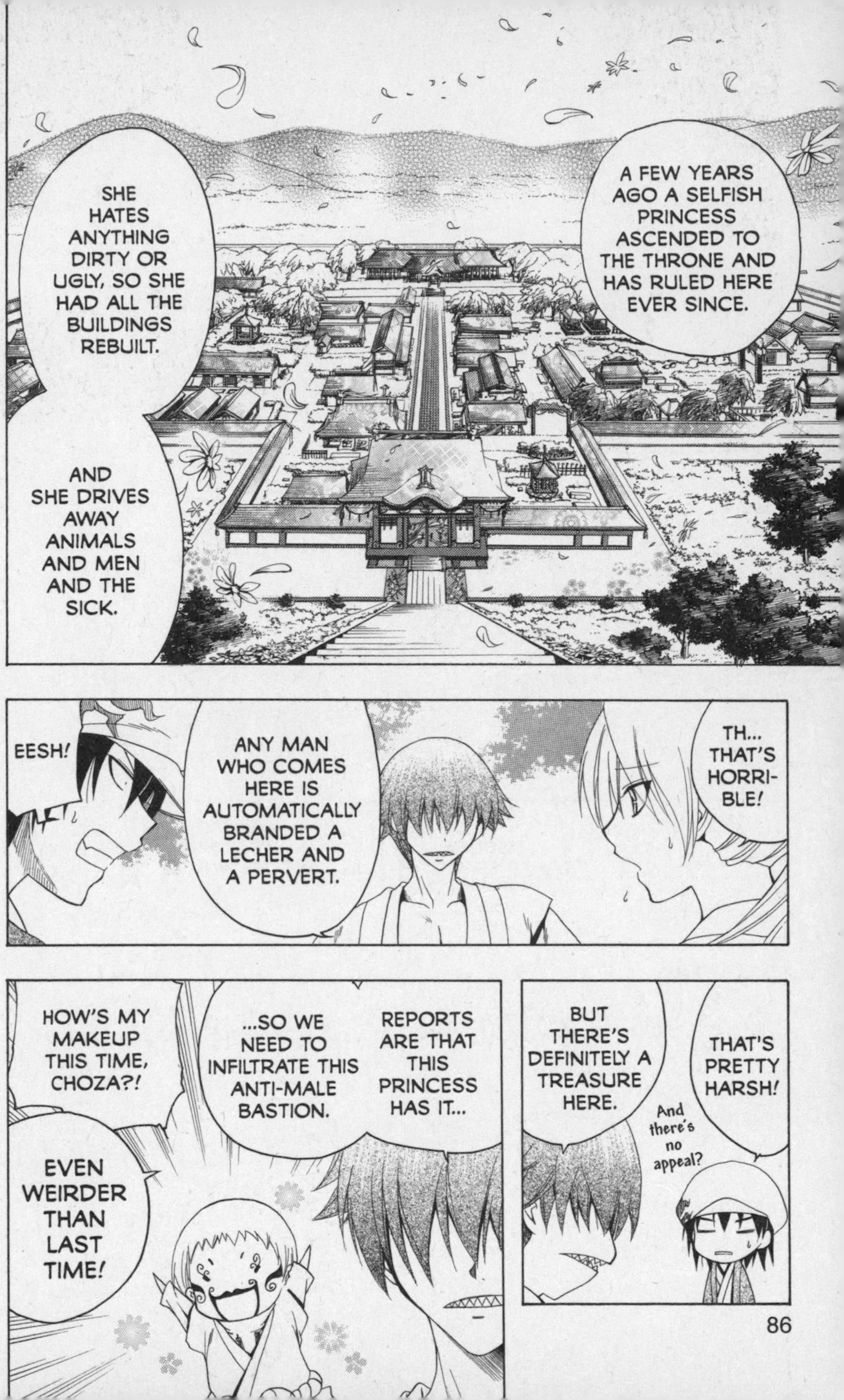
A FEW YEARS AGO A SELFISH PRINCESS ASCENDED TO THE THRONE AND HAS RULED HERE EVER SINCE.
SHE HATES ANYTHING DIRTY OR UGLY, SO SHE HAD ALL THE BUILDINGS REBUILT.
AND SHE DRIVES AWAY ANIMALS AND MEN AND THE SICK.
TH... THAT'S HORRIBLE!
ANY MAN WHO COMES HERE IS AUTOMATICALLY BRANDED A LECHER AND A PERVERT.
EESH!
THAT'S PRETTY HARSH!
And there's no appeal?
BUT THERE'S DEFINITELY A TREASURE HERE.
REPORTS ARE THAT THIS PRINCESS HAS IT...
...SO WE NEED TO INFILTRATE THIS ANTI-MALE BASTION.
HOW'S MY MAKEUP THIS TIME, CHOZA?!
EVEN WEIRDER THAN LAST TIME!

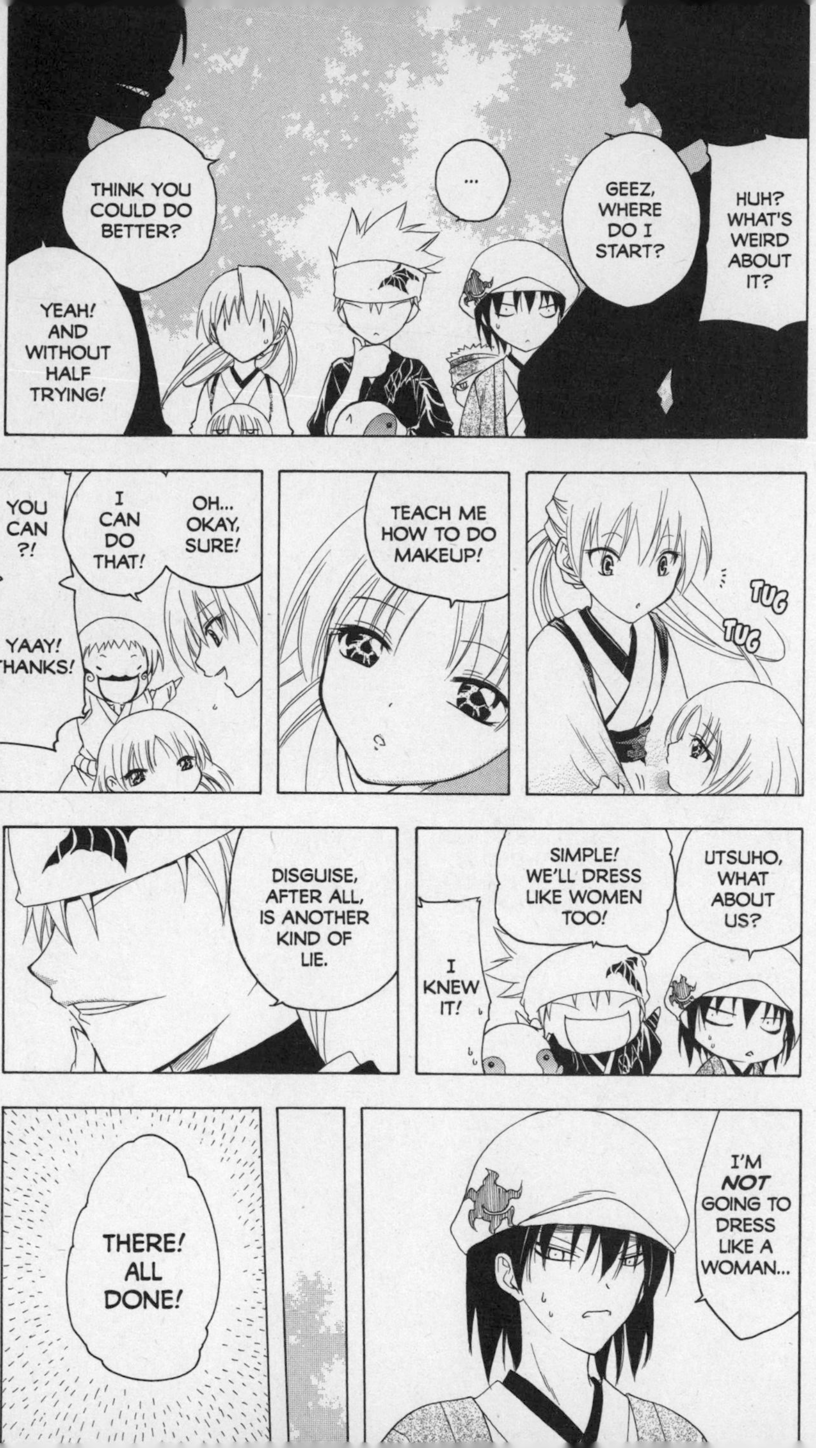
HUH? WHAT'S WEIRD ABOUT IT?
GEEZ, WHERE DO I START?
...
THINK YOU COULD DO BETTER?
YEAH! AND WITHOUT HALF TRYING!
TUG
TUG
TEACH ME HOW TO DO MAKEUP!
OH... OKAY, SURE!
I CAN DO THAT!
YOU CAN?!
YAAY! THANKS!
UTSUHO, WHAT ABOUT US?
SIMPLE! WE'LL DRESS LIKE WOMEN TOO!
I KNEW IT!
DISGUISE, AFTER ALL, IS ANOTHER KIND OF LIE.
I'M *NOT* GOING TO DRESS LIKE A WOMAN...
THERE! ALL DONE!

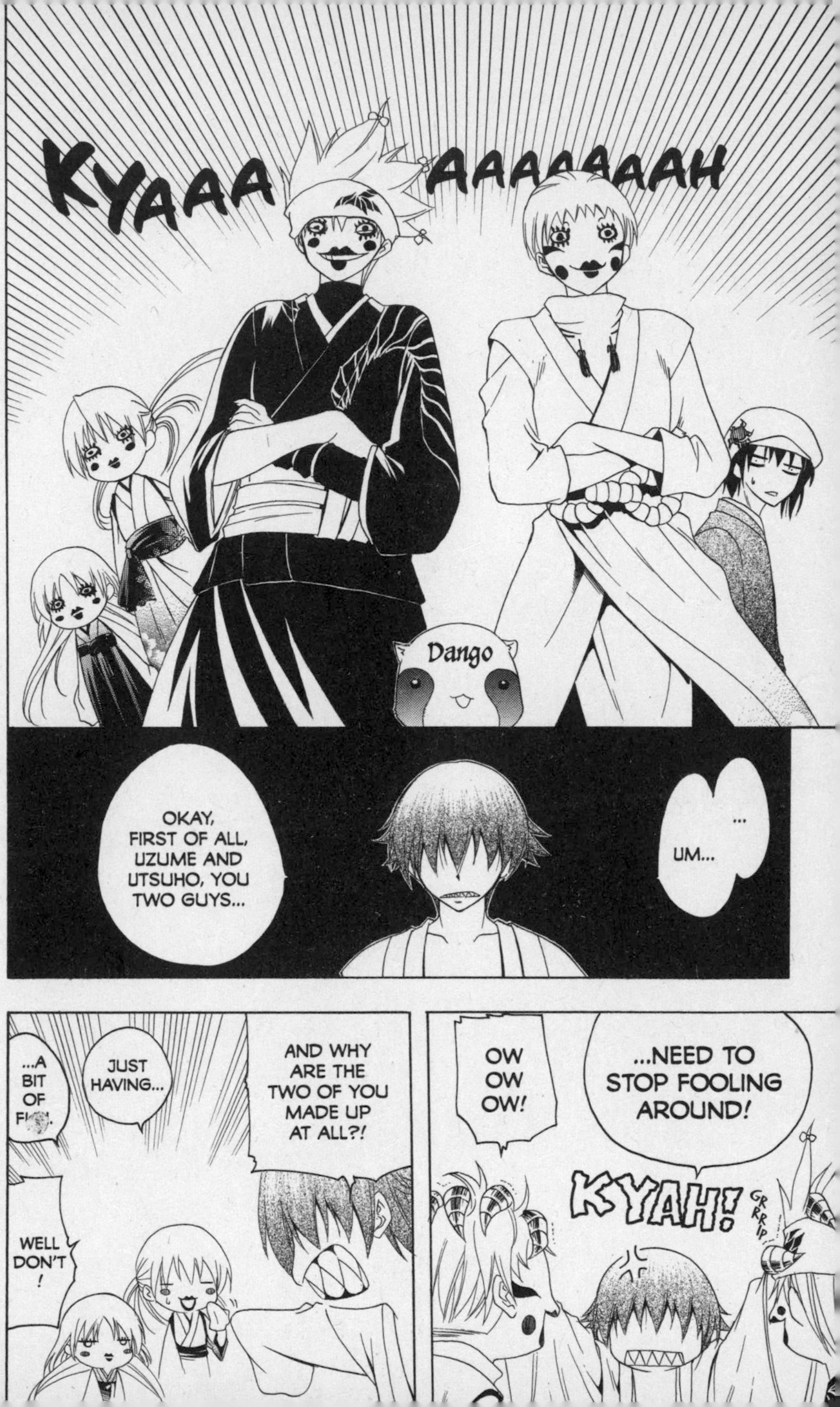
KYAAA AAAAAAAH
Dango
... UM...
OKAY, FIRST OF ALL, UZUME AND UTSUHO, YOU TWO GUYS...
...NEED TO STOP FOOLING AROUND!
OW OW OW!
KYAH!
GRRRIP
AND WHY ARE THE TWO OF YOU MADE UP AT ALL?!
JUST HAVING...
...A BIT OF
WELL DON'T!

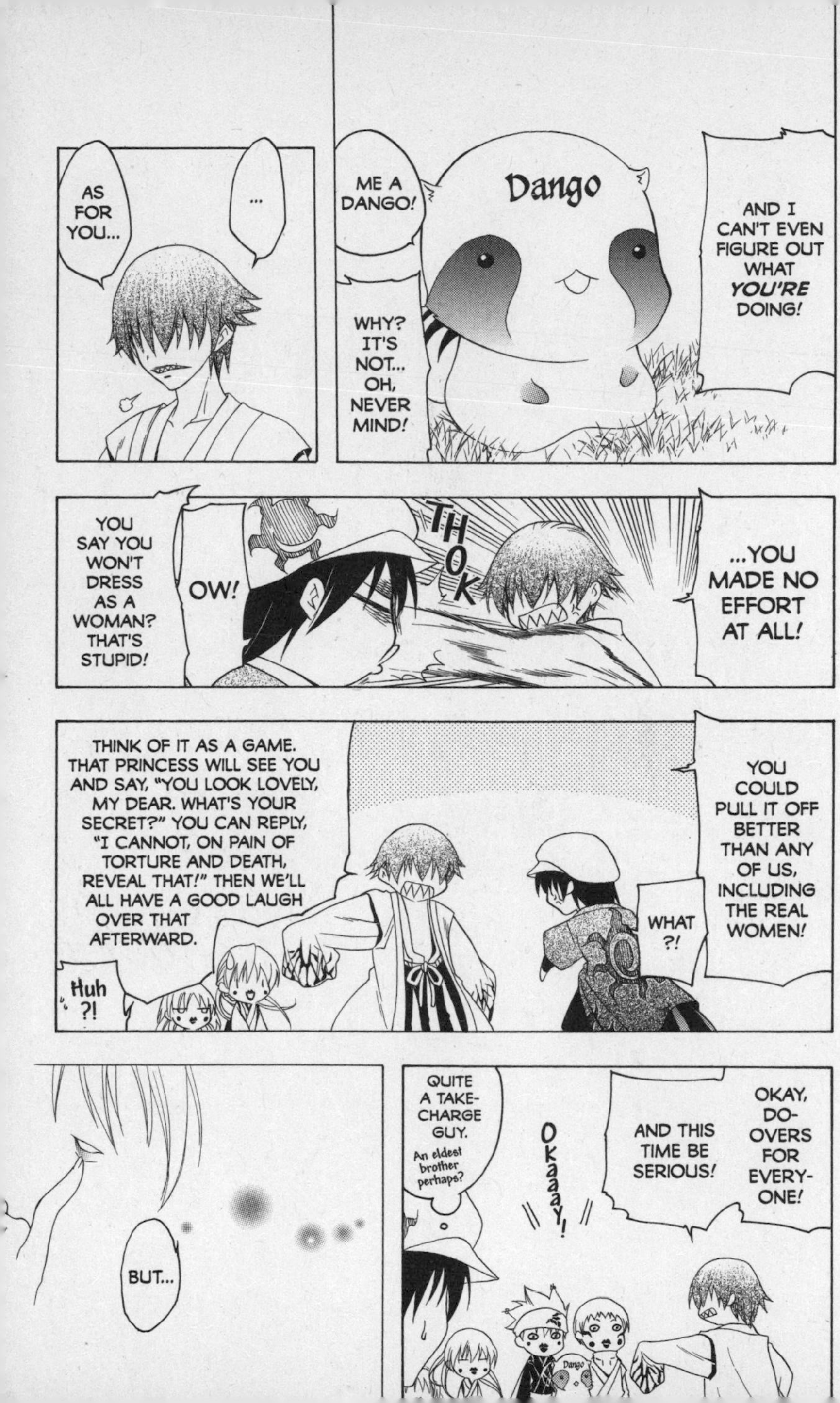
AND I CAN'T EVEN FIGURE OUT WHAT *YOU'RE* DOING!
ME A DANGO!
Dango
WHY? IT'S NOT... OH, NEVER MIND!
...
AS FOR YOU...
...YOU MADE NO EFFORT AT ALL!
THOK
OW!
YOU SAY YOU WON'T DRESS AS A WOMAN? THAT'S STUPID!
YOU COULD PULL IT OFF BETTER THAN ANY OF US, INCLUDING THE REAL WOMEN!
WHAT ?!
THINK OF IT AS A GAME. THAT PRINCESS WILL SEE YOU AND SAY, "YOU LOOK LOVELY, MY DEAR. WHAT'S YOUR SECRET?" YOU CAN REPLY, "I CANNOT, ON PAIN OF TORTURE AND DEATH, REVEAL THAT!" THEN WE'LL ALL HAVE A GOOD LAUGH OVER THAT AFTERWARD.
Huh ?!
OKAY, DO-OVERS FOR EVERY-ONE!
AND THIS TIME BE SERIOUS!
Okaaay!
QUITE A TAKE-CHARGE GUY.
An eldest brother perhaps?
Dango
BUT...

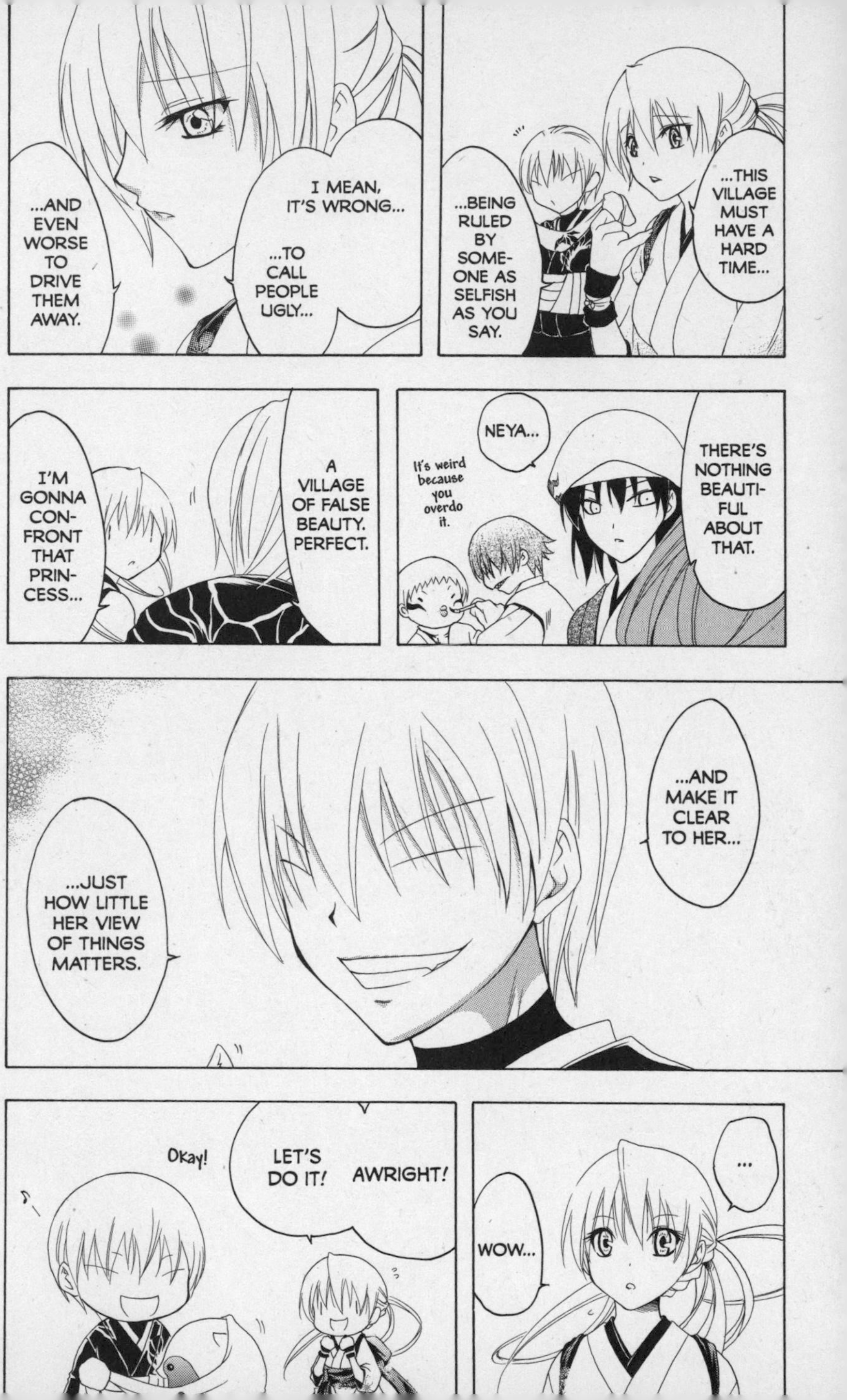
...THIS VILLAGE MUST HAVE A HARD TIME...
...BEING RULED BY SOMEONE AS SELFISH AS YOU SAY.
I MEAN, IT'S WRONG...
...TO CALL PEOPLE UGLY...
...AND EVEN WORSE TO DRIVE THEM AWAY.
THERE'S NOTHING BEAUTIFUL ABOUT THAT.
NEYA...
It's weird because you overdo it.
A VILLAGE OF FALSE BEAUTY. PERFECT.
I'M GONNA CONFRONT THAT PRINCESS...
...AND MAKE IT CLEAR TO HER...
...JUST HOW LITTLE HER VIEW OF THINGS MATTERS.
...
WOW...
AWRIGHT!
LET'S DO IT!
Okay!

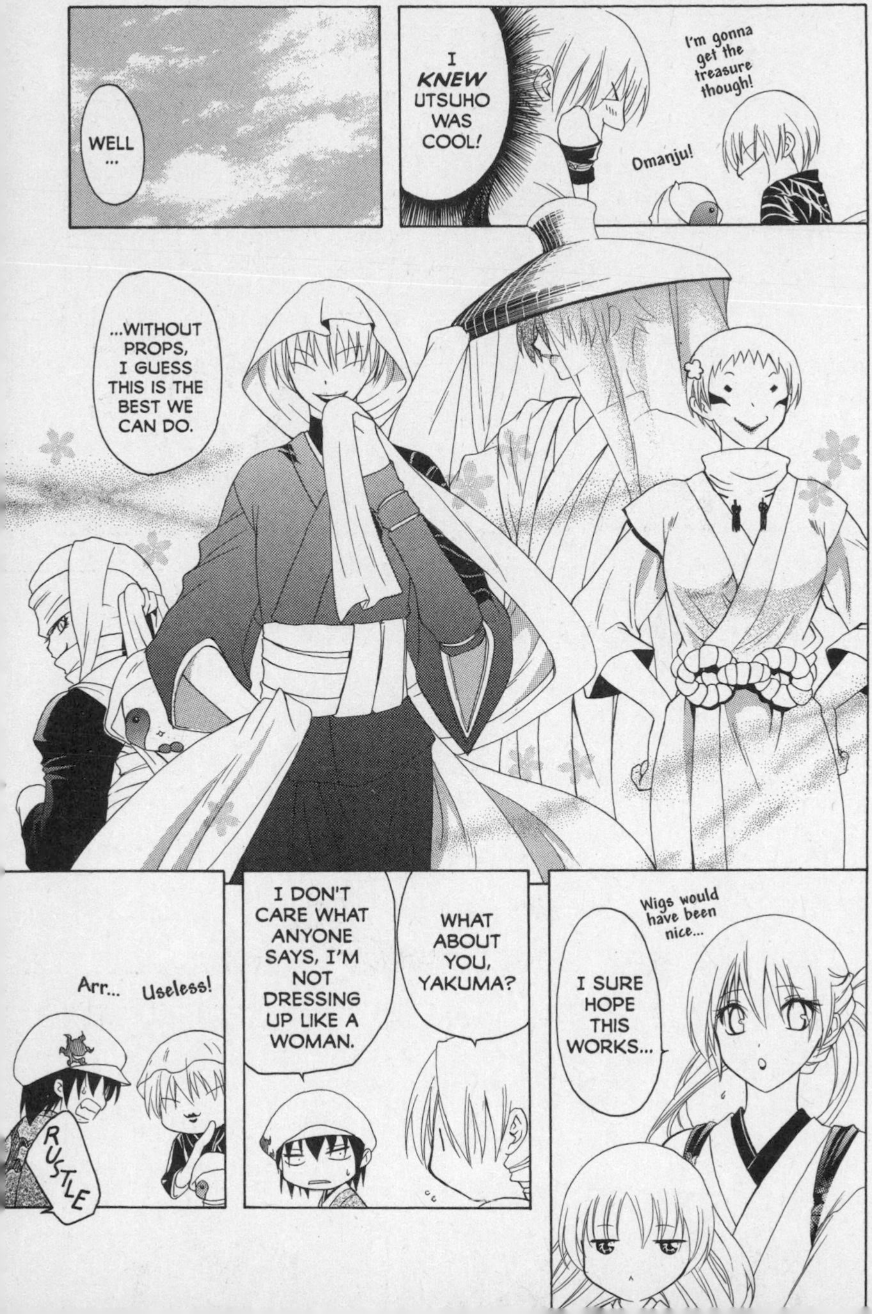
I'm gonna get the treasure though!
I *KNEW* UTSUHO WAS COOL!
Omanju!
WELL ...
...WITHOUT PROPS, I GUESS THIS IS THE BEST WE CAN DO.
Wigs would have been nice...
I SURE HOPE THIS WORKS...
WHAT ABOUT YOU, YAKUMA?
I DON'T CARE WHAT ANYONE SAYS, I'M NOT DRESSING UP LIKE A WOMAN.
Useless!
Arr...
RUSTLE

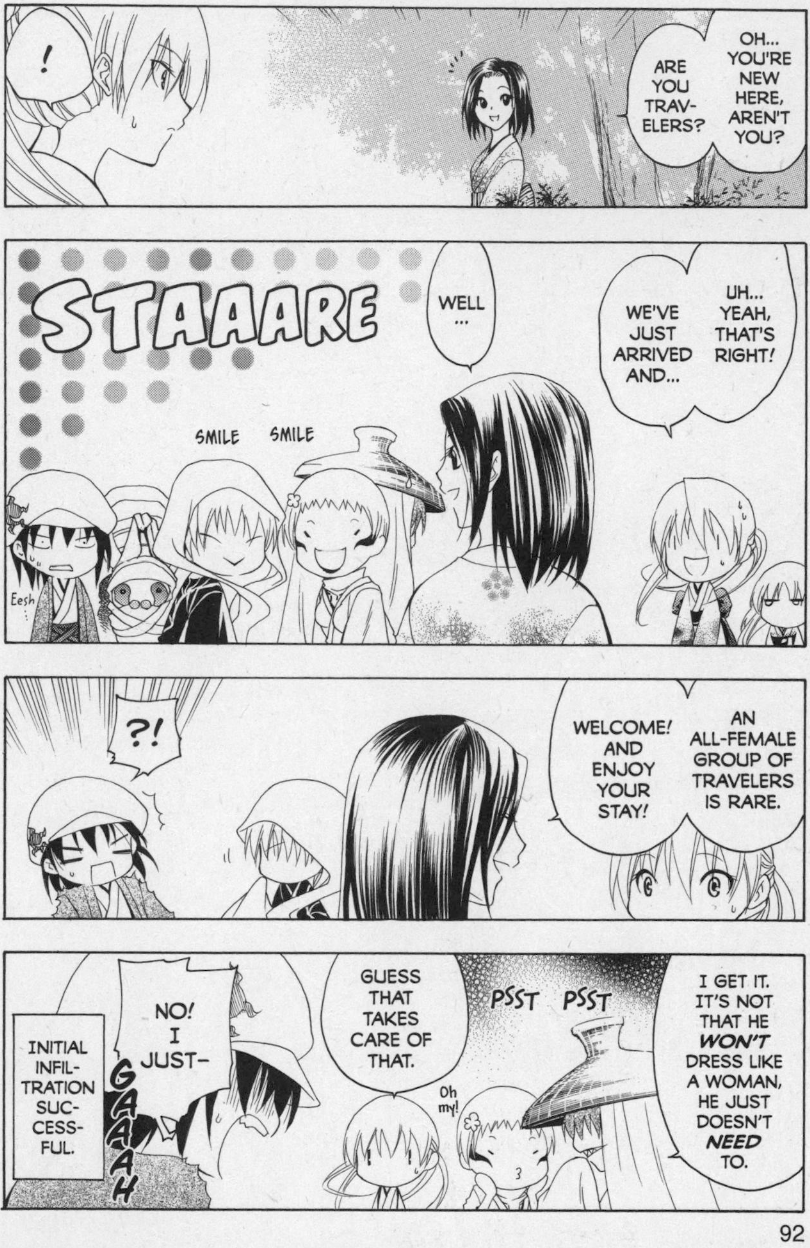
OH... YOU'RE NEW HERE, AREN'T YOU?
ARE YOU TRAV-ELERS?
!
UH... YEAH, THAT'S RIGHT!
WE'VE JUST ARRIVED AND...
WELL ...
STAAARE
SMILE SMILE
Eesh
AN ALL-FEMALE GROUP OF TRAVELERS IS RARE.
WELCOME! AND ENJOY YOUR STAY!
?!
I GET IT. IT'S NOT THAT HE *WON'T* DRESS LIKE A WOMAN, HE JUST DOESN'T *NEED* TO.
PSST PSST
GUESS THAT TAKES CARE OF THAT.
Oh my!
NO! I JUST-
GAAAAH
INITIAL INFIL-TRATION SUC-CESS-FUL.

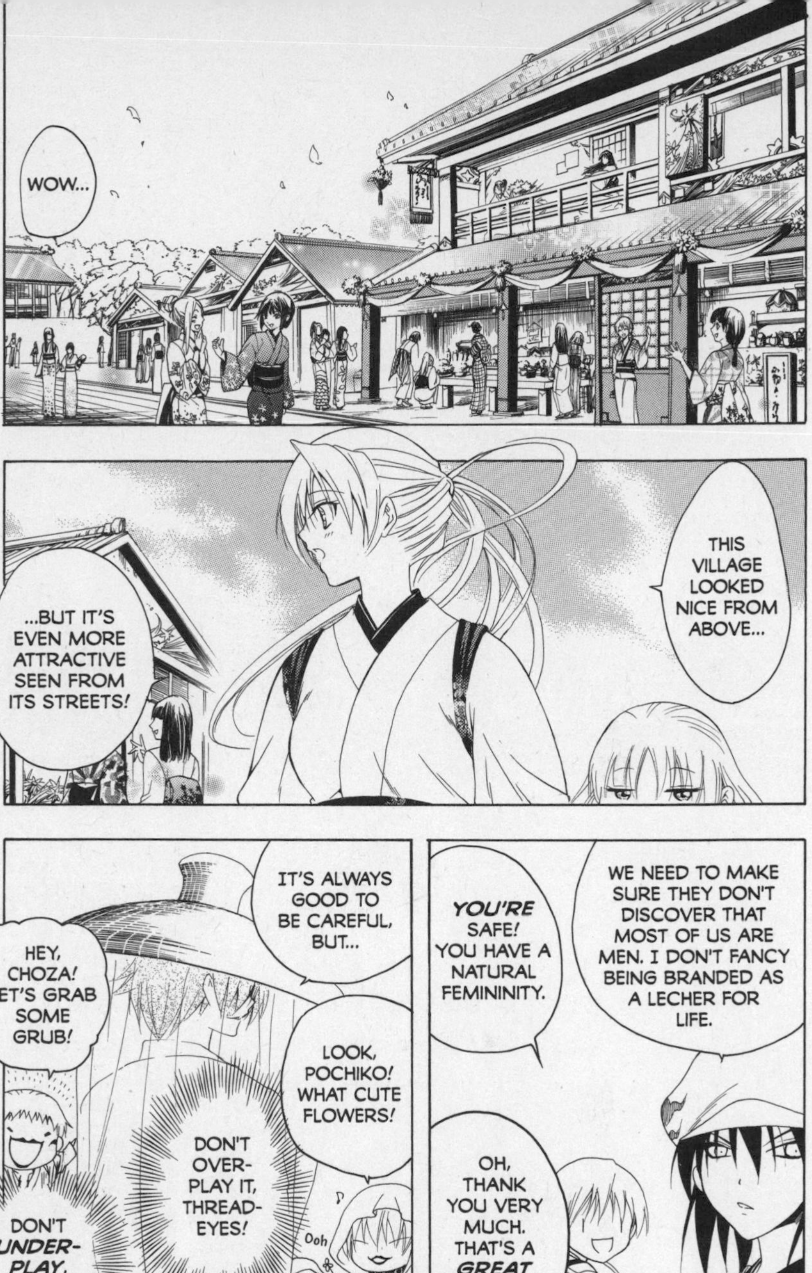
WOW...
THIS VILLAGE LOOKED NICE FROM ABOVE...
...BUT IT'S EVEN MORE ATTRACTIVE SEEN FROM ITS STREETS!
WE NEED TO MAKE SURE THEY DON'T DISCOVER THAT MOST OF US ARE MEN. I DON'T FANCY BEING BRANDED AS A LECHER FOR LIFE.
YOU'RE SAFE! YOU HAVE A NATURAL FEMININITY.
OH, THANK YOU VERY MUCH. THAT'S A *GREAT* COMFORT!
IT'S ALWAYS GOOD TO BE CAREFUL, BUT...
HEY, CHOZA! LET'S GRAB SOME GRUB!
LOOK, POCHIKO! WHAT CUTE FLOWERS!
Ooh
DON'T OVER-PLAY IT, THREAD-EYES!
DON'T *UNDER-PLAY*, UZUME! GEEZ...

Chapter 83 Iwashihime

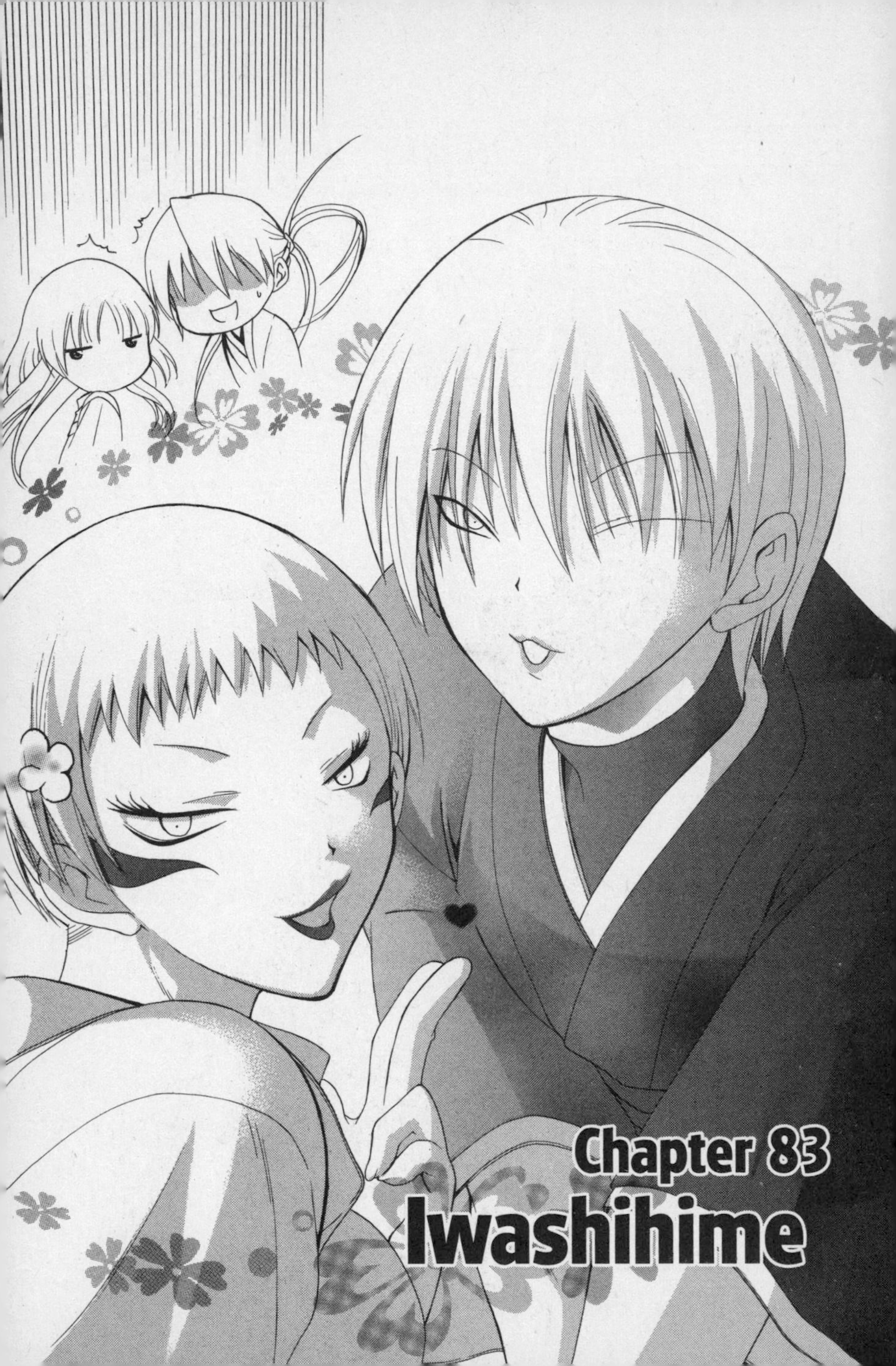
Chapter 83
Iwashihime

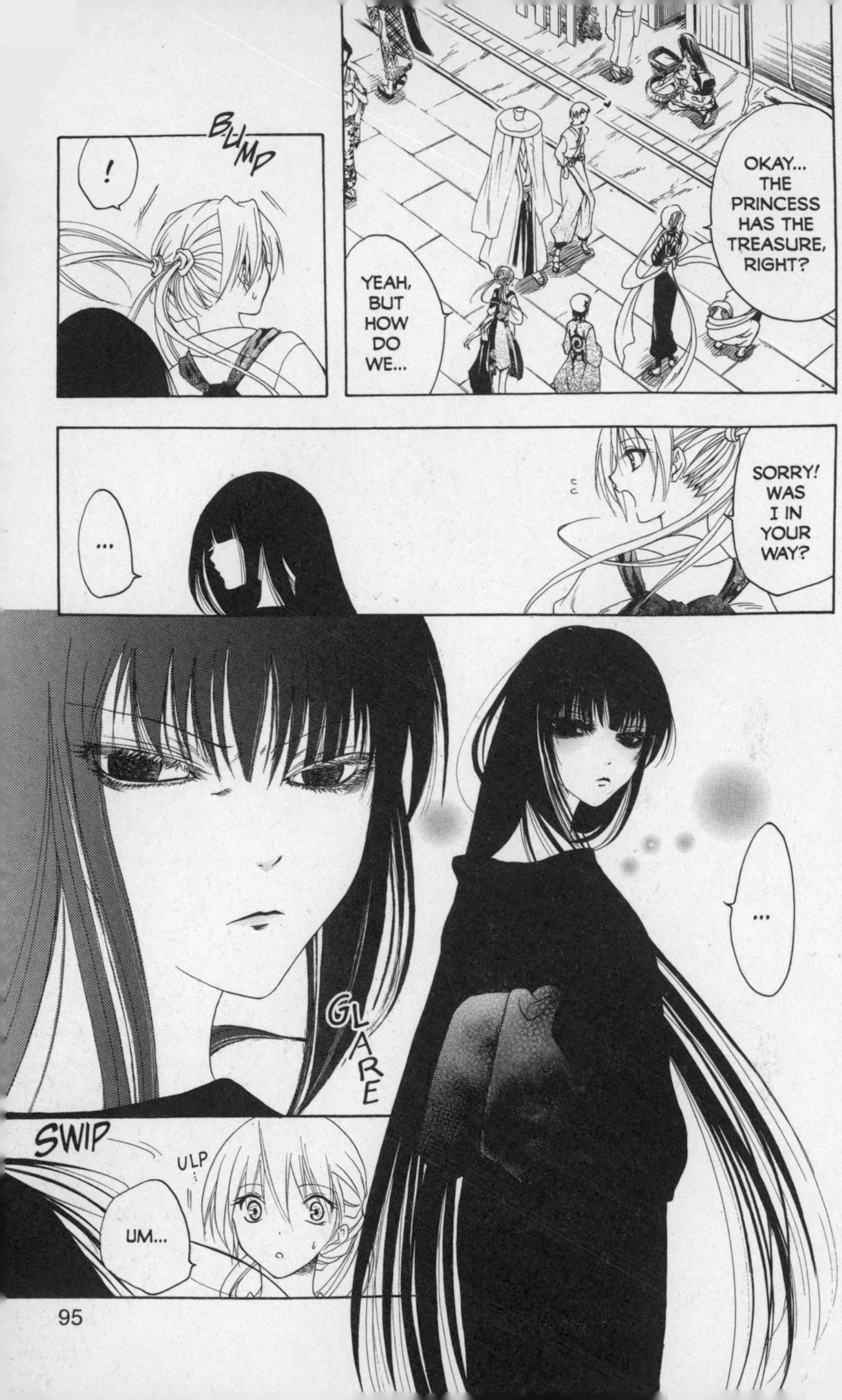

OKAY... THE PRINCESS HAS THE TREASURE, RIGHT?
YEAH, BUT HOW DO WE...
B-LUMP
!
SORRY! WAS I IN YOUR WAY?
...
...
GLARE
SWIP
ULP
UM...

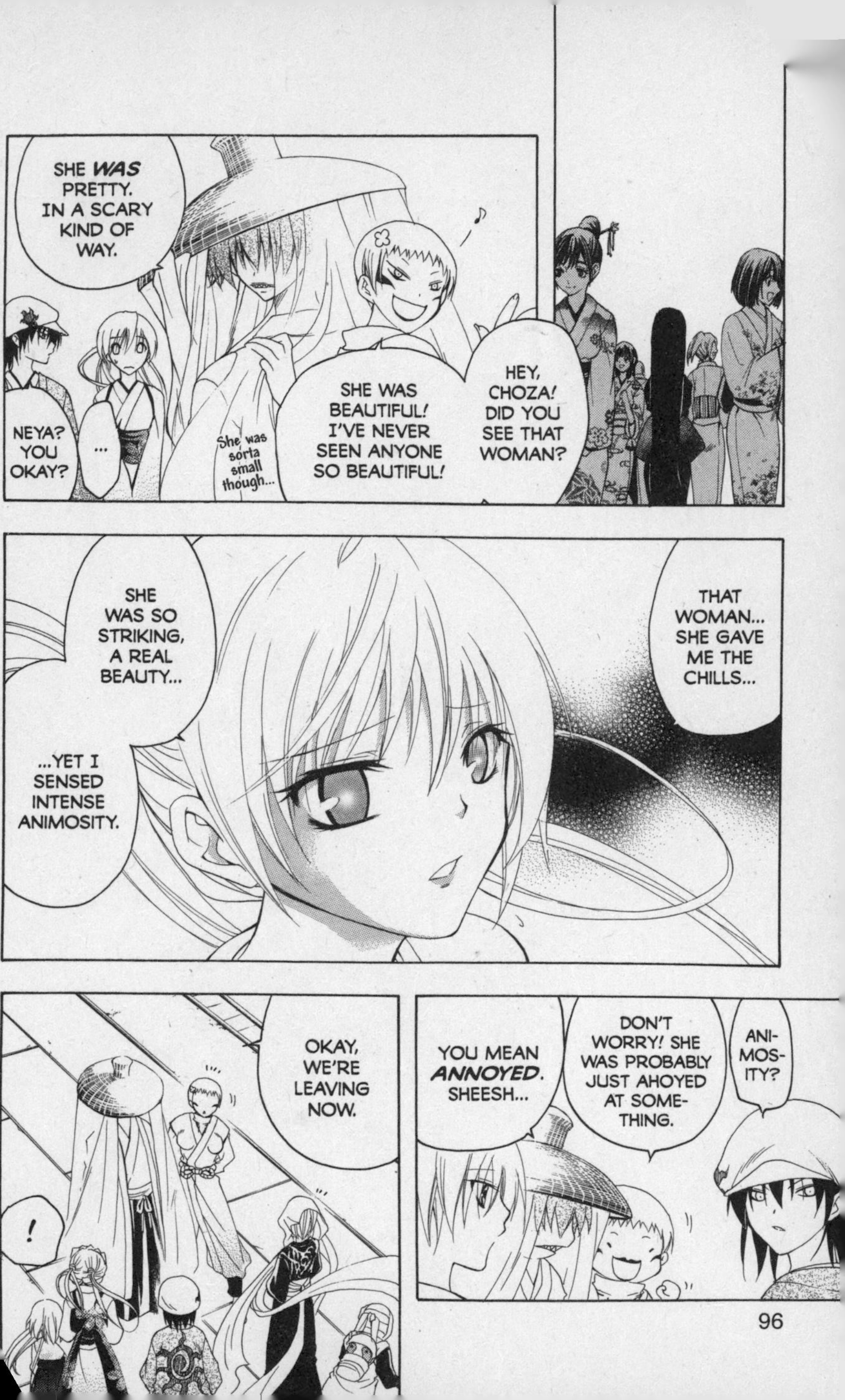
HEY, CHOZA! DID YOU SEE THAT WOMAN?
SHE WAS BEAUTIFUL! I'VE NEVER SEEN ANYONE SO BEAUTIFUL!
She was sorta small though...
SHE ***WAS*** PRETTY. IN A SCARY KIND OF WAY.
...
NEYA? YOU OKAY?
THAT WOMAN... SHE GAVE ME THE CHILLS...
SHE WAS SO STRIKING, A REAL BEAUTY...
...YET I SENSED INTENSE ANIMOSITY.
ANI-MOS-ITY?
DON'T WORRY! SHE WAS PROBABLY JUST AHOYED AT SOME-THING.
YOU MEAN ***ANNOYED***. SHEESH...
OKAY, WE'RE LEAVING NOW.
!

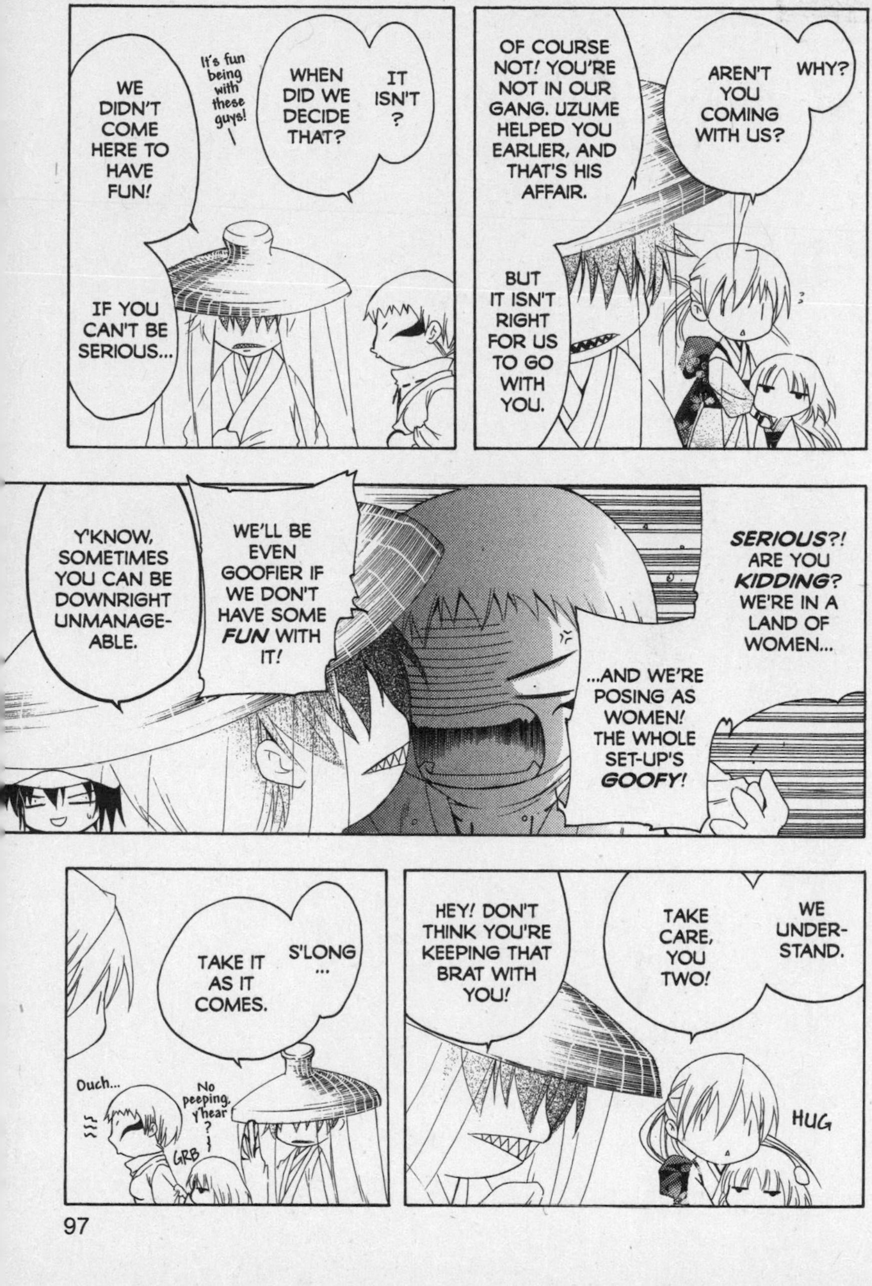
WHY?
AREN'T YOU COMING WITH US?
OF COURSE NOT! YOU'RE NOT IN OUR GANG. UZUME HELPED YOU EARLIER, AND THAT'S HIS AFFAIR.
BUT IT ISN'T RIGHT FOR US TO GO WITH YOU.
IT ISN'T?
WHEN DID WE DECIDE THAT?
It's fun being with these guys!
WE DIDN'T COME HERE TO HAVE FUN!
IF YOU CAN'T BE SERIOUS...
SERIOUS?! ARE YOU KIDDING? WE'RE IN A LAND OF WOMEN...
...AND WE'RE POSING AS WOMEN! THE WHOLE SET-UP'S GOOFY!
WE'LL BE EVEN GOOFIER IF WE DON'T HAVE SOME FUN WITH IT!
Y'KNOW, SOMETIMES YOU CAN BE DOWNRIGHT UNMANAGE-ABLE.
WE UNDER-STAND.
TAKE CARE, YOU TWO!
HUG
HEY! DON'T THINK YOU'RE KEEPING THAT BRAT WITH YOU!
S'LONG...
TAKE IT AS IT COMES.
No peeping, y'hear?
Ouch...
GRB

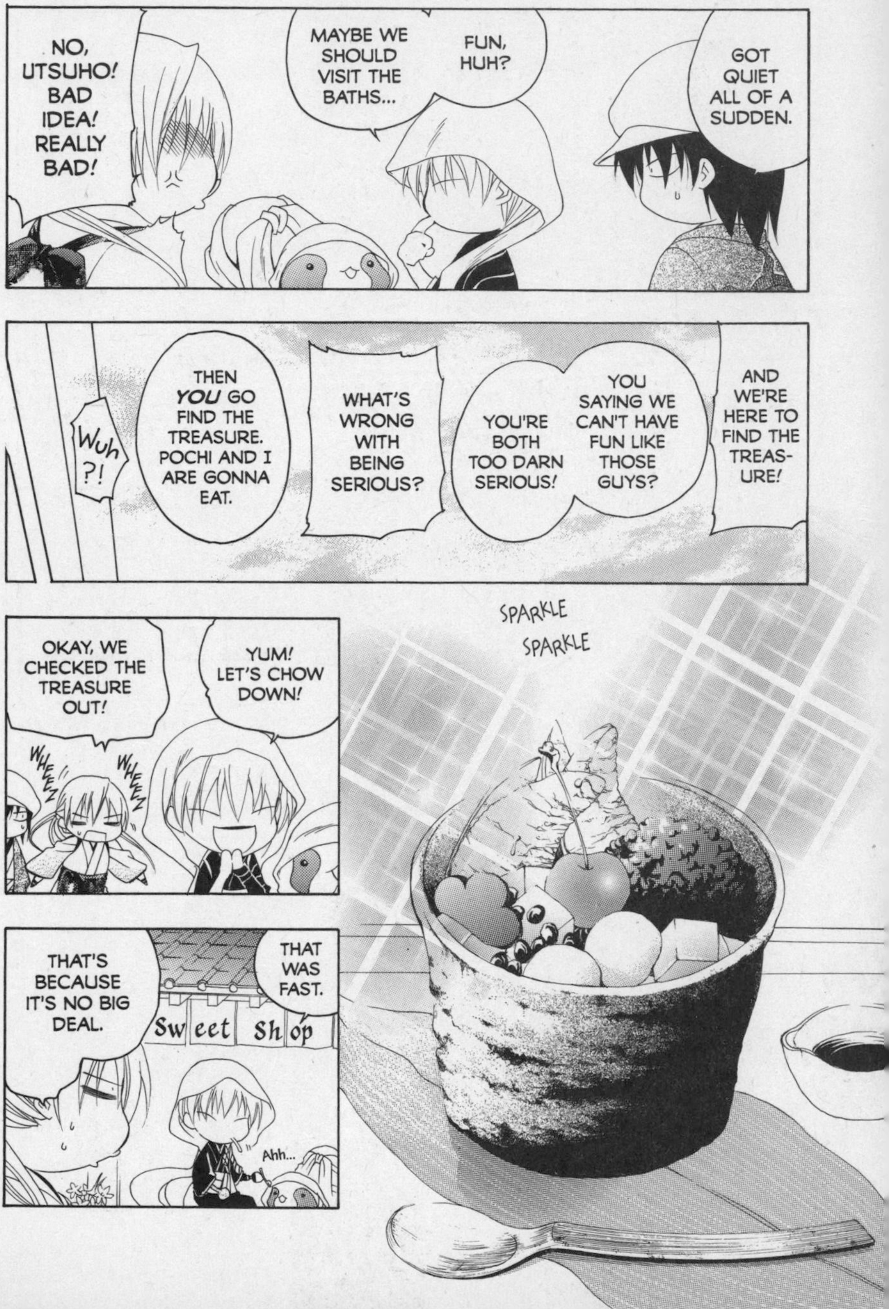
GOT QUIET ALL OF A SUDDEN.
FUN, HUH?
MAYBE WE SHOULD VISIT THE BATHS...
NO, UTSUHO! BAD IDEA! REALLY BAD!
AND WE'RE HERE TO FIND THE TREAS-URE!
YOU SAYING WE CAN'T HAVE FUN LIKE THOSE GUYS?
YOU'RE BOTH TOO DARN SERIOUS!
WHAT'S WRONG WITH BEING SERIOUS?
THEN *YOU* GO FIND THE TREASURE. POCHI AND I ARE GONNA EAT.
Wuh?!
SPARKLE
SPARKLE
YUM! LET'S CHOW DOWN!
OKAY, WE CHECKED THE TREASURE OUT!
WHEEZE
WHEEZE
THAT WAS FAST.
THAT'S BECAUSE IT'S NO BIG DEAL.
Sweet Shop
Ahh...

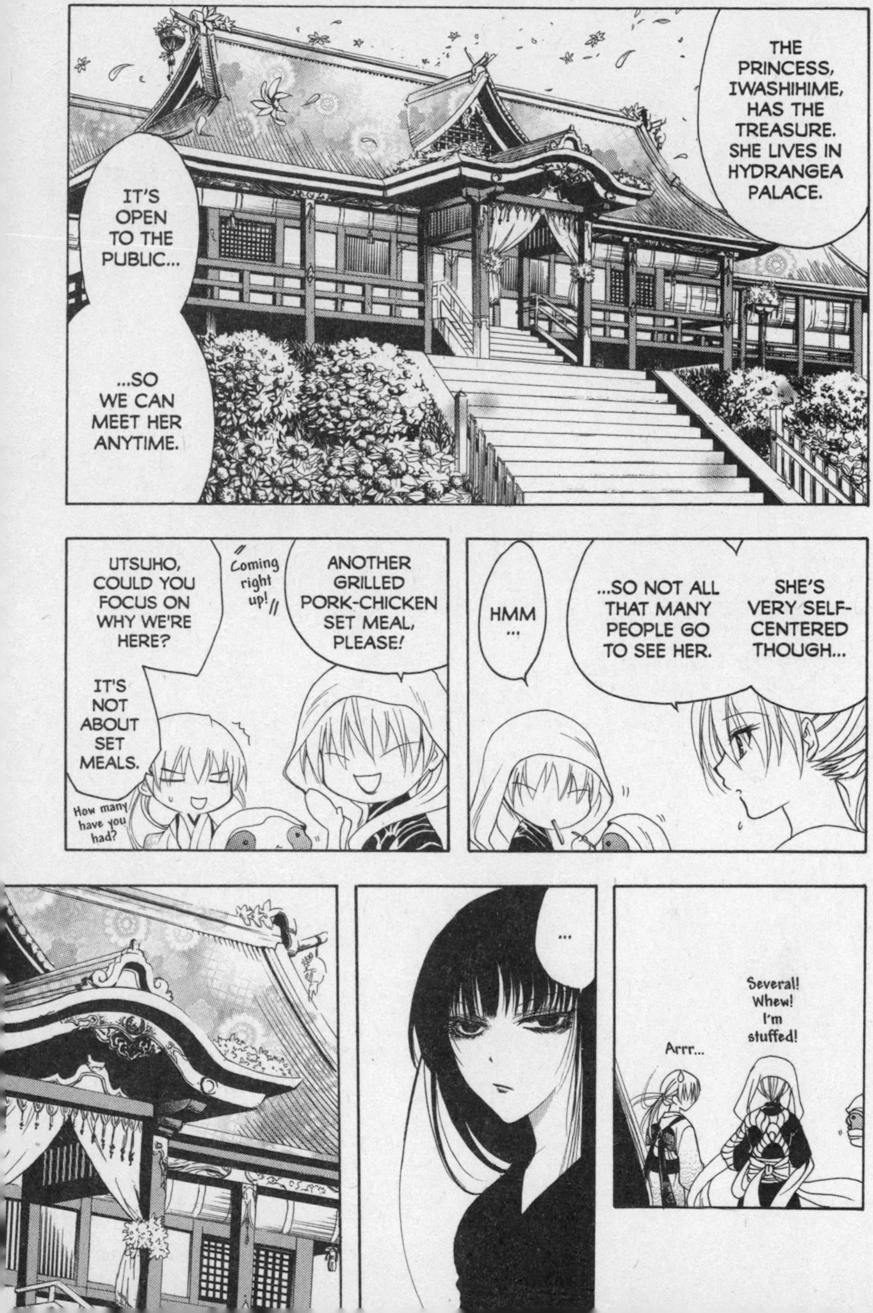
THE PRINCESS, IWASHIHIME, HAS THE TREASURE. SHE LIVES IN HYDRANGEA PALACE.
IT'S OPEN TO THE PUBLIC...
...SO WE CAN MEET HER ANYTIME.
SHE'S VERY SELF-CENTERED THOUGH...
...SO NOT ALL THAT MANY PEOPLE GO TO SEE HER.
HMM...
ANOTHER GRILLED PORK-CHICKEN SET MEAL, PLEASE!
Coming right up!
UTSUHO, COULD YOU FOCUS ON WHY WE'RE HERE?
IT'S NOT ABOUT SET MEALS.
How many have you had?
Several! Whew! I'm stuffed!
Arrr...
...

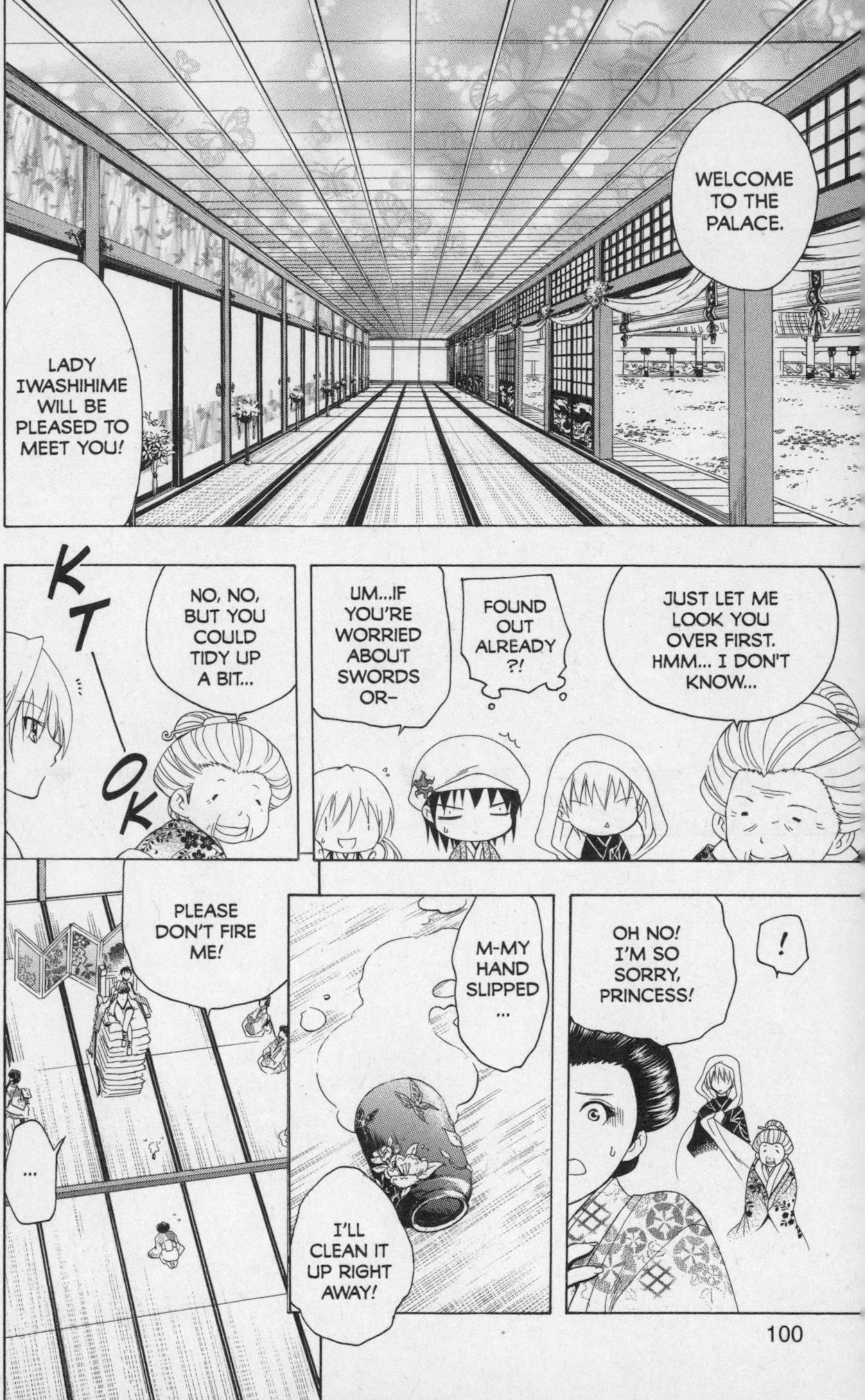
WELCOME TO THE PALACE.
LADY IWASHIHIME WILL BE PLEASED TO MEET YOU!
JUST LET ME LOOK YOU OVER FIRST. HMM... I DON'T KNOW...
FOUND OUT ALREADY?!
UM...IF YOU'RE WORRIED ABOUT SWORDS OR–
NO, NO, BUT YOU COULD TIDY UP A BIT...
KTOK
!
OH NO! I'M SO SORRY, PRINCESS!
M-MY HAND SLIPPED ...
I'LL CLEAN IT UP RIGHT AWAY!
PLEASE DON'T FIRE ME!
...

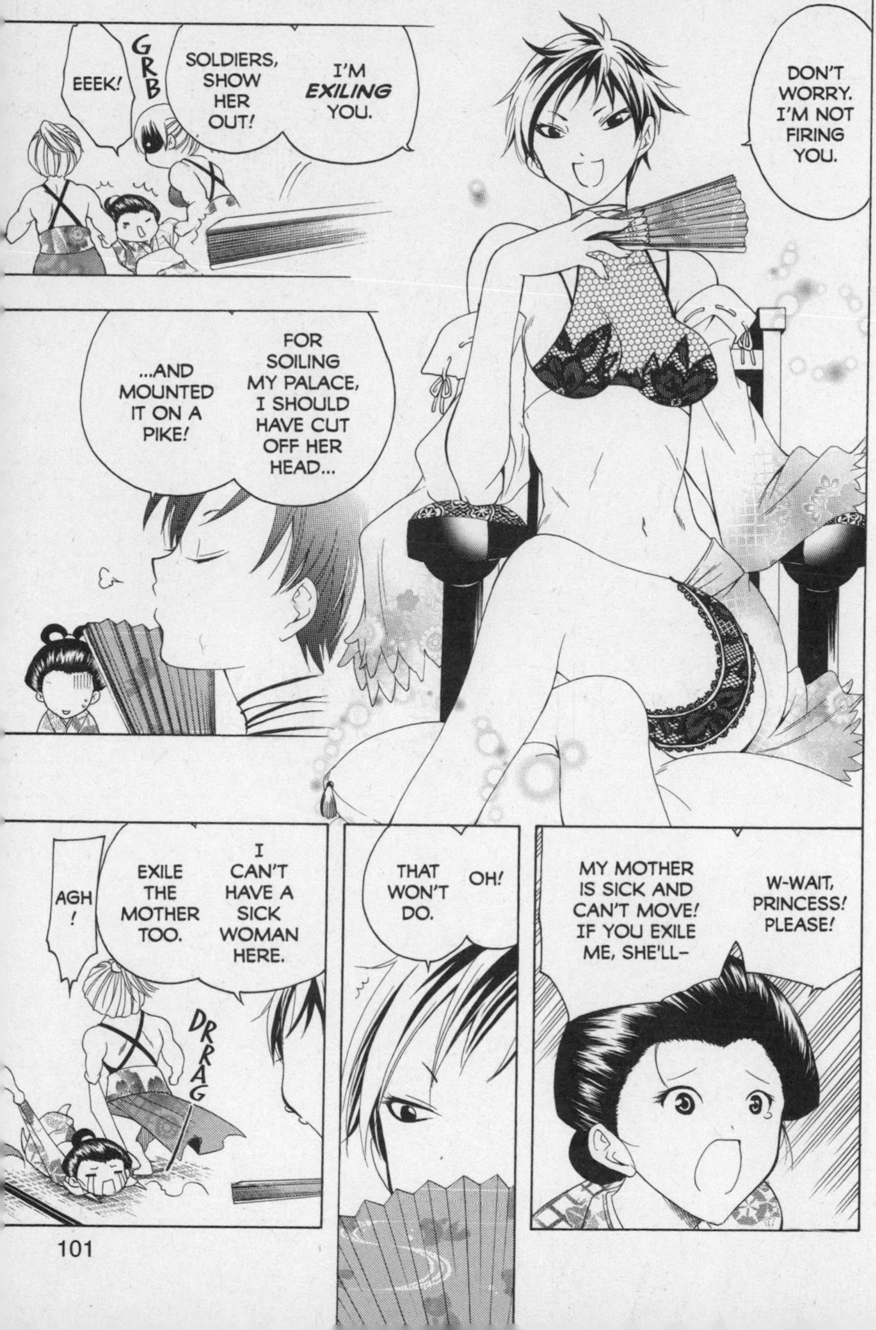
DON'T WORRY. I'M NOT FIRING YOU.
I'M EXILING YOU.
SOLDIERS, SHOW HER OUT!
GRB
EEEK!
FOR SOILING MY PALACE, I SHOULD HAVE CUT OFF HER HEAD...
...AND MOUNTED IT ON A PIKE!
W-WAIT, PRINCESS! PLEASE!
MY MOTHER IS SICK AND CAN'T MOVE! IF YOU EXILE ME, SHE'LL–
OH!
THAT WON'T DO.
I CAN'T HAVE A SICK WOMAN HERE.
EXILE THE MOTHER TOO.
AGH!
DRRRAG

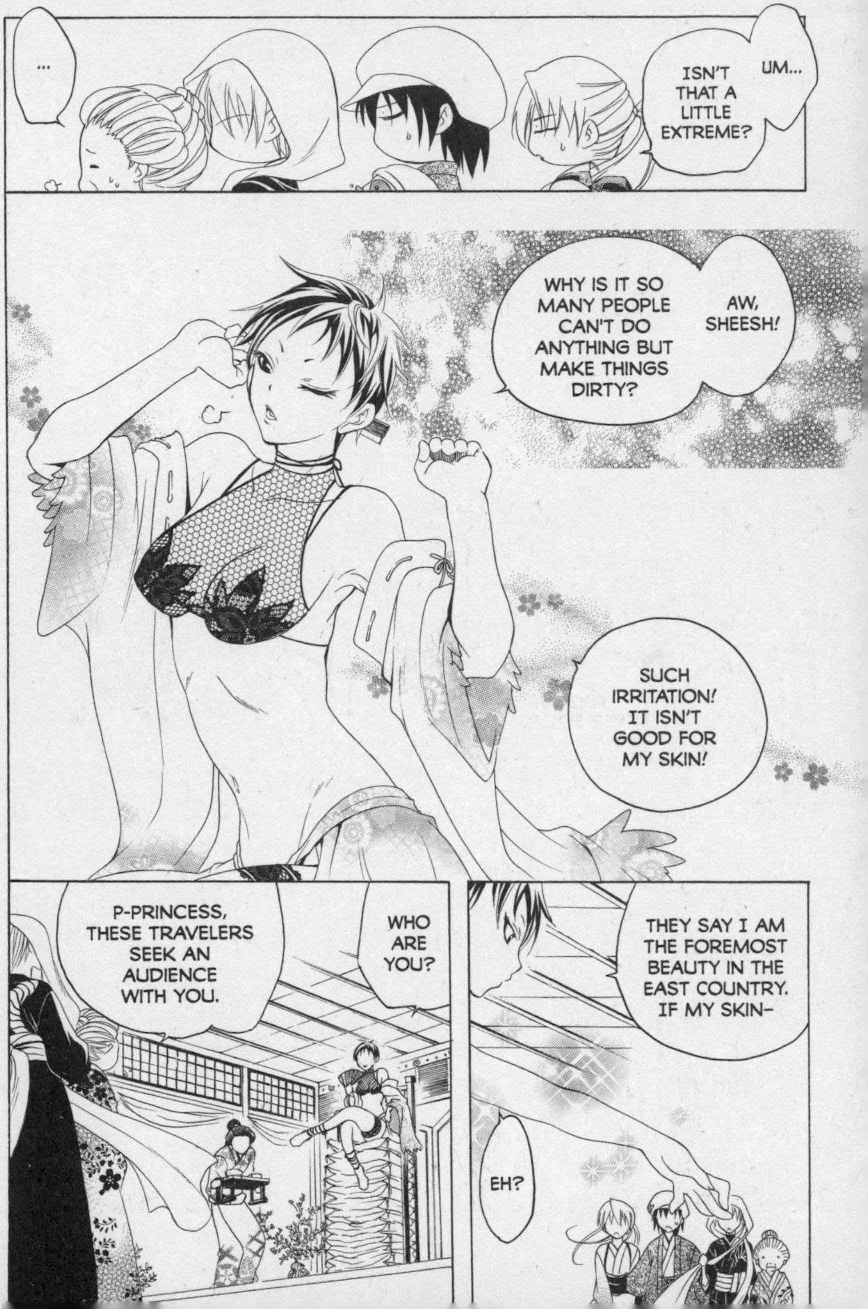
UM...
ISN'T THAT A LITTLE EXTREME?
...
AW, SHEESH!
WHY IS IT SO MANY PEOPLE CAN'T DO ANYTHING BUT MAKE THINGS DIRTY?
SUCH IRRITATION! IT ISN'T GOOD FOR MY SKIN!
THEY SAY I AM THE FOREMOST BEAUTY IN THE EAST COUNTRY. IF MY SKIN–
EH?
WHO ARE YOU?
P-PRINCESS, THESE TRAVELERS SEEK AN AUDIENCE WITH YOU.

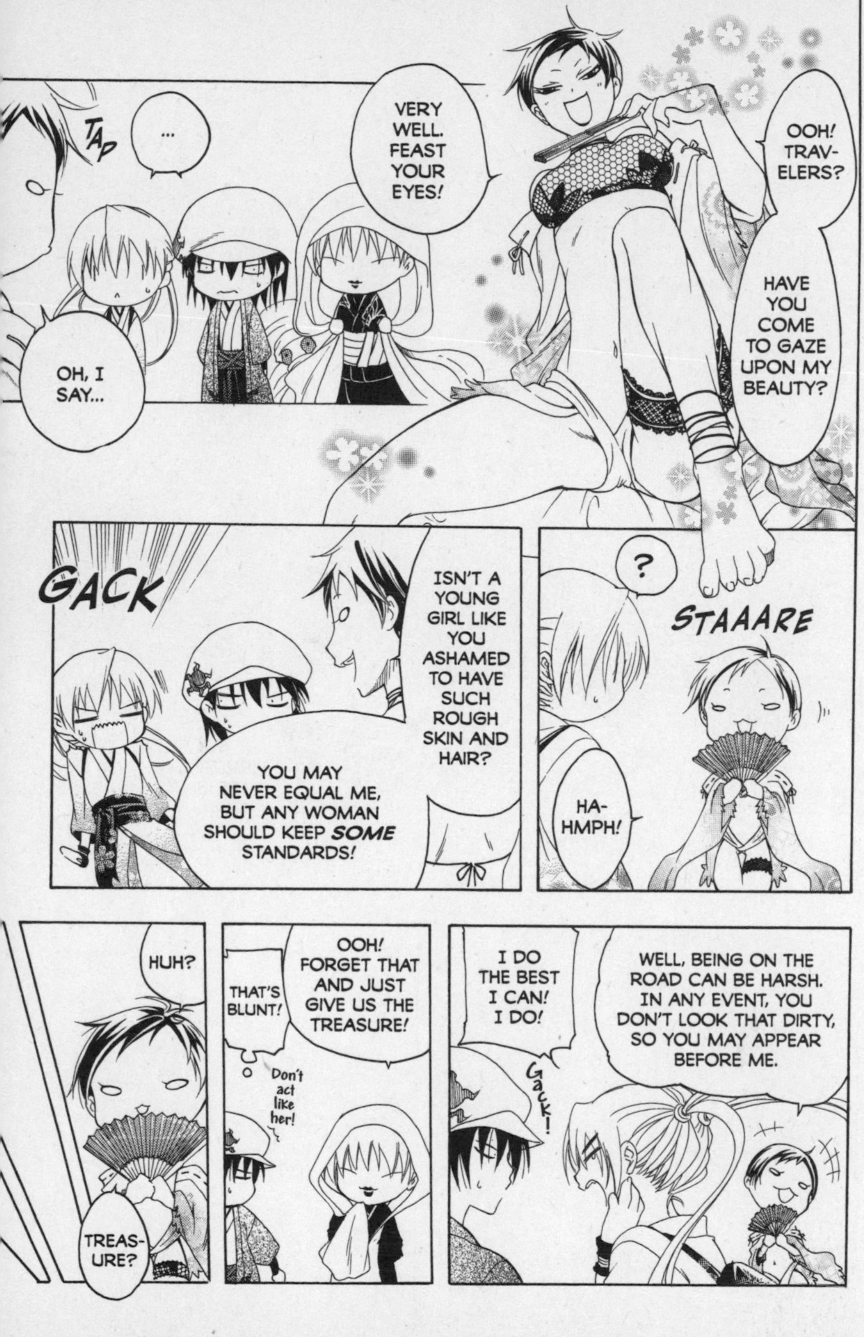
OOH! TRAVELERS?
HAVE YOU COME TO GAZE UPON MY BEAUTY?
VERY WELL. FEAST YOUR EYES!
...
TAP
OH, I SAY...
?
STAAARE
HA-HMPH!
ISN'T A YOUNG GIRL LIKE YOU ASHAMED TO HAVE SUCH ROUGH SKIN AND HAIR?
GACK
YOU MAY NEVER EQUAL ME, BUT ANY WOMAN SHOULD KEEP *SOME* STANDARDS!
WELL, BEING ON THE ROAD CAN BE HARSH. IN ANY EVENT, YOU DON'T LOOK THAT DIRTY, SO YOU MAY APPEAR BEFORE ME.
I DO THE BEST I CAN! I DO!
Gack!
OOH! FORGET THAT AND JUST GIVE US THE TREASURE!
THAT'S BLUNT!
Don't act like her!
HUH?
TREASURE?

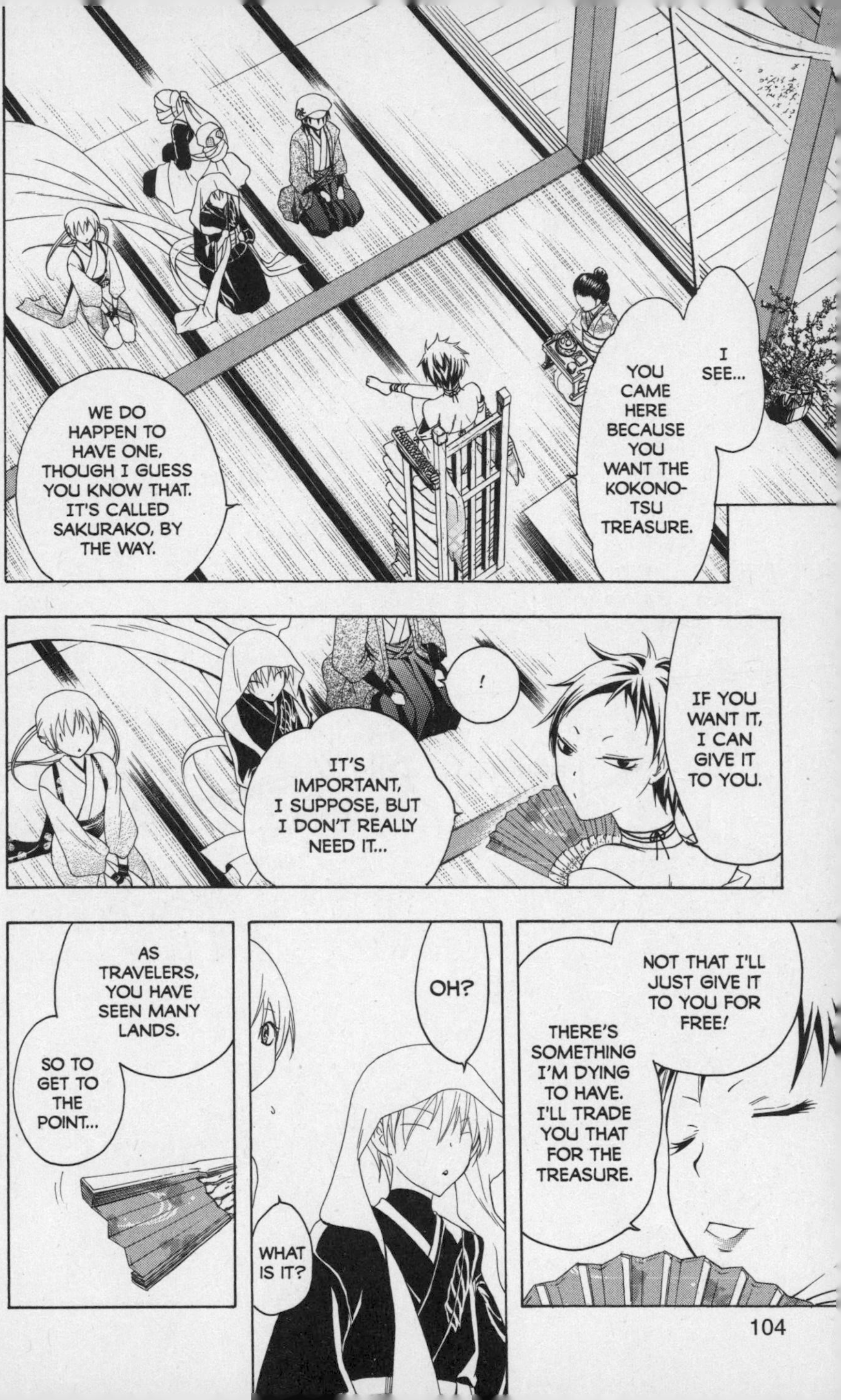
I SEE...
YOU CAME HERE BECAUSE YOU WANT THE KOKONO-TSU TREASURE.
WE DO HAPPEN TO HAVE ONE, THOUGH I GUESS YOU KNOW THAT. IT'S CALLED SAKURAKO, BY THE WAY.
IF YOU WANT IT, I CAN GIVE IT TO YOU.
!
IT'S IMPORTANT, I SUPPOSE, BUT I DON'T REALLY NEED IT...
NOT THAT I'LL JUST GIVE IT TO YOU FOR FREE!
THERE'S SOMETHING I'M DYING TO HAVE. I'LL TRADE YOU THAT FOR THE TREASURE.
OH?
WHAT IS IT?
AS TRAVELERS, YOU HAVE SEEN MANY LANDS.
SO TO GET TO THE POINT...

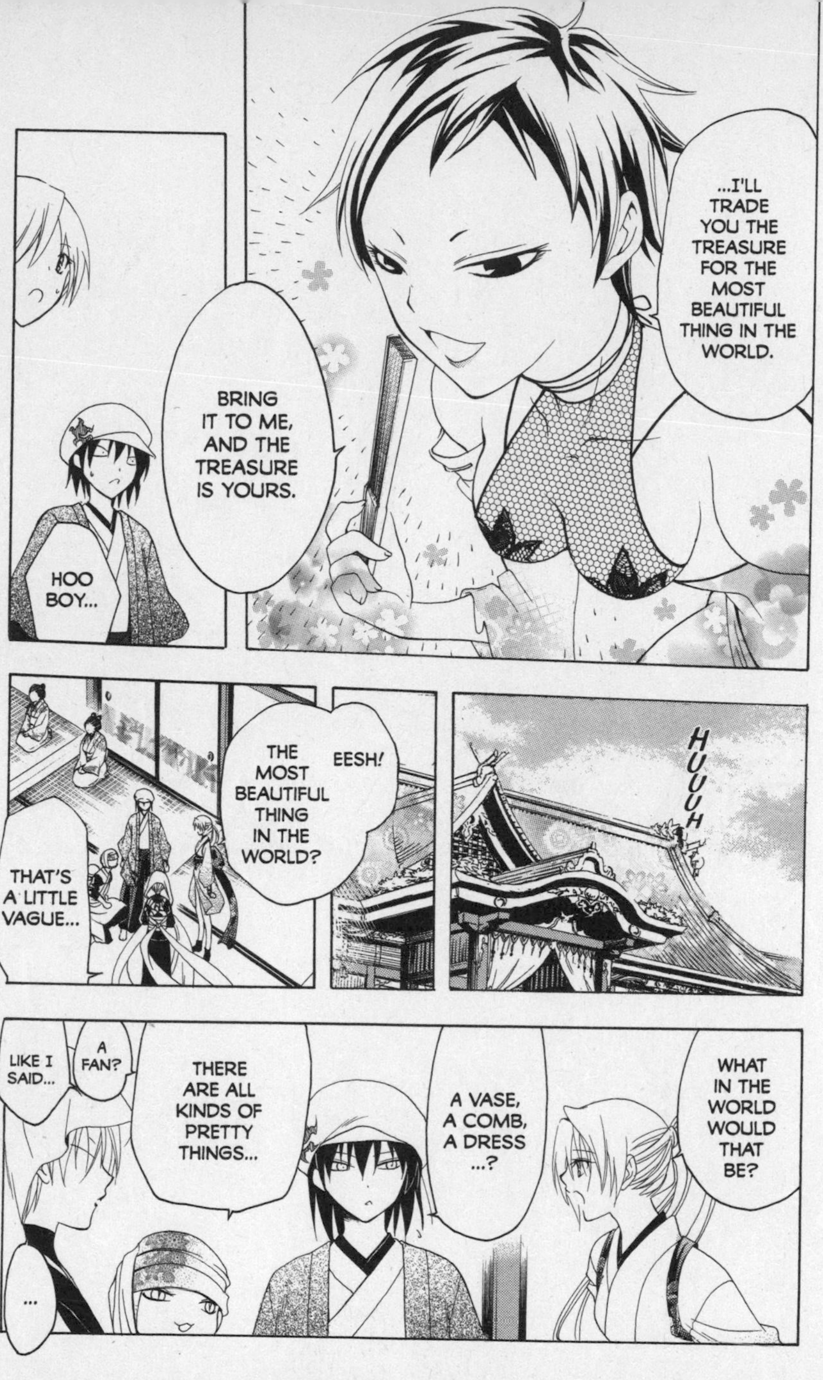
...I'LL TRADE YOU THE TREASURE FOR THE MOST BEAUTIFUL THING IN THE WORLD.
BRING IT TO ME, AND THE TREASURE IS YOURS.
HOO BOY...
HUUUH
EESH!
THE MOST BEAUTIFUL THING IN THE WORLD?
THAT'S A LITTLE VAGUE...
WHAT IN THE WORLD WOULD THAT BE?
A VASE, A COMB, A DRESS ...?
THERE ARE ALL KINDS OF PRETTY THINGS...
A FAN?
LIKE I SAID...
...

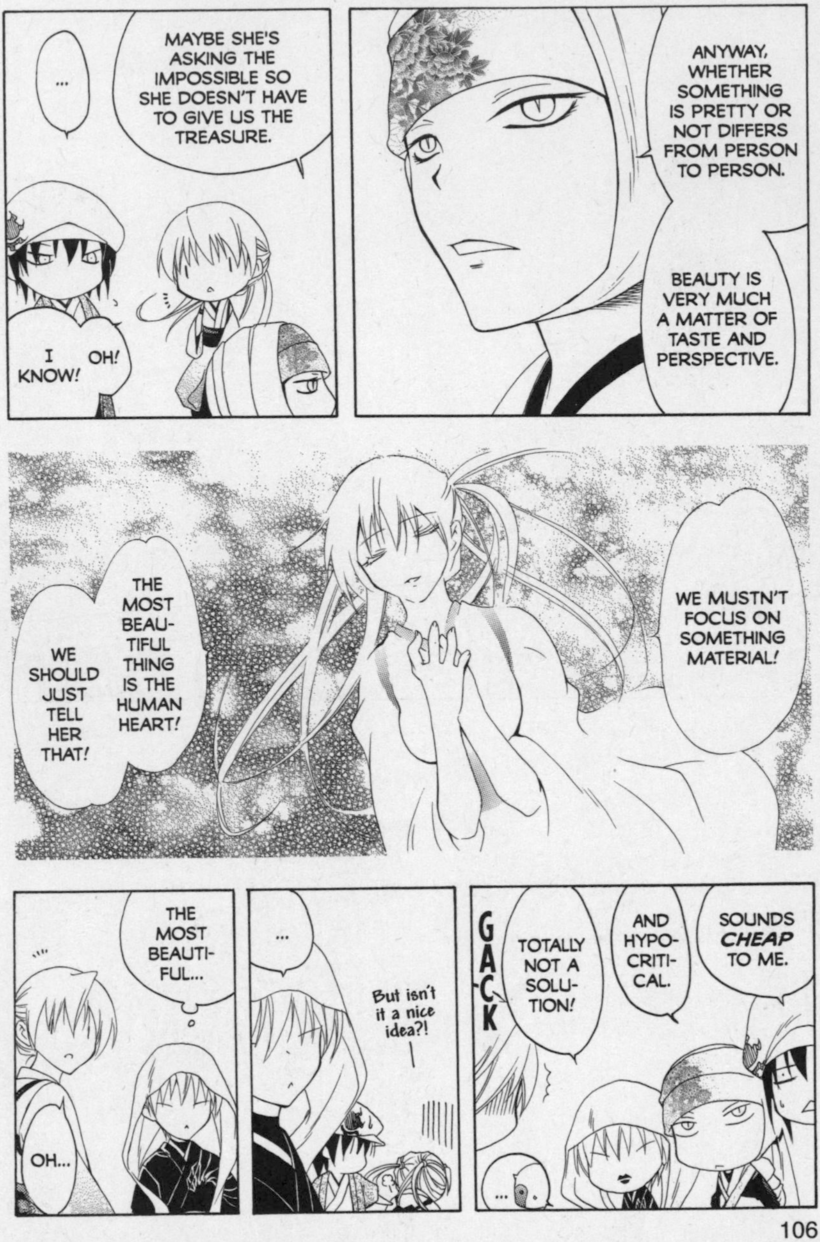
ANYWAY, WHETHER SOMETHING IS PRETTY OR NOT DIFFERS FROM PERSON TO PERSON.
BEAUTY IS VERY MUCH A MATTER OF TASTE AND PERSPECTIVE.
MAYBE SHE'S ASKING THE IMPOSSIBLE SO SHE DOESN'T HAVE TO GIVE US THE TREASURE.
...
OH! I KNOW!
WE MUSTN'T FOCUS ON SOMETHING MATERIAL!
THE MOST BEAU-TIFUL THING IS THE HUMAN HEART!
WE SHOULD JUST TELL HER THAT!
SOUNDS *CHEAP* TO ME.
AND HYPO-CRITI-CAL.
TOTALLY NOT A SOLU-TION!
GACK
...
...
But isn't it a nice idea?!
THE MOST BEAUTI-FUL...
OH...

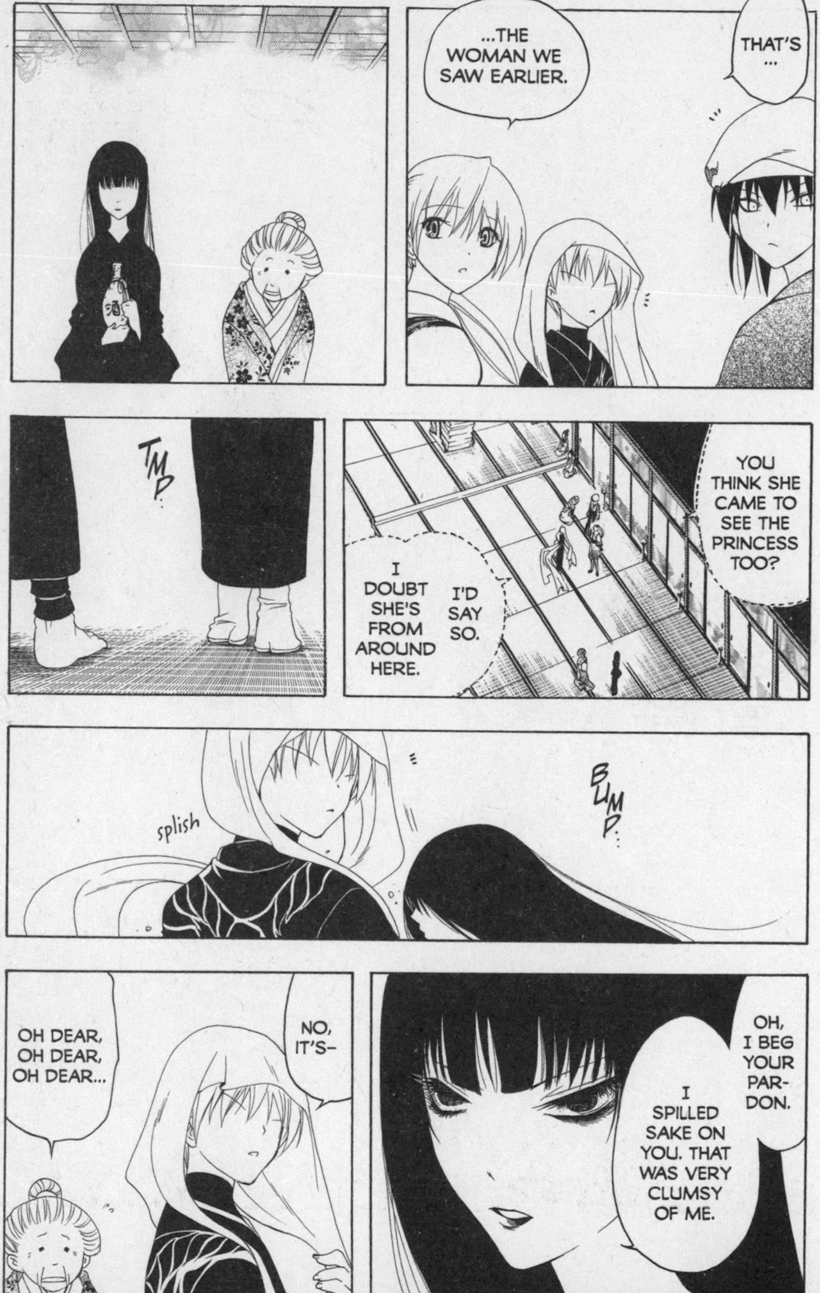
THAT'S ...
...THE WOMAN WE SAW EARLIER.
YOU THINK SHE CAME TO SEE THE PRINCESS TOO?
I'D SAY SO.
I DOUBT SHE'S FROM AROUND HERE.
TMP
BUMP
splish
OH, I BEG YOUR PARDON.
I SPILLED SAKE ON YOU. THAT WAS VERY CLUMSY OF ME.
NO, IT'S–
OH DEAR, OH DEAR, OH DEAR...

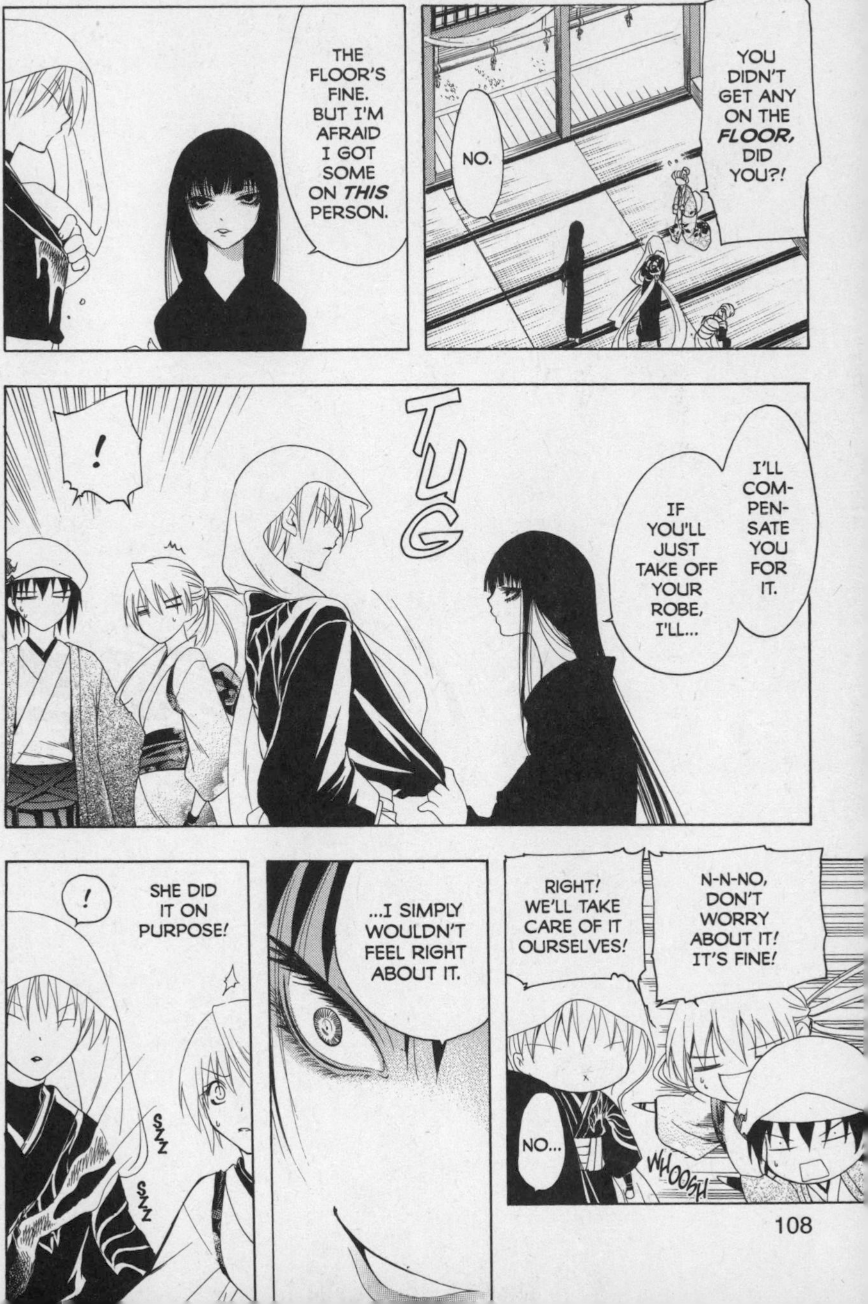
YOU DIDN'T GET ANY ON THE *FLOOR,* DID YOU?!
NO.
THE FLOOR'S FINE. BUT I'M AFRAID I GOT SOME ON *THIS* PERSON.
I'LL COM-PEN-SATE YOU FOR IT.
IF YOU'LL JUST TAKE OFF YOUR ROBE, I'LL...
TUG
!
N-N-NO, DON'T WORRY ABOUT IT! IT'S FINE!
RIGHT! WE'LL TAKE CARE OF IT OURSELVES!
NO...
WHOOSH
...I SIMPLY WOULDN'T FEEL RIGHT ABOUT IT.
SHE DID IT ON PURPOSE!
!
SZZ
SZZ

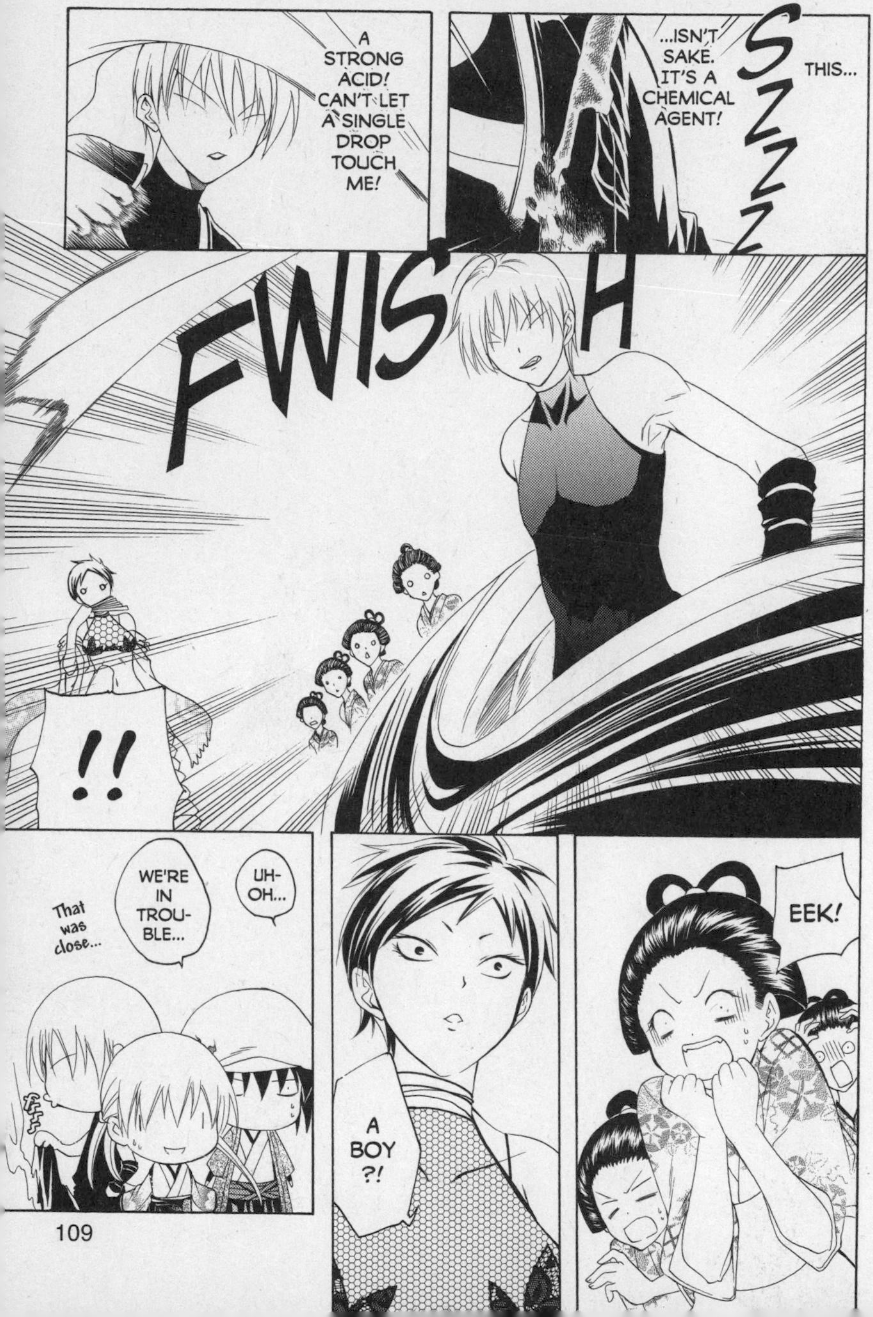
THIS...
...ISN'T SAKE. IT'S A CHEMICAL AGENT!
SZZZZ
A STRONG ACID! CAN'T LET A SINGLE DROP TOUCH ME!
FWISH
!!
EEK!
A BOY?!
UH-OH...
WE'RE IN TROUBLE...
That was close...

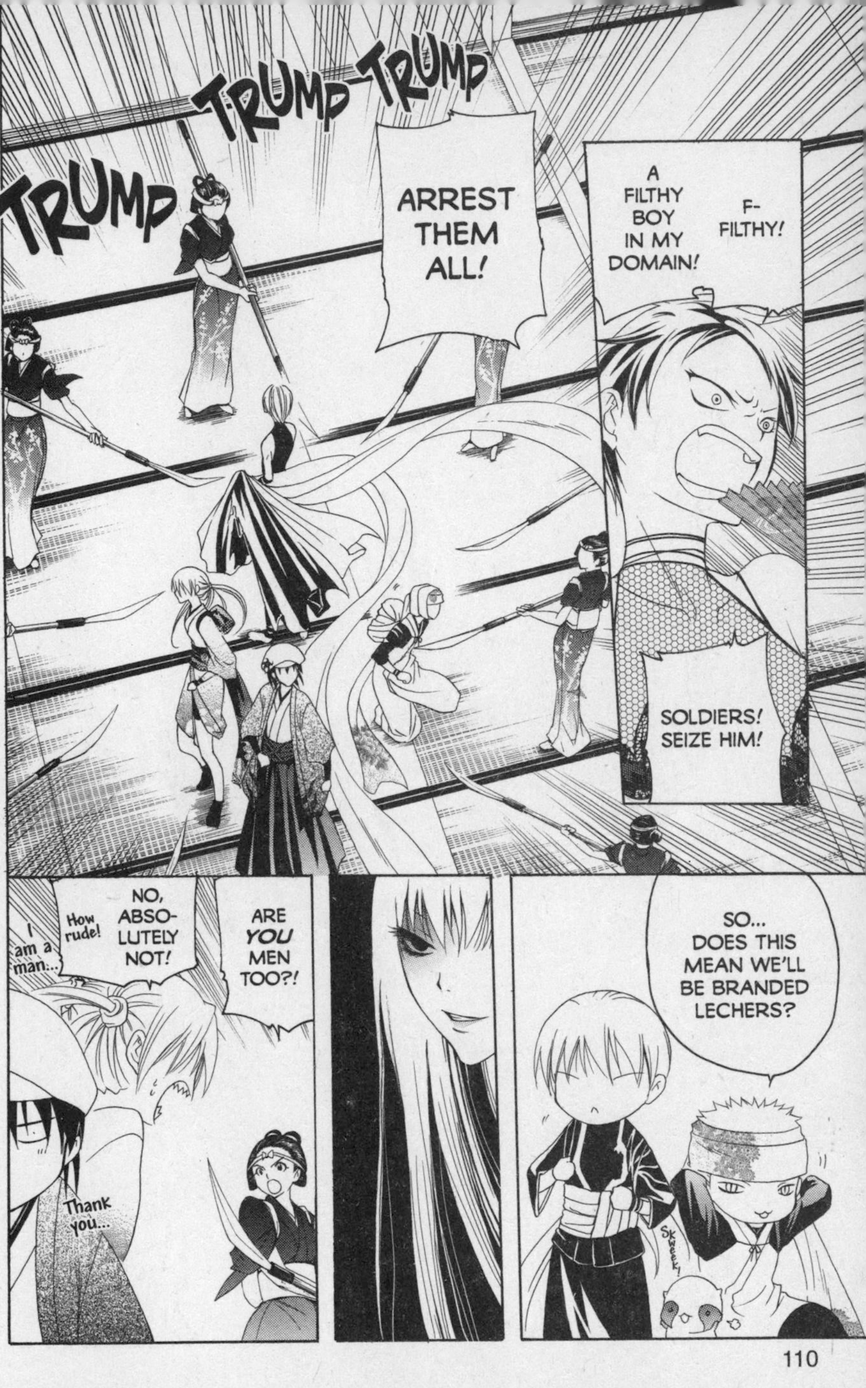
A FILTHY BOY IN MY DOMAIN!
F-FILTHY!
SOLDIERS! SEIZE HIM!
ARREST THEM ALL!
TRUMP TRUMP TRUMP
TRUMP
SO... DOES THIS MEAN WE'LL BE BRANDED LECHERS?
SKWEEK!
ARE YOU MEN TOO?!
NO, ABSOLUTELY NOT!
How rude!
I am a man...
Thank you...

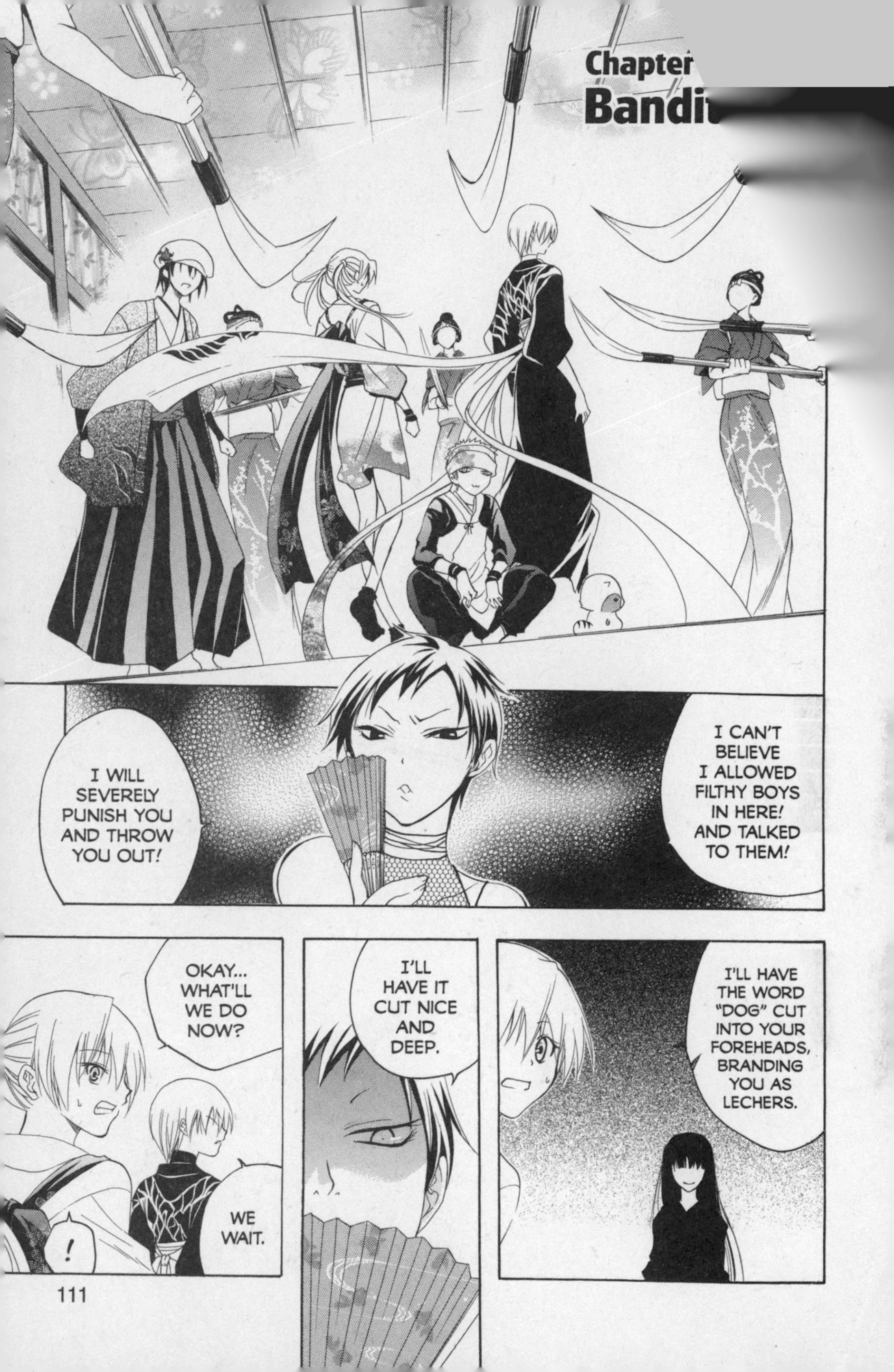
Chapter
Bandit
I CAN'T BELIEVE I ALLOWED FILTHY BOYS IN HERE! AND TALKED TO THEM!
I WILL SEVERELY PUNISH YOU AND THROW YOU OUT!
I'LL HAVE THE WORD "DOG" CUT INTO YOUR FOREHEADS, BRANDING YOU AS LECHERS.
I'LL HAVE IT CUT NICE AND DEEP.
OKAY... WHAT'LL WE DO NOW?
WE WAIT.
!

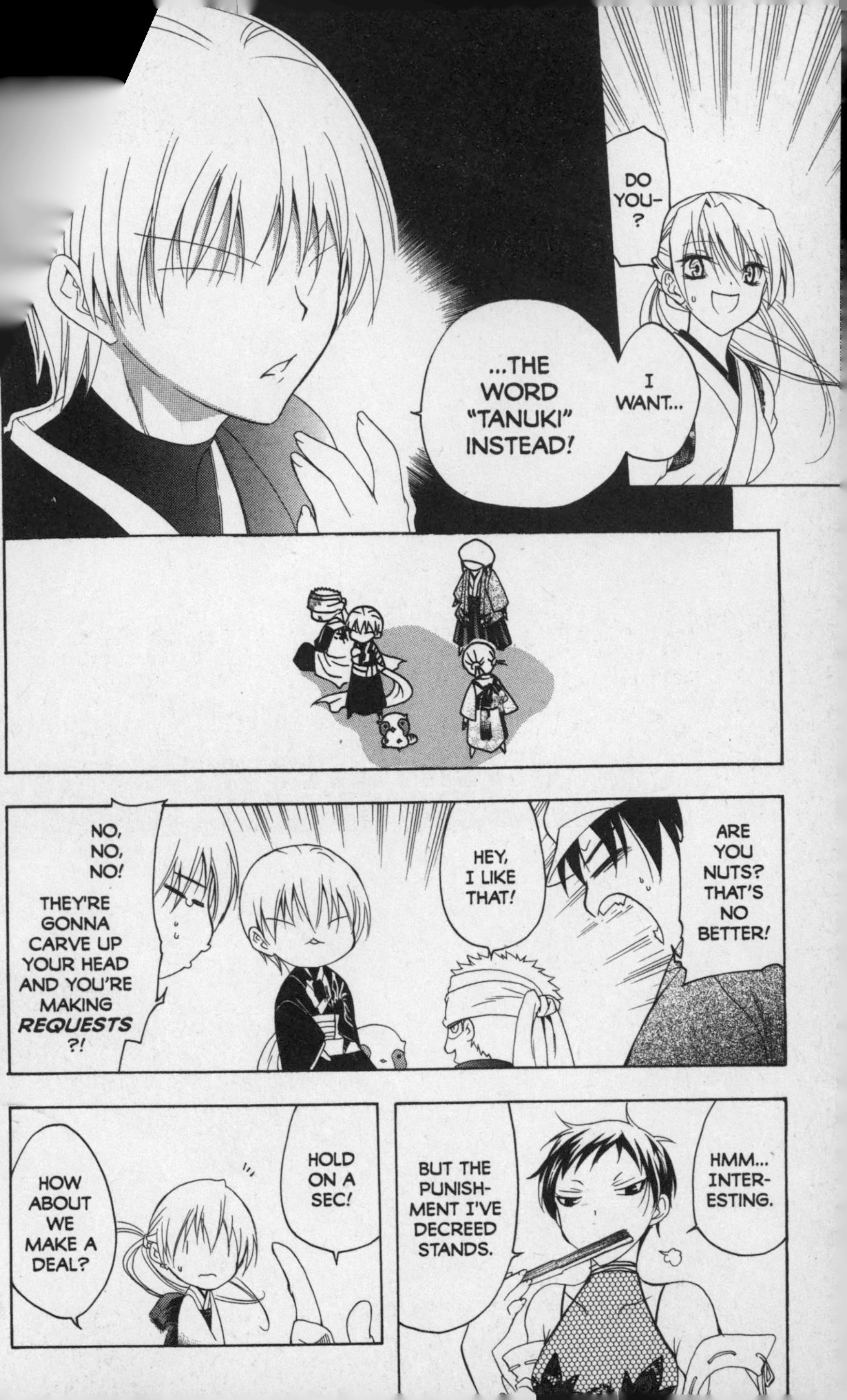
DO YOU-?
I WANT...
...THE WORD "TANUKI" INSTEAD!
ARE YOU NUTS? THAT'S NO BETTER!
HEY, I LIKE THAT!
NO, NO, NO!
THEY'RE GONNA CARVE UP YOUR HEAD AND YOU'RE MAKING *REQUESTS*?!
HMM... INTERESTING.
BUT THE PUNISHMENT I'VE DECREED STANDS.
HOLD ON A SEC!
HOW ABOUT WE MAKE A DEAL?

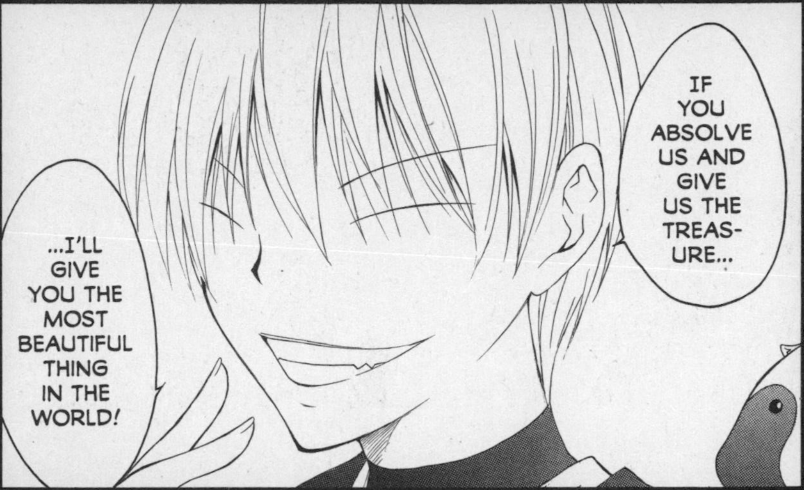
IF YOU ABSOLVE US AND GIVE US THE TREAS-URE...
...I'LL GIVE YOU THE MOST BEAUTIFUL THING IN THE WORLD!

Chapter 84 Bandits

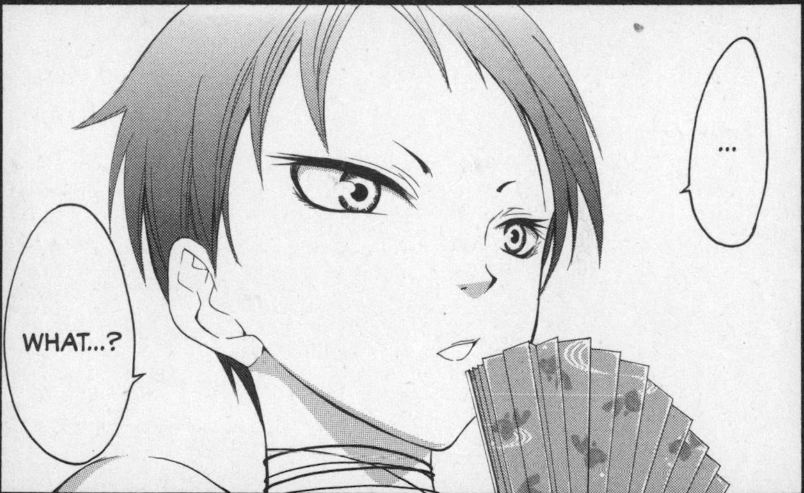
...
WHAT...?

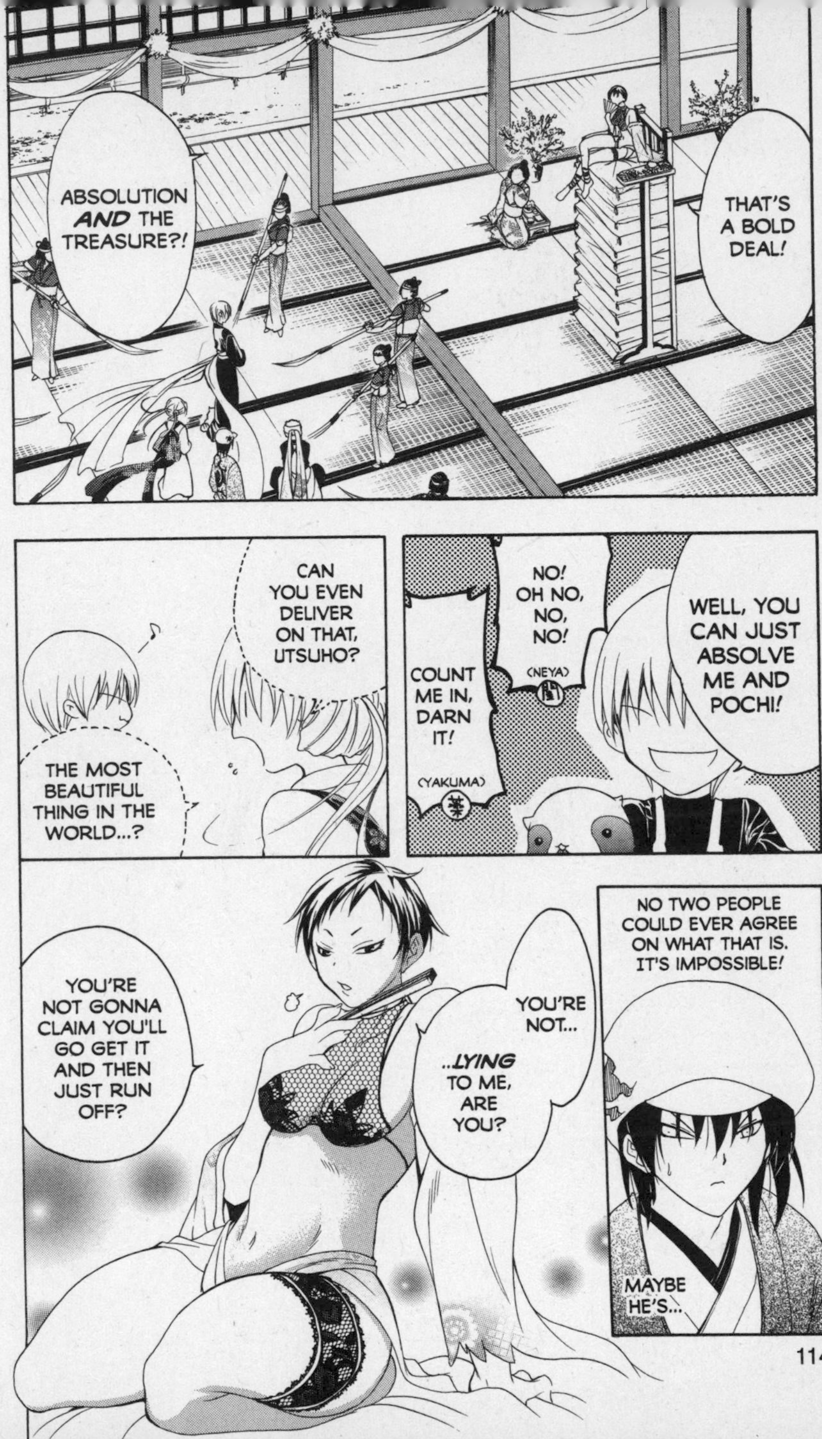
THAT'S A BOLD DEAL!
ABSOLUTION AND THE TREASURE?!
WELL, YOU CAN JUST ABSOLVE ME AND POCHI!
NO! OH NO, NO, NO!
(NEYA)
COUNT ME IN, DARN IT!
(YAKUMA)
CAN YOU EVEN DELIVER ON THAT, UTSUHO?
THE MOST BEAUTIFUL THING IN THE WORLD...?
NO TWO PEOPLE COULD EVER AGREE ON WHAT THAT IS. IT'S IMPOSSIBLE!
MAYBE HE'S...
YOU'RE NOT...
...LYING TO ME, ARE YOU?
YOU'RE NOT GONNA CLAIM YOU'LL GO GET IT AND THEN JUST RUN OFF?

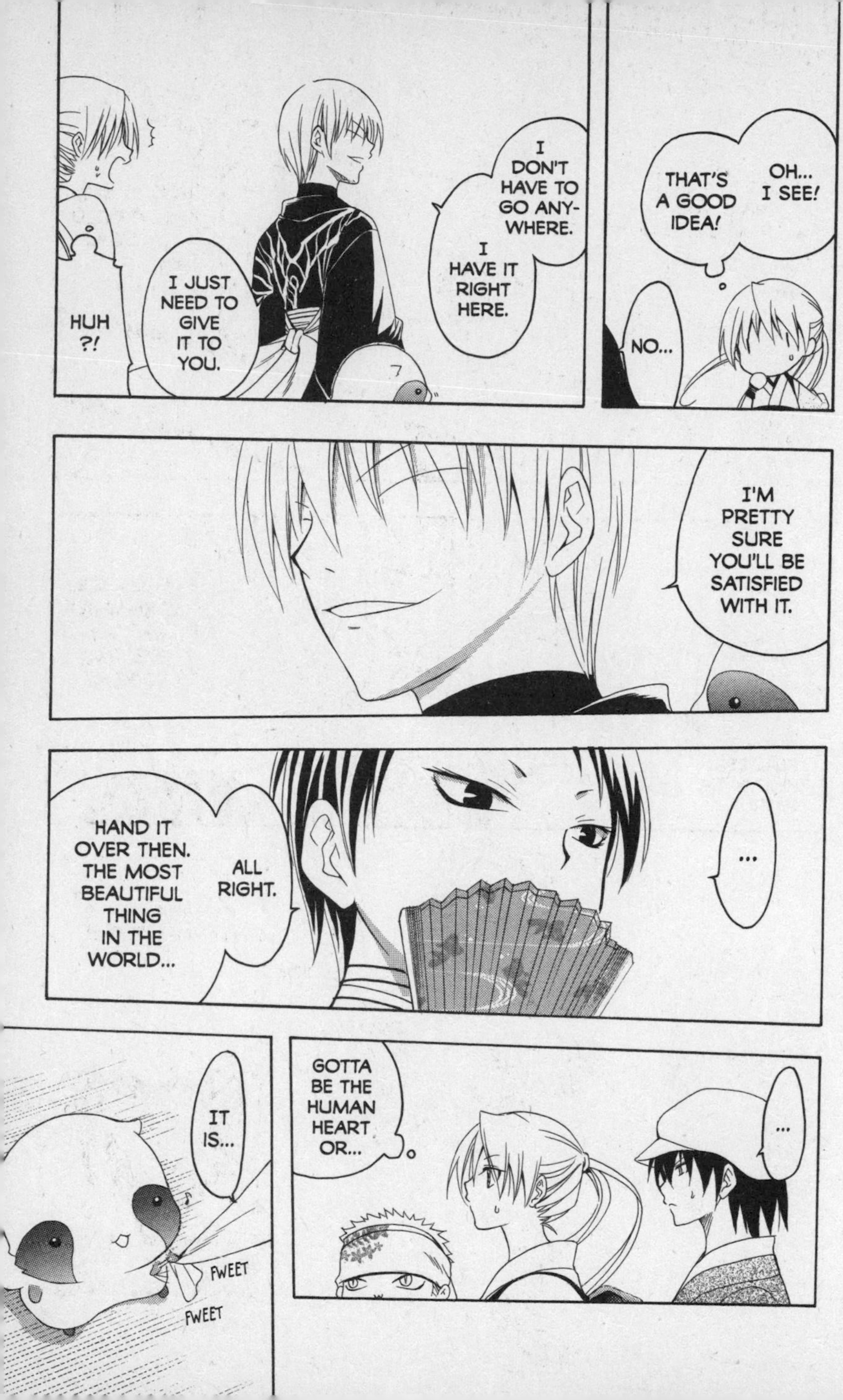
OH... I SEE! THAT'S A GOOD IDEA!
NO...
I DON'T HAVE TO GO ANY-WHERE.
I HAVE IT RIGHT HERE.
I JUST NEED TO GIVE IT TO YOU.
HUH ?!
I'M PRETTY SURE YOU'LL BE SATISFIED WITH IT.
...
ALL RIGHT.
HAND IT OVER THEN. THE MOST BEAUTIFUL THING IN THE WORLD...
...
GOTTA BE THE HUMAN HEART OR...
IT IS...
FWEET
FWEET

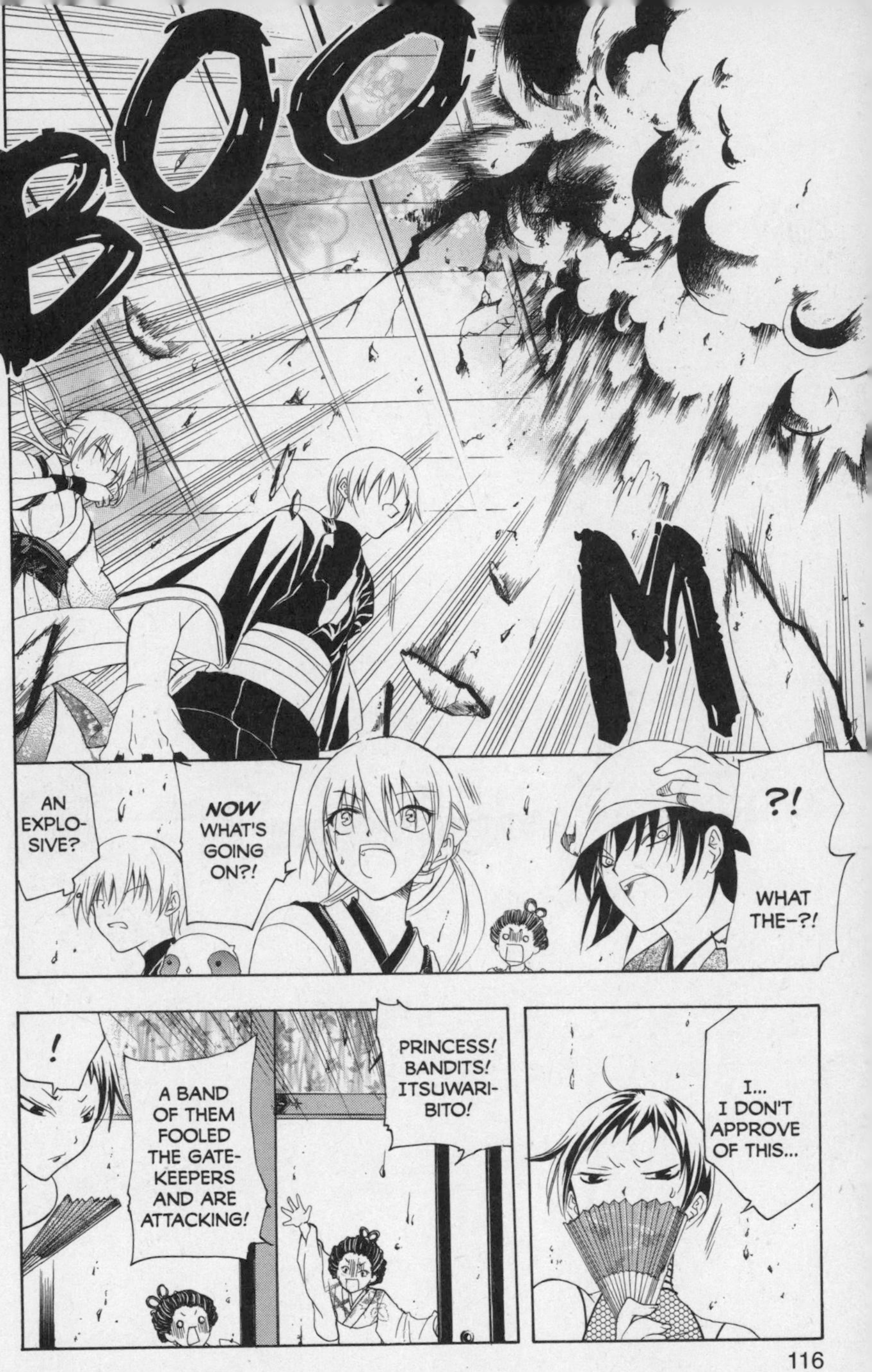
BOOOM
?!
WHAT THE-?!
NOW WHAT'S GOING ON?!
AN EXPLOSIVE?
I... I DON'T APPROVE OF THIS...
PRINCESS! BANDITS! ITSUWARIBITO!
!
A BAND OF THEM FOOLED THE GATEKEEPERS AND ARE ATTACKING!

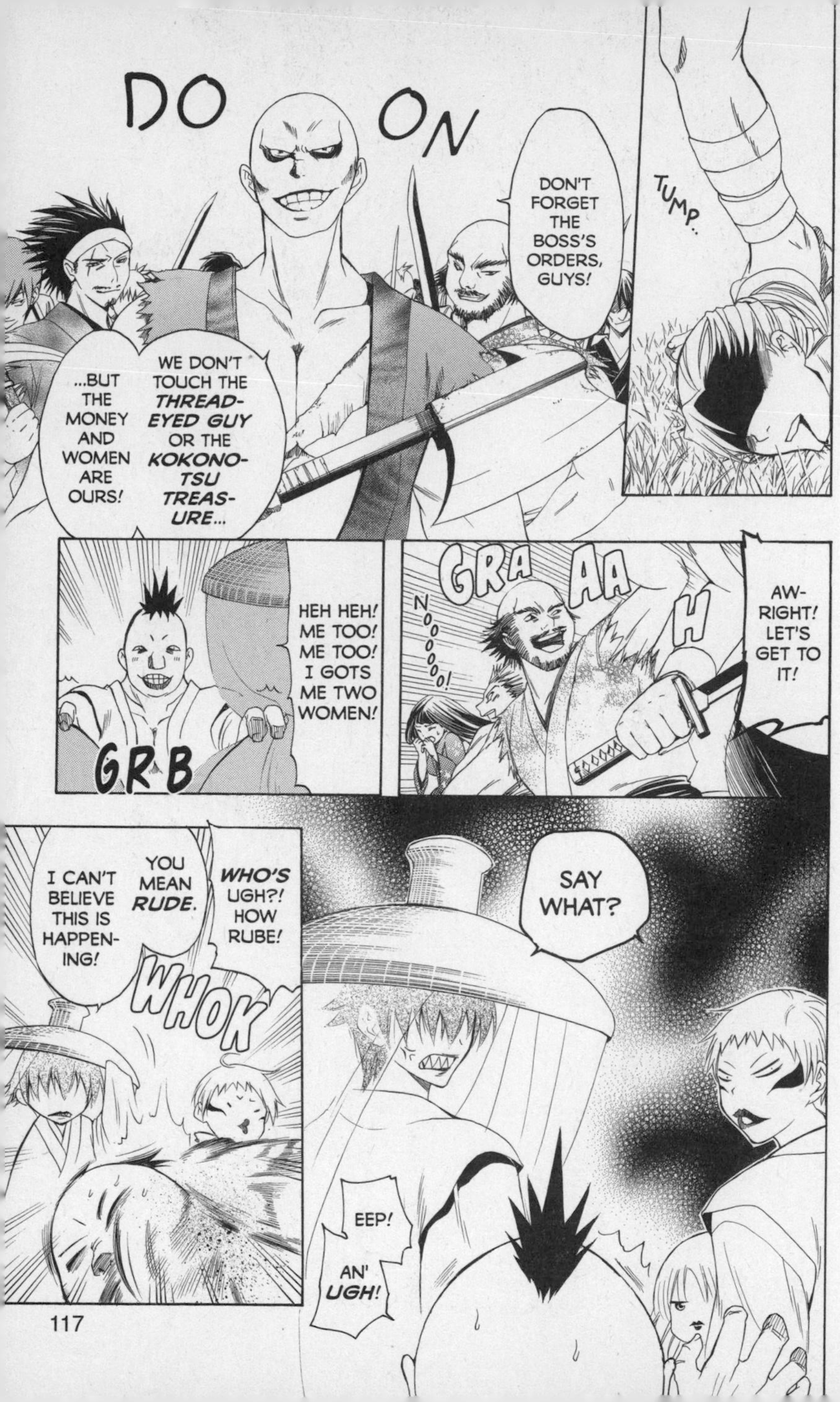
TUMP..
DO ON
DON'T FORGET THE BOSS'S ORDERS, GUYS!
WE DON'T TOUCH THE *THREAD-EYED GUY* OR THE *KOKONO-TSU TREAS-URE*...
...BUT THE MONEY AND WOMEN ARE OURS!
AW-RIGHT! LET'S GET TO IT!
GRAAAH
NOOOOOO!
HEH HEH! ME TOO! ME TOO! I GOTS ME TWO WOMEN!
GRB
SAY WHAT?
EEP!
AN' *UGH*!
WHO'S UGH?! HOW RUBE!
YOU MEAN *RUDE*.
I CAN'T BELIEVE THIS IS HAPPEN-ING!
WHOK

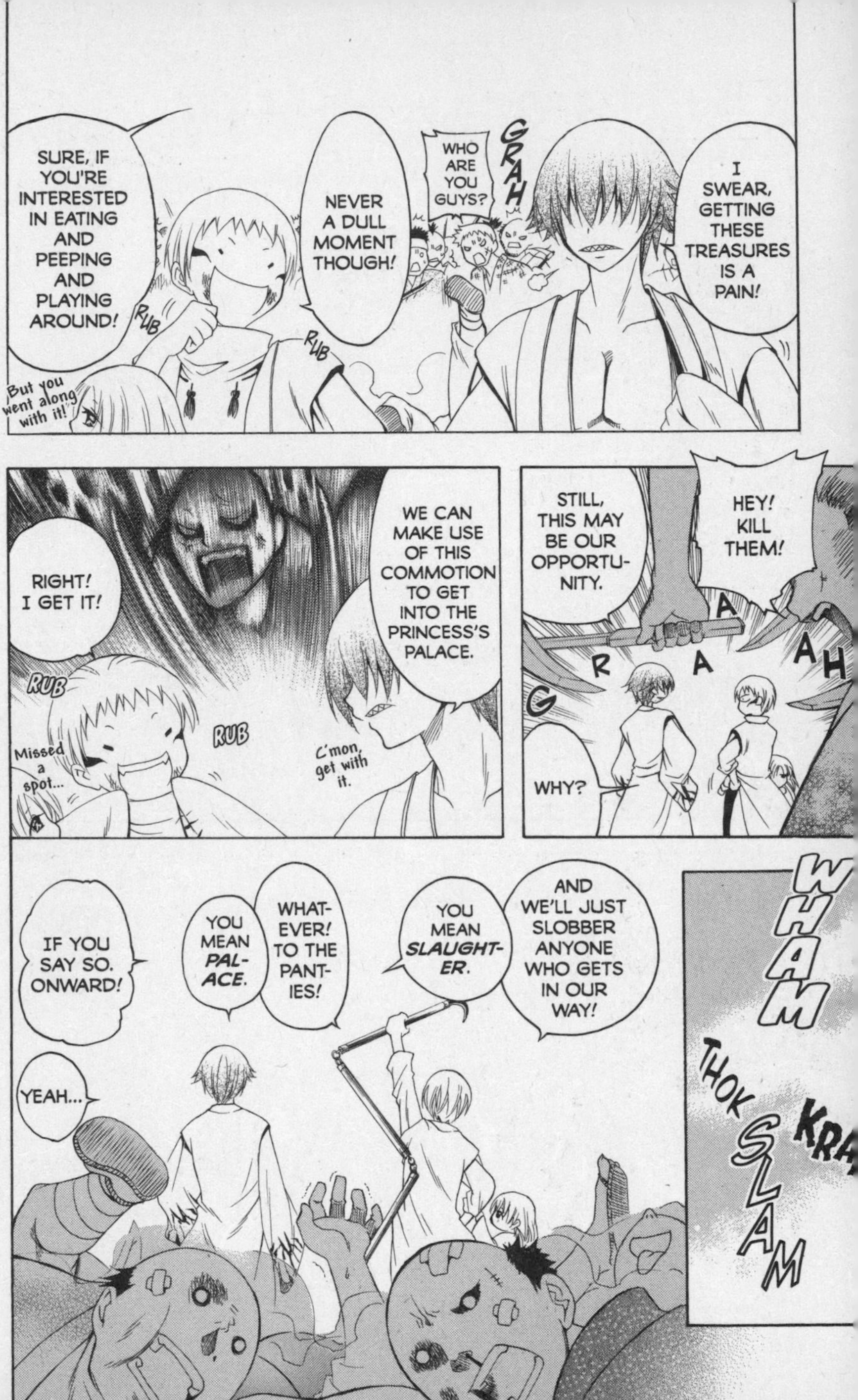
I SWEAR, GETTING THESE TREASURES IS A PAIN!
GRAH
WHO ARE YOU GUYS?
NEVER A DULL MOMENT THOUGH!
SURE, IF YOU'RE INTERESTED IN EATING AND PEEPING AND PLAYING AROUND!
RUB
RUB
But you went along with it!
HEY! KILL THEM!
STILL, THIS MAY BE OUR OPPORTUNITY.
GRAAAH
WHY?
WE CAN MAKE USE OF THIS COMMOTION TO GET INTO THE PRINCESS'S PALACE.
RIGHT! I GET IT!
C'mon, get with it.
RUB
RUB
Missed a spot...
WHAM
THOK
KRA
SLAM
AND WE'LL JUST SLOBBER ANYONE WHO GETS IN OUR WAY!
YOU MEAN *SLAUGHTER*.
WHATEVER! TO THE PANTIES!
YOU MEAN *PALACE*.
IF YOU SAY SO. ONWARD!
YEAH...

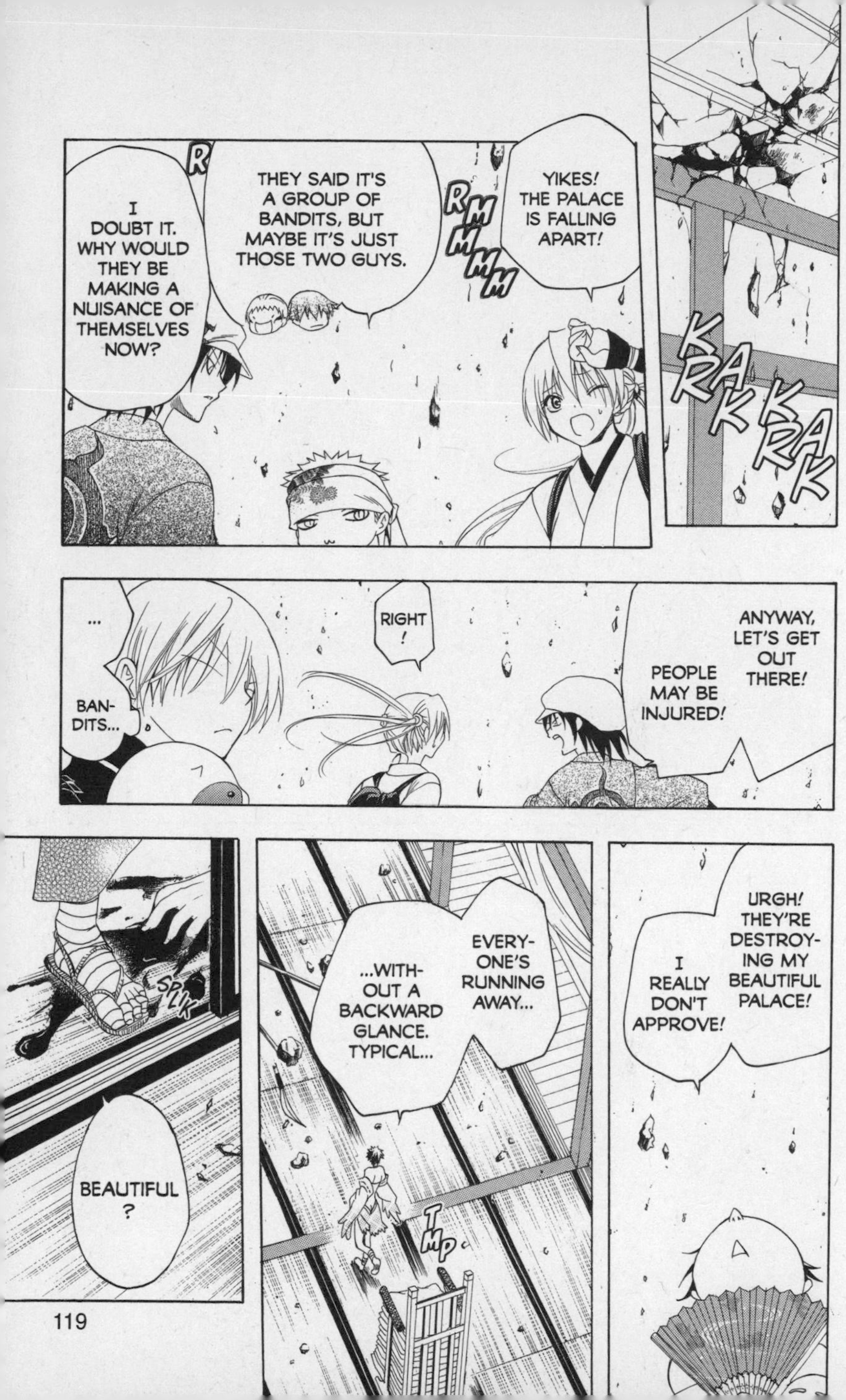
KRAK KRAK
YIKES! THE PALACE IS FALLING APART!
RMMMM
THEY SAID IT'S A GROUP OF BANDITS, BUT MAYBE IT'S JUST THOSE TWO GUYS.
R
I DOUBT IT. WHY WOULD THEY BE MAKING A NUISANCE OF THEMSELVES NOW?
ANYWAY, LET'S GET OUT THERE!
PEOPLE MAY BE INJURED!
RIGHT!
...
BAN-DITS...
URGH! THEY'RE DESTROY-ING MY BEAUTIFUL PALACE!
I REALLY DON'T APPROVE!
EVERY-ONE'S RUNNING AWAY...
...WITH-OUT A BACKWARD GLANCE. TYPICAL...
TMP
SPLIK
BEAUTIFUL?

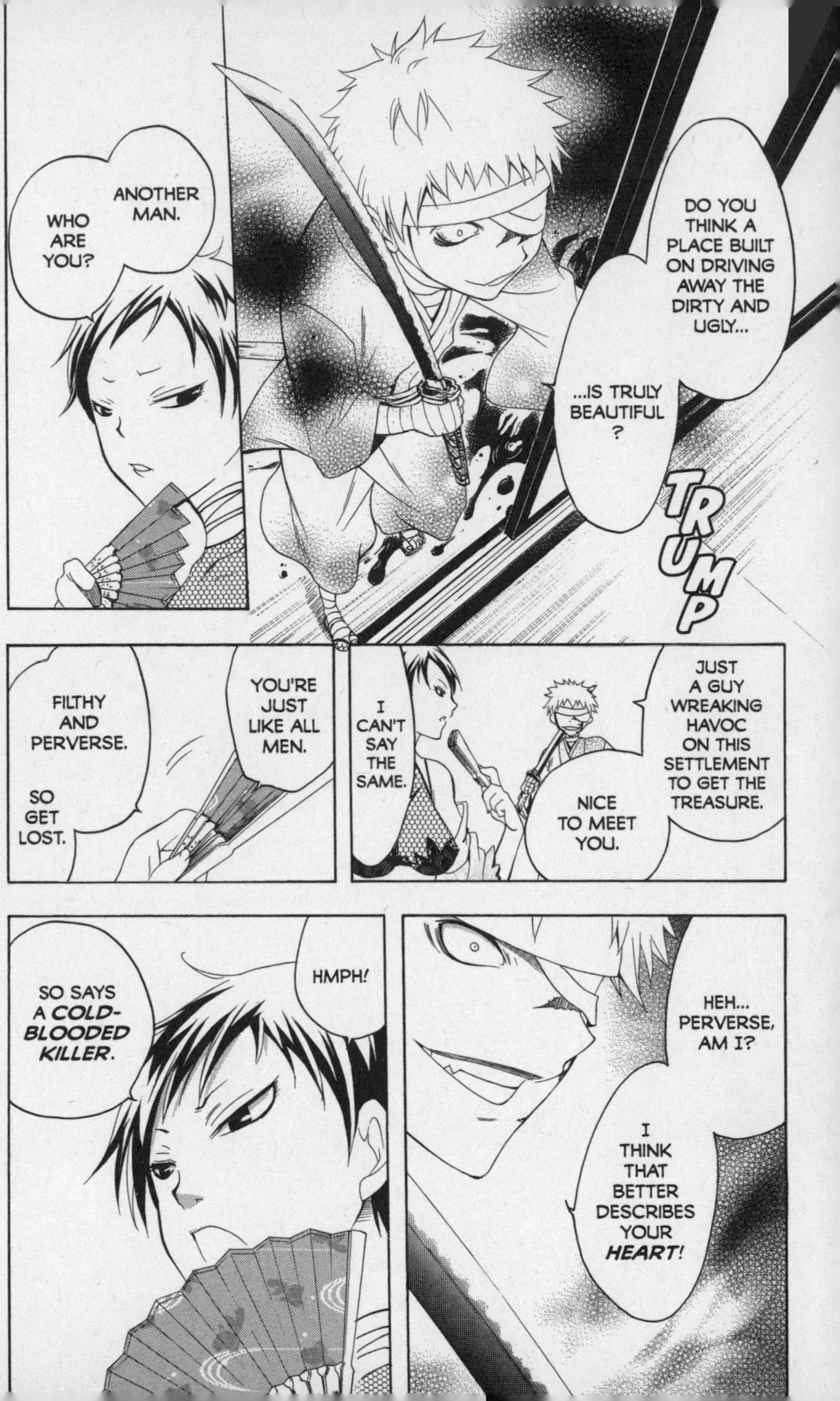
DO YOU THINK A PLACE BUILT ON DRIVING AWAY THE DIRTY AND UGLY...
...IS TRULY BEAUTIFUL?
TRUMP
ANOTHER MAN.
WHO ARE YOU?
JUST A GUY WREAKING HAVOC ON THIS SETTLEMENT TO GET THE TREASURE.
NICE TO MEET YOU.
I CAN'T SAY THE SAME.
YOU'RE JUST LIKE ALL MEN.
FILTHY AND PERVERSE.
SO GET LOST.
HEH... PERVERSE, AM I?
I THINK THAT BETTER DESCRIBES YOUR HEART!
HMPH!
SO SAYS A COLD-BLOODED KILLER.

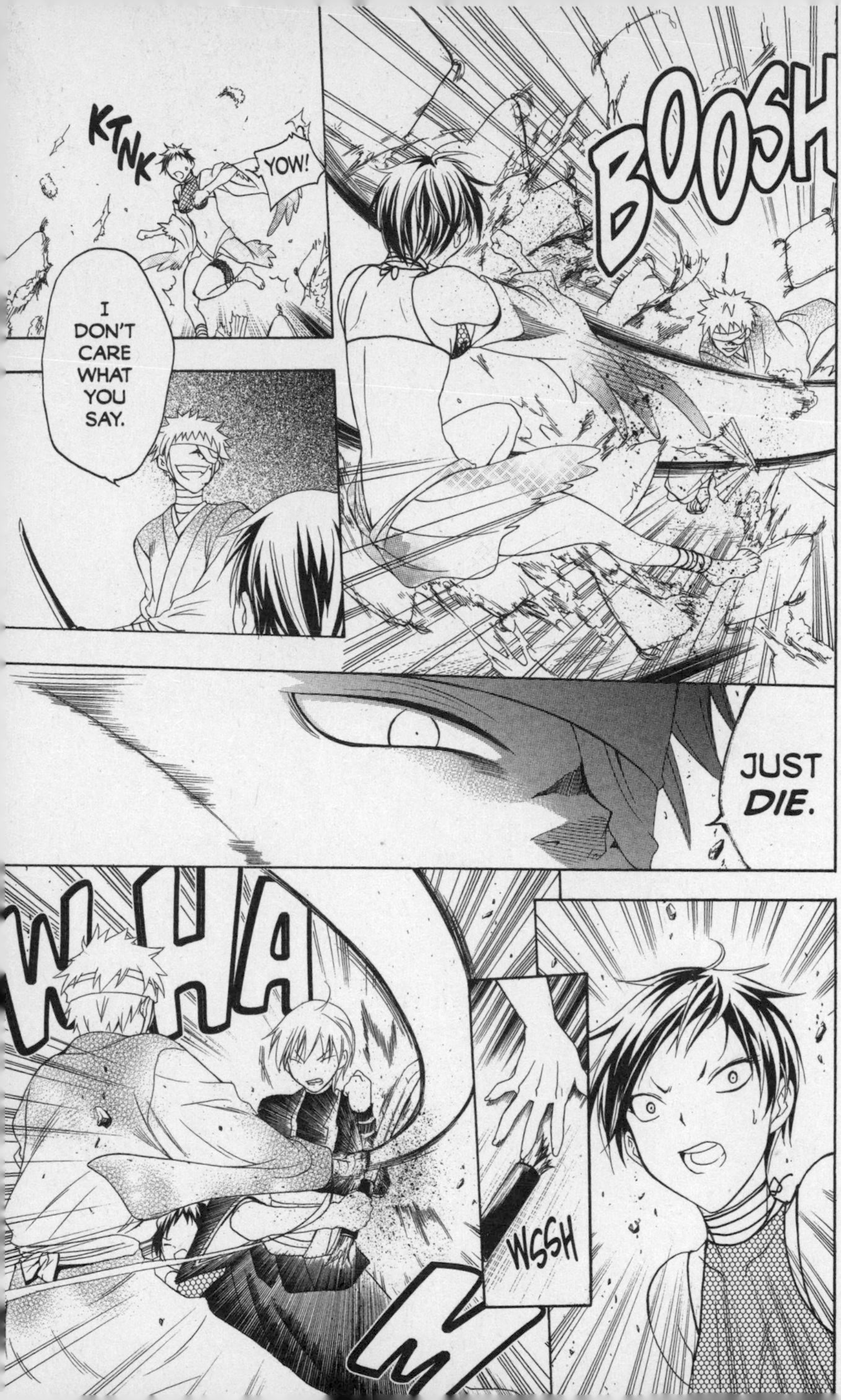
BOOSH
KTNK
YOW!
I DON'T CARE WHAT YOU SAY.
JUST *DIE*.
WSSH
WHAM

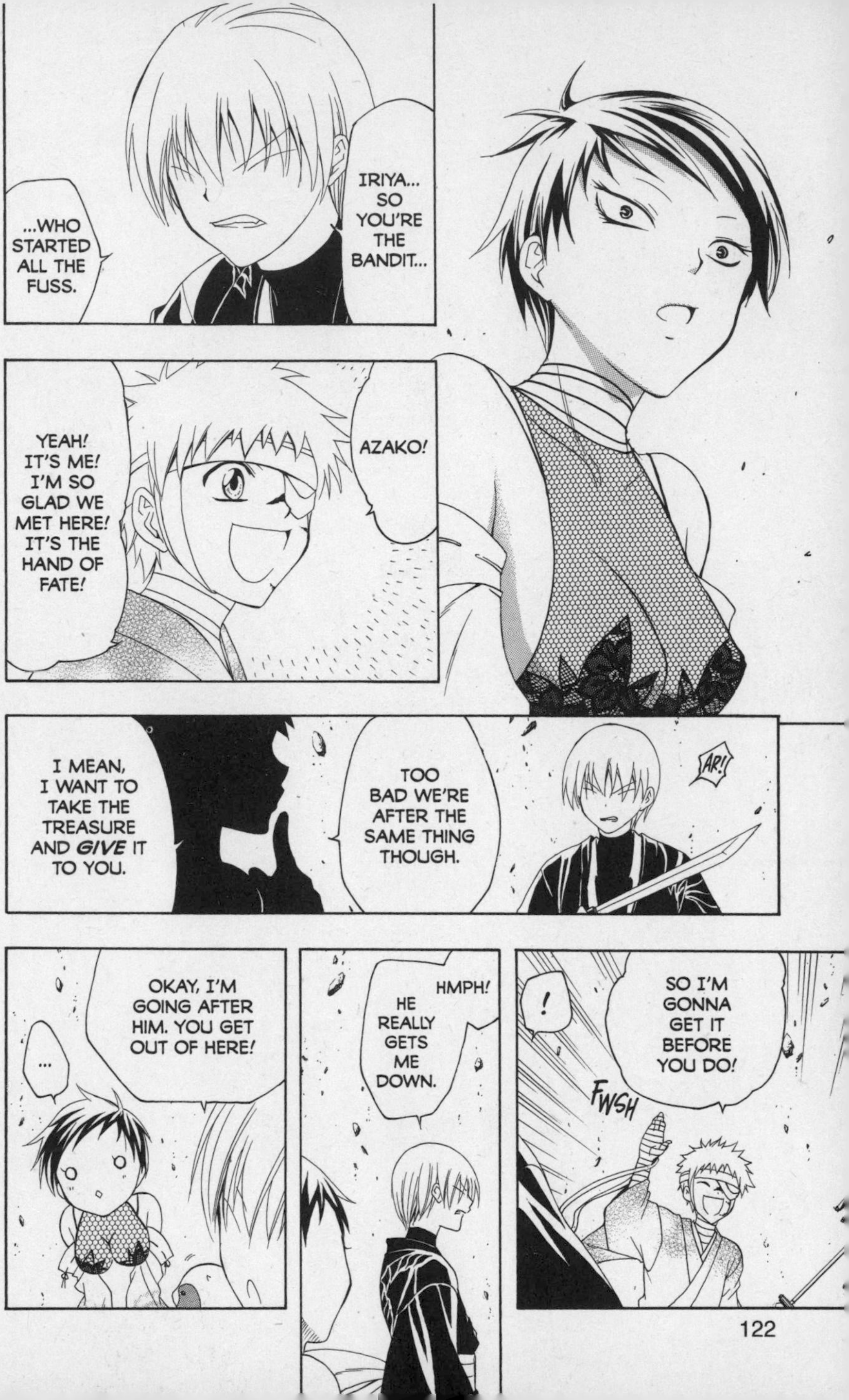
IRIYA... SO YOU'RE THE BANDIT...
...WHO STARTED ALL THE FUSS.
AZAKO!
YEAH! IT'S ME! I'M SO GLAD WE MET HERE! IT'S THE HAND OF FATE!
AR!
TOO BAD WE'RE AFTER THE SAME THING THOUGH.
I MEAN, I WANT TO TAKE THE TREASURE AND *GIVE* IT TO YOU.
SO I'M GONNA GET IT BEFORE YOU DO!
!
FWSH
HMPH!
HE REALLY GETS ME DOWN.
OKAY, I'M GOING AFTER HIM. YOU GET OUT OF HERE!
...

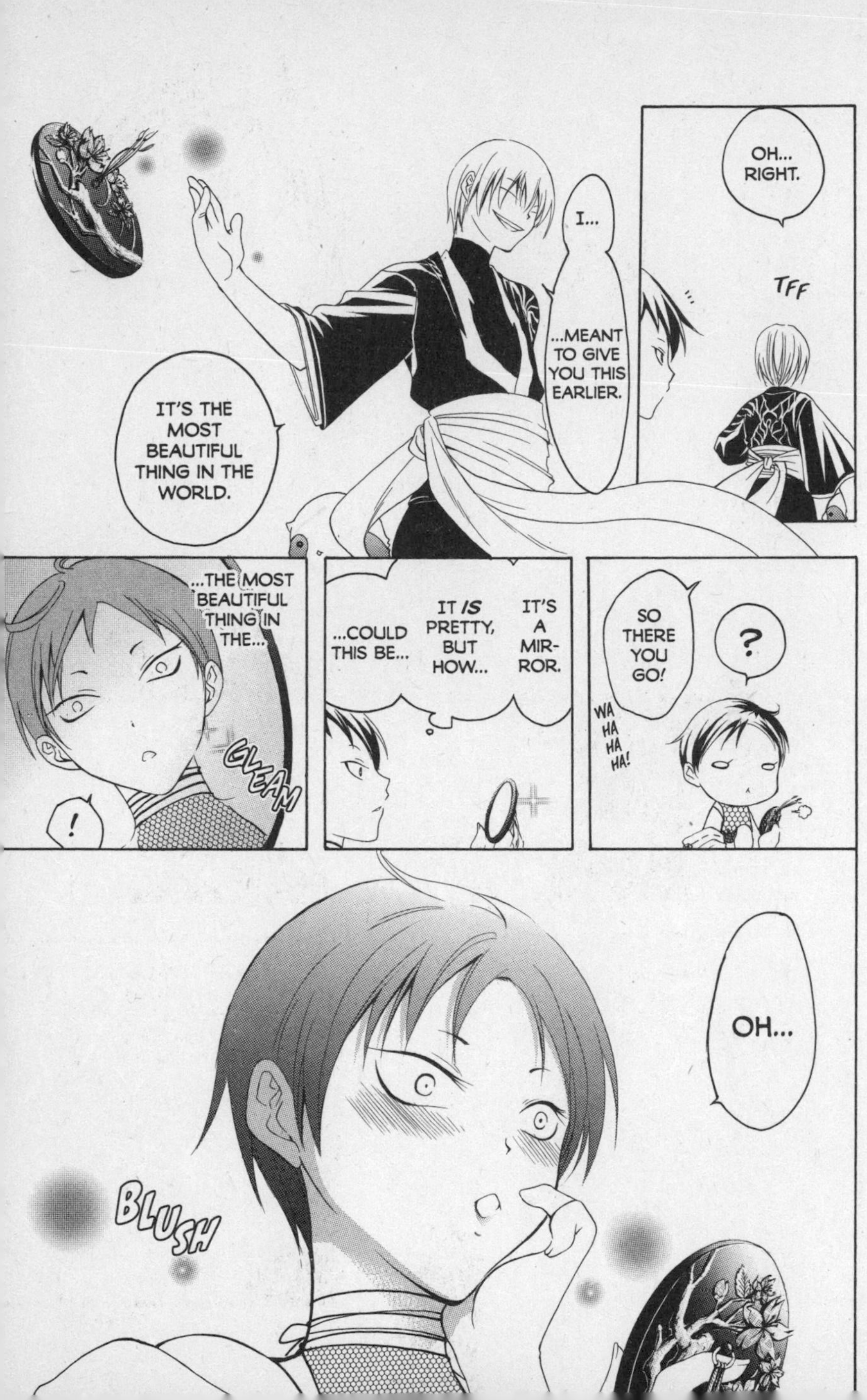

OH... RIGHT.
TFF
I...
...MEANT TO GIVE YOU THIS EARLIER.
IT'S THE MOST BEAUTIFUL THING IN THE WORLD.
SO THERE YOU GO!
?
WA HA HA HA!
IT'S A MIR-ROR.
IT *IS* PRETTY, BUT HOW...
...COULD THIS BE...
...THE MOST BEAUTIFUL THING IN THE...
GLEAM
!
OH...
BLUSH

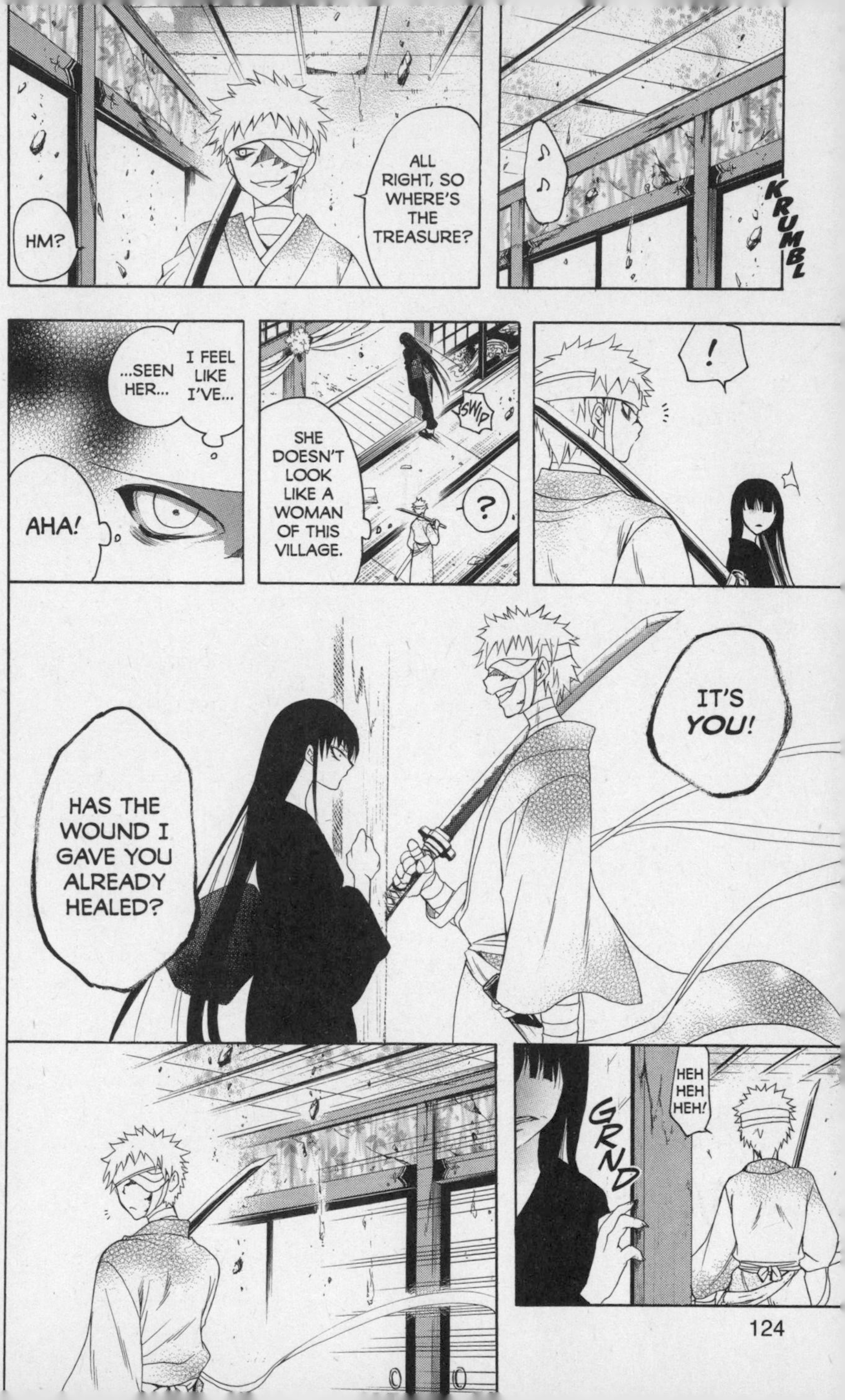
♪ ♪
KRUMBL
ALL RIGHT, SO WHERE'S THE TREASURE?
HM?
!
SWIP
SHE DOESN'T LOOK LIKE A WOMAN OF THIS VILLAGE.
?
I FEEL LIKE I'VE...
...SEEN HER...
AHA!
IT'S YOU!
HAS THE WOUND I GAVE YOU ALREADY HEALED?
HEH HEH HEH!
GRND

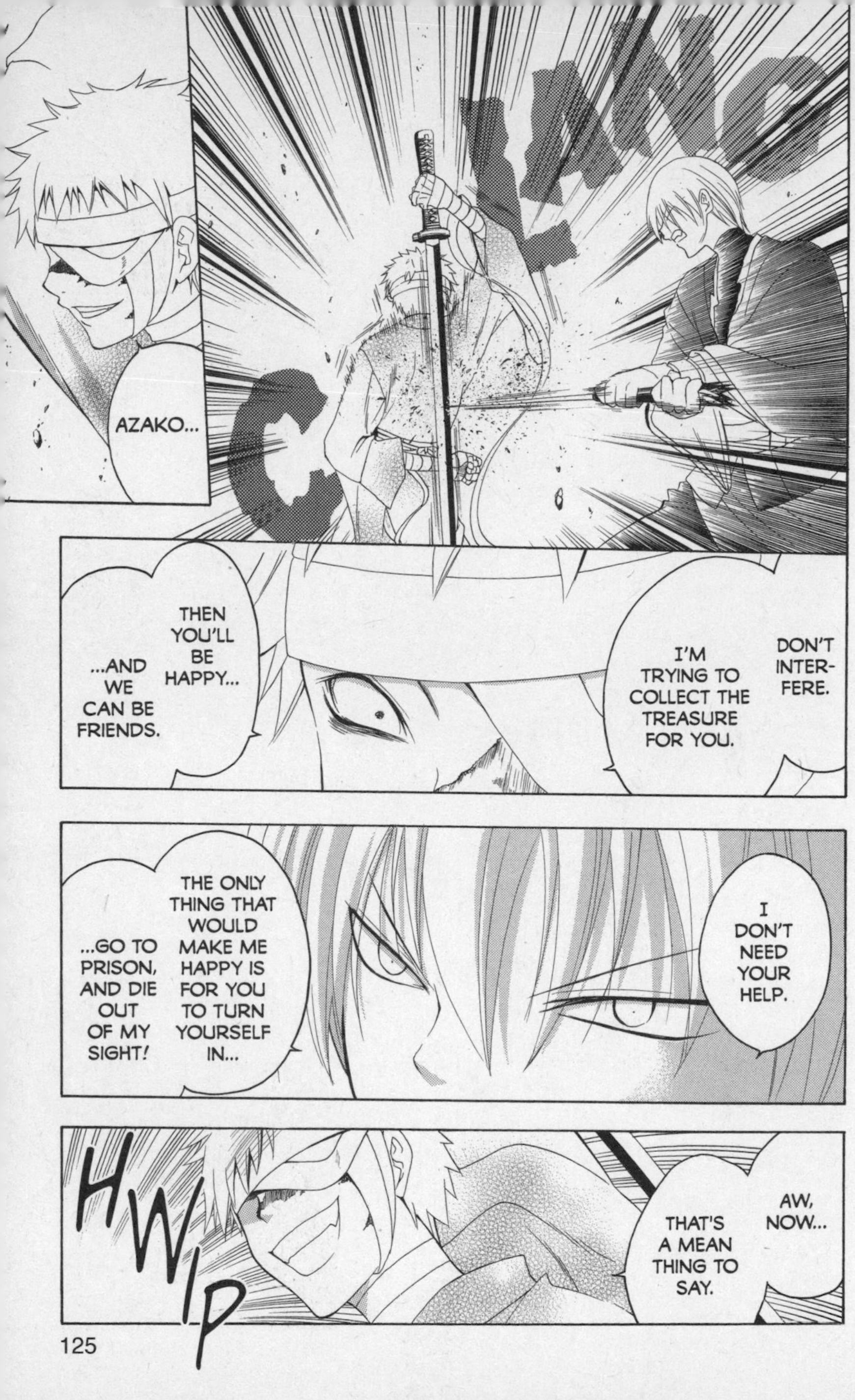
CLANG
AZAKO...
DON'T INTERFERE.
I'M TRYING TO COLLECT THE TREASURE FOR YOU.
THEN YOU'LL BE HAPPY...
...AND WE CAN BE FRIENDS.
I DON'T NEED YOUR HELP.
THE ONLY THING THAT WOULD MAKE ME HAPPY IS FOR YOU TO TURN YOURSELF IN...
...GO TO PRISON, AND DIE OUT OF MY SIGHT!
AW, NOW...
THAT'S A MEAN THING TO SAY.
HWIP

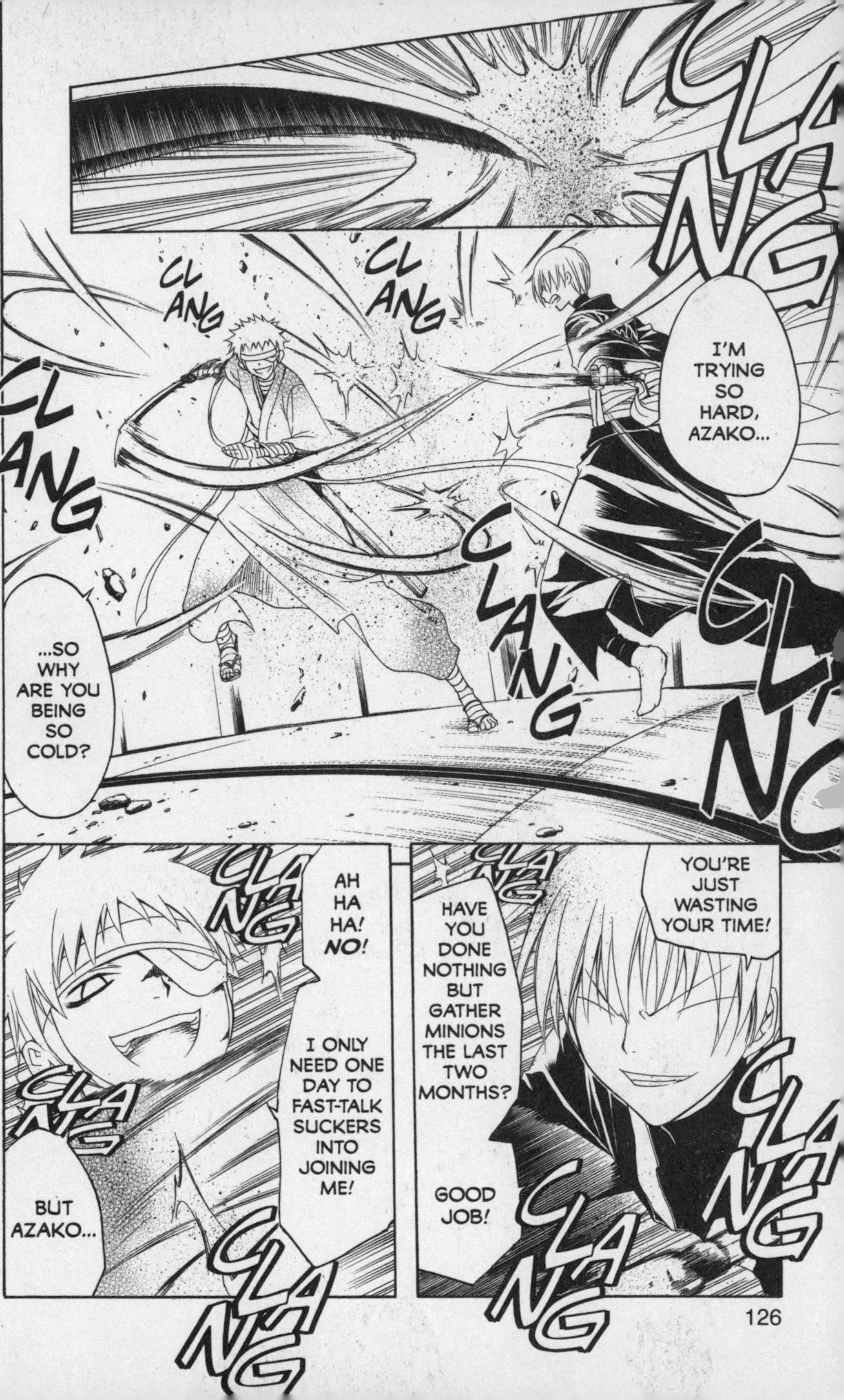
CLANG
CLANG
CLANG
CLANG
I'M TRYING SO HARD, AZAKO...
CLANG
CLANG
CLANG
...SO WHY ARE YOU BEING SO COLD?
CLANG
YOU'RE JUST WASTING YOUR TIME!
HAVE YOU DONE NOTHING BUT GATHER MINIONS THE LAST TWO MONTHS?
GOOD JOB!
CLANG
CLANG
CLANG
AH HA HA! *NO*!
I ONLY NEED ONE DAY TO FAST-TALK SUCKERS INTO JOINING ME!
CLANG
BUT AZAKO...
CLANG

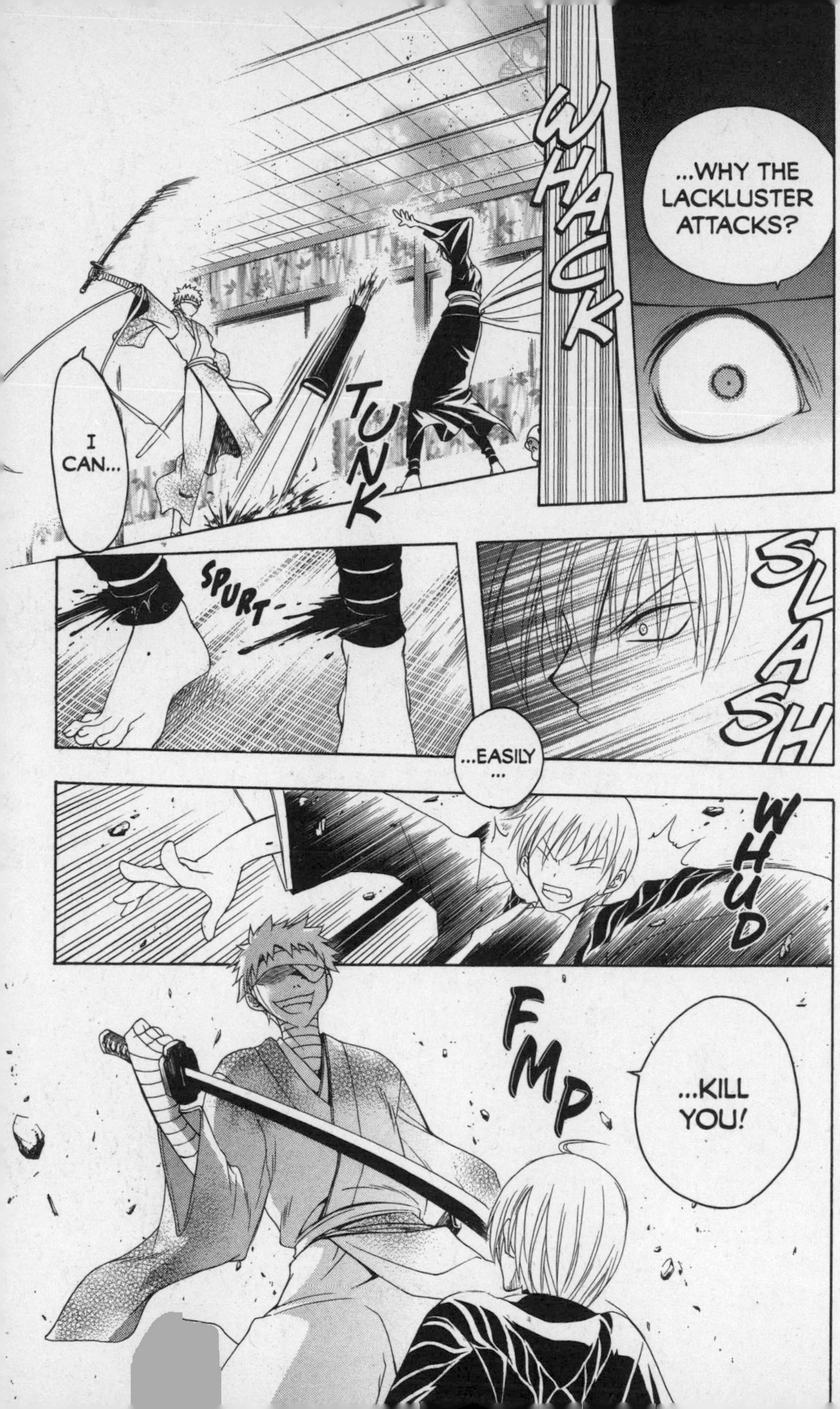
...WHY THE LACKLUSTER ATTACKS?
WHACK
TUNK
I CAN...
SLASH
...EASILY ...
SPURT
WHUD
FMP
...KILL YOU!

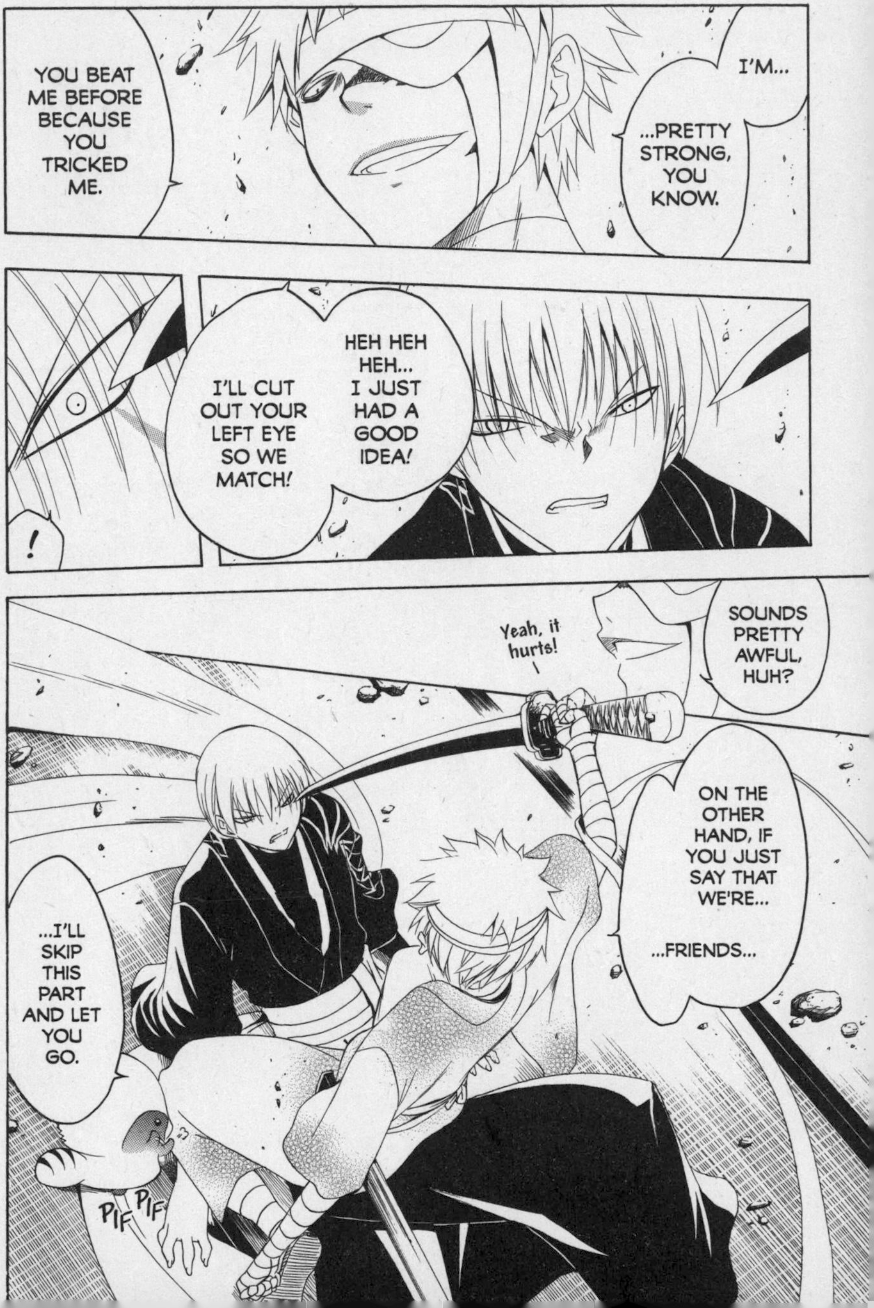
I'M...
...PRETTY STRONG, YOU KNOW.
YOU BEAT ME BEFORE BECAUSE YOU TRICKED ME.
HEH HEH HEH... I JUST HAD A GOOD IDEA!
I'LL CUT OUT YOUR LEFT EYE SO WE MATCH!
!
SOUNDS PRETTY AWFUL, HUH?
Yeah, it hurts!
ON THE OTHER HAND, IF YOU JUST SAY THAT WE'RE...
...FRIENDS...
...I'LL SKIP THIS PART AND LET YOU GO.
PIF PIF

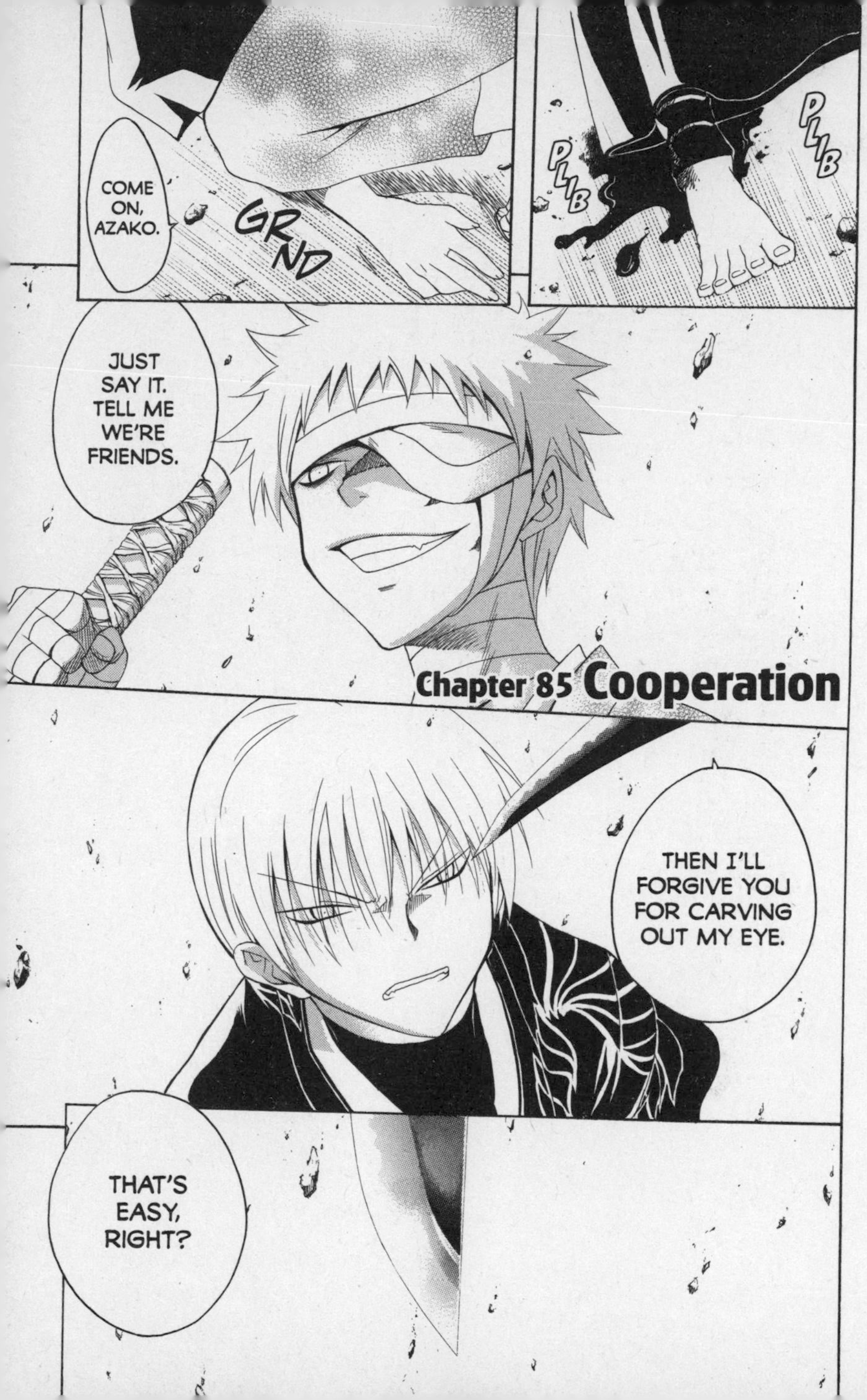
PLIB
PLIB
COME ON, AZAKO.
GRND
JUST SAY IT. TELL ME WE'RE FRIENDS.
Chapter 85 Cooperation
THEN I'LL FORGIVE YOU FOR CARVING OUT MY EYE.
THAT'S EASY, RIGHT?

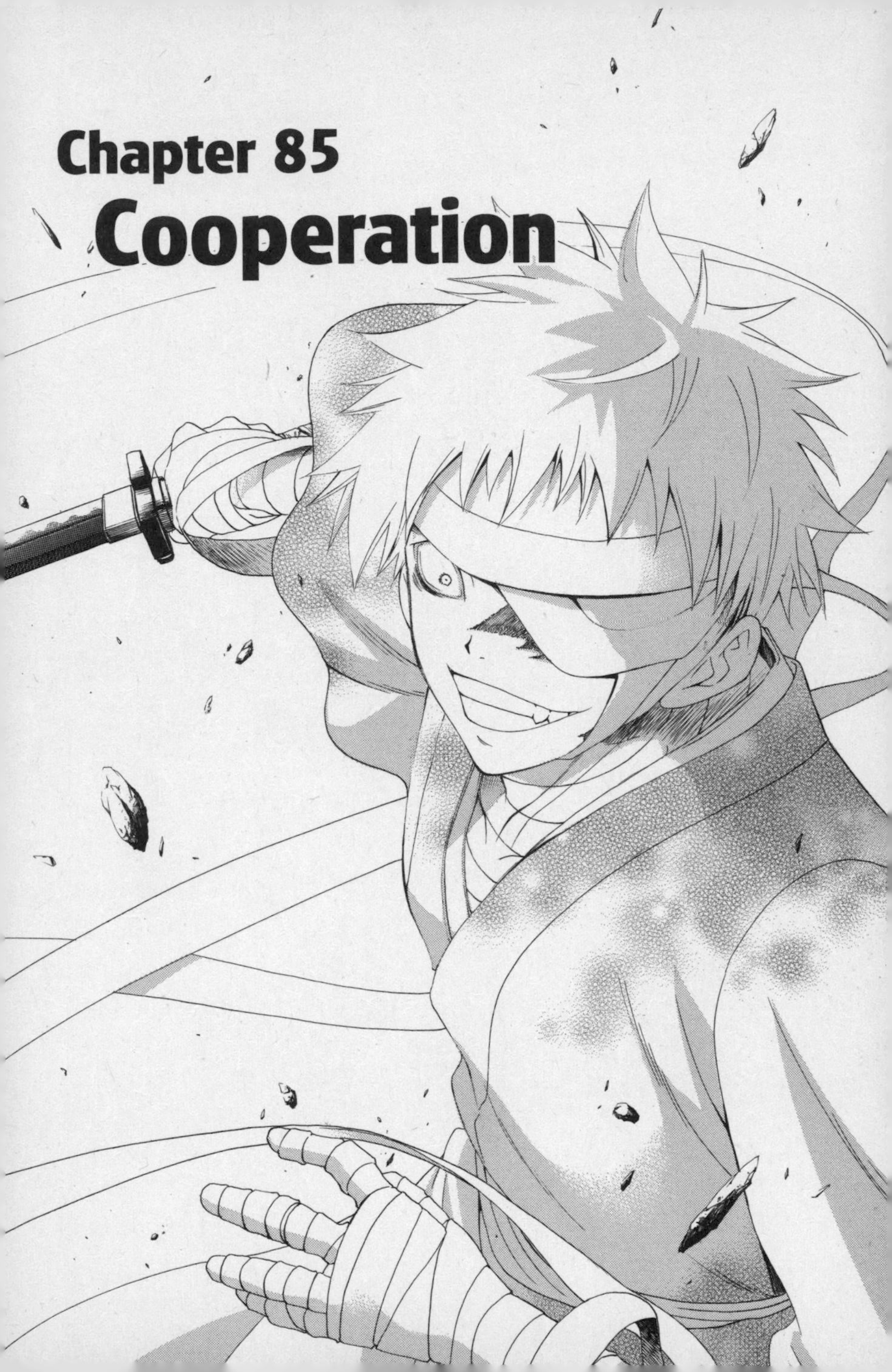
Chapter 85
Cooperation

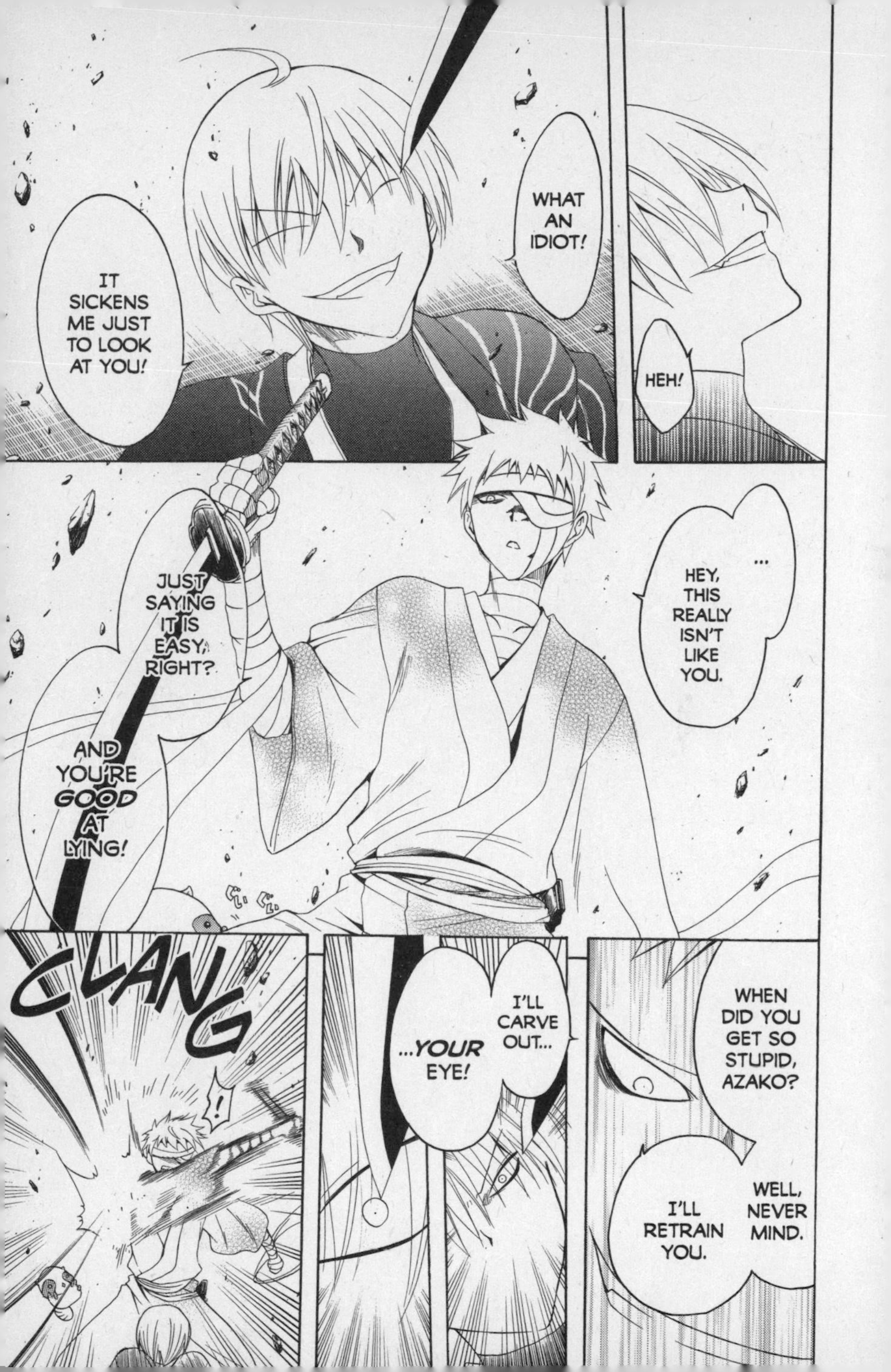
HEH!
WHAT AN IDIOT!
IT SICKENS ME JUST TO LOOK AT YOU!
... HEY, THIS REALLY ISN'T LIKE YOU.
JUST SAYING IT IS EASY, RIGHT?
AND YOU'RE GOOD AT LYING!
WHEN DID YOU GET SO STUPID, AZAKO?
WELL, NEVER MIND.
I'LL RETRAIN YOU.
I'LL CARVE OUT...
...YOUR EYE!
CLANG
!

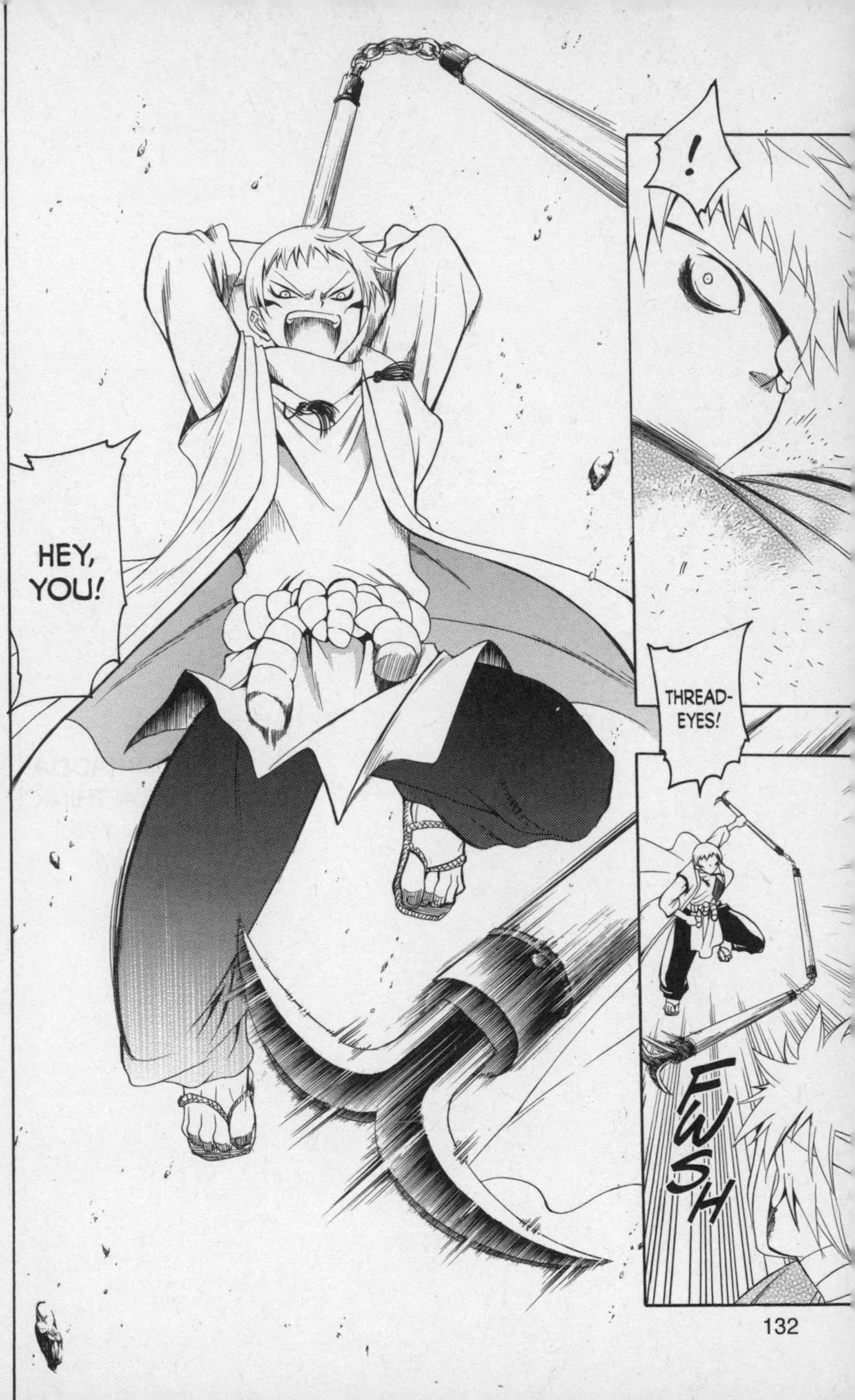
!
THREAD-EYES!
FWSH
HEY, YOU!

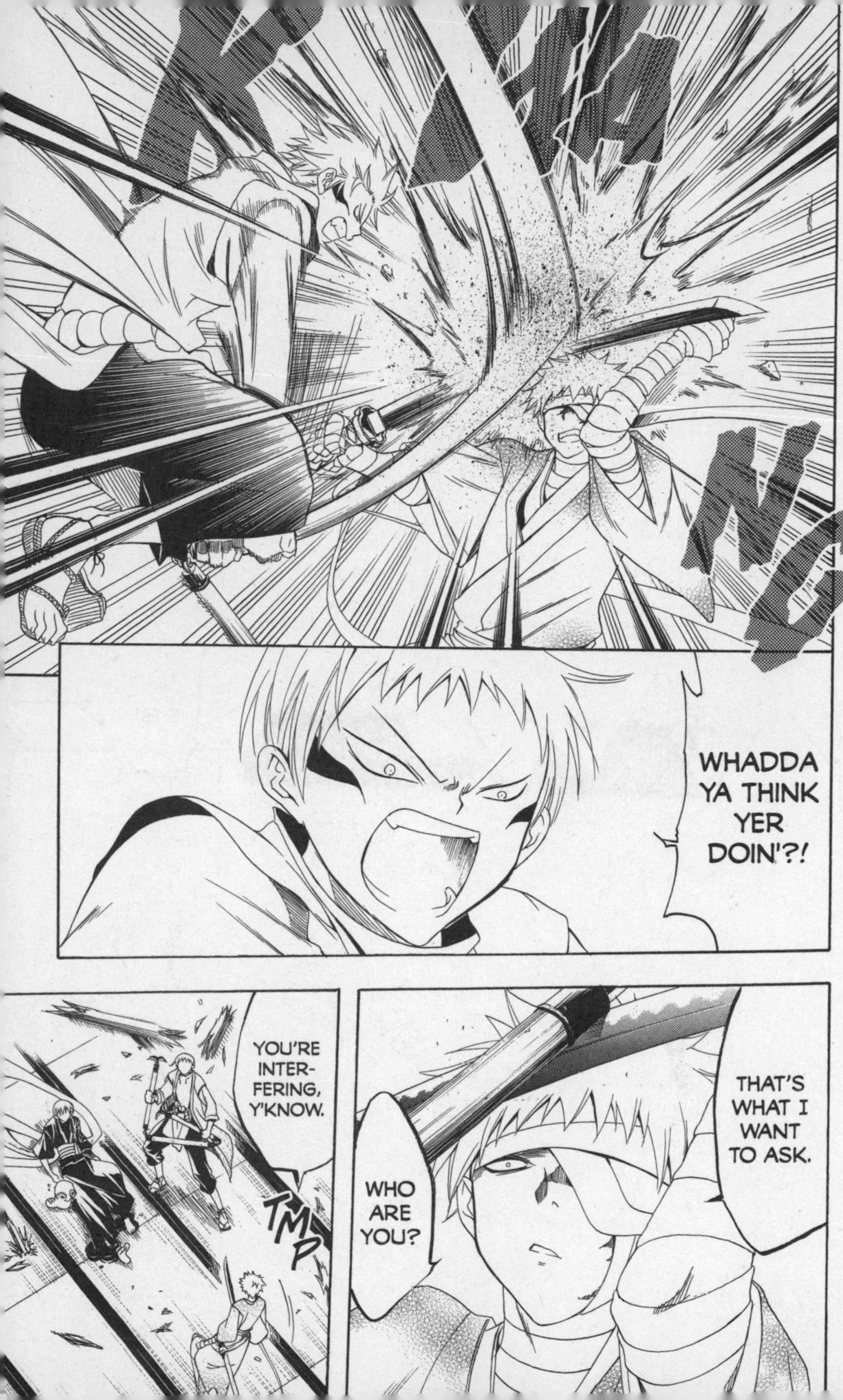
NG
WHADDA YA THINK YER DOIN'?!
THAT'S WHAT I WANT TO ASK.
WHO ARE YOU?
YOU'RE INTER-FERING, Y'KNOW.
TMP

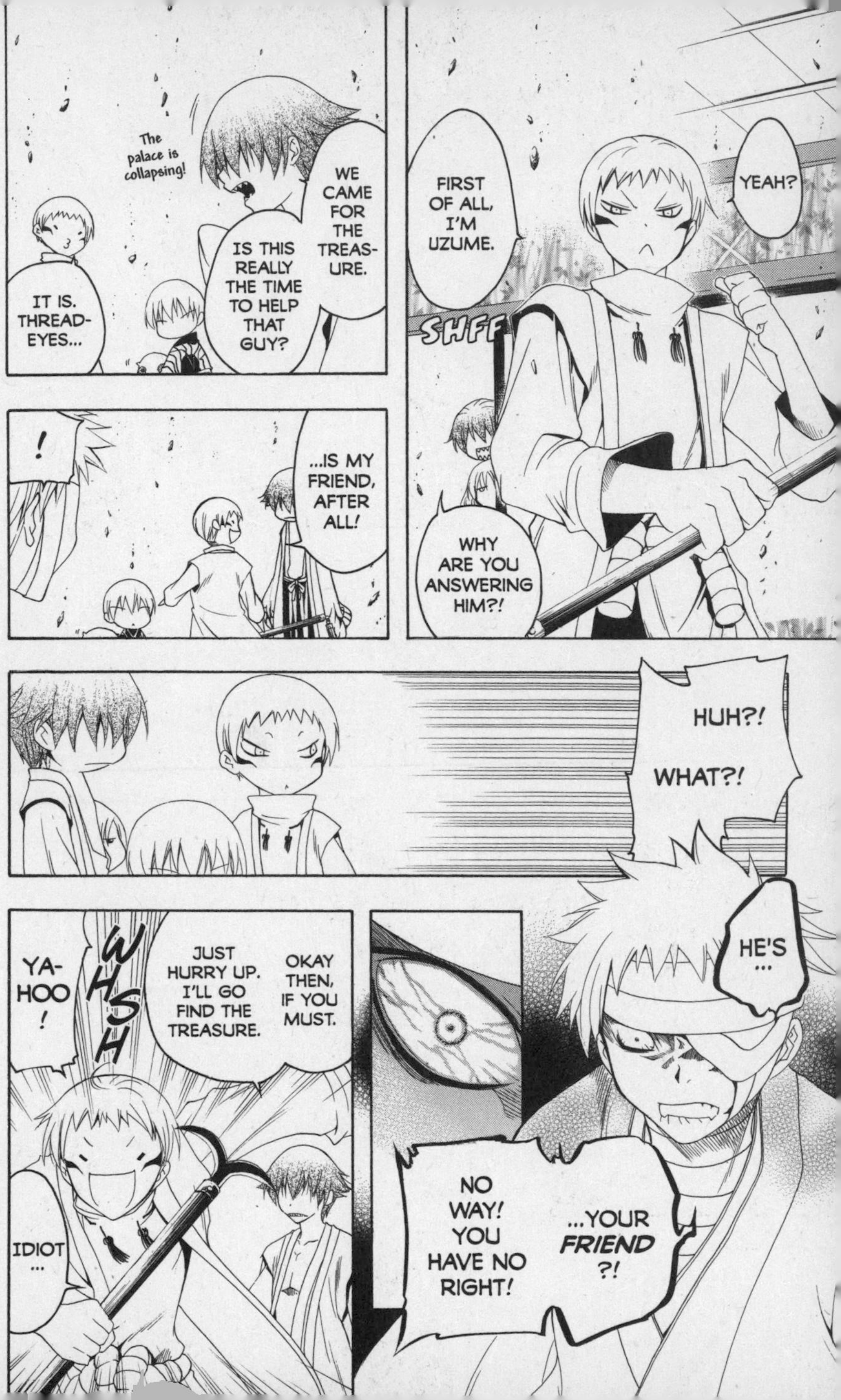
YEAH?
FIRST OF ALL, I'M UZUME.
SHFF
WHY ARE YOU ANSWERING HIM?!
WE CAME FOR THE TREASURE.
IS THIS REALLY THE TIME TO HELP THAT GUY?
The palace is collapsing!
IT IS. THREAD-EYES...
...IS MY FRIEND, AFTER ALL!
!
HUH?!
WHAT?!
HE'S...
...YOUR FRIEND?!
NO WAY! YOU HAVE NO RIGHT!
OKAY THEN, IF YOU MUST.
JUST HURRY UP. I'LL GO FIND THE TREASURE.
WHSH
YA-HOO!
IDIOT...

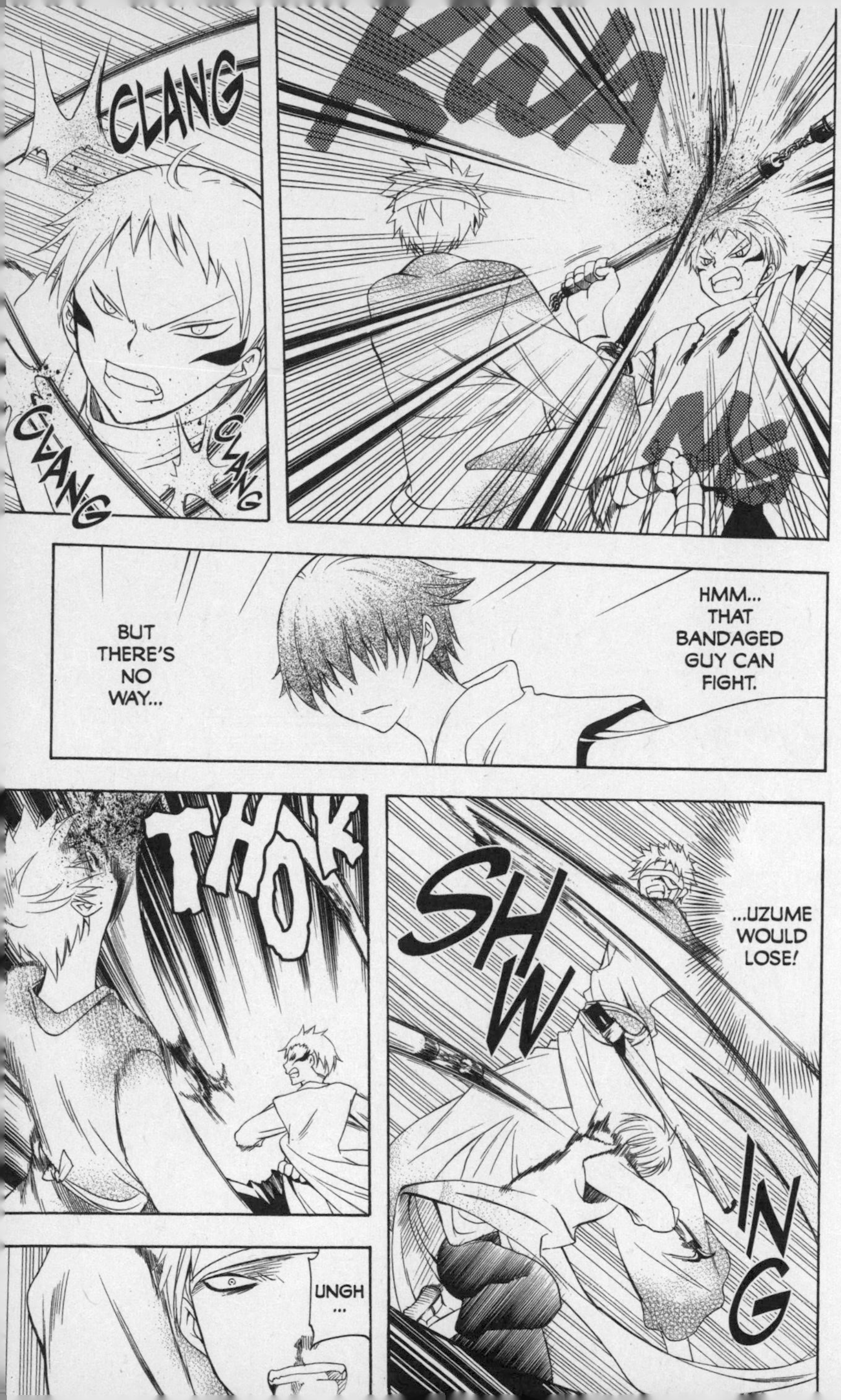
KAJA
CLANG
CLANG
CLANG
HMM... THAT BANDAGED GUY CAN FIGHT.
BUT THERE'S NO WAY...
SHWING
...UZUME WOULD LOSE!
THOK
UNGH ...

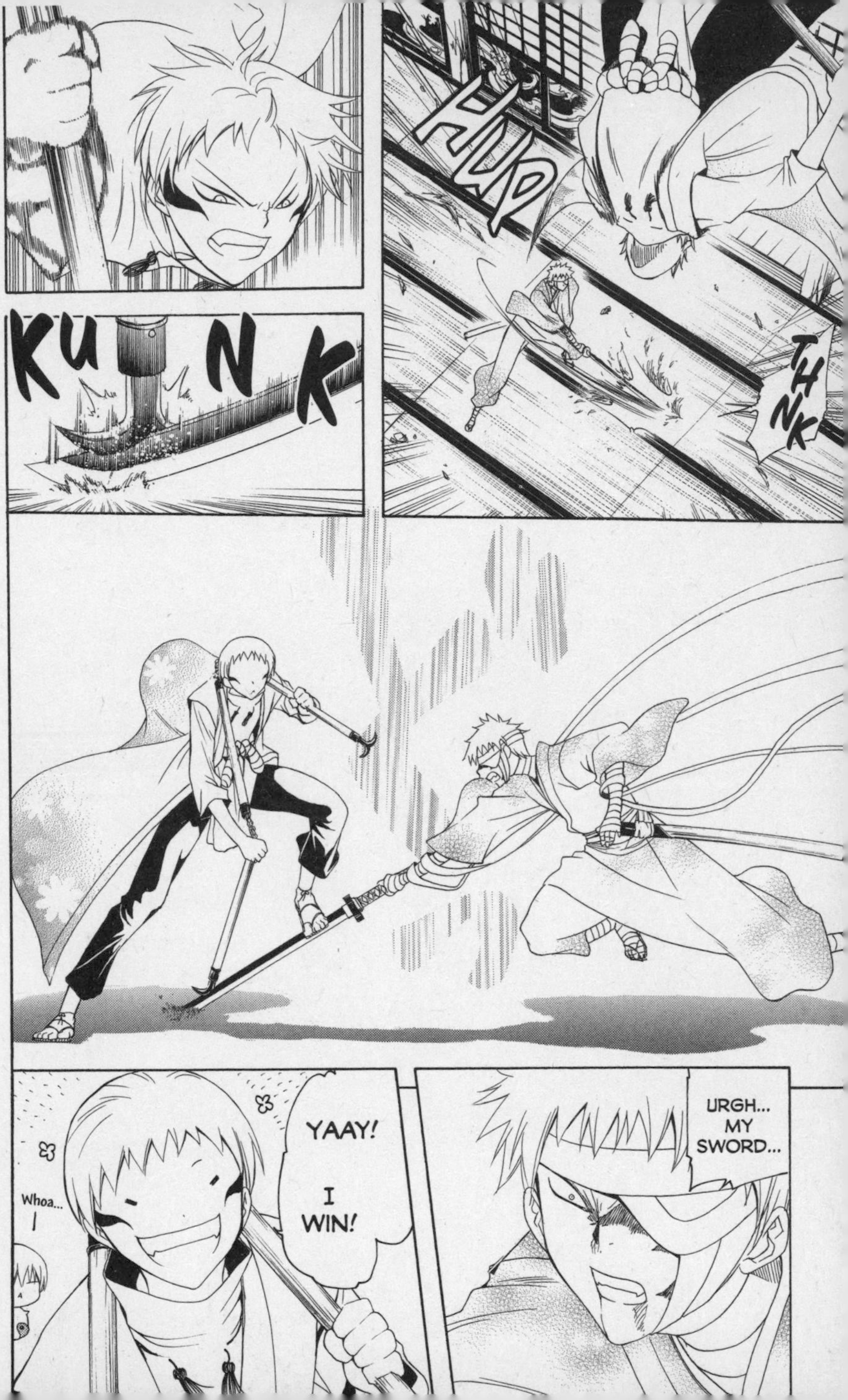
HUP
THNK
KUNK
URGH... MY SWORD...
YAAY!
I WIN!
Whoa...

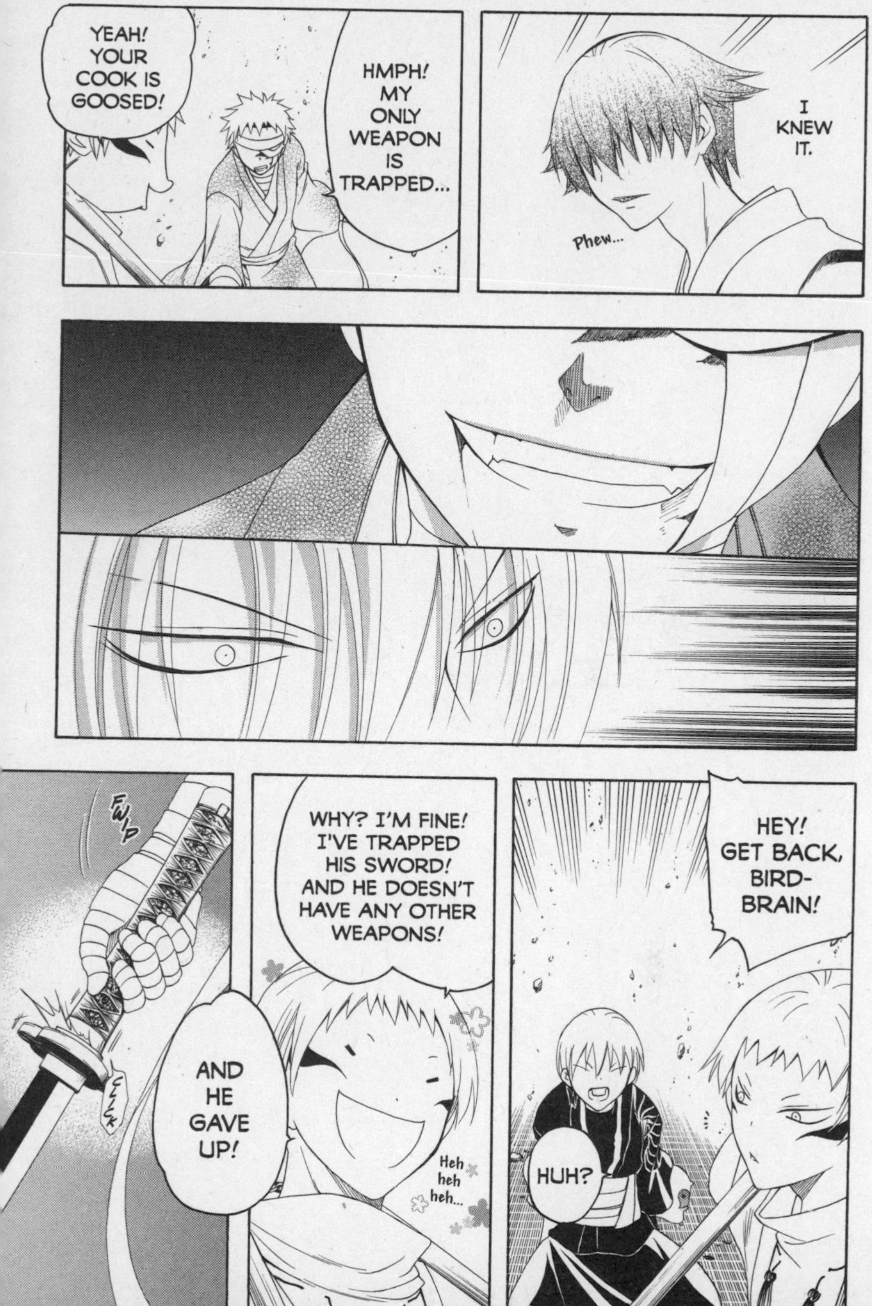
I KNEW IT.
Phew...
HMPH! MY ONLY WEAPON IS TRAPPED...
YEAH! YOUR COOK IS GOOSED!
HEY! GET BACK, BIRD-BRAIN!
HUH?
WHY? I'M FINE! I'VE TRAPPED HIS SWORD! AND HE DOESN'T HAVE ANY OTHER WEAPONS!
AND HE GAVE UP!
Heh heh heh...
FWIP
CLICK

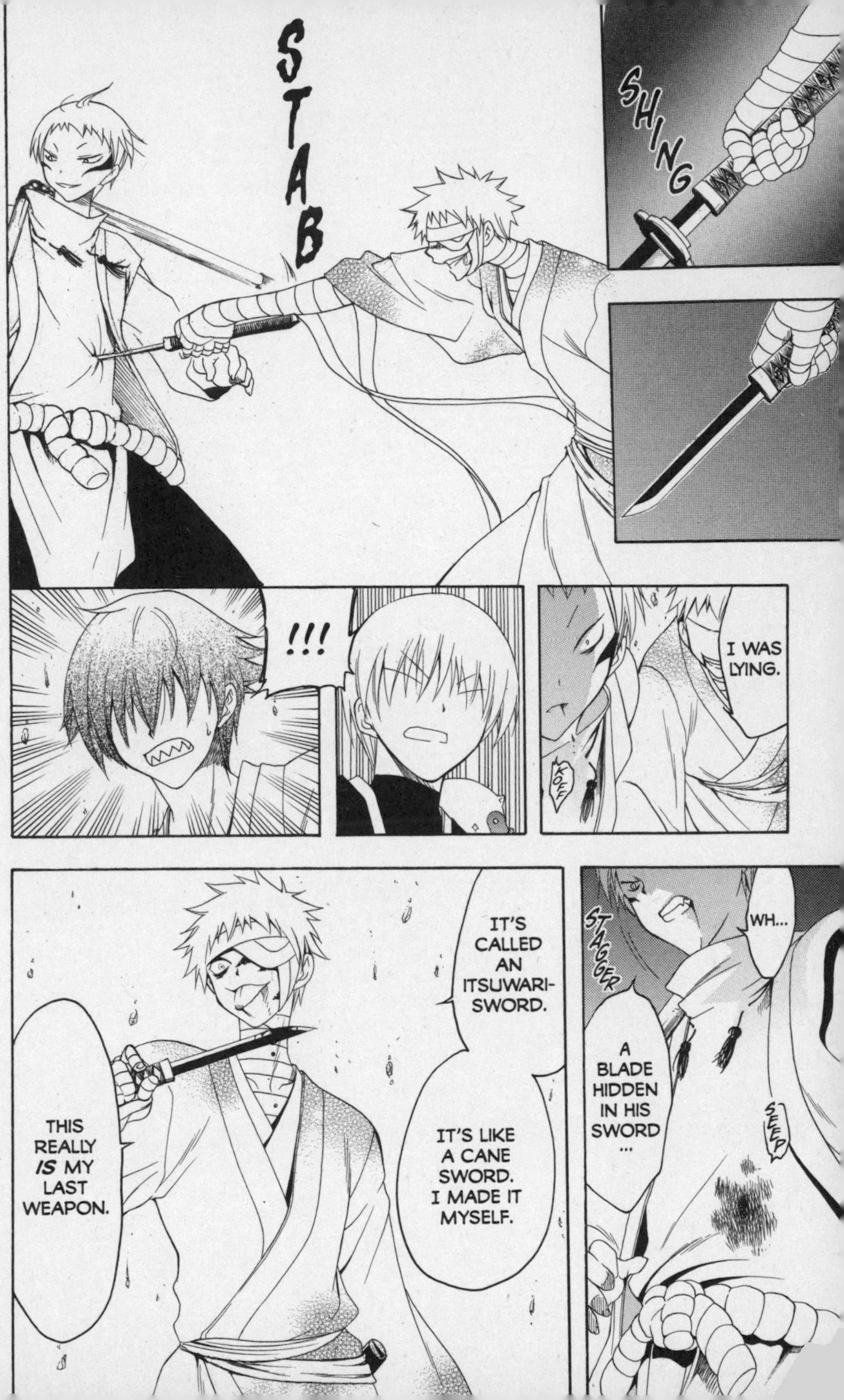
SHING
STAB
I WAS LYING.
KOFF
!!!
WH...
STAGGER
A BLADE HIDDEN IN HIS SWORD...
SEEP
IT'S CALLED AN ITSUWARI-SWORD.
IT'S LIKE A CANE SWORD. I MADE IT MYSELF.
THIS REALLY *IS* MY LAST WEAPON.

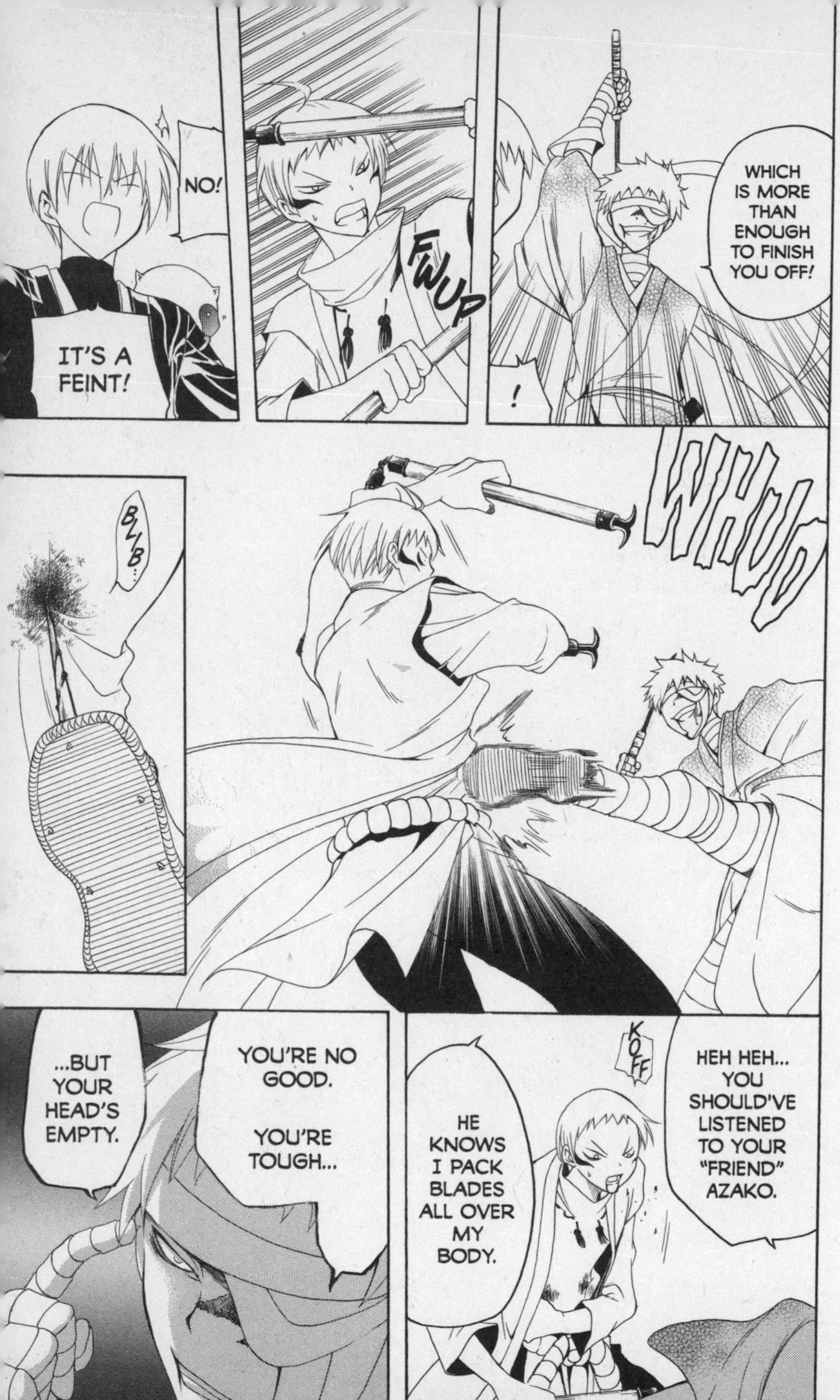
WHICH IS MORE THAN ENOUGH TO FINISH YOU OFF!
!
FWUP
NO!
IT'S A FEINT!
WHUD
BLB...
KOFF
HEH HEH... YOU SHOULD'VE LISTENED TO YOUR "FRIEND" AZAKO.
HE KNOWS I PACK BLADES ALL OVER MY BODY.
YOU'RE NO GOOD.
YOU'RE TOUGH...
...BUT YOUR HEAD'S EMPTY.

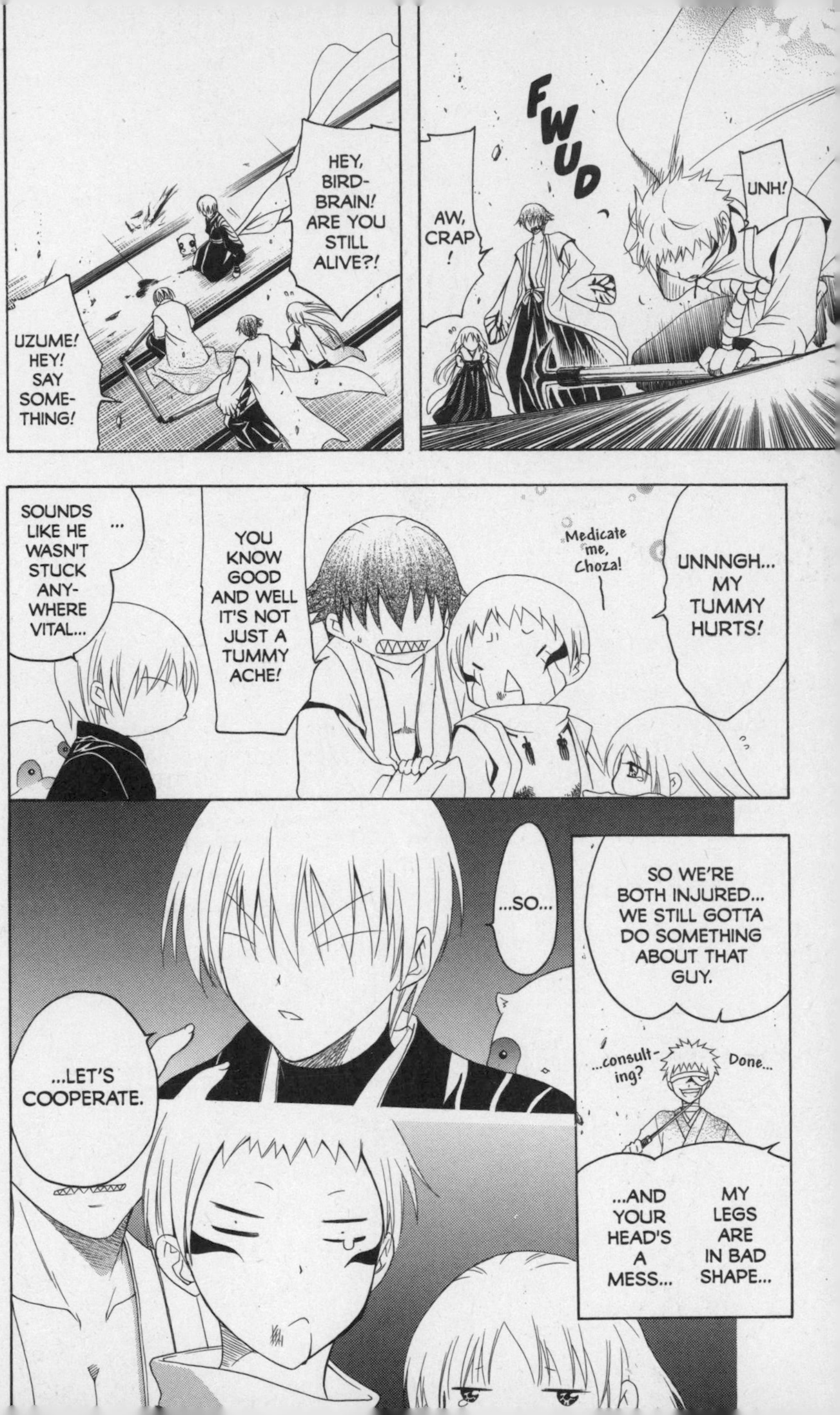
UNH!
FWUD
AW, CRAP!
HEY, BIRD-BRAIN! ARE YOU STILL ALIVE?!
UZUME! HEY! SAY SOMETHING!
UNNNGH... MY TUMMY HURTS!
Medicate me, Choza!
YOU KNOW GOOD AND WELL IT'S NOT JUST A TUMMY ACHE!
...
SOUNDS LIKE HE WASN'T STUCK ANYWHERE VITAL...
SO WE'RE BOTH INJURED... WE STILL GOTTA DO SOMETHING ABOUT THAT GUY.
Done...
...consulting?
MY LEGS ARE IN BAD SHAPE...
...AND YOUR HEAD'S A MESS...
...SO...
...LET'S COOPERATE.

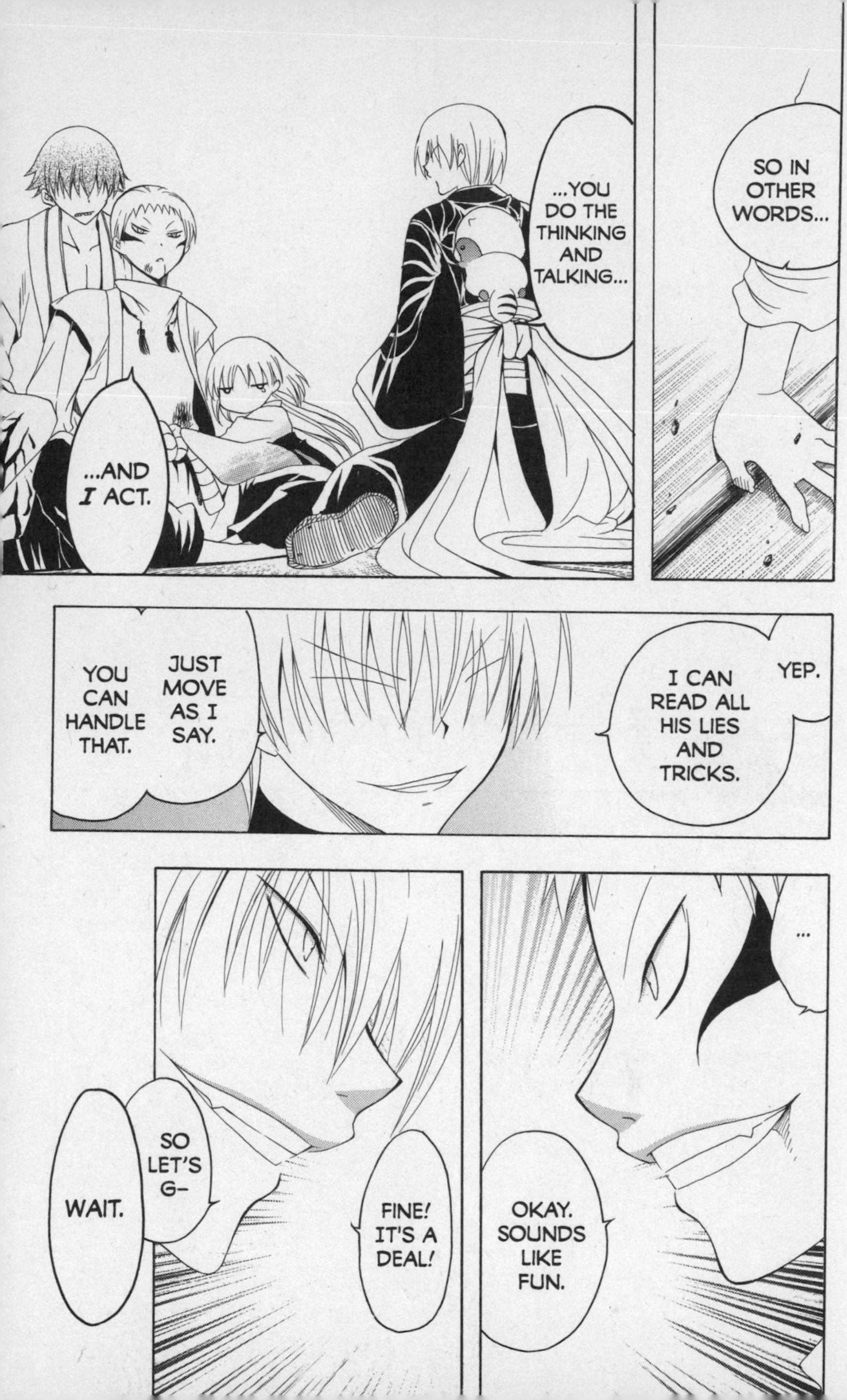
SO IN OTHER WORDS...
...YOU DO THE THINKING AND TALKING...
...AND *I* ACT.
YEP.
I CAN READ ALL HIS LIES AND TRICKS.
JUST MOVE AS I SAY.
YOU CAN HANDLE THAT.
...
OKAY. SOUNDS LIKE FUN.
FINE! IT'S A DEAL!
SO LET'S G–
WAIT.

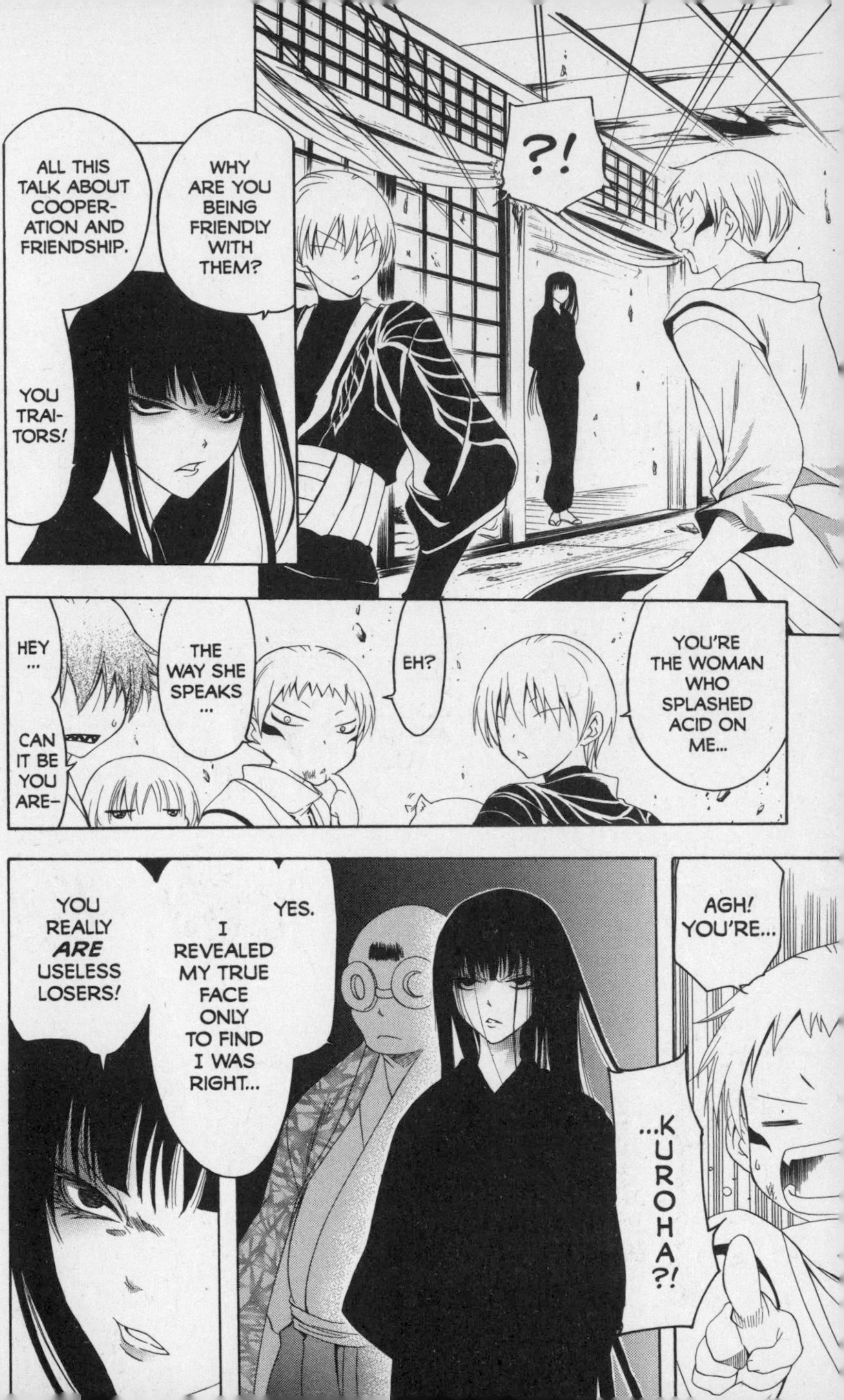
?!
WHY ARE YOU BEING FRIENDLY WITH THEM?
ALL THIS TALK ABOUT COOPERATION AND FRIENDSHIP.
YOU TRAITORS!
YOU'RE THE WOMAN WHO SPLASHED ACID ON ME...
EH?
THE WAY SHE SPEAKS...
HEY...
CAN IT BE YOU ARE–
AGH! YOU'RE...
...KUROHA?!
YES.
I REVEALED MY TRUE FACE ONLY TO FIND I WAS RIGHT...
YOU REALLY *ARE* USELESS LOSERS!

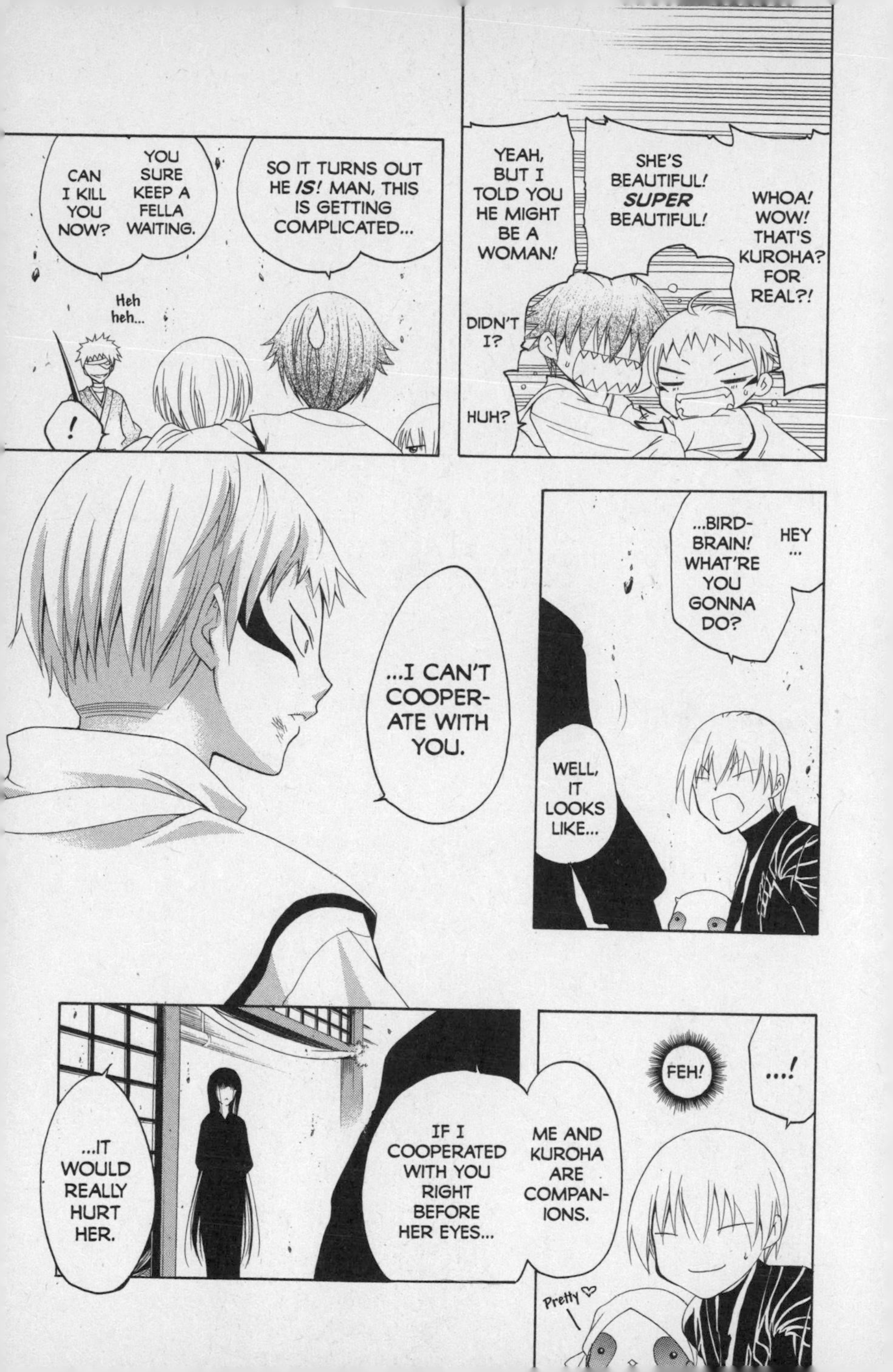
WHOA! WOW! THAT'S KUROHA? FOR REAL?!
SHE'S BEAUTIFUL! SUPER BEAUTIFUL!
YEAH, BUT I TOLD YOU HE MIGHT BE A WOMAN!
DIDN'T I?
HUH?
SO IT TURNS OUT HE IS! MAN, THIS IS GETTING COMPLICATED...
YOU SURE KEEP A FELLA WAITING.
CAN I KILL YOU NOW?
Heh heh...
!
HEY ...
...BIRD-BRAIN! WHAT'RE YOU GONNA DO?
WELL, IT LOOKS LIKE...
...I CAN'T COOPERATE WITH YOU.
...!
FEH!
ME AND KUROHA ARE COMPANIONS.
Pretty
IF I COOPERATED WITH YOU RIGHT BEFORE HER EYES...
...IT WOULD REALLY HURT HER.

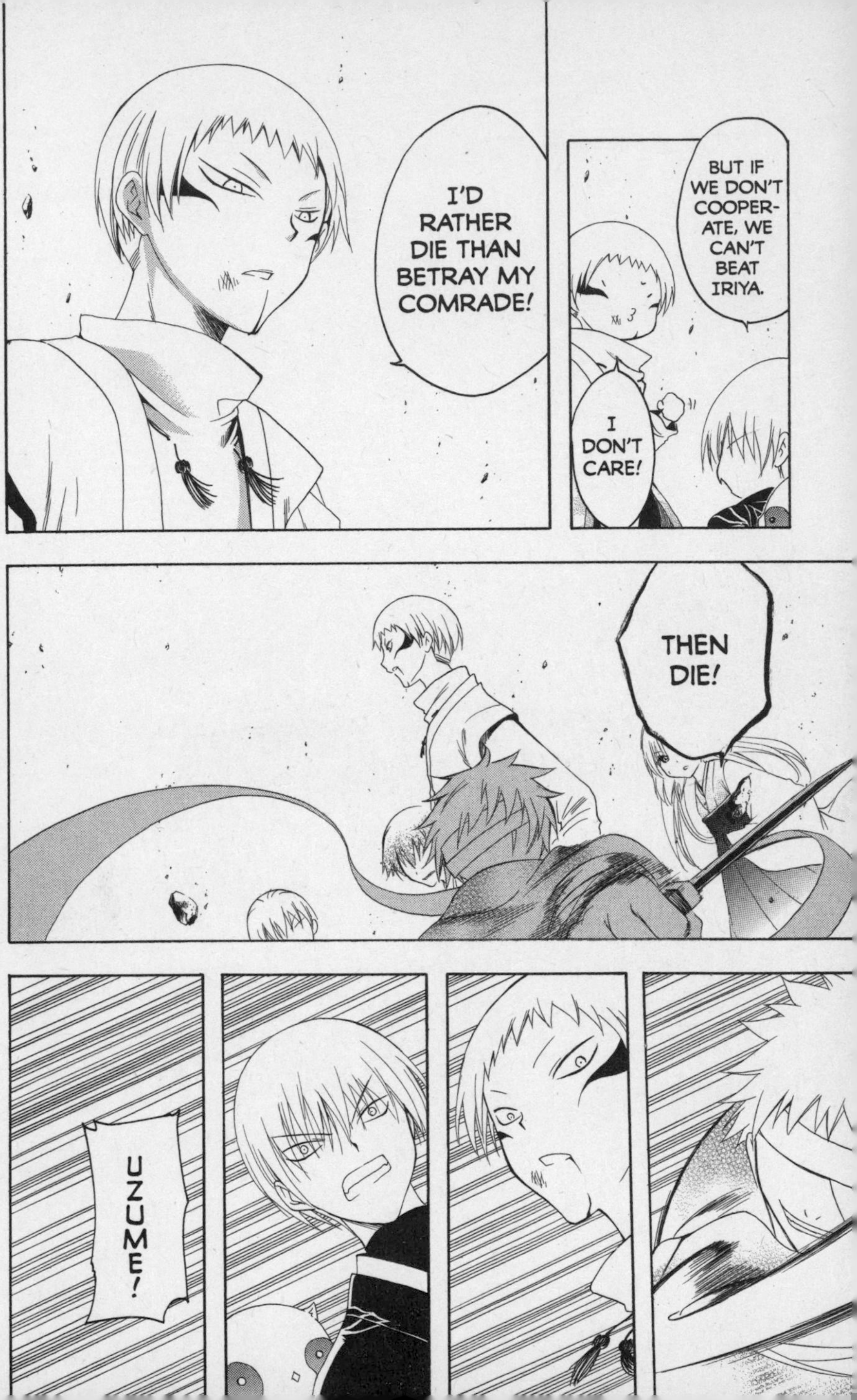
BUT IF WE DON'T COOPER-ATE, WE CAN'T BEAT IRIYA.
I DON'T CARE!
I'D RATHER DIE THAN BETRAY MY COMRADE!
THEN DIE!
UZUME!

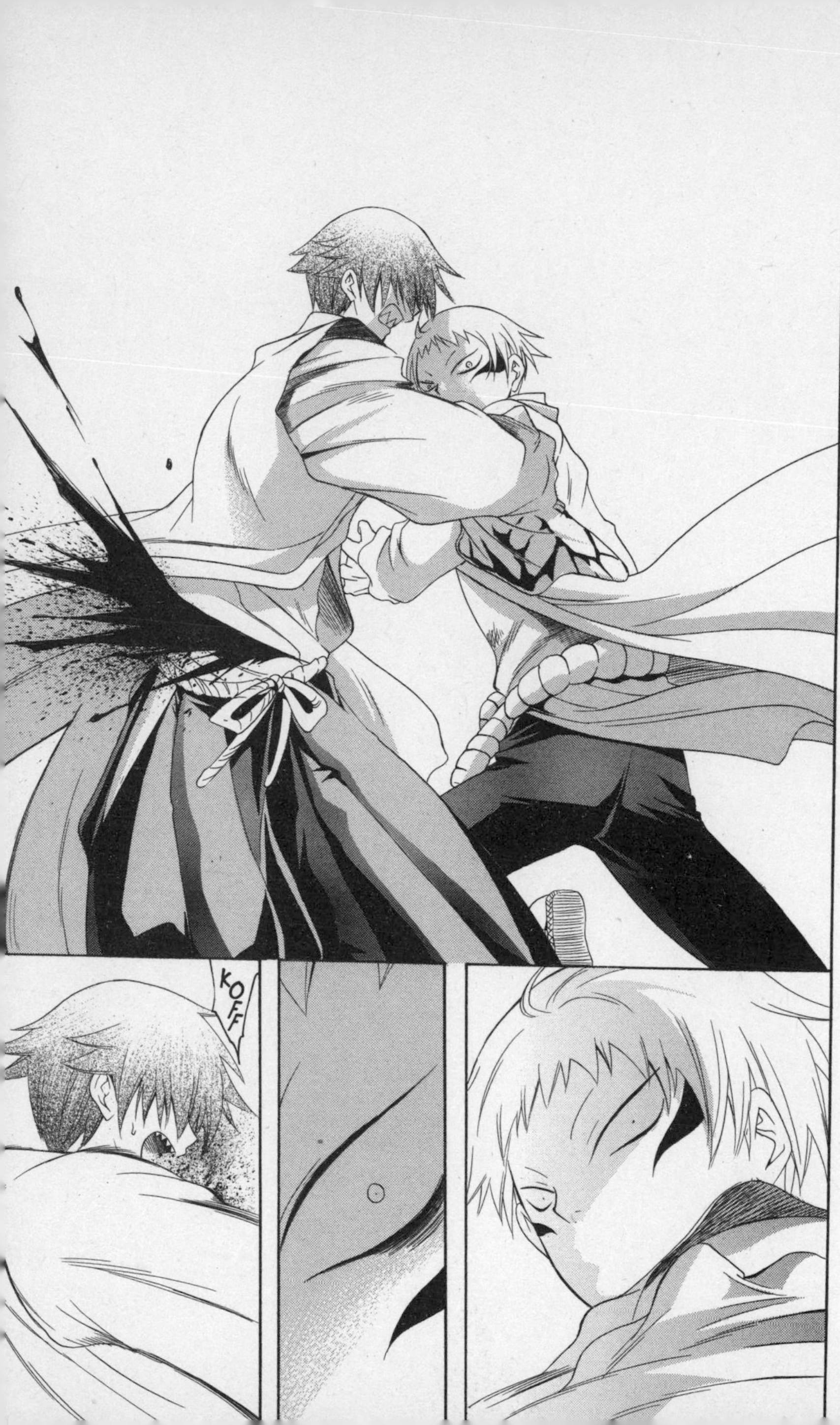
KOFF

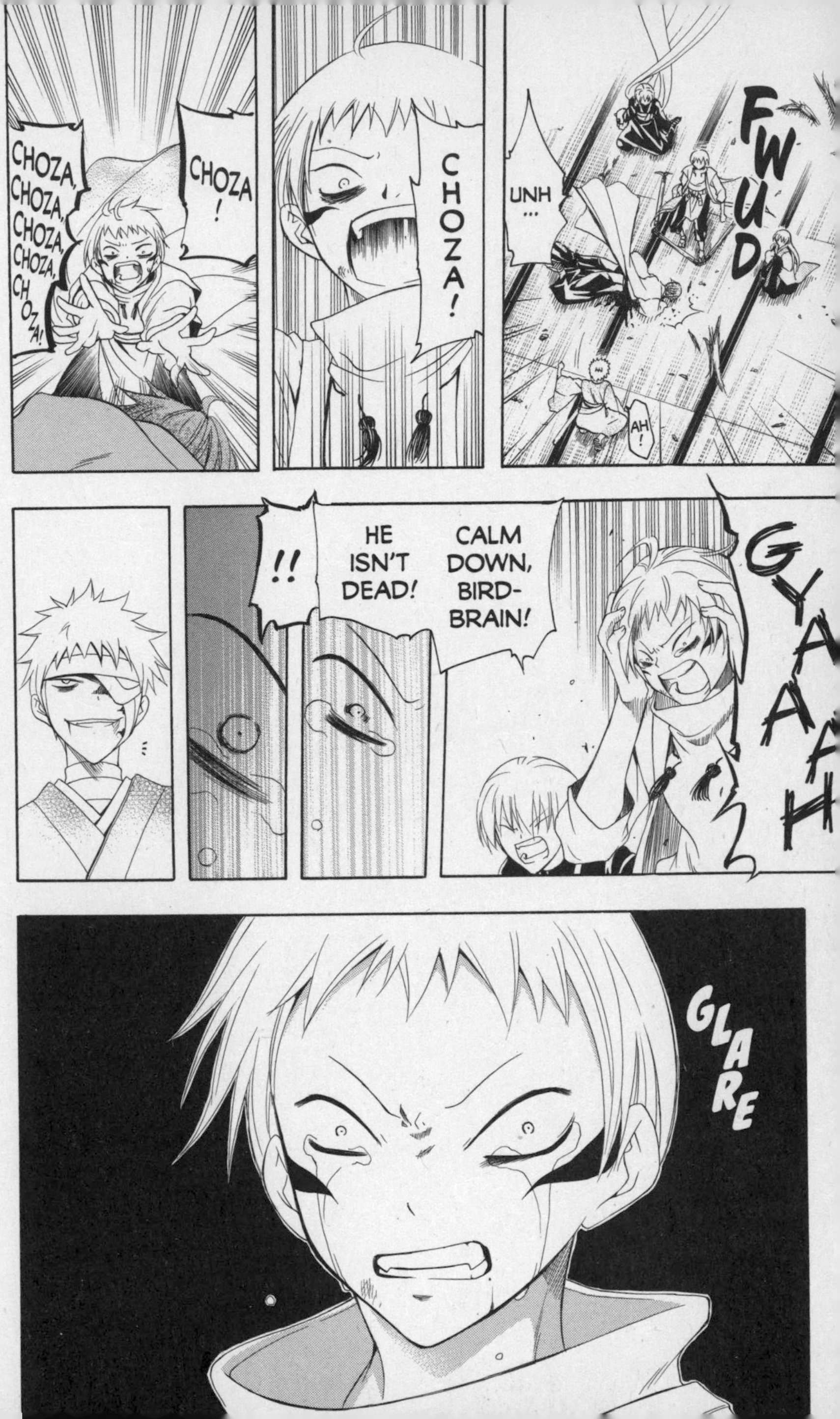
FWUD
UNH ...
AH!
CHOZA!
CHOZA!
CHOZA, CHOZA, CHOZA, CHOZA, CHOZA!
GYAAAH
CALM DOWN, BIRD-BRAIN!
HE ISN'T DEAD!
!!
GLARE

Chapter 86 Sakurako

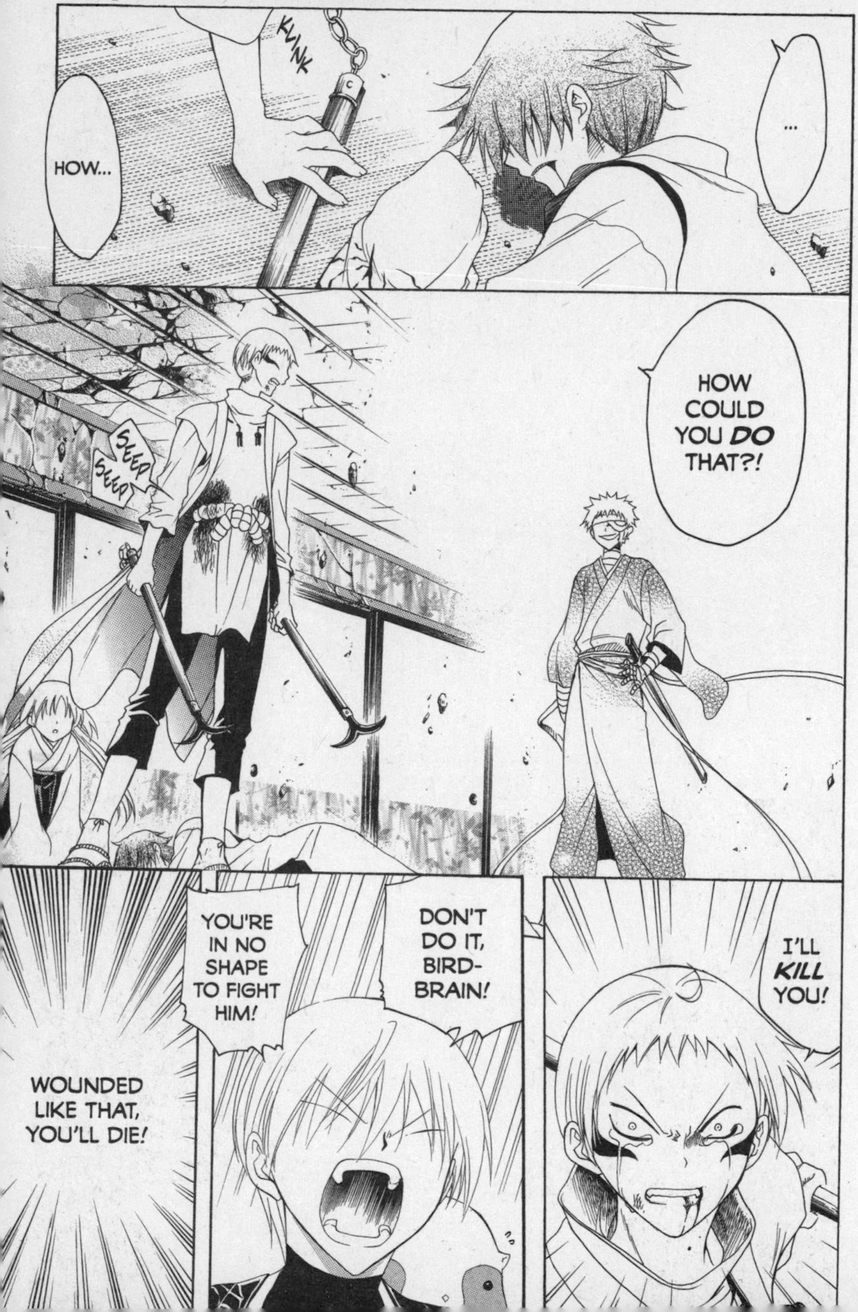
...
KLINK
HOW...
HOW COULD YOU *DO* THAT?!
SEEP SEEP
I'LL *KILL* YOU!
DON'T DO IT, BIRD-BRAIN!
YOU'RE IN NO SHAPE TO FIGHT HIM!
WOUNDED LIKE THAT, YOU'LL DIE!

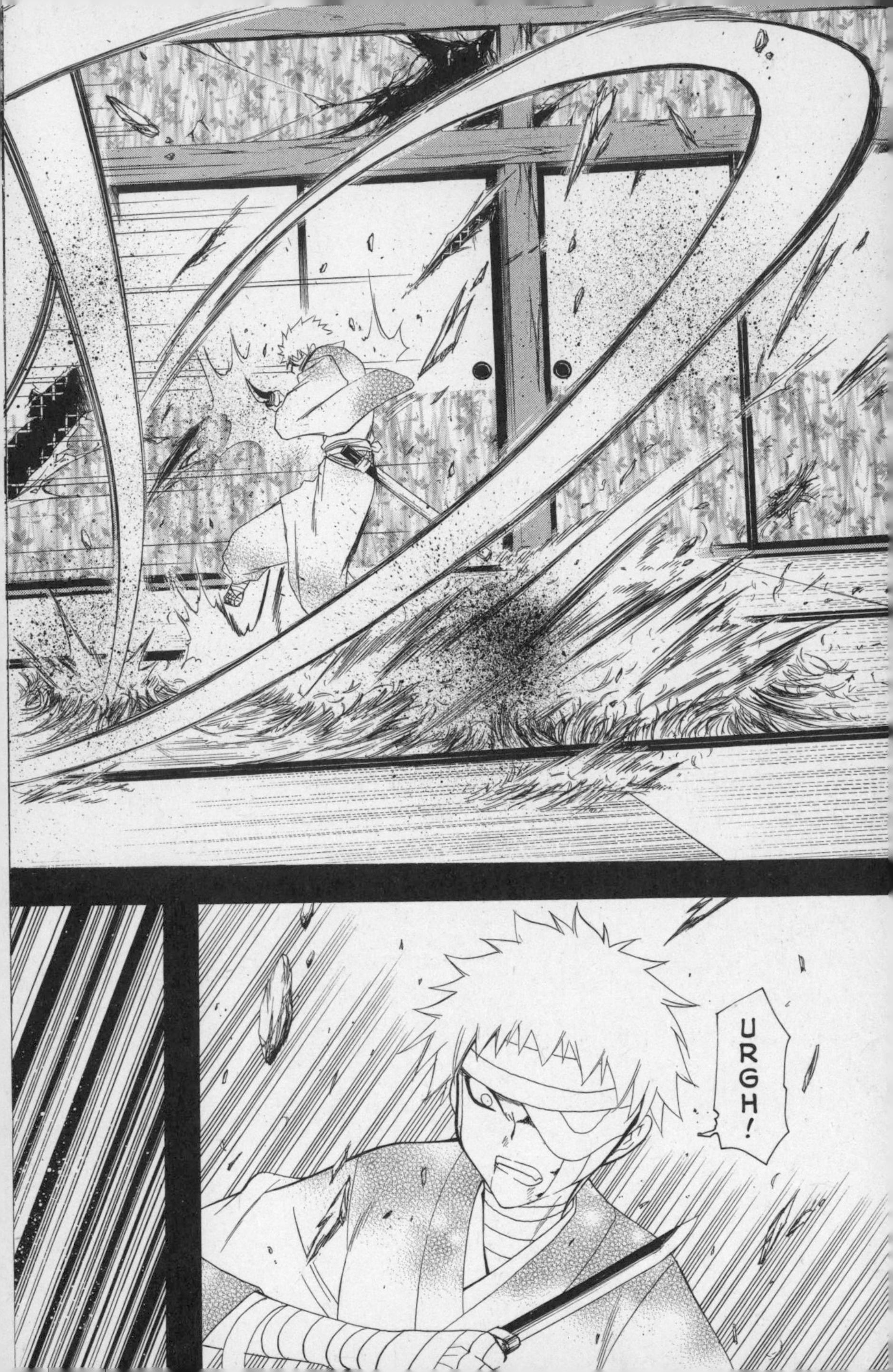
URGH!

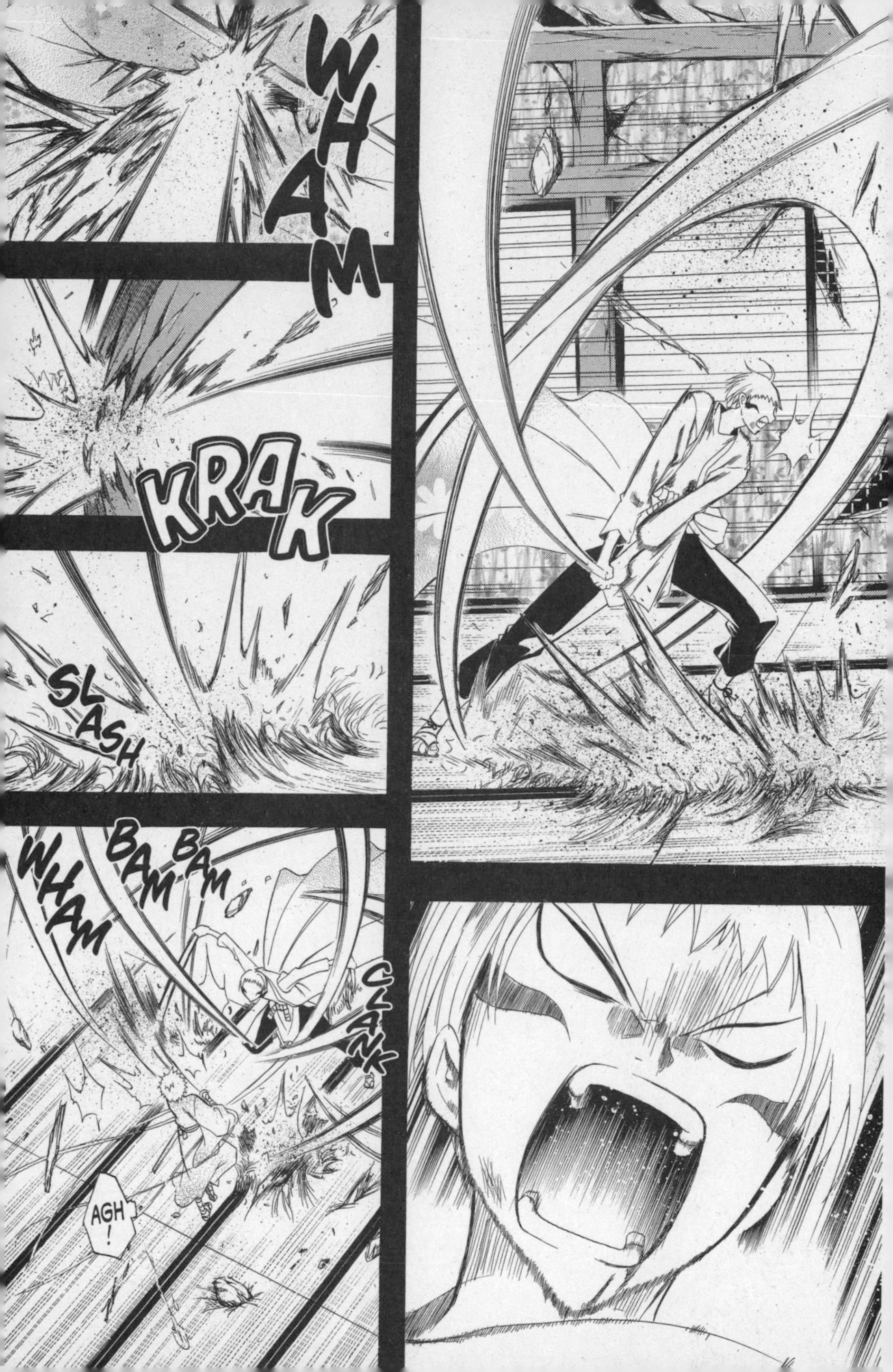
WHAM
KRAK
SLASH
BAM BAM
WHAM
CLANK
AGH!

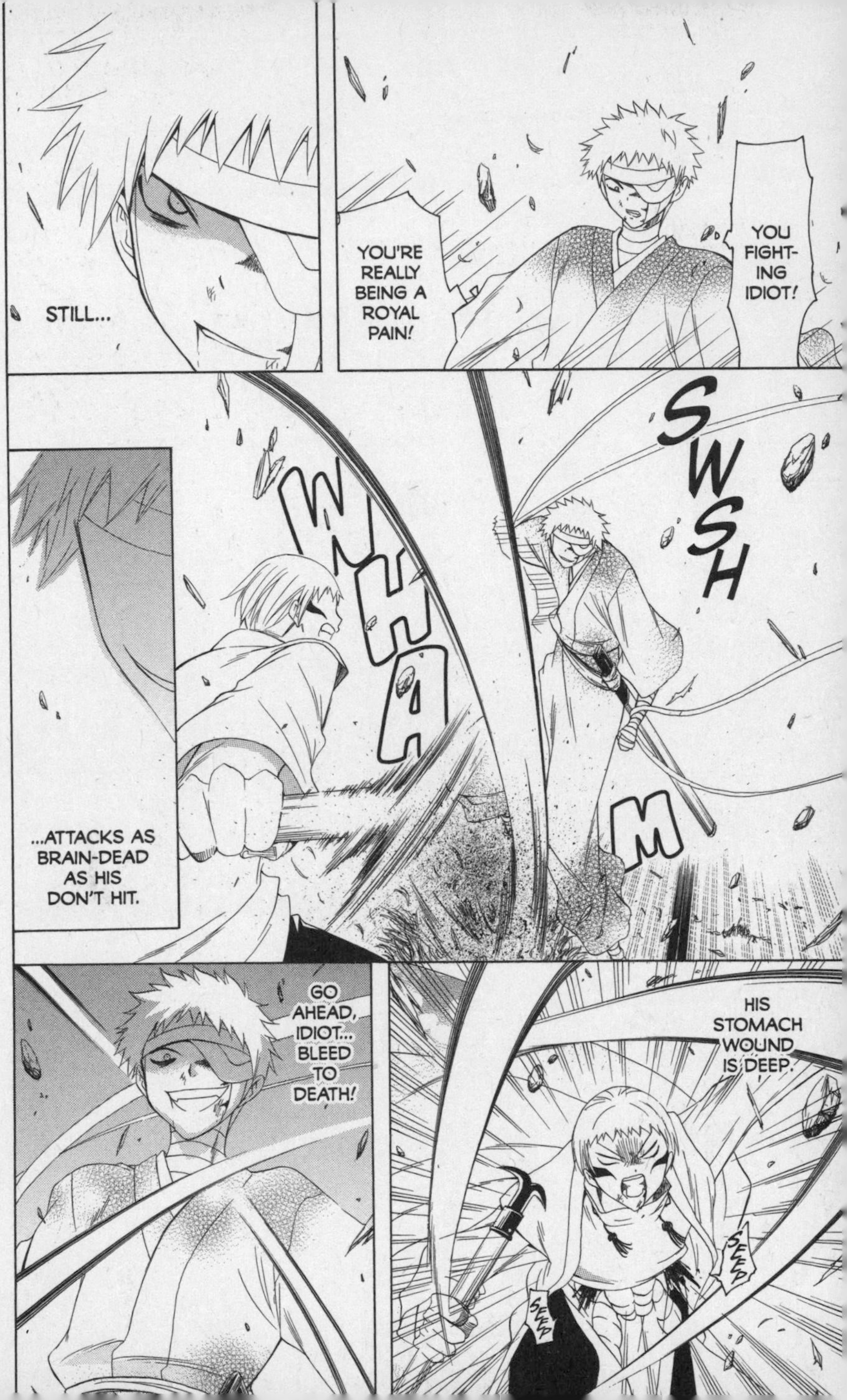
YOU FIGHTING IDIOT!
YOU'RE REALLY BEING A ROYAL PAIN!
STILL...
SWSH
WHAM
...ATTACKS AS BRAIN-DEAD AS HIS DON'T HIT.
HIS STOMACH WOUND IS DEEP.
SEEP
SEEP
GO AHEAD, IDIOT... BLEED TO DEATH!

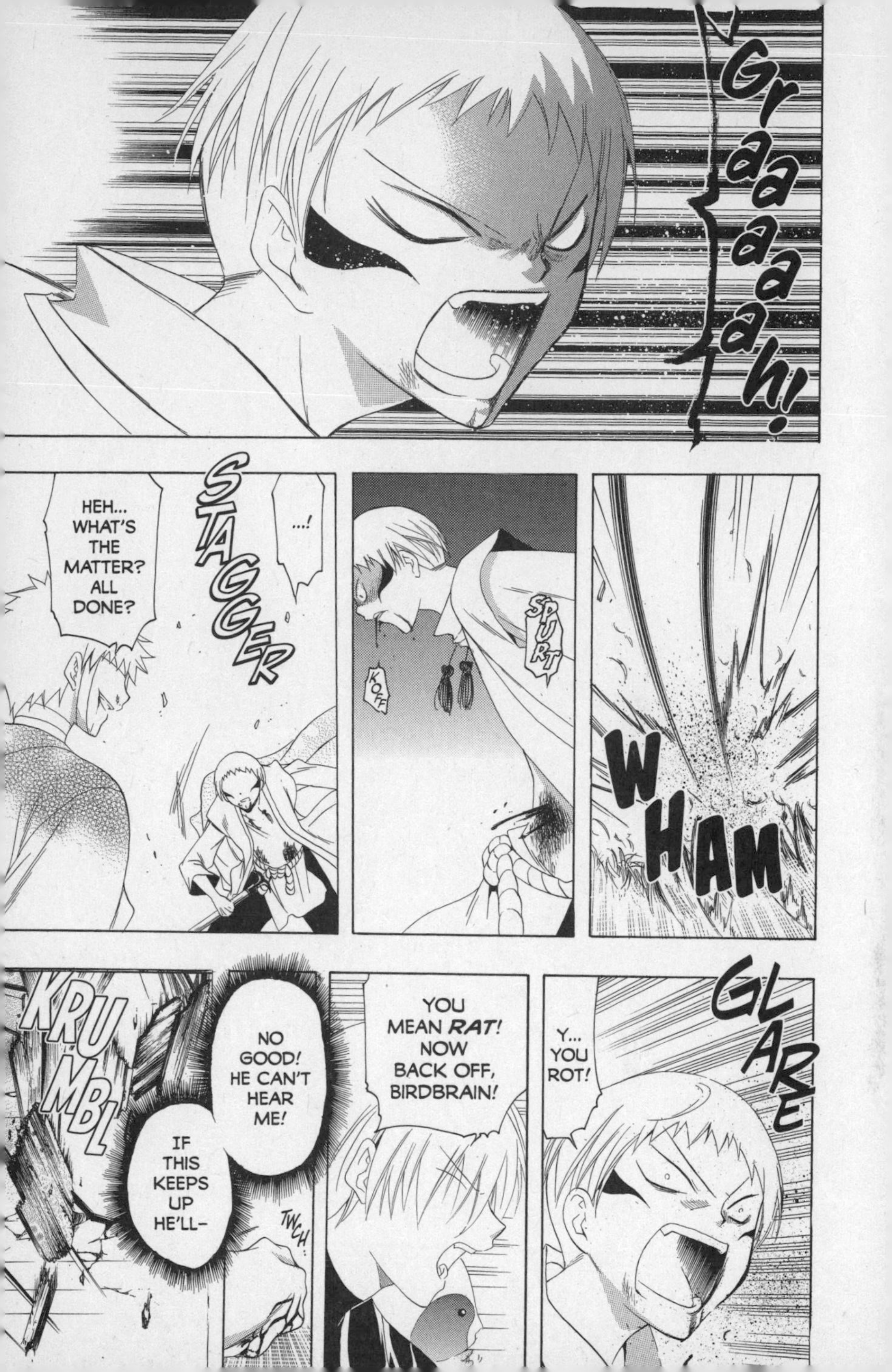
Graaaaaah!
WHAM
SPURT
KOFF
...!
STAGGER
HEH... WHAT'S THE MATTER? ALL DONE?
GLARE
Y... YOU ROT!
YOU MEAN RAT! NOW BACK OFF, BIRDBRAIN!
TWCH
NO GOOD! HE CAN'T HEAR ME!
IF THIS KEEPS UP HE'LL–
KRUMBL

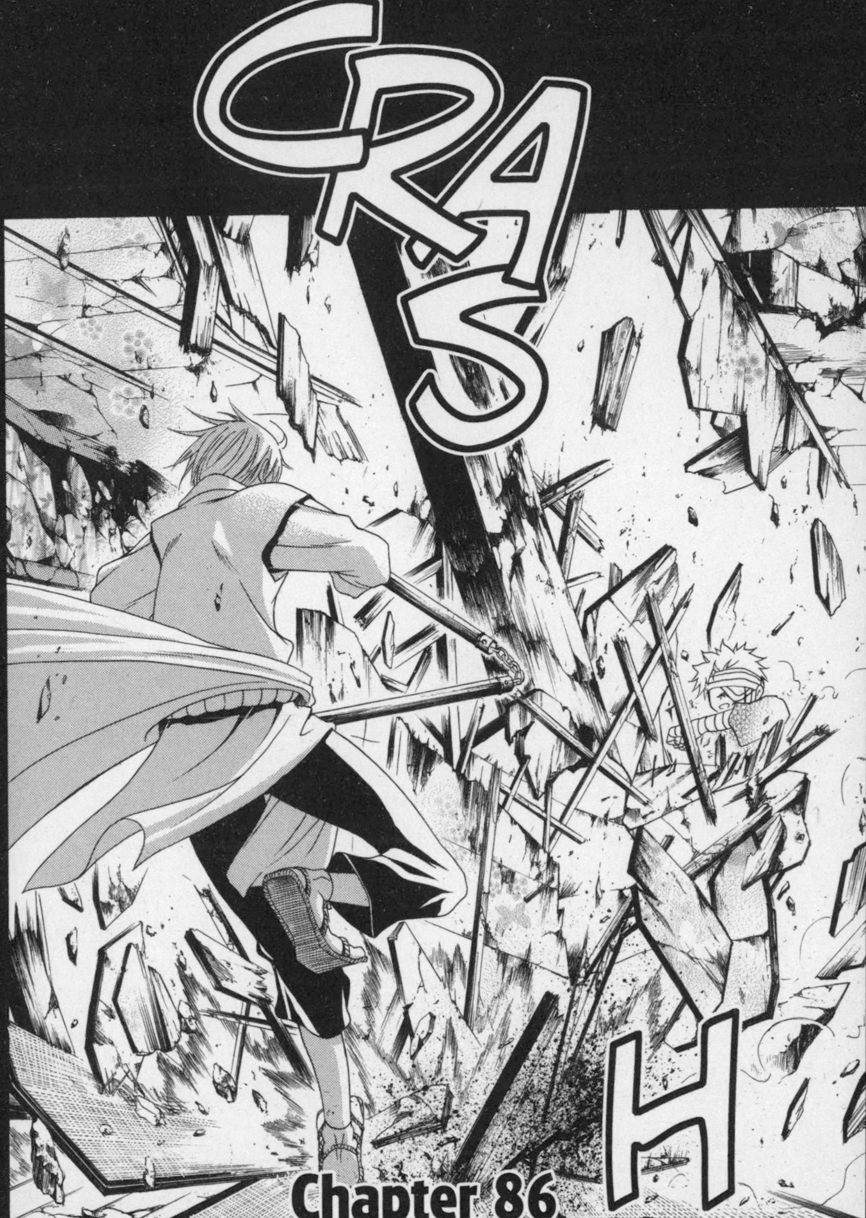
CRASH

Chapter 86
Sakurako

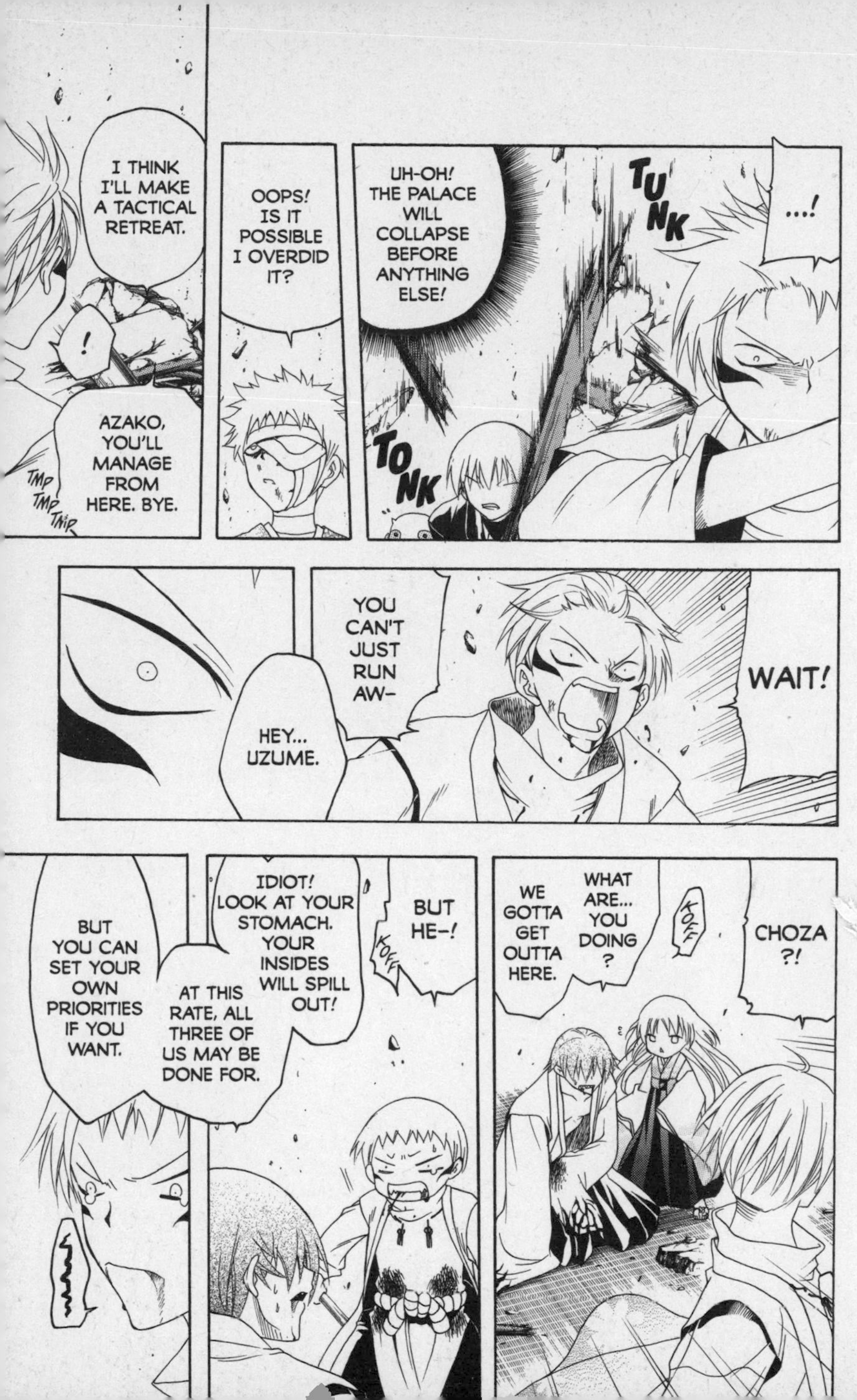
...!
TUNK
TONK
UH-OH! THE PALACE WILL COLLAPSE BEFORE ANYTHING ELSE!
OOPS! IS IT POSSIBLE I OVERDID IT?
I THINK I'LL MAKE A TACTICAL RETREAT.
!
AZAKO, YOU'LL MANAGE FROM HERE. BYE.
TMP TMP TMP
WAIT!
YOU CAN'T JUST RUN AW–
HEY... UZUME.
CHOZA ?!
KOFF
WHAT ARE... YOU DOING ?
WE GOTTA GET OUTTA HERE.
BUT HE–!
KOFF
IDIOT! LOOK AT YOUR STOMACH. YOUR INSIDES WILL SPILL OUT!
AT THIS RATE, ALL THREE OF US MAY BE DONE FOR.
BUT YOU CAN SET YOUR OWN PRIORITIES IF YOU WANT.

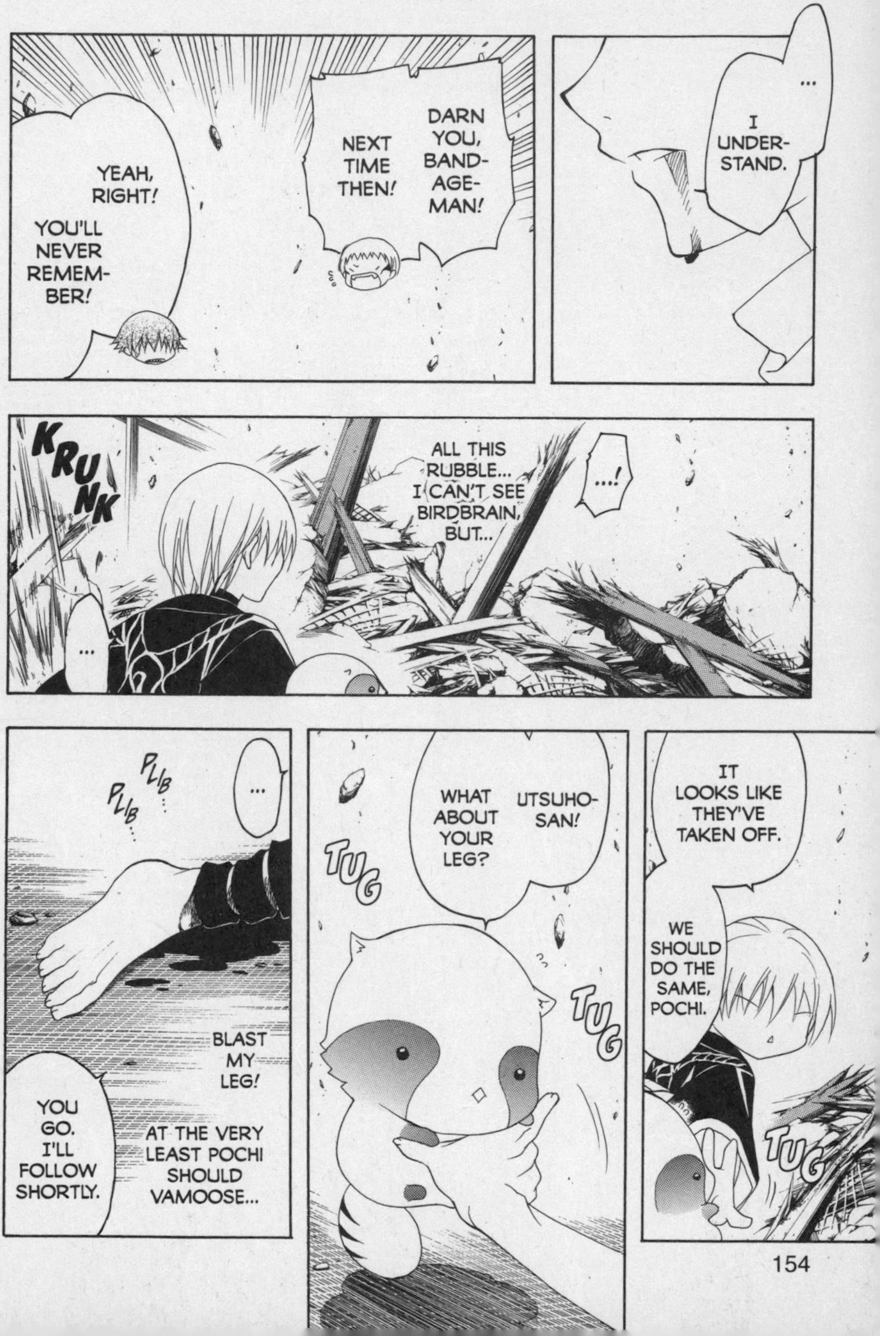
...
I UNDER-STAND.
DARN YOU, BAND-AGE-MAN!
NEXT TIME THEN!
YEAH, RIGHT!
YOU'LL NEVER REMEM-BER!
....!
ALL THIS RUBBLE... I CAN'T SEE BIRDBRAIN, BUT...
KRUNK
...
IT LOOKS LIKE THEY'VE TAKEN OFF.
WE SHOULD DO THE SAME, POCHI.
TUG
UTSUHO-SAN!
WHAT ABOUT YOUR LEG?
TUG
TUG
...
PLIB...
PLIB...
BLAST MY LEG!
AT THE VERY LEAST POCHI SHOULD VAMOOSE...
YOU GO. I'LL FOLLOW SHORTLY.

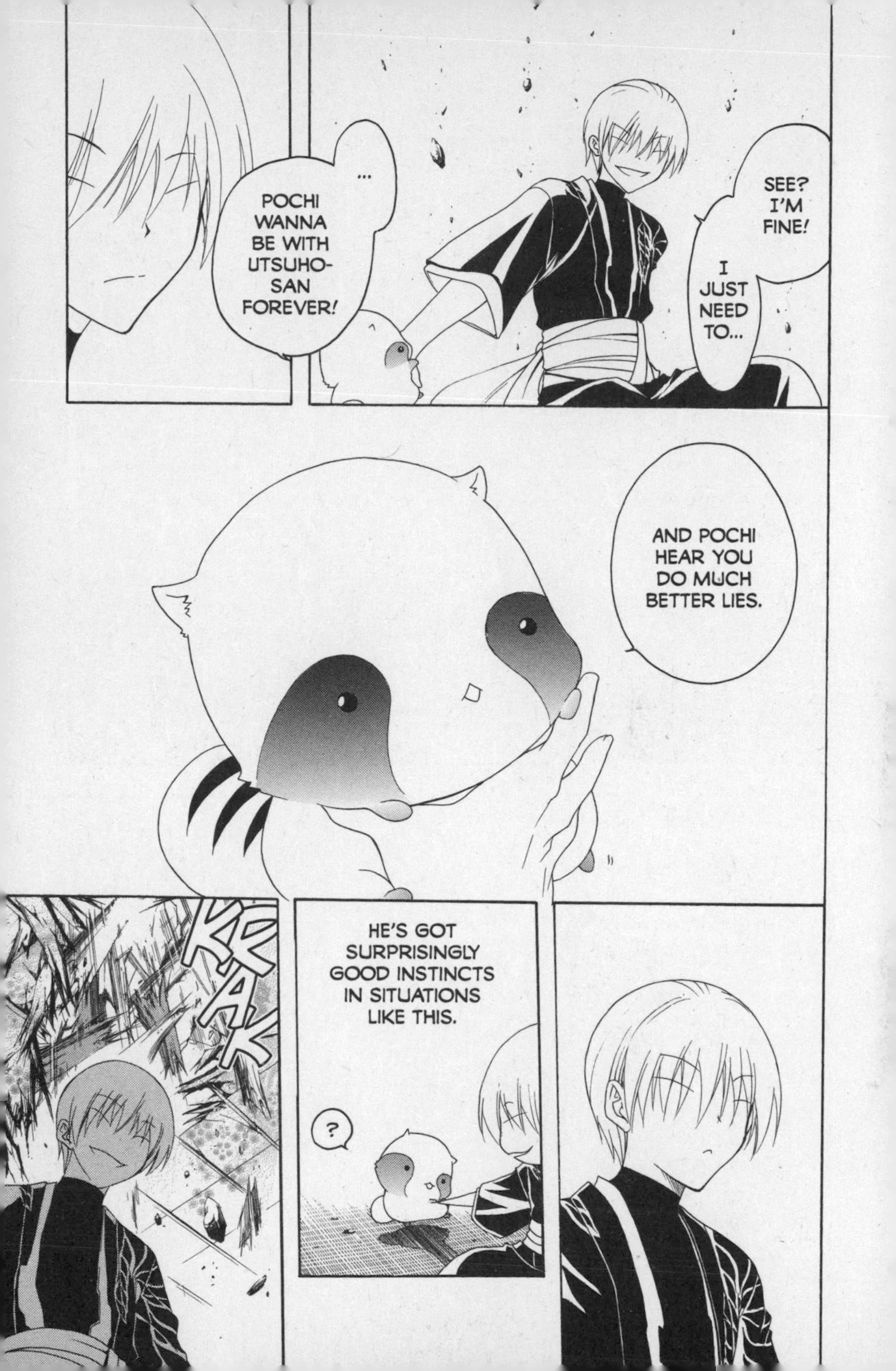
SEE? I'M FINE!
I JUST NEED TO...
...
POCHI WANNA BE WITH UTSUHO-SAN FOREVER!
AND POCHI HEAR YOU DO MUCH BETTER LIES.
HE'S GOT SURPRISINGLY GOOD INSTINCTS IN SITUATIONS LIKE THIS.
?
KRAK

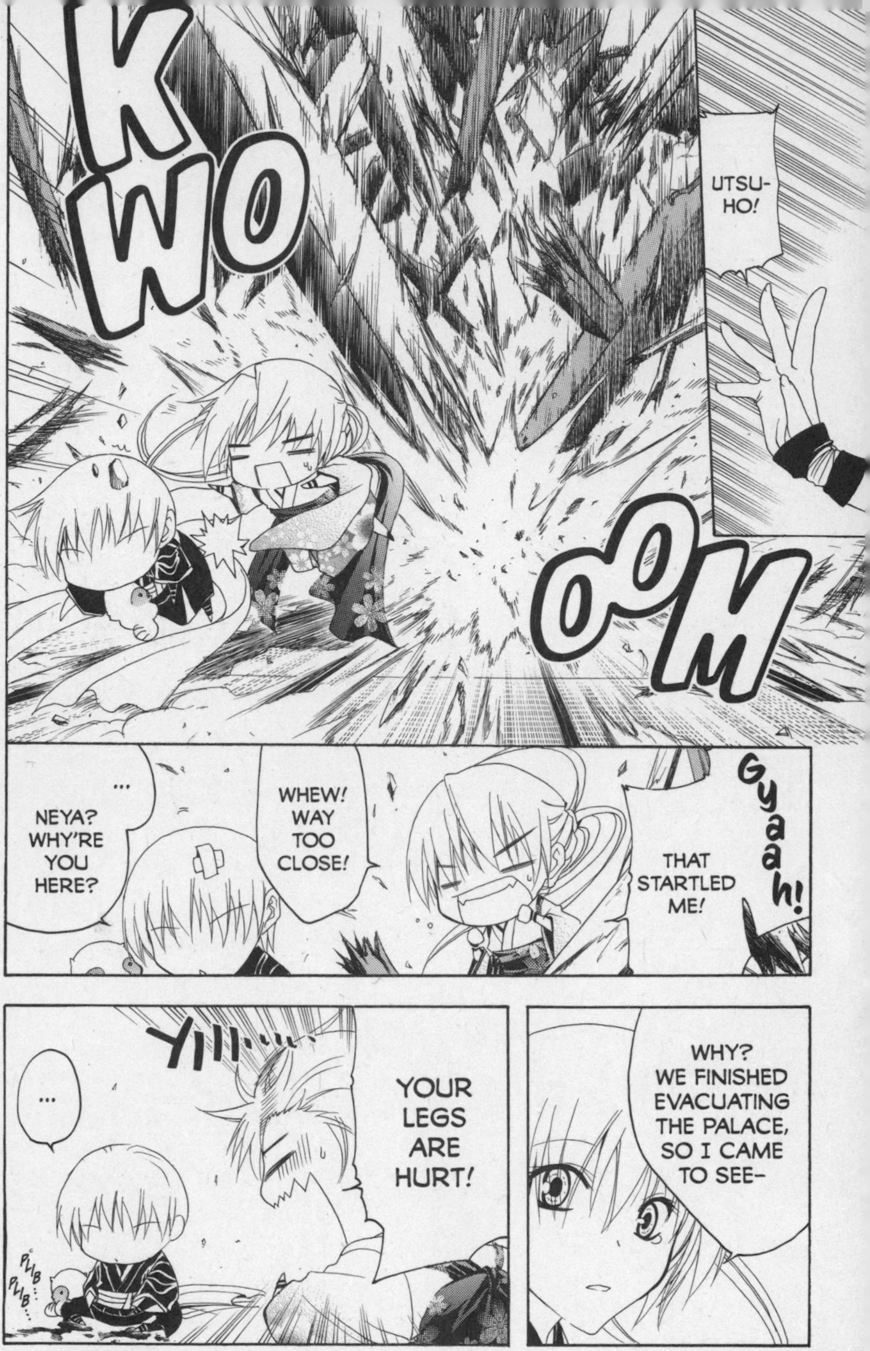
UTSU-HO!
KWO
OOM
Gyaaah!
THAT STARTLED ME!
WHEW! WAY TOO CLOSE!
...
NEYA? WHY'RE YOU HERE?
WHY? WE FINISHED EVACUATING THE PALACE, SO I CAME TO SEE–
YOUR LEGS ARE HURT!
...
PLIB PLIB

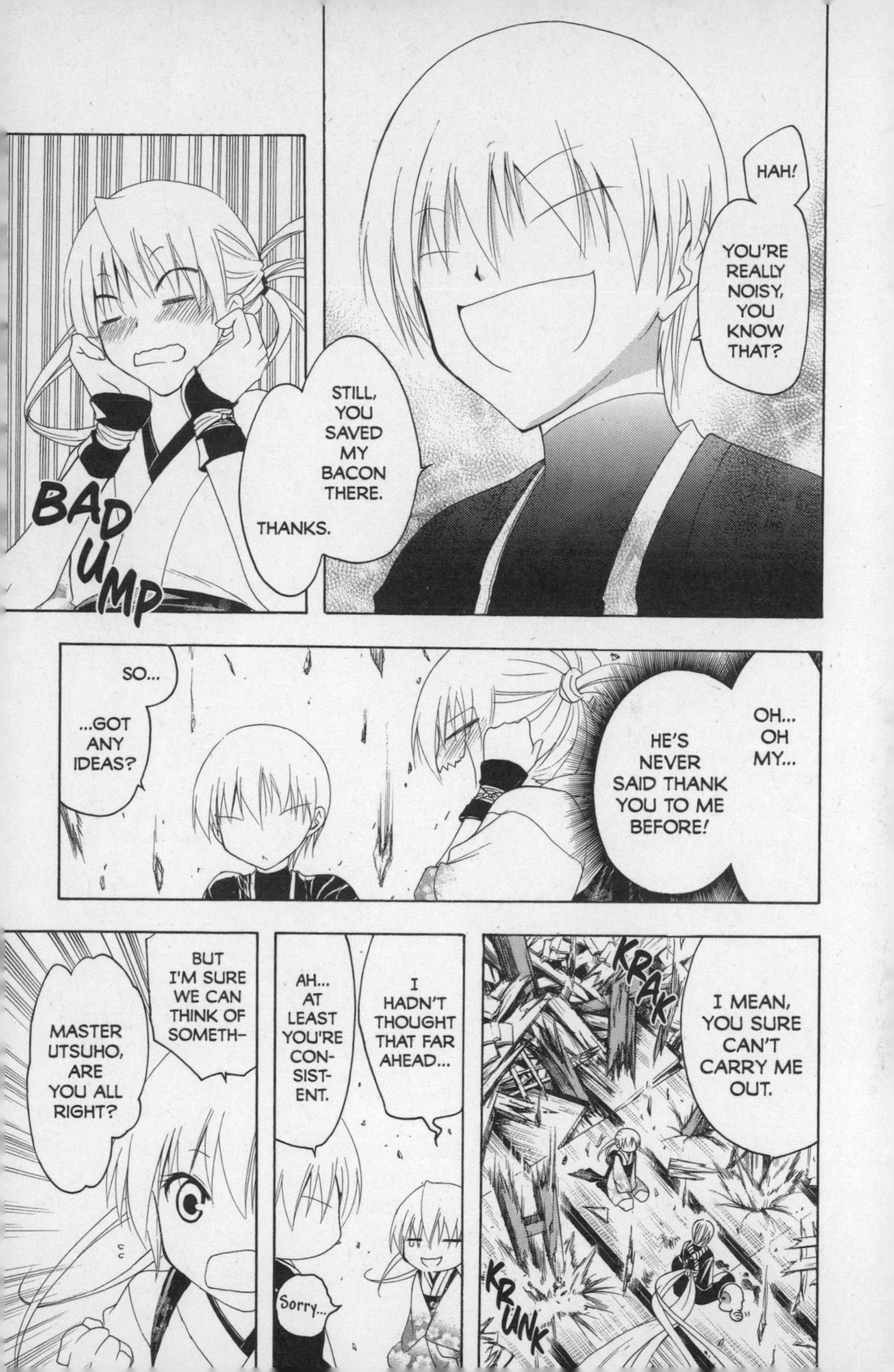
HAH!
YOU'RE REALLY NOISY, YOU KNOW THAT?
STILL, YOU SAVED MY BACON THERE.
THANKS.
BADUMP
OH... OH MY...
HE'S NEVER SAID THANK YOU TO ME BEFORE!
SO...
...GOT ANY IDEAS?
KRAK
I MEAN, YOU SURE CAN'T CARRY ME OUT.
KRUNK
I HADN'T THOUGHT THAT FAR AHEAD...
AH... AT LEAST YOU'RE CON-SIST-ENT.
Sorry...
BUT I'M SURE WE CAN THINK OF SOMETH–
MASTER UTSUHO, ARE YOU ALL RIGHT?

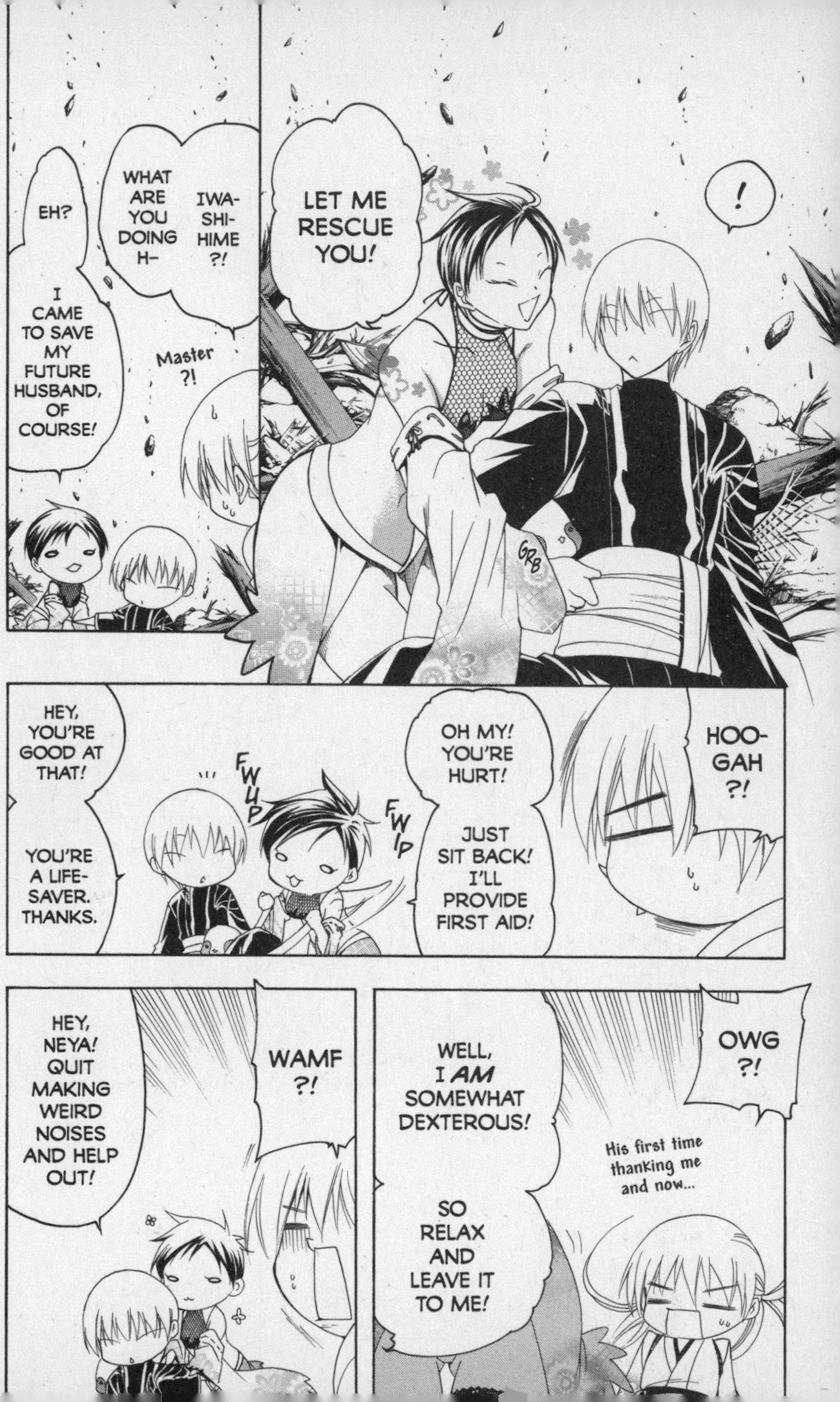
!
LET ME RESCUE YOU!
GRB
WHAT ARE YOU DOING H- IWA-SHI-HIME?!
Master?!
EH?
I CAME TO SAVE MY FUTURE HUSBAND, OF COURSE!
HOO-GAH?!
OH MY! YOU'RE HURT!
JUST SIT BACK! I'LL PROVIDE FIRST AID!
FWIP
FWUP
HEY, YOU'RE GOOD AT THAT!
YOU'RE A LIFE-SAVER. THANKS.
OWG?!
WELL, I *AM* SOMEWHAT DEXTEROUS!
SO RELAX AND LEAVE IT TO ME!
His first time thanking me and now...
WAMF?!
HEY, NEYA! QUIT MAKING WEIRD NOISES AND HELP OUT!

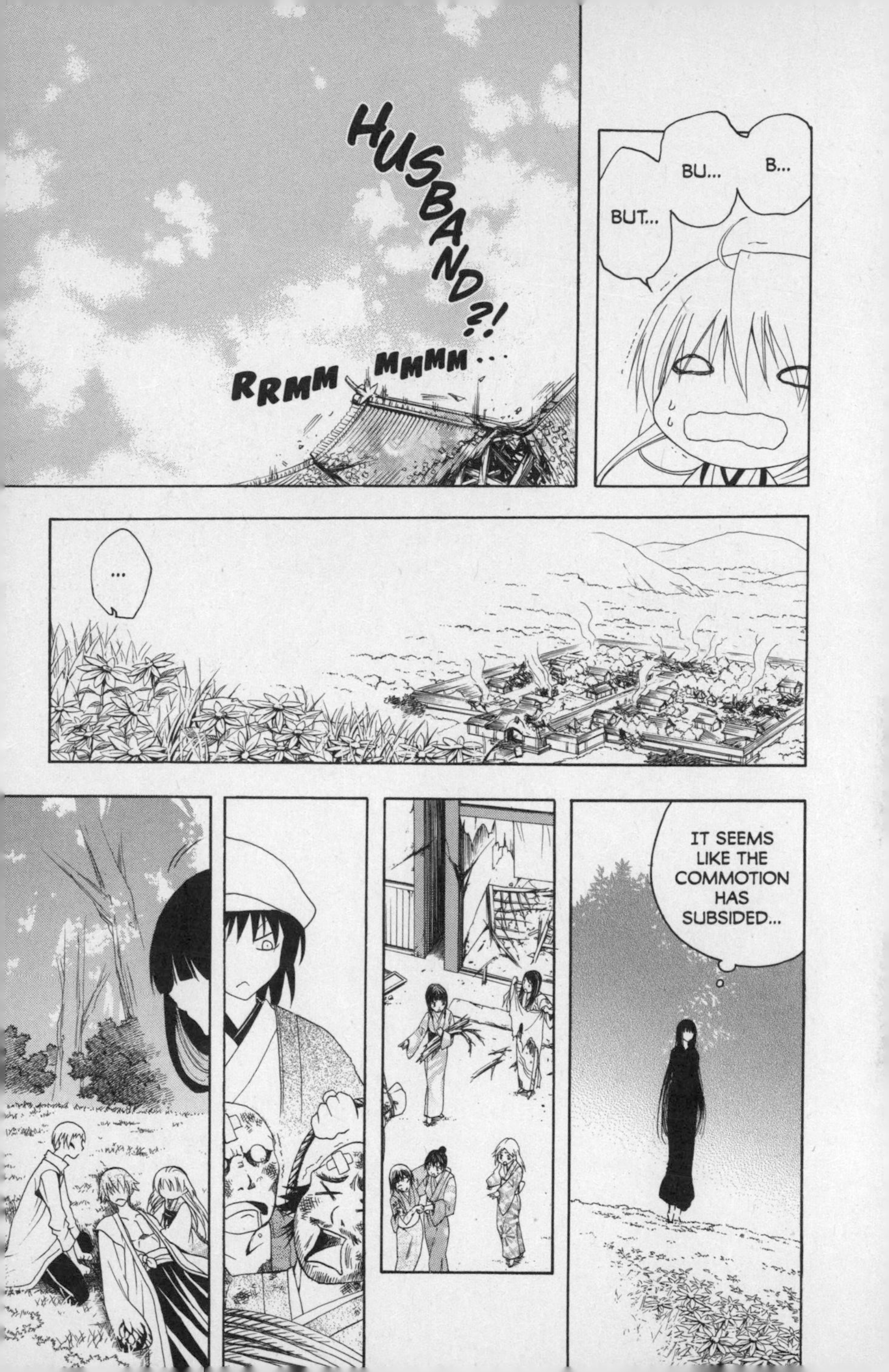
B...
BU...
BUT...
HUSBAND?!
RRMM MMMM...
...
IT SEEMS LIKE THE COMMOTION HAS SUBSIDED...

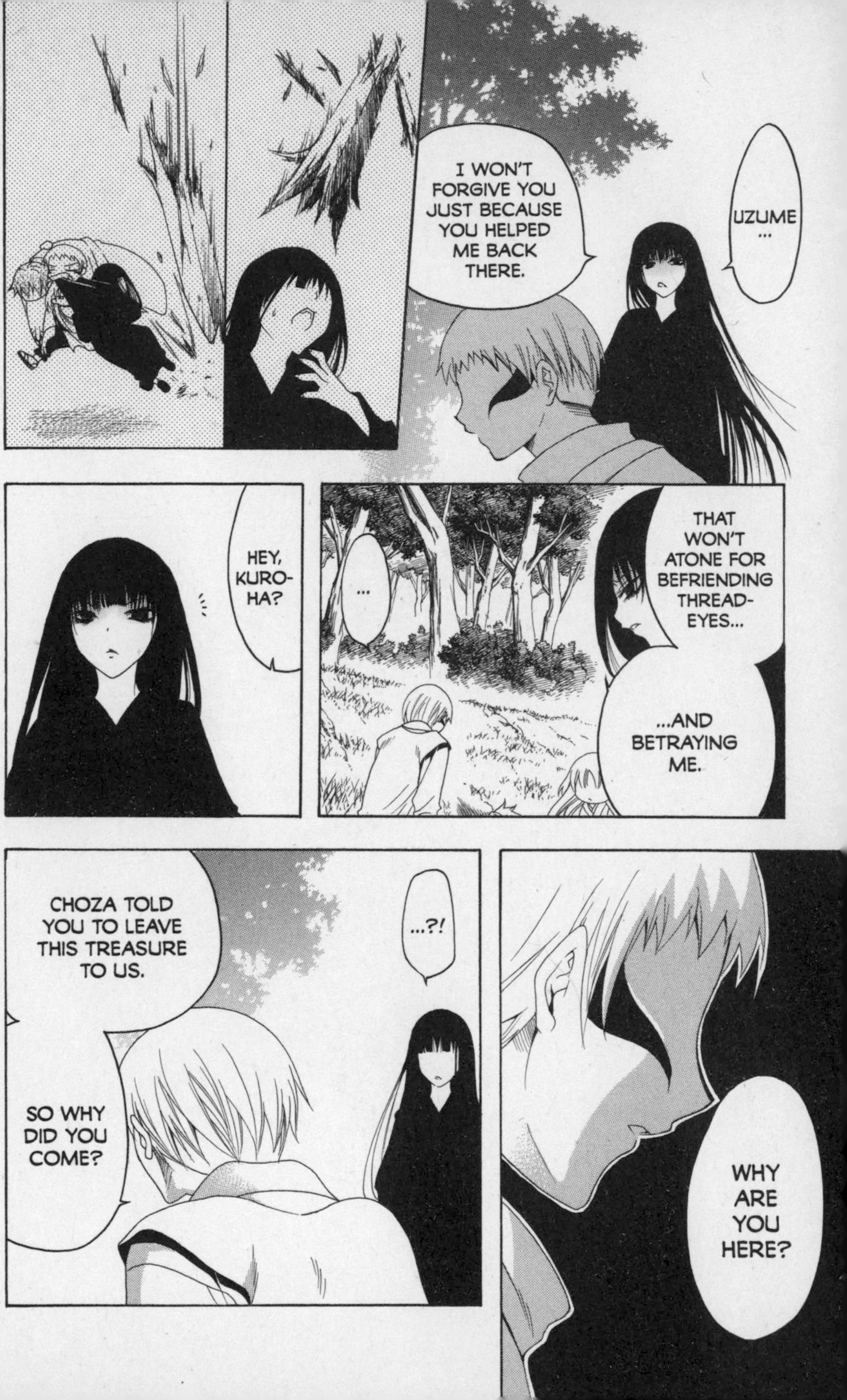
UZUME ...
I WON'T FORGIVE YOU JUST BECAUSE YOU HELPED ME BACK THERE.
THAT WON'T ATONE FOR BEFRIENDING THREAD-EYES...
...AND BETRAYING ME.
...
HEY, KURO-HA?
WHY ARE YOU HERE?
...?!
CHOZA TOLD YOU TO LEAVE THIS TREASURE TO US.
SO WHY DID YOU COME?

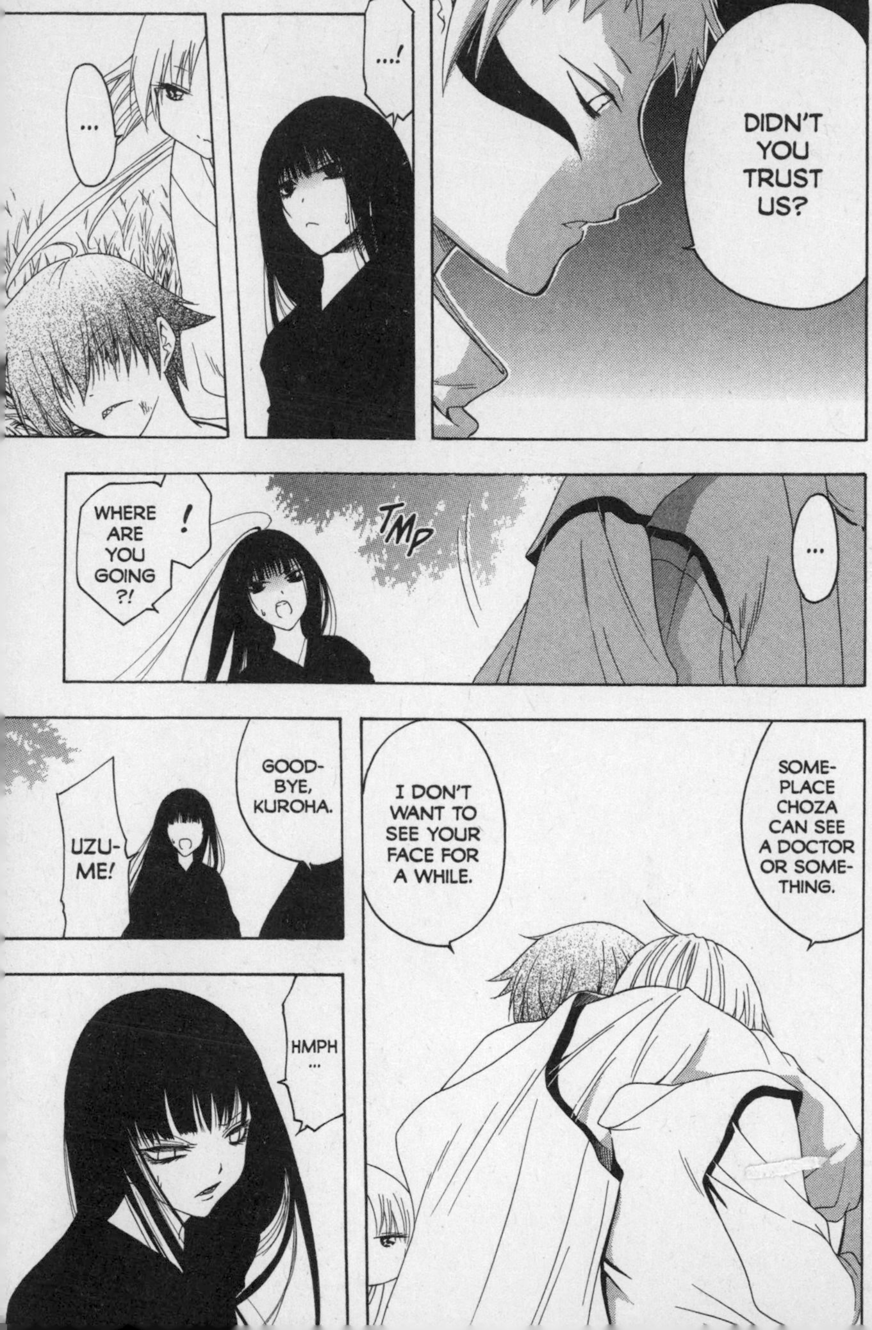
DIDN'T YOU TRUST US?
...!
...
...
TMP
WHERE ARE YOU GOING ?!
SOME-PLACE CHOZA CAN SEE A DOCTOR OR SOME-THING.
I DON'T WANT TO SEE YOUR FACE FOR A WHILE.
GOOD-BYE, KUROHA.
UZU-ME!
HMPH ...

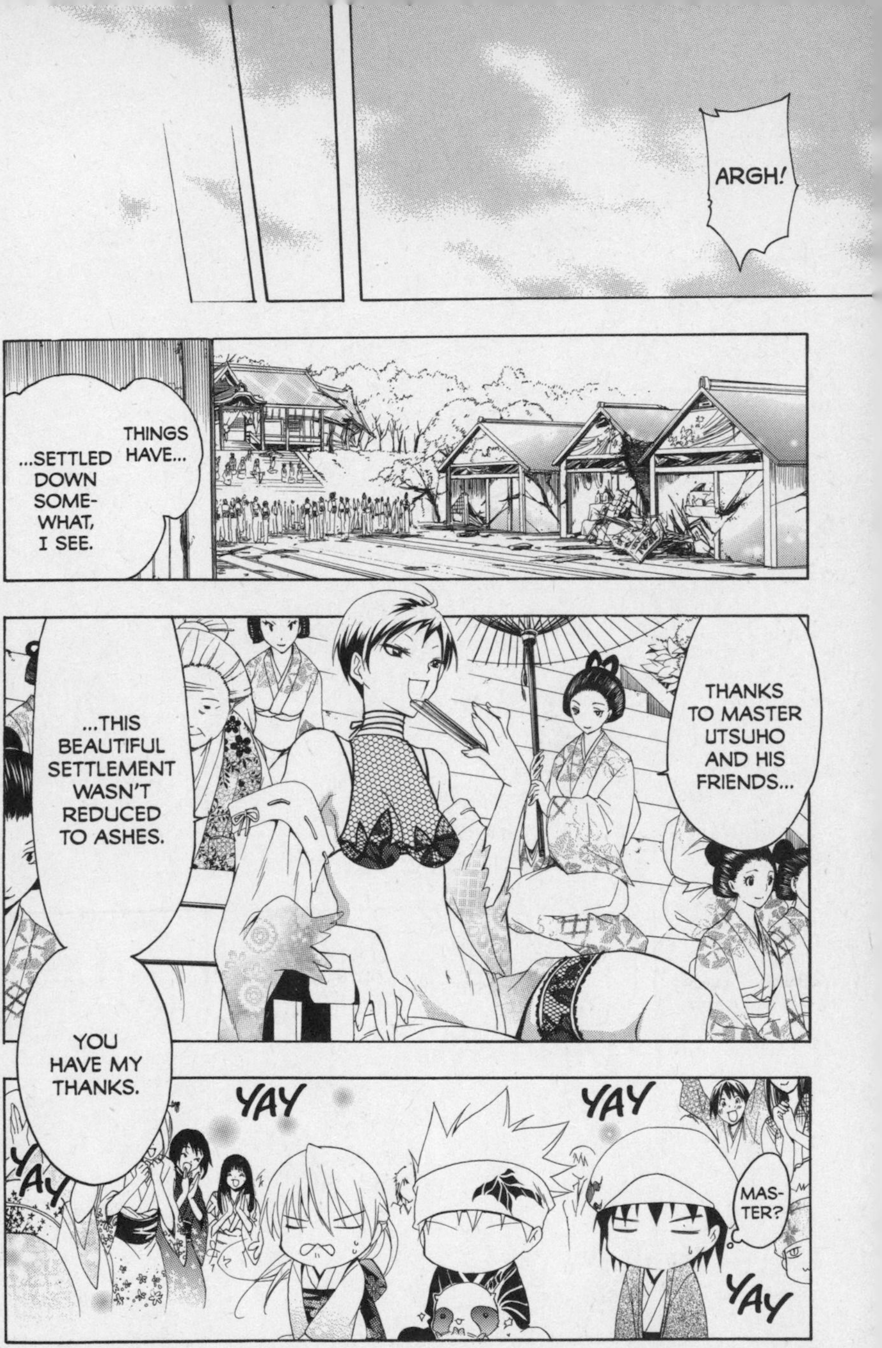
ARGH!
THINGS HAVE...
...SETTLED DOWN SOME-WHAT, I SEE.
THANKS TO MASTER UTSUHO AND HIS FRIENDS...
...THIS BEAUTIFUL SETTLEMENT WASN'T REDUCED TO ASHES.
YOU HAVE MY THANKS.
YAY
YAY
MAS-TER?
YAY
YAY
YAY

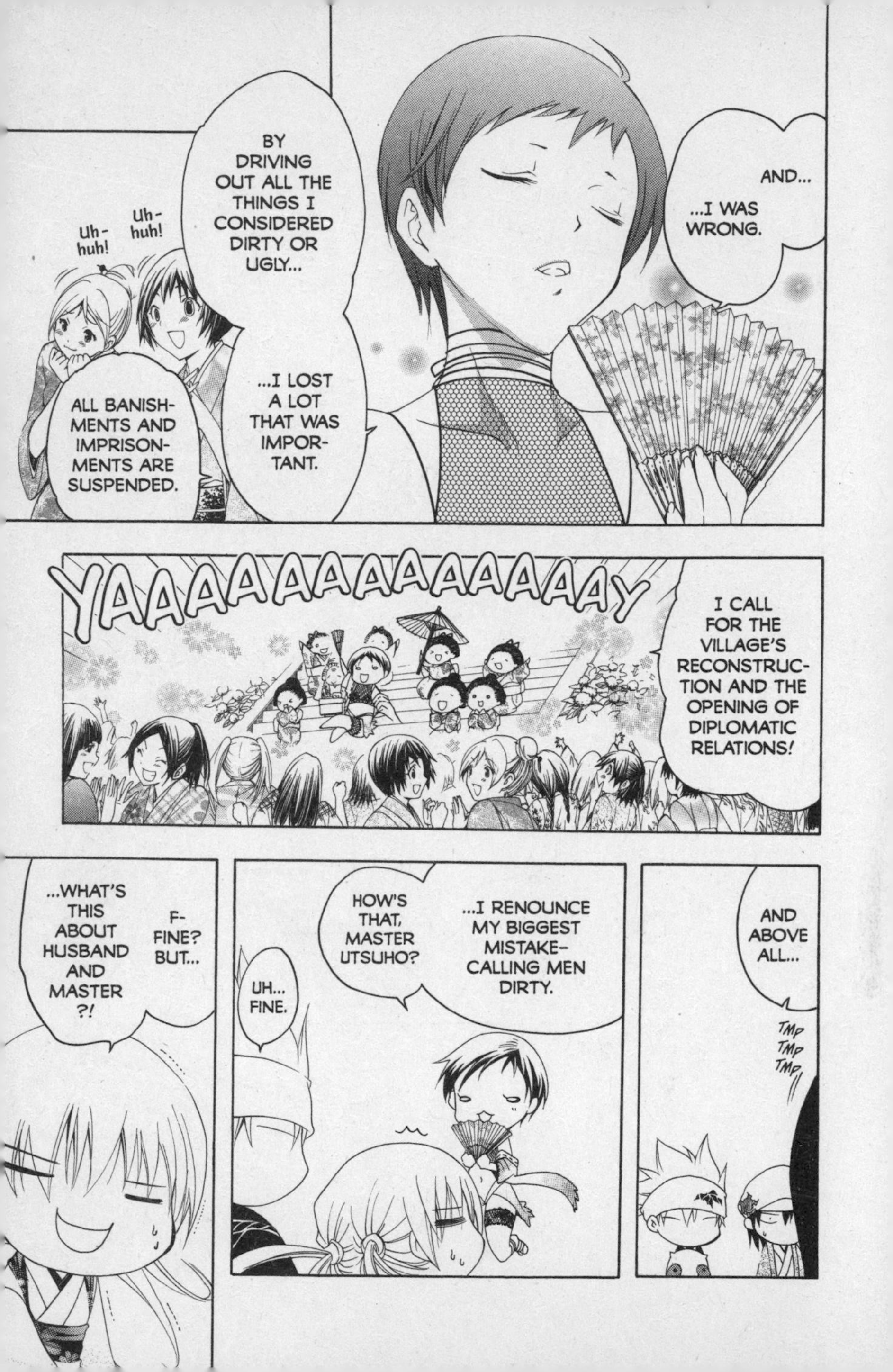
AND...
...I WAS WRONG.
BY DRIVING OUT ALL THE THINGS I CONSIDERED DIRTY OR UGLY...
...I LOST A LOT THAT WAS IMPORTANT.
ALL BANISHMENTS AND IMPRISONMENTS ARE SUSPENDED.
Uh-huh!
Uh-huh!
I CALL FOR THE VILLAGE'S RECONSTRUCTION AND THE OPENING OF DIPLOMATIC RELATIONS!
YAAAAAAAAAAAAY
AND ABOVE ALL...
TMP TMP TMP
...I RENOUNCE MY BIGGEST MISTAKE–CALLING MEN DIRTY.
HOW'S THAT, MASTER UTSUHO?
UH... FINE.
F-FINE? BUT...
...WHAT'S THIS ABOUT HUSBAND AND MASTER?!

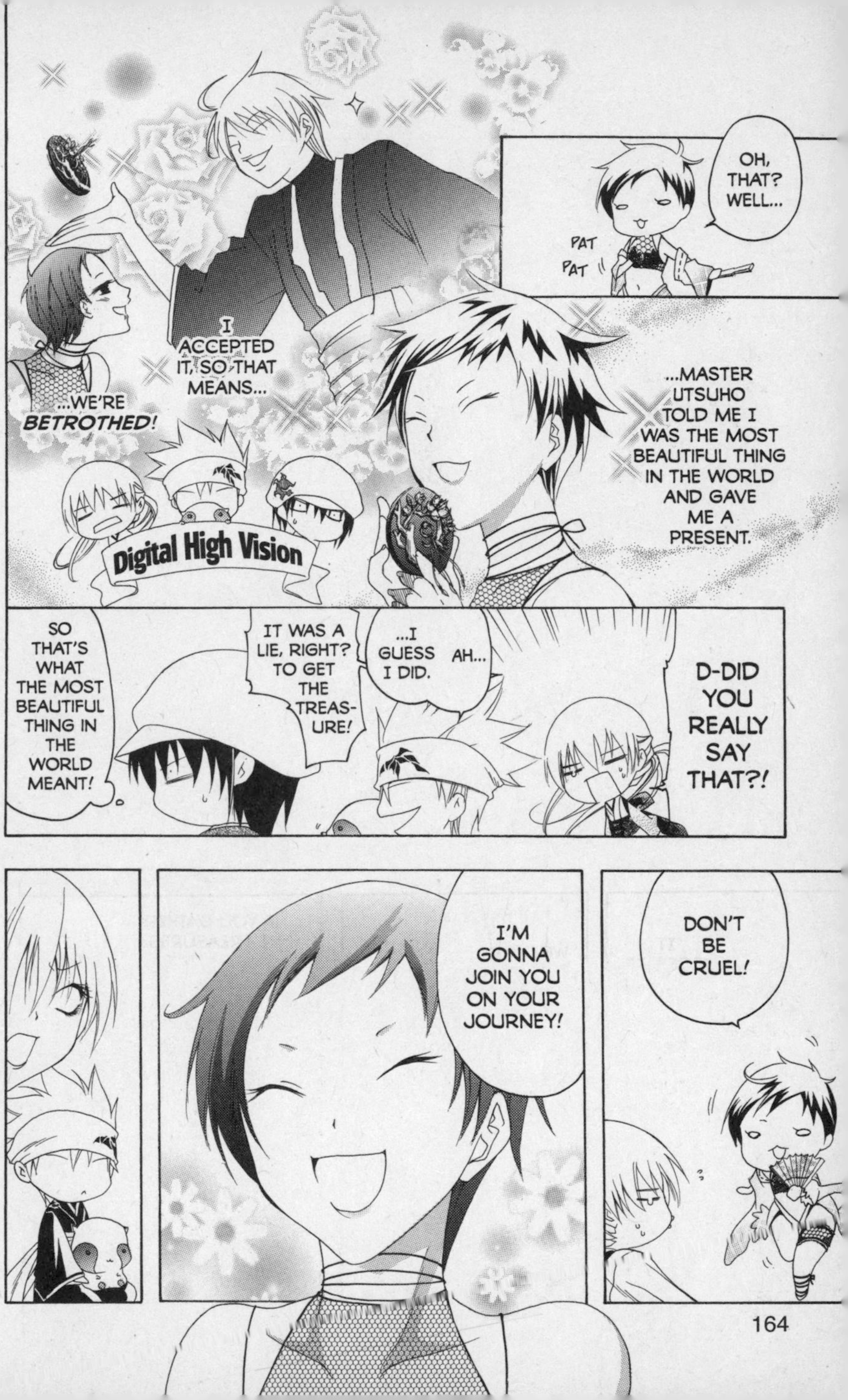
OH, THAT? WELL...
PAT PAT
...MASTER UTSUHO TOLD ME I WAS THE MOST BEAUTIFUL THING IN THE WORLD AND GAVE ME A PRESENT.
I ACCEPTED IT, SO THAT MEANS...
...WE'RE *BETROTHED*!
Digital High Vision
D-DID YOU REALLY SAY THAT?!
AH...
...I GUESS I DID.
IT WAS A LIE, RIGHT? TO GET THE TREASURE!
SO THAT'S WHAT THE MOST BEAUTIFUL THING IN THE WORLD MEANT!
DON'T BE CRUEL!
I'M GONNA JOIN YOU ON YOUR JOURNEY!

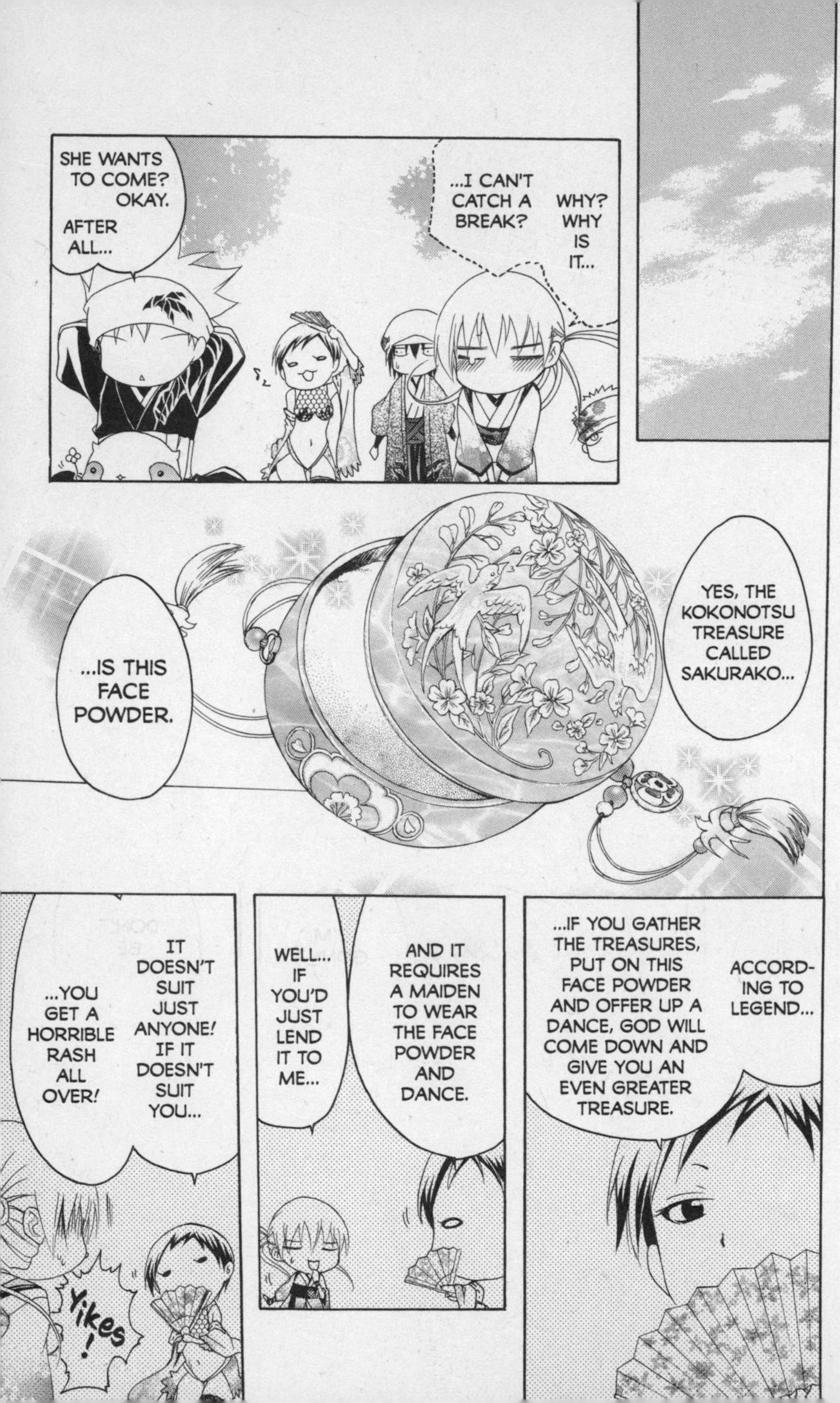
WHY? WHY IS IT...
...I CAN'T CATCH A BREAK?
SHE WANTS TO COME? OKAY. AFTER ALL...
YES, THE KOKONOTSU TREASURE CALLED SAKURAKO...
...IS THIS FACE POWDER.
ACCORD-ING TO LEGEND...
...IF YOU GATHER THE TREASURES, PUT ON THIS FACE POWDER AND OFFER UP A DANCE, GOD WILL COME DOWN AND GIVE YOU AN EVEN GREATER TREASURE.
AND IT REQUIRES A MAIDEN TO WEAR THE FACE POWDER AND DANCE.
WELL... IF YOU'D JUST LEND IT TO ME...
IT DOESN'T SUIT JUST ANYONE! IF IT DOESN'T SUIT YOU...
...YOU GET A HORRIBLE RASH ALL OVER!
Yikes!

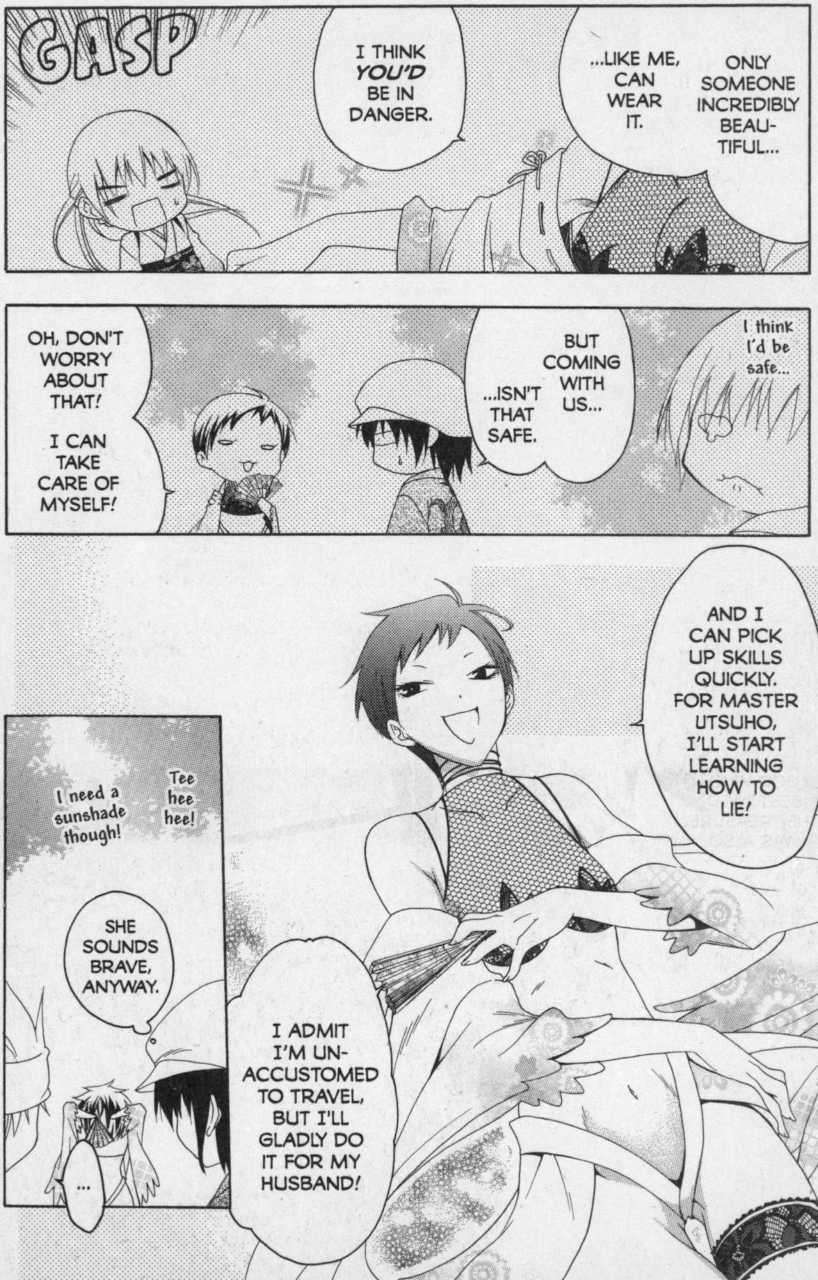
ONLY SOMEONE INCREDIBLY BEAU-TIFUL...
...LIKE ME, CAN WEAR IT.
I THINK *YOU'D* BE IN DANGER.
GASP
I think I'd be safe...
BUT COMING WITH US...
...ISN'T THAT SAFE.
OH, DON'T WORRY ABOUT THAT!
I CAN TAKE CARE OF MYSELF!
AND I CAN PICK UP SKILLS QUICKLY. FOR MASTER UTSUHO, I'LL START LEARNING HOW TO LIE!
I ADMIT I'M UN-ACCUSTOMED TO TRAVEL, BUT I'LL GLADLY DO IT FOR MY HUSBAND!
Tee hee hee!
I need a sunshade though!
SHE SOUNDS BRAVE, ANYWAY.
...

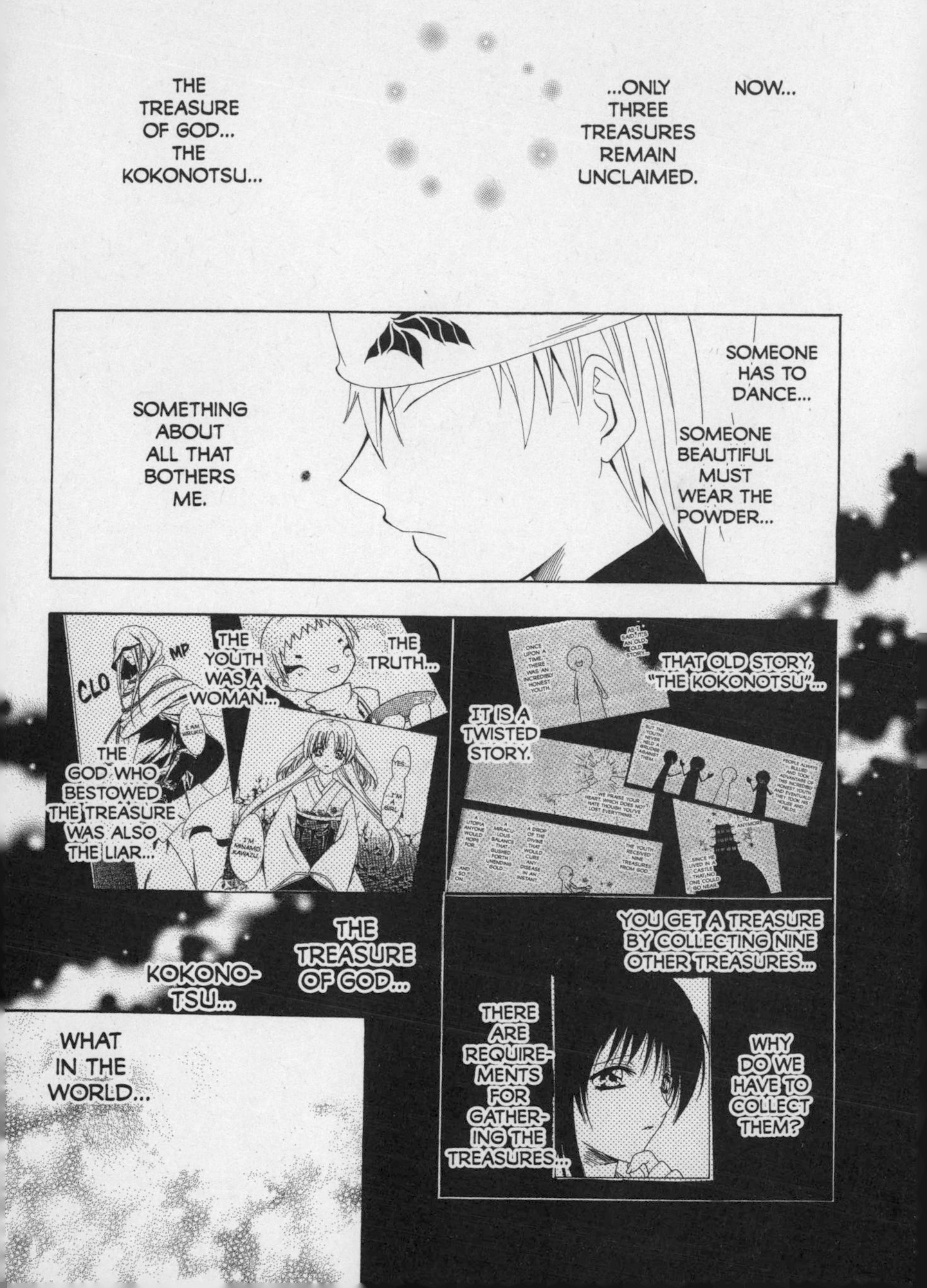
NOW...
...ONLY THREE TREASURES REMAIN UNCLAIMED.
THE TREASURE OF GOD... THE KOKONOTSU...
SOMEONE HAS TO DANCE...
SOMEONE BEAUTIFUL MUST WEAR THE POWDER...
SOMETHING ABOUT ALL THAT BOTHERS ME.
THAT OLD STORY, "THE KOKONOTSU"...
AS I SAID, IT'S AN OLD, OLD STORY...
ONCE UPON A TIME, THERE WAS AN INCREDIBLY HONEST YOUTH.
IT IS A TWISTED STORY.
PEOPLE ALWAYS BULLIED AND TOOK ADVANTAGE OF THIS INCREDIBLY HONEST YOUTH AND EVENTUALLY THEY TOOK HIS HOUSE AND FIELDS.
BUT THE YOUTH NEVER HELD A GRUDGE AGAINST THEM.
...WE PRAISE YOUR HEART, WHICH DOES NOT HATE THOUGH YOU'VE LOST EVERYTHING.
ANYMORE
SINCE HE LIVED IN A CASTLE THAT NO ONE COULD GO NEAR.
THE YOUTH RECEIVED NINE TREASURES FROM GOD.
A DROP OF THE DIVINE THAT WOULD CURE ANY DISEASE IN AN INSTANT.
A MIRACULOUS BALANCE THAT GUSHED FORTH UNENDING GOLD.
A UTOPIA ANYONE WOULD HOPE FOR.
...AND SO ON.
THE TRUTH...
THE YOUTH WAS A WOMAN...
YES...
...I'M A GIRL.
I'M MINAMO KAWAZU.
CLOMP
I AM HIRUKO.
THE GOD WHO BESTOWED THE TREASURE WAS ALSO THE LIAR...
YOU GET A TREASURE BY COLLECTING NINE OTHER TREASURES...
WHY DO WE HAVE TO COLLECT THEM?
THERE ARE REQUIREMENTS FOR GATHERING THE TREASURES...
THE TREASURE OF GOD...
KOKONO-TSU...
WHAT IN THE WORLD...

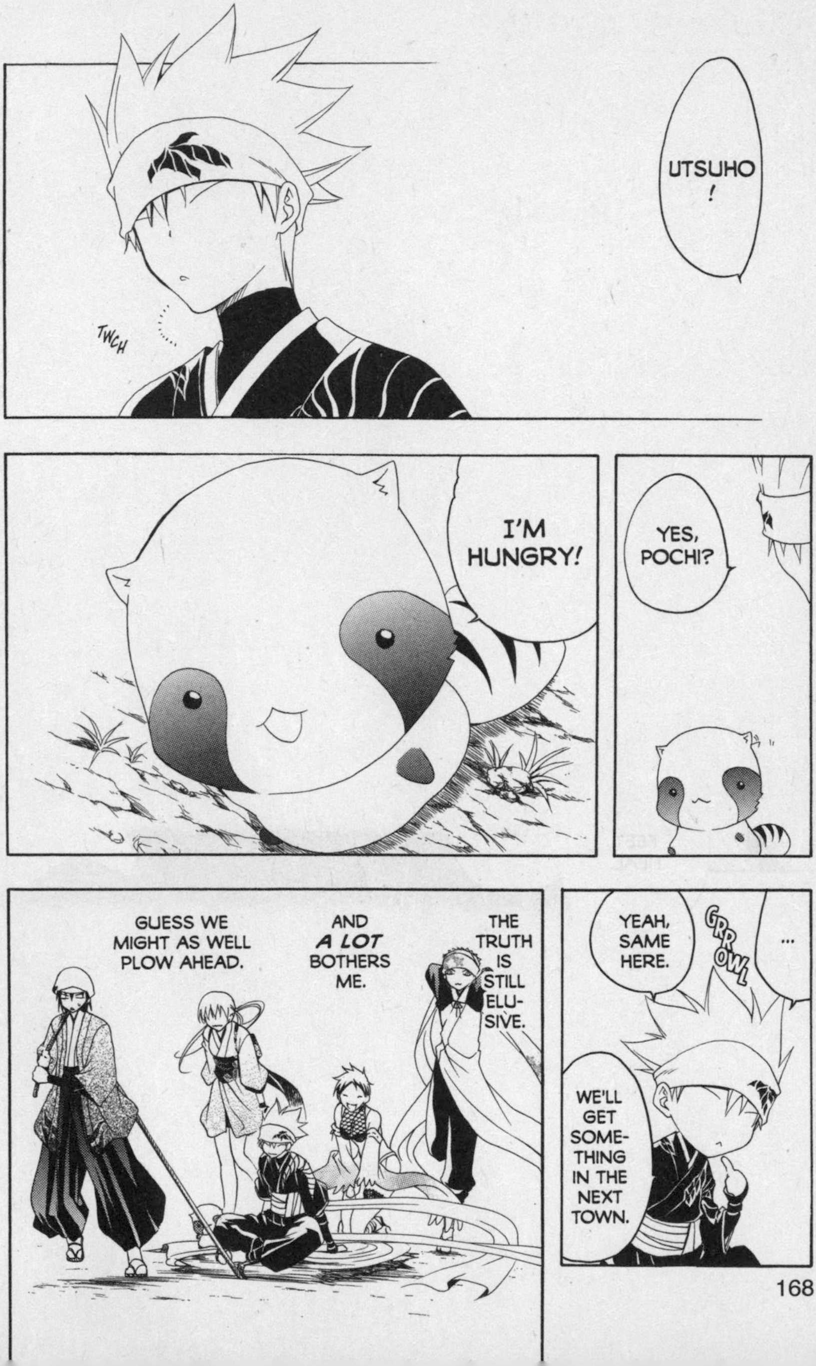
UTSUHO!
TWCH
YES, POCHI?
I'M HUNGRY!
...
GRROWL
YEAH, SAME HERE.
WE'LL GET SOMETHING IN THE NEXT TOWN.
THE TRUTH IS STILL ELUSIVE.
AND *A LOT* BOTHERS ME.
GUESS WE MIGHT AS WELL PLOW AHEAD.

Chapter 87 Sasaka

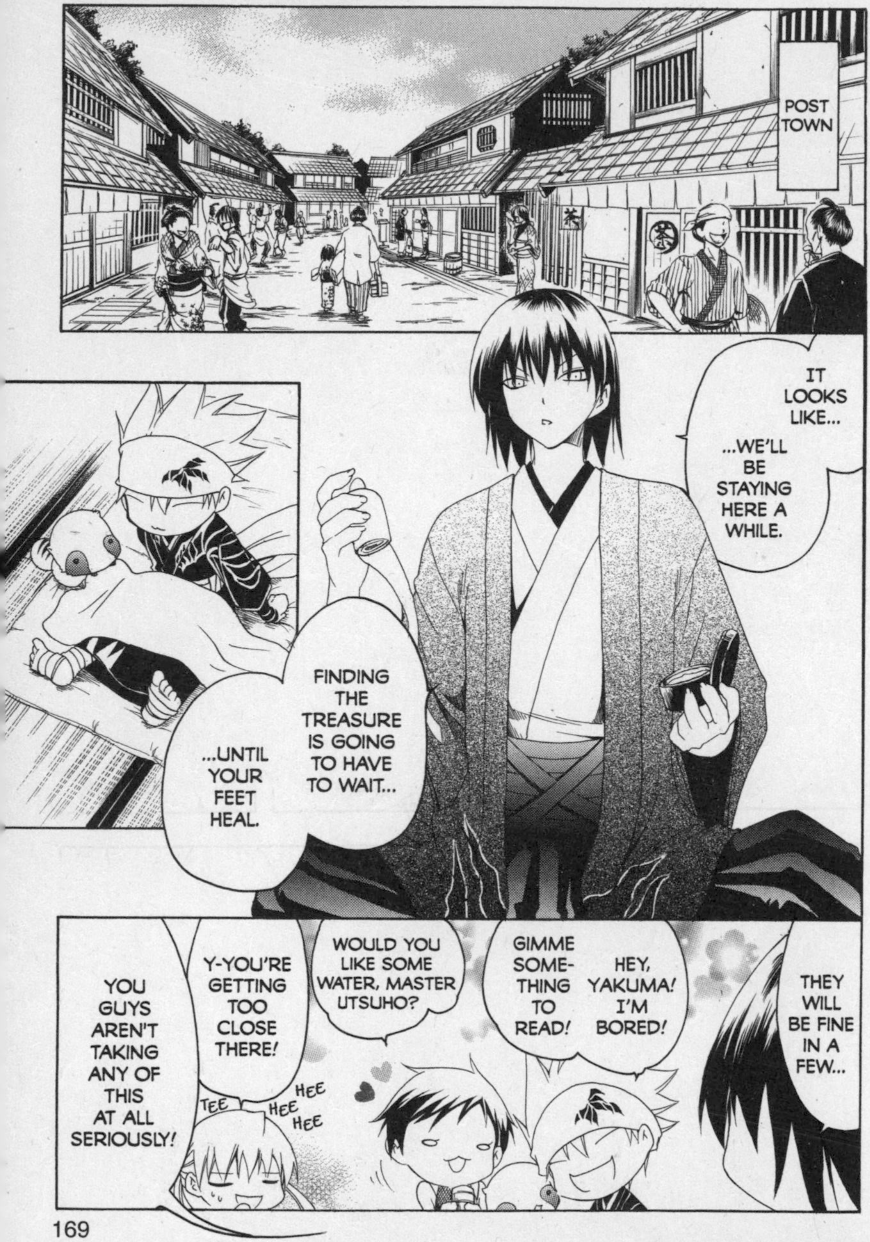
POST TOWN
IT LOOKS LIKE...
...WE'LL BE STAYING HERE A WHILE.
FINDING THE TREASURE IS GOING TO HAVE TO WAIT...
...UNTIL YOUR FEET HEAL.
THEY WILL BE FINE IN A FEW...
HEY, YAKUMA! I'M BORED!
GIMME SOME-THING TO READ!
WOULD YOU LIKE SOME WATER, MASTER UTSUHO?
Y-YOU'RE GETTING TOO CLOSE THERE!
HEE HEE HEE
TEE HEE
YOU GUYS AREN'T TAKING ANY OF THIS AT ALL SERIOUSLY!

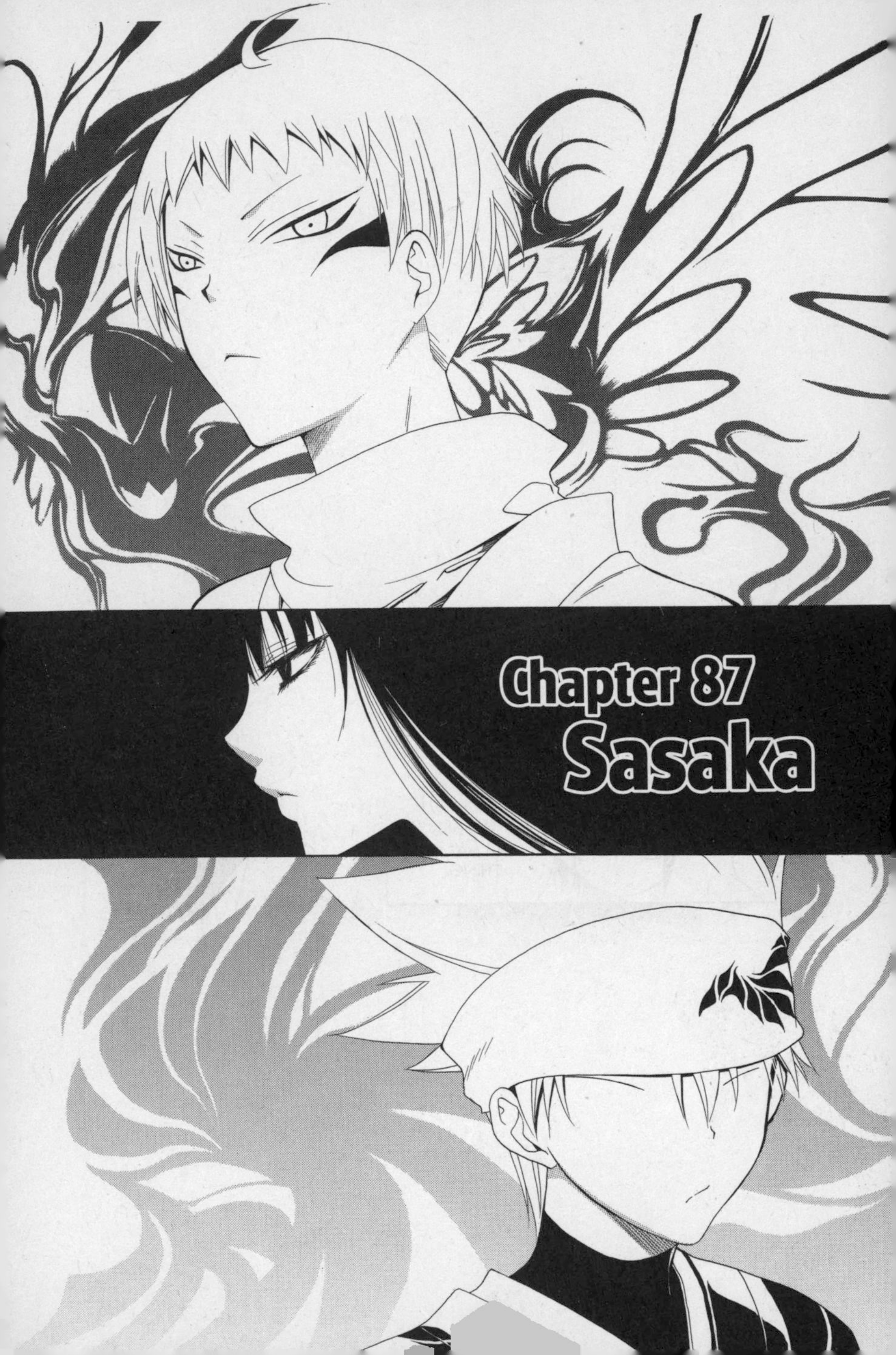
Chapter 87
Sasaka

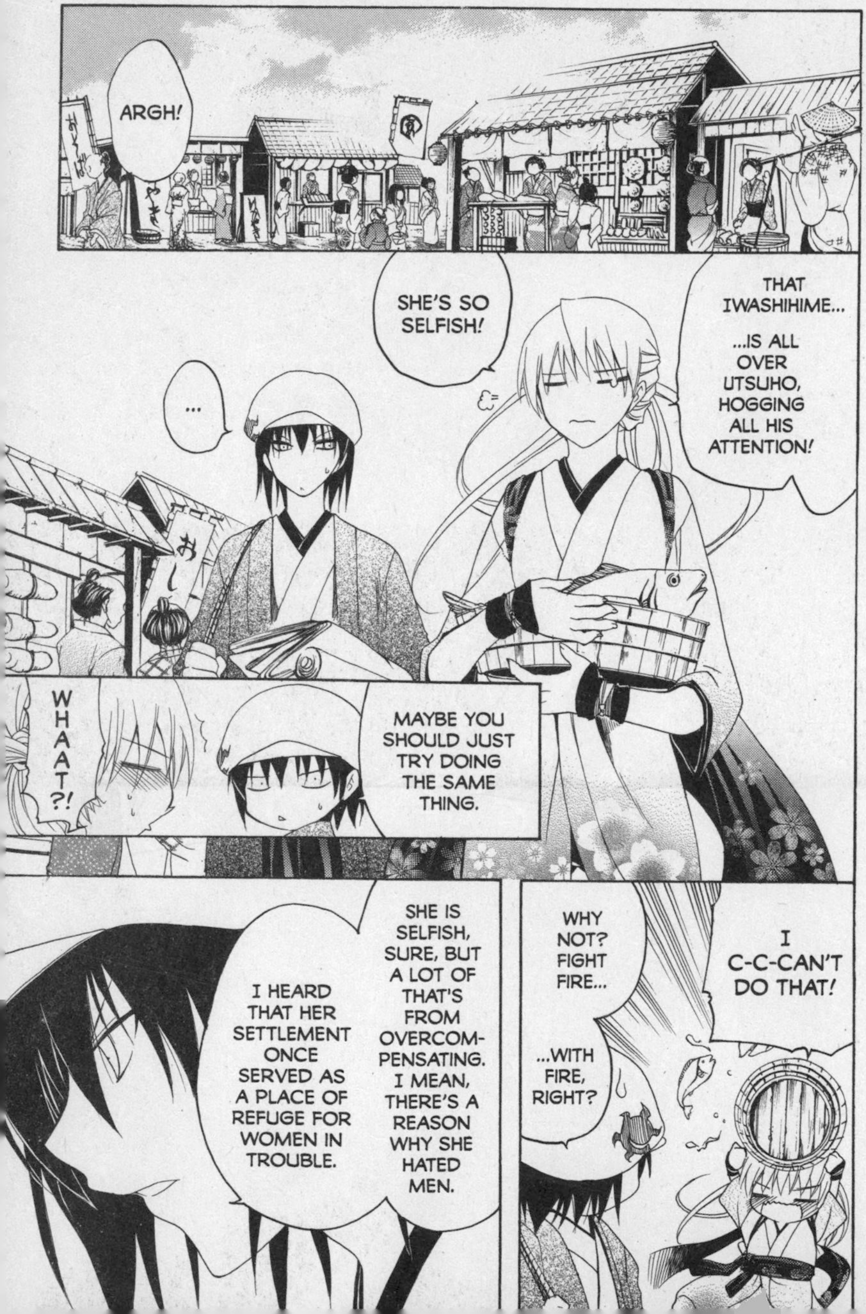
ARGH!
THAT IWASHIHIME... ...IS ALL OVER UTSUHO, HOGGING ALL HIS ATTENTION!
SHE'S SO SELFISH!
...
MAYBE YOU SHOULD JUST TRY DOING THE SAME THING.
WHAAT?!
I C-C-CAN'T DO THAT!
WHY NOT? FIGHT FIRE...
...WITH FIRE, RIGHT?
SHE IS SELFISH, SURE, BUT A LOT OF THAT'S FROM OVERCOMPENSATING. I MEAN, THERE'S A REASON WHY SHE HATED MEN.
I HEARD THAT HER SETTLEMENT ONCE SERVED AS A PLACE OF REFUGE FOR WOMEN IN TROUBLE.

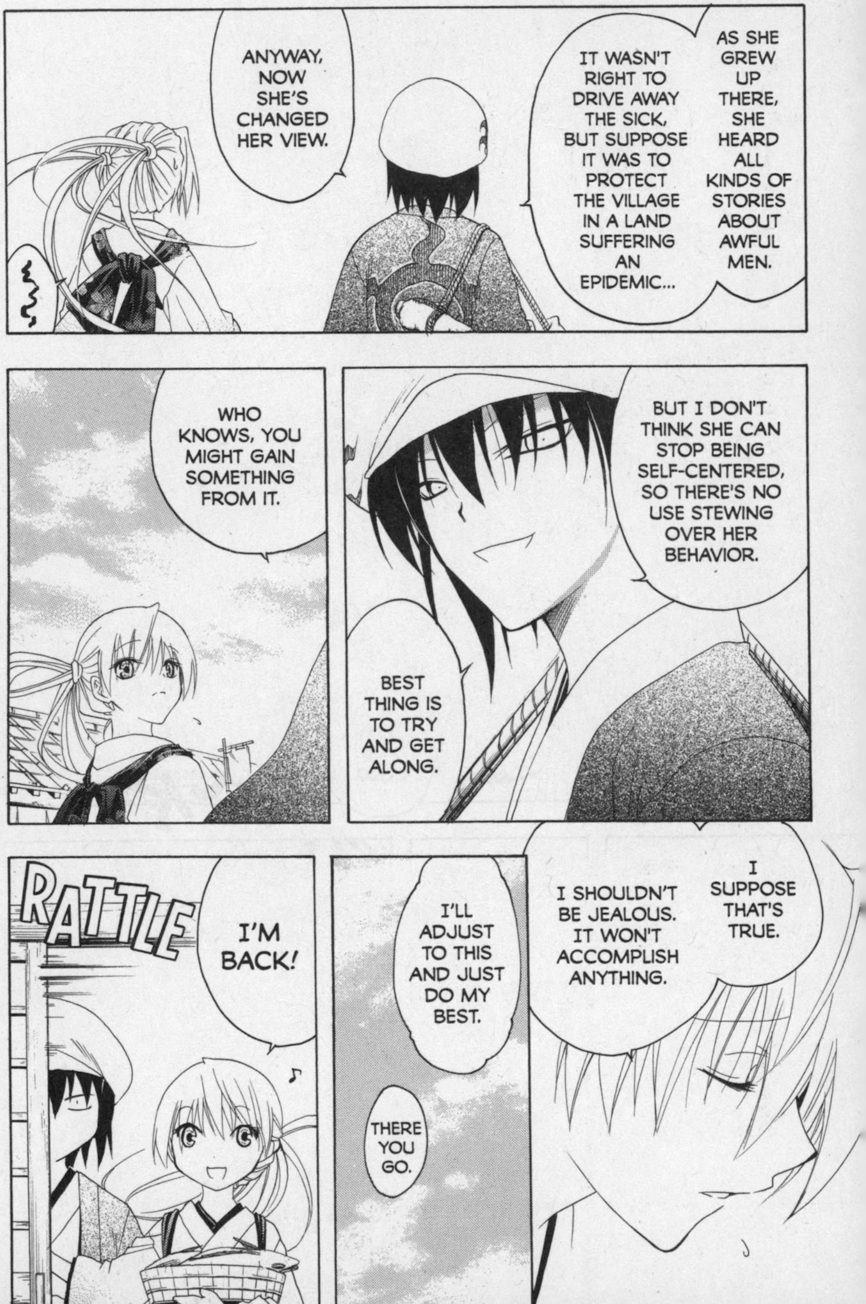
AS SHE GREW UP THERE, SHE HEARD ALL KINDS OF STORIES ABOUT AWFUL MEN.
IT WASN'T RIGHT TO DRIVE AWAY THE SICK, BUT SUPPOSE IT WAS TO PROTECT THE VILLAGE IN A LAND SUFFERING AN EPIDEMIC...
ANYWAY, NOW SHE'S CHANGED HER VIEW.
BUT I DON'T THINK SHE CAN STOP BEING SELF-CENTERED, SO THERE'S NO USE STEWING OVER HER BEHAVIOR.
BEST THING IS TO TRY AND GET ALONG.
WHO KNOWS, YOU MIGHT GAIN SOMETHING FROM IT.
I SUPPOSE THAT'S TRUE.
I SHOULDN'T BE JEALOUS. IT WON'T ACCOMPLISH ANYTHING.
I'LL ADJUST TO THIS AND JUST DO MY BEST.
THERE YOU GO.
I'M BACK!
RATTLE

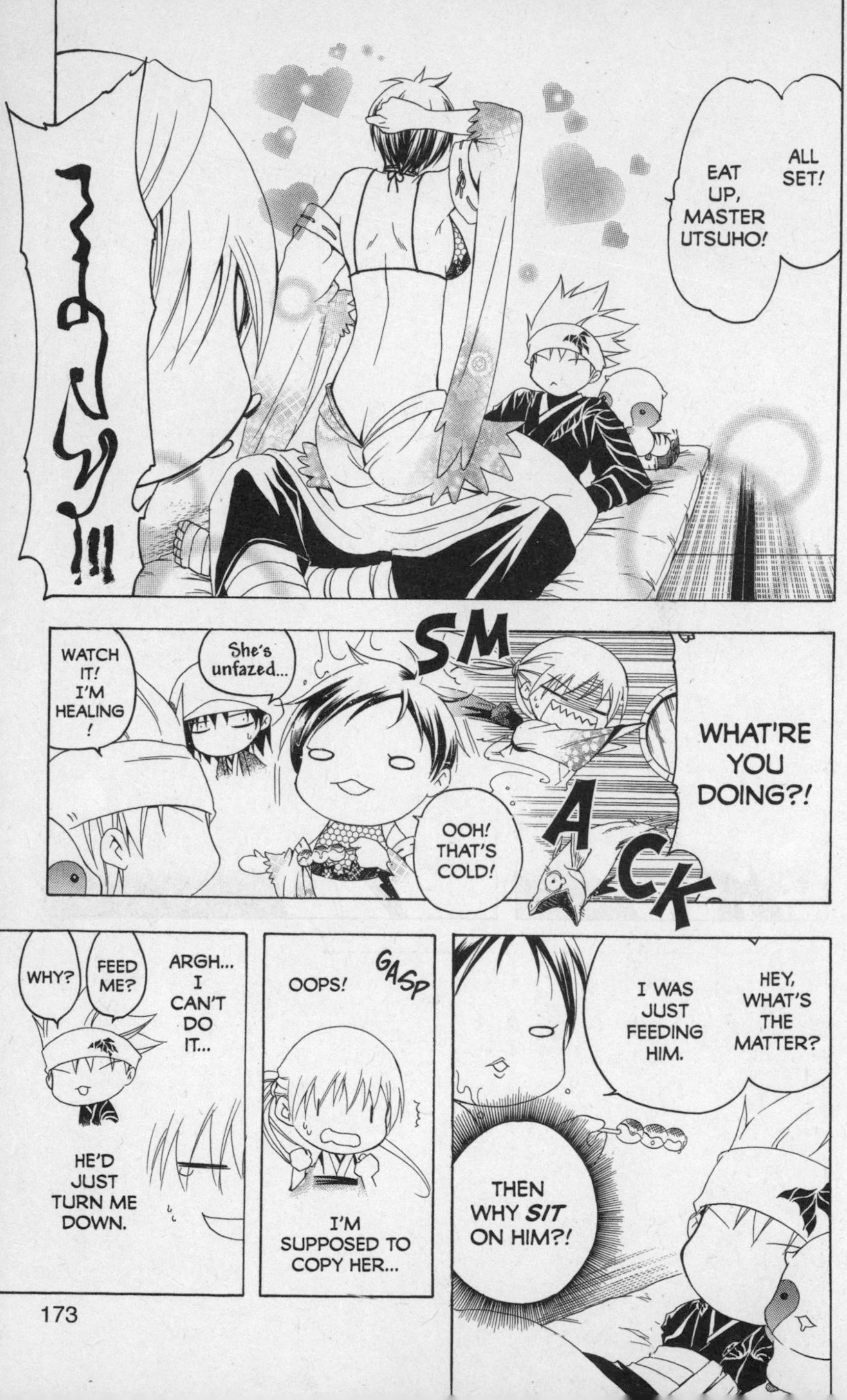
ALL SET!
EAT UP, MASTER UTSUHO!
WHAT'RE YOU DOING?!
SMACK
OOH! THAT'S COLD!
She's unfazed...
WATCH IT! I'M HEALING!
HEY, WHAT'S THE MATTER?
I WAS JUST FEEDING HIM.
THEN WHY SIT ON HIM?!
GASP
OOPS!
I'M SUPPOSED TO COPY HER...
ARGH... I CAN'T DO IT...
FEED ME?
WHY?
HE'D JUST TURN ME DOWN.

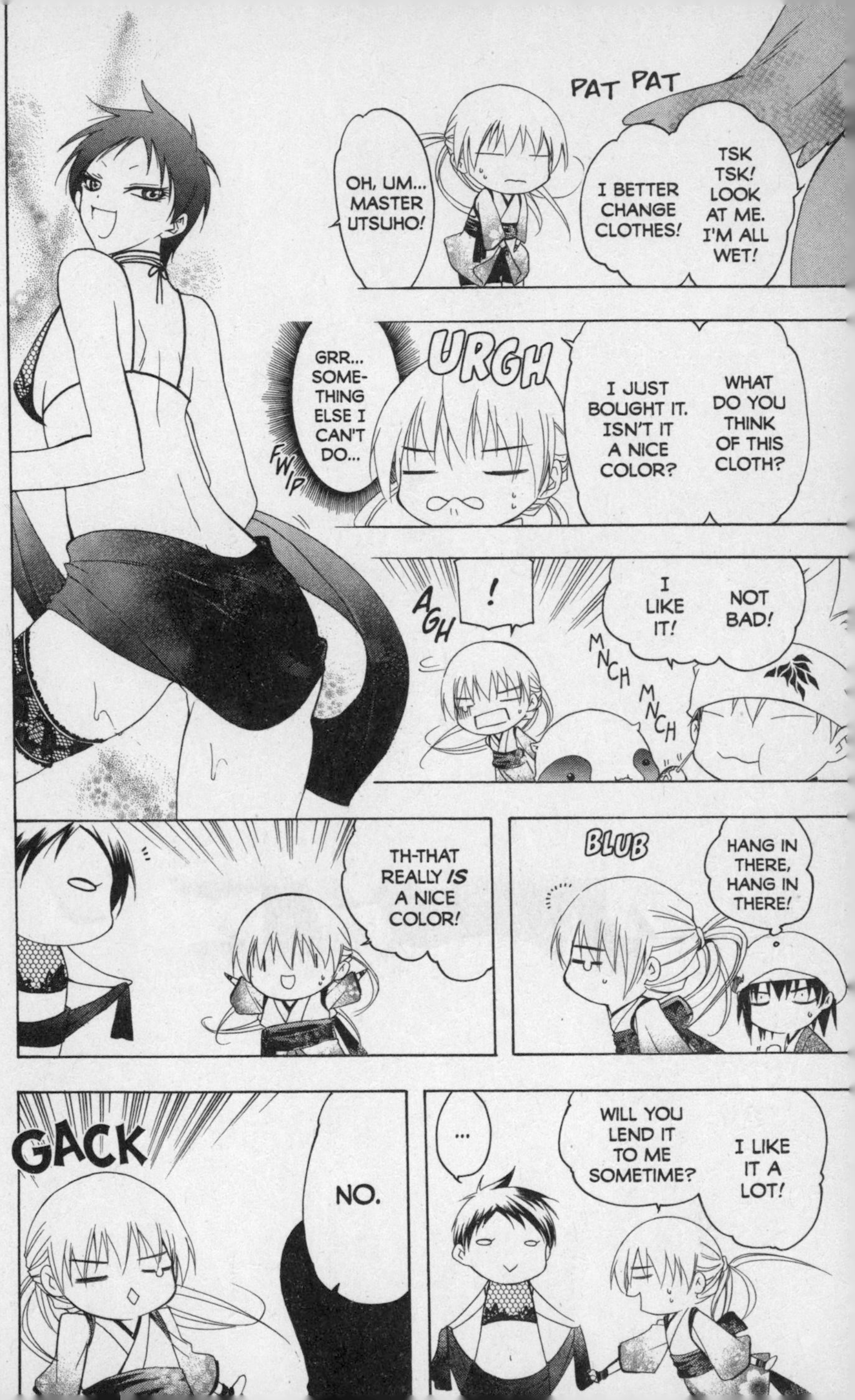
PAT PAT
TSK TSK! LOOK AT ME. I'M ALL WET!
I BETTER CHANGE CLOTHES!
OH, UM... MASTER UTSUHO!
WHAT DO YOU THINK OF THIS CLOTH?
I JUST BOUGHT IT. ISN'T IT A NICE COLOR?
URGH
GRR... SOME-THING ELSE I CAN'T DO...
NOT BAD!
I LIKE IT!
MNCH MNCH
!
AGH
FWIP
HANG IN THERE, HANG IN THERE!
BLUB
TH-THAT REALLY *IS* A NICE COLOR!
I LIKE IT A LOT!
WILL YOU LEND IT TO ME SOMETIME?
...
NO.
GACK

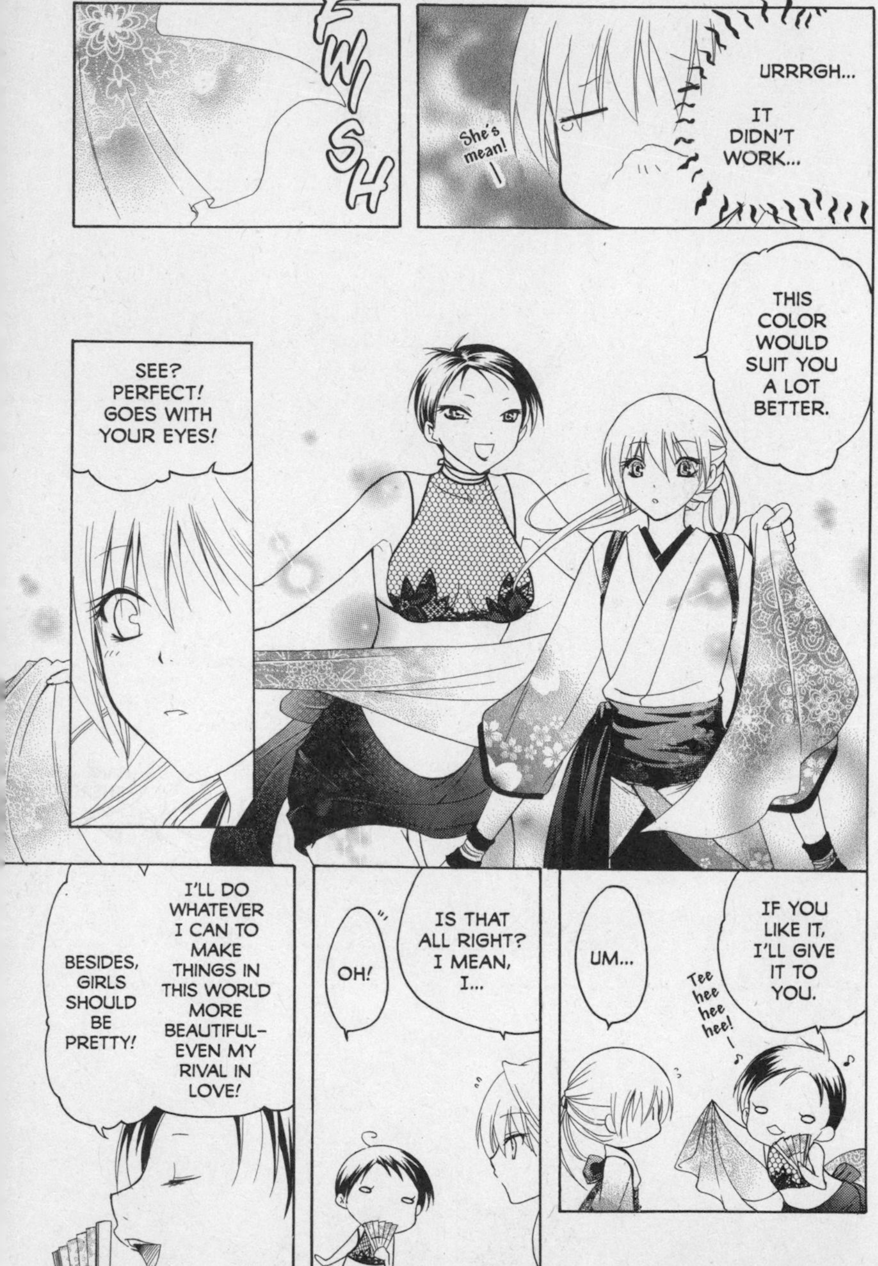
URRRGH...
IT DIDN'T WORK...
She's mean!
FWISH
THIS COLOR WOULD SUIT YOU A LOT BETTER.
SEE? PERFECT! GOES WITH YOUR EYES!
IF YOU LIKE IT, I'LL GIVE IT TO YOU.
Tee hee hee hee!
UM...
IS THAT ALL RIGHT? I MEAN, I...
OH!
I'LL DO WHATEVER I CAN TO MAKE THINGS IN THIS WORLD MORE BEAUTIFUL- EVEN MY RIVAL IN LOVE!
BESIDES, GIRLS SHOULD BE PRETTY!

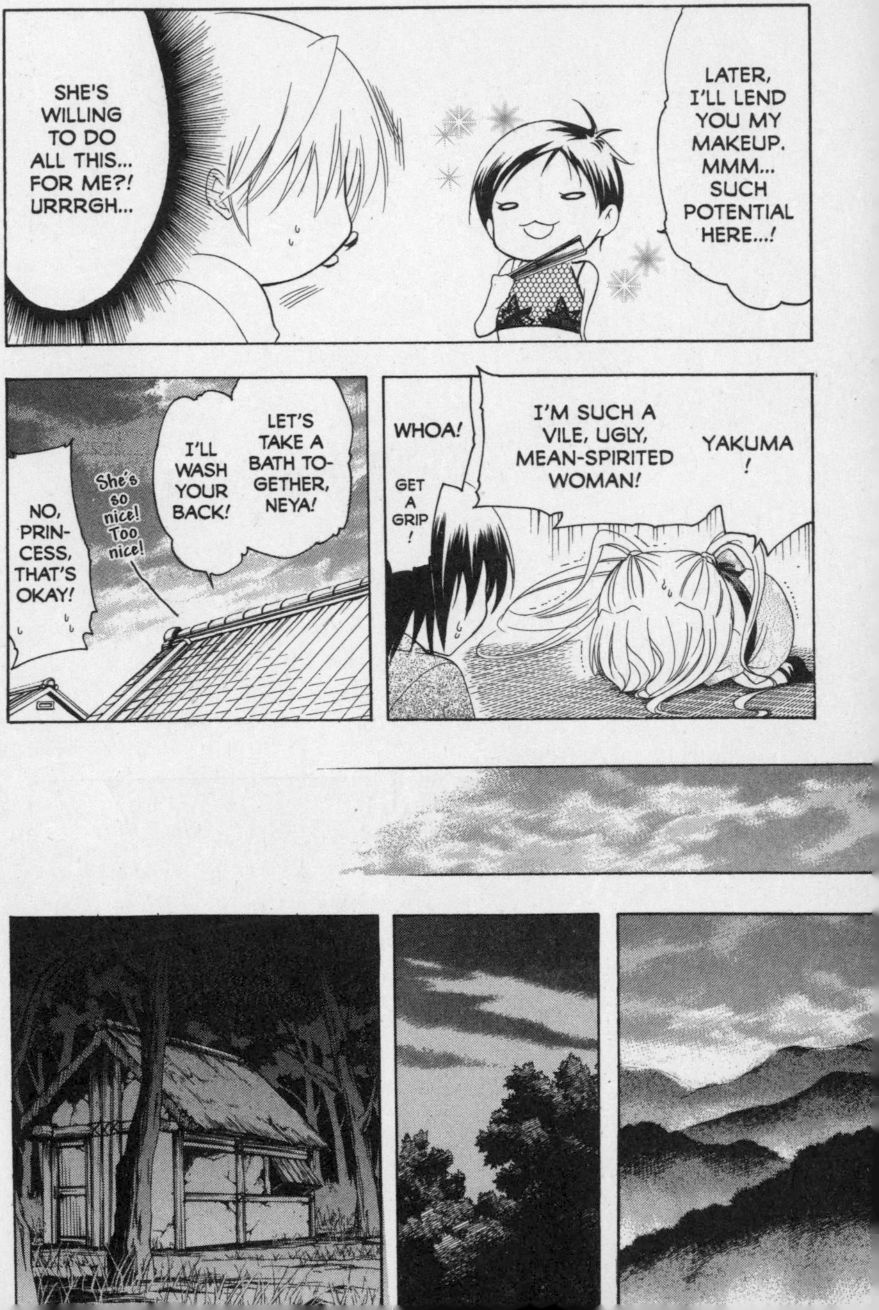
LATER, I'LL LEND YOU MY MAKEUP. MMM... SUCH POTENTIAL HERE...!
SHE'S WILLING TO DO ALL THIS... FOR ME?! URRRGH...
YAKUMA!
I'M SUCH A VILE, UGLY, MEAN-SPIRITED WOMAN!
WHOA!
GET A GRIP!
LET'S TAKE A BATH TOGETHER, NEYA!
I'LL WASH YOUR BACK!
She's so nice! Too nice!
NO, PRINCESS, THAT'S OKAY!

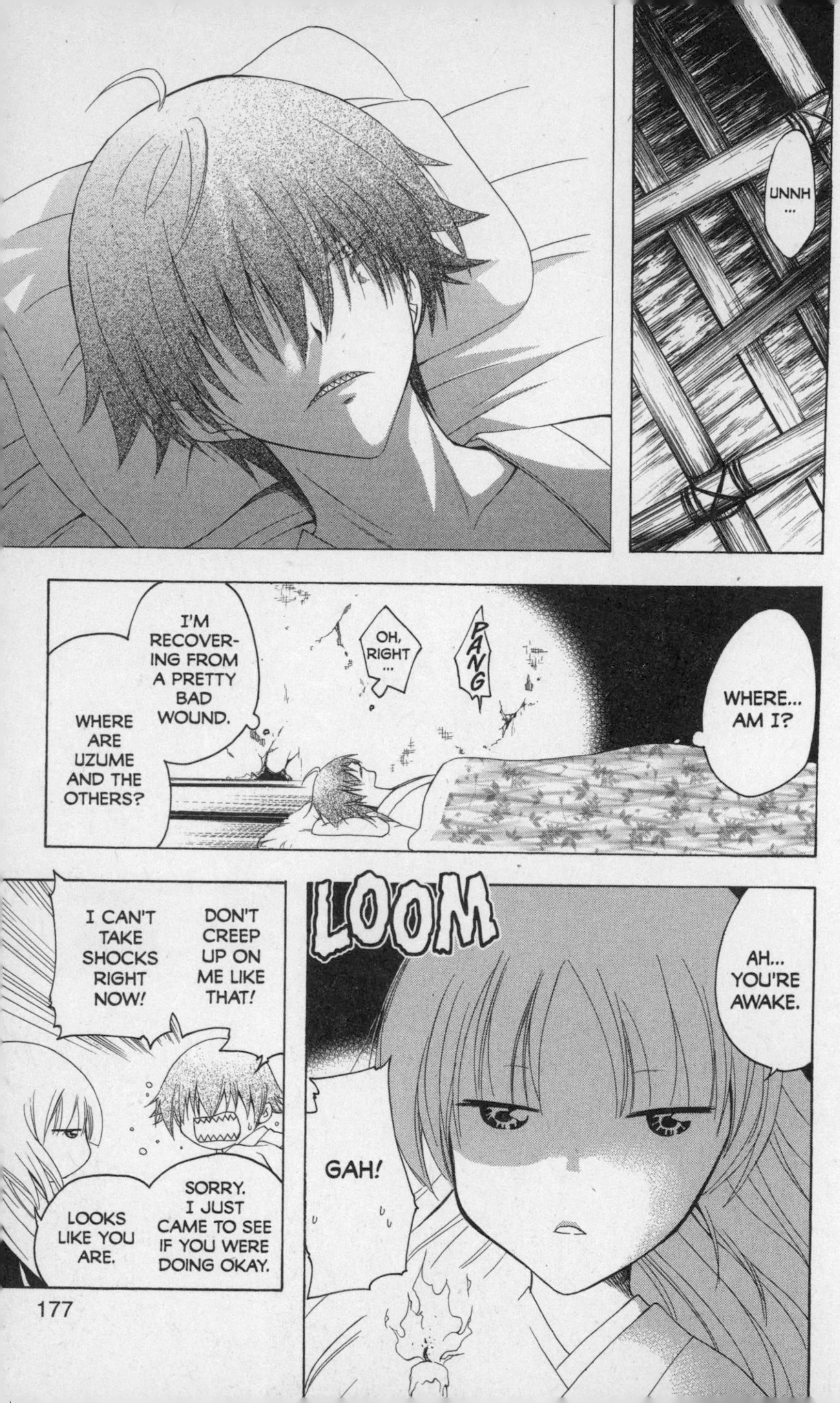
UNNH...
WHERE... AM I?
PANG
OH, RIGHT...
I'M RECOVERING FROM A PRETTY BAD WOUND.
WHERE ARE UZUME AND THE OTHERS?
LOOM
AH... YOU'RE AWAKE.
GAH!
DON'T CREEP UP ON ME LIKE THAT!
I CAN'T TAKE SHOCKS RIGHT NOW!
SORRY. I JUST CAME TO SEE IF YOU WERE DOING OKAY.
LOOKS LIKE YOU ARE.

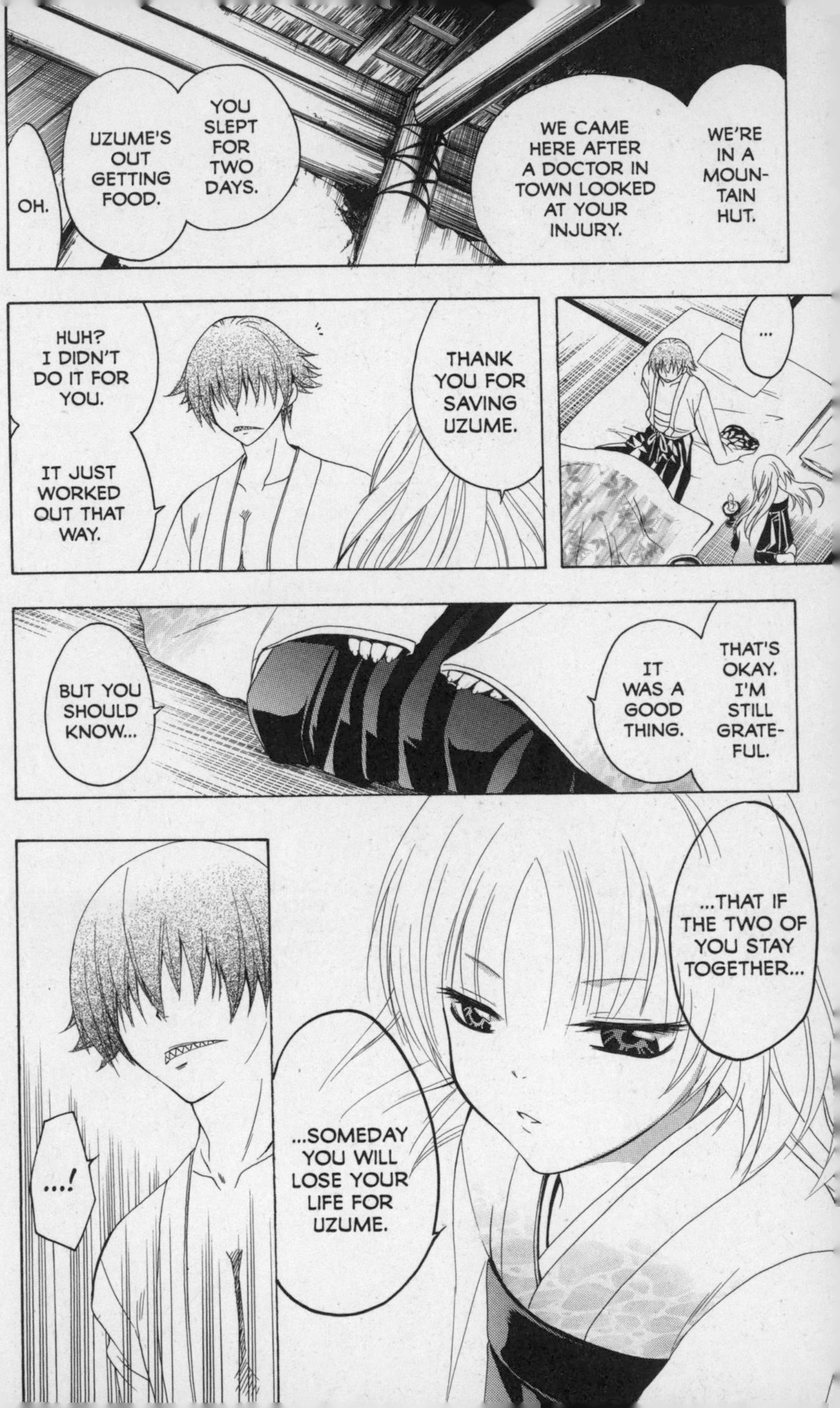
WE'RE IN A MOUNTAIN HUT.
WE CAME HERE AFTER A DOCTOR IN TOWN LOOKED AT YOUR INJURY.
YOU SLEPT FOR TWO DAYS.
UZUME'S OUT GETTING FOOD.
OH.
...
THANK YOU FOR SAVING UZUME.
HUH? I DIDN'T DO IT FOR YOU.
IT JUST WORKED OUT THAT WAY.
THAT'S OKAY. I'M STILL GRATEFUL.
IT WAS A GOOD THING.
BUT YOU SHOULD KNOW...
...THAT IF THE TWO OF YOU STAY TOGETHER...
...SOMEDAY YOU WILL LOSE YOUR LIFE FOR UZUME.
...!

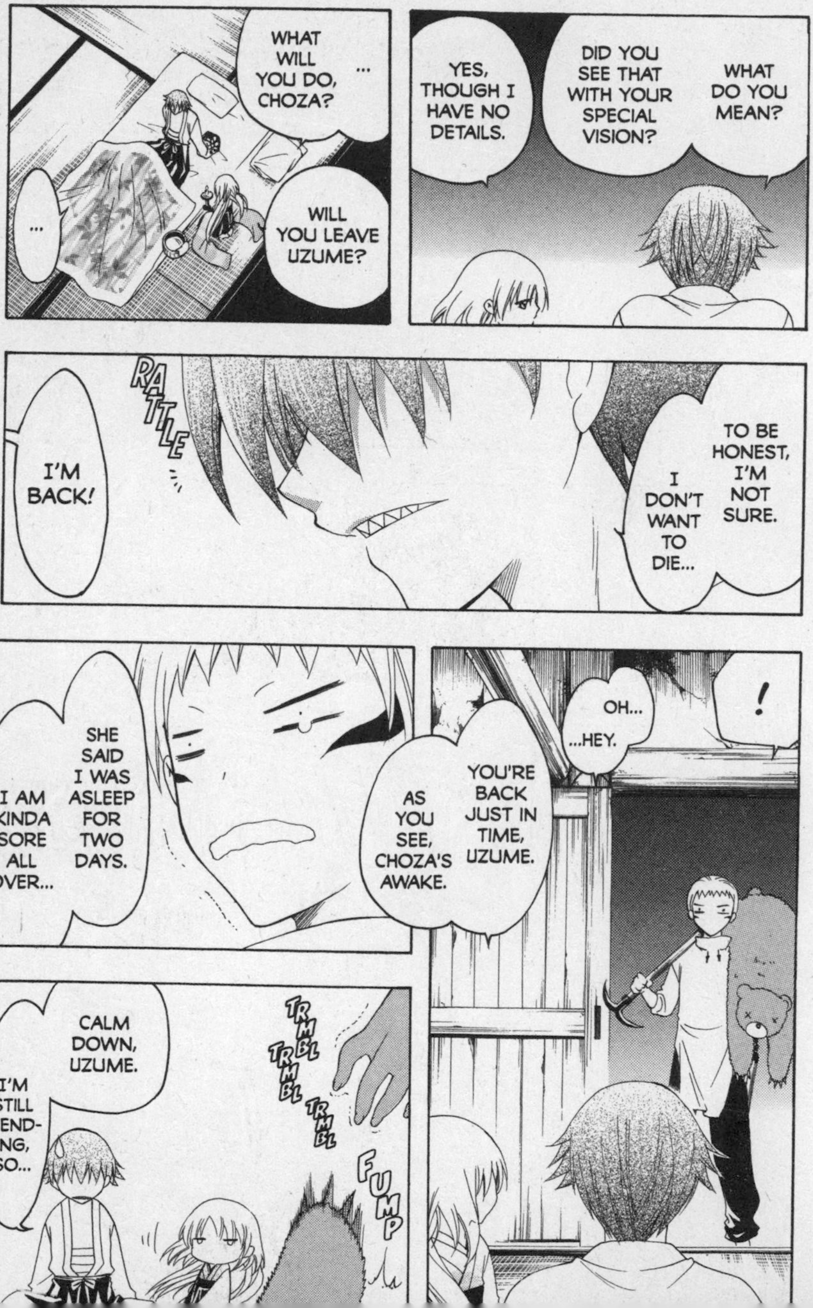
WHAT DO YOU MEAN?
DID YOU SEE THAT WITH YOUR SPECIAL VISION?
YES, THOUGH I HAVE NO DETAILS.
WHAT WILL YOU DO, CHOZA?
...
WILL YOU LEAVE UZUME?
...
TO BE HONEST, I'M NOT SURE.
I DON'T WANT TO DIE...
RATTLE
I'M BACK!
!
OH... ...HEY.
YOU'RE BACK JUST IN TIME, UZUME.
AS YOU SEE, CHOZA'S AWAKE.
SHE SAID I WAS ASLEEP FOR TWO DAYS.
I AM KINDA SORE ALL OVER...
TRMBL TRMBL TRMBL
FUMP
CALM DOWN, UZUME.
I'M STILL MEND-ING, SO...

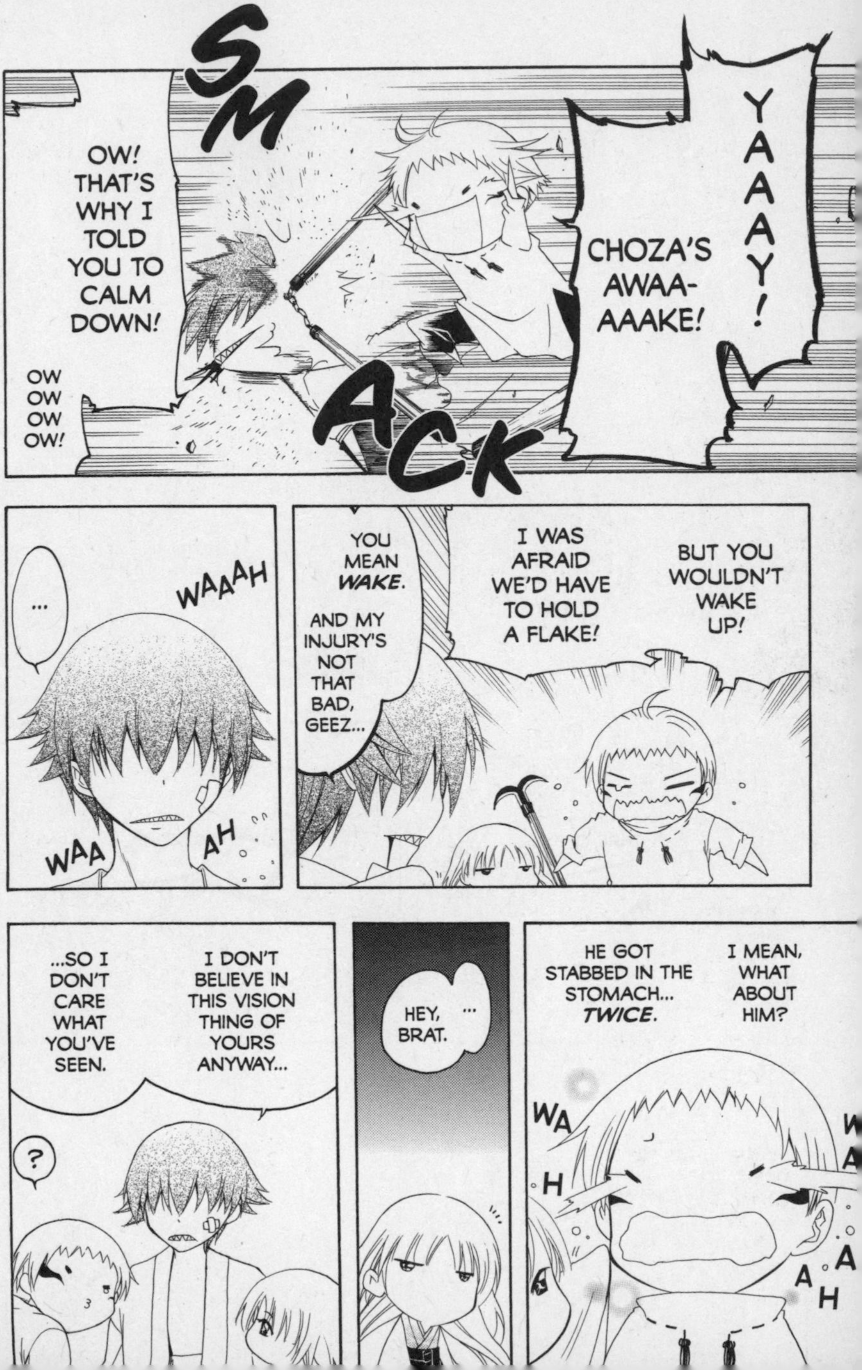
YAAAAY!
CHOZA'S AWAAAAAKE!
SMACK
OW! THAT'S WHY I TOLD YOU TO CALM DOWN!
OW OW OW OW!
BUT YOU WOULDN'T WAKE UP!
I WAS AFRAID WE'D HAVE TO HOLD A FLAKE!
YOU MEAN *WAKE*.
AND MY INJURY'S NOT THAT BAD, GEEZ...
WAAAH
...
WAA AH
I MEAN, WHAT ABOUT HIM?
HE GOT STABBED IN THE STOMACH... *TWICE*.
WAAAH
WAH
...
HEY, BRAT.
I DON'T BELIEVE IN THIS VISION THING OF YOURS ANYWAY...
...SO I DON'T CARE WHAT YOU'VE SEEN.
?

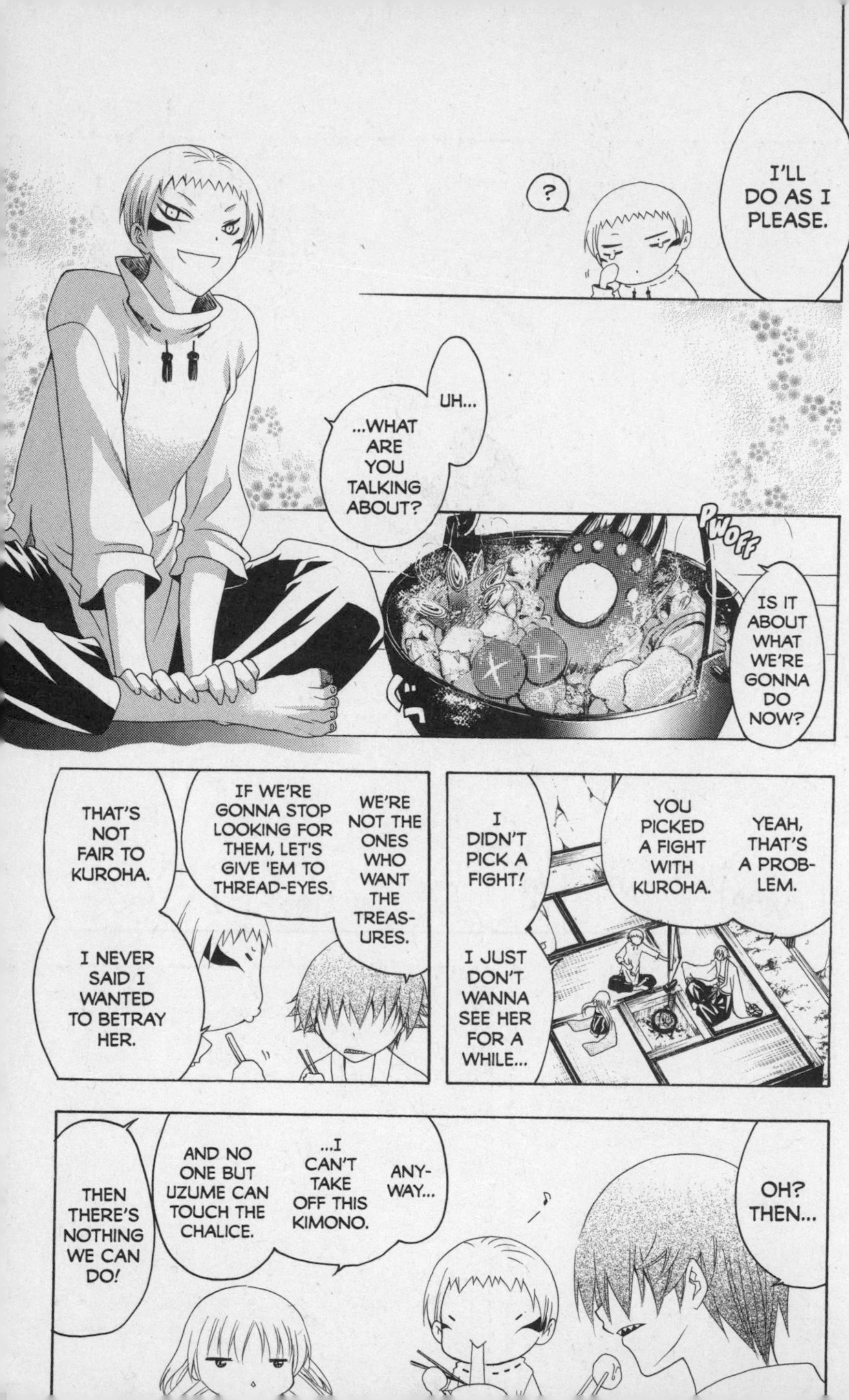
I'LL DO AS I PLEASE.
?
PWOFF
IS IT ABOUT WHAT WE'RE GONNA DO NOW?
UH...
...WHAT ARE YOU TALKING ABOUT?
YEAH, THAT'S A PROB-LEM.
YOU PICKED A FIGHT WITH KUROHA.
I DIDN'T PICK A FIGHT!
I JUST DON'T WANNA SEE HER FOR A WHILE...
WE'RE NOT THE ONES WHO WANT THE TREAS-URES.
IF WE'RE GONNA STOP LOOKING FOR THEM, LET'S GIVE 'EM TO THREAD-EYES.
THAT'S NOT FAIR TO KUROHA.
I NEVER SAID I WANTED TO BETRAY HER.
OH? THEN...
ANY-WAY...
...I CAN'T TAKE OFF THIS KIMONO.
AND NO ONE BUT UZUME CAN TOUCH THE CHALICE.
THEN THERE'S NOTHING WE CAN DO!

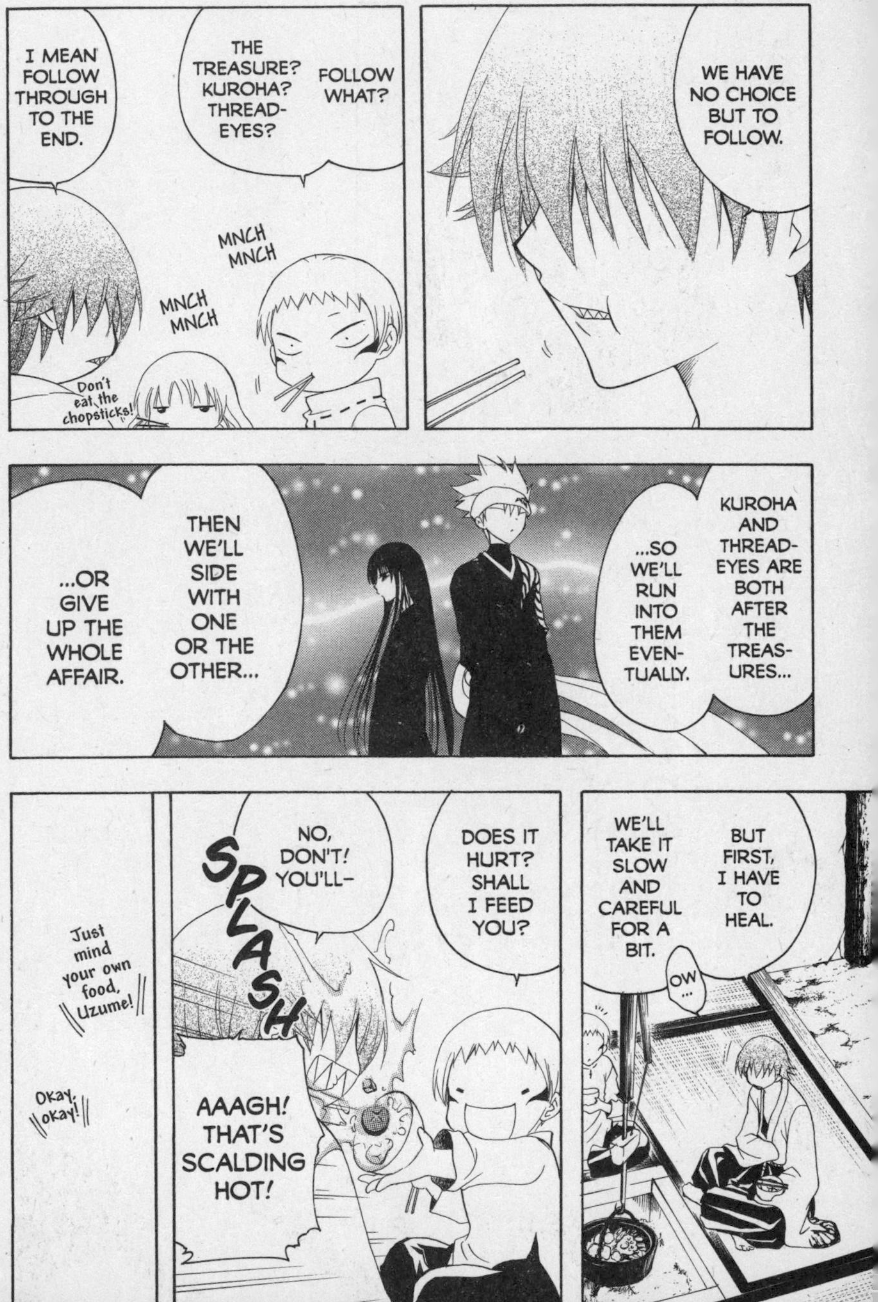
WE HAVE NO CHOICE BUT TO FOLLOW.
FOLLOW WHAT?
THE TREASURE? KUROHA? THREAD-EYES?
I MEAN FOLLOW THROUGH TO THE END.
MNCH MNCH
MNCH MNCH
Don't eat the chopsticks!
KUROHA AND THREAD-EYES ARE BOTH AFTER THE TREASURES...
...SO WE'LL RUN INTO THEM EVEN-TUALLY.
THEN WE'LL SIDE WITH ONE OR THE OTHER...
...OR GIVE UP THE WHOLE AFFAIR.
BUT FIRST, I HAVE TO HEAL.
WE'LL TAKE IT SLOW AND CAREFUL FOR A BIT.
OW...
DOES IT HURT? SHALL I FEED YOU?
NO, DON'T! YOU'LL-
SPLASH
AAAGH! THAT'S SCALDING HOT!
Just mind your own food, Uzume!
Okay, okay!

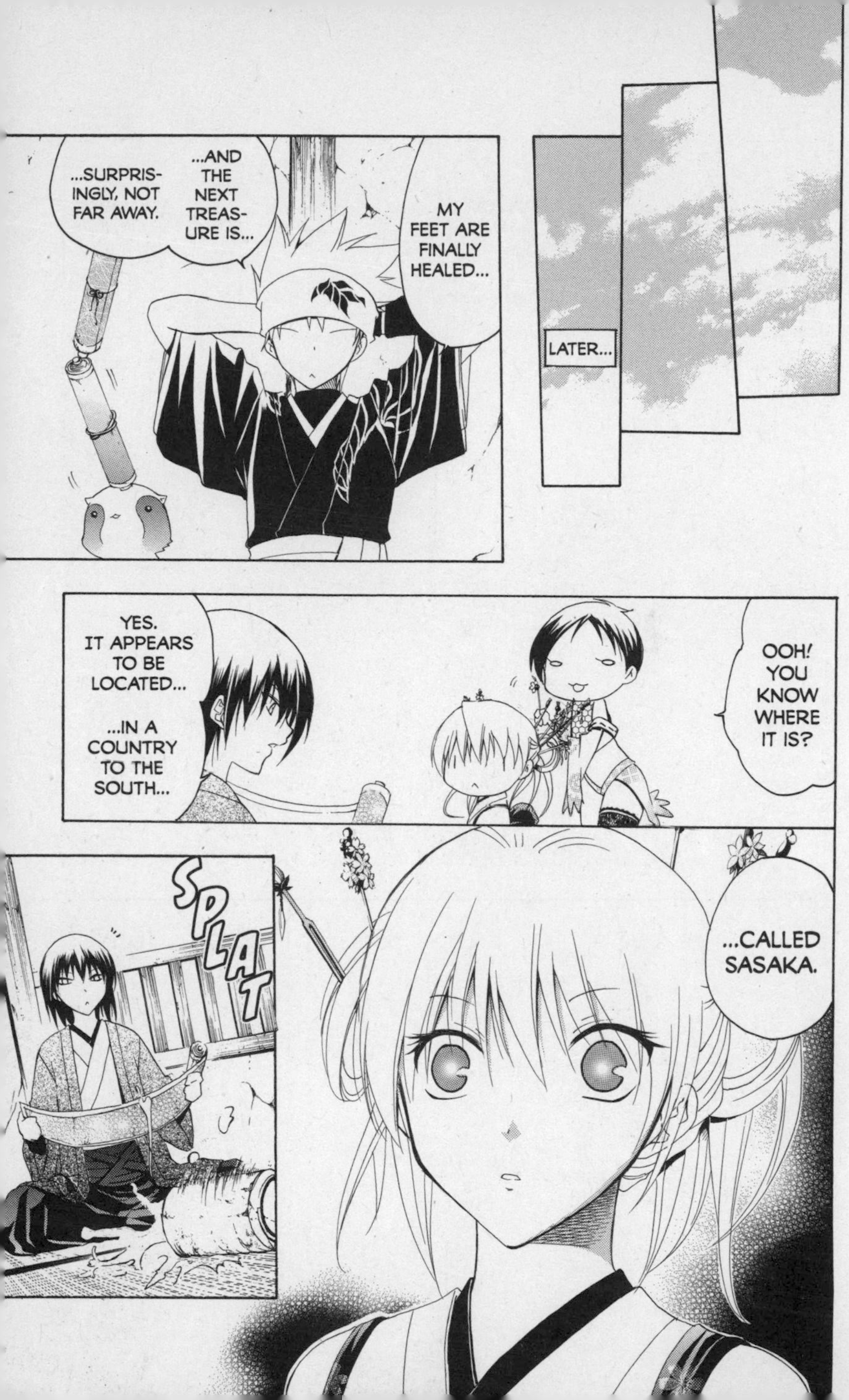
LATER...
MY FEET ARE FINALLY HEALED...
...AND THE NEXT TREAS-URE IS...
...SURPRIS-INGLY, NOT FAR AWAY.
OOH! YOU KNOW WHERE IT IS?
YES. IT APPEARS TO BE LOCATED...
...IN A COUNTRY TO THE SOUTH...
...CALLED SASAKA.
SPLAT

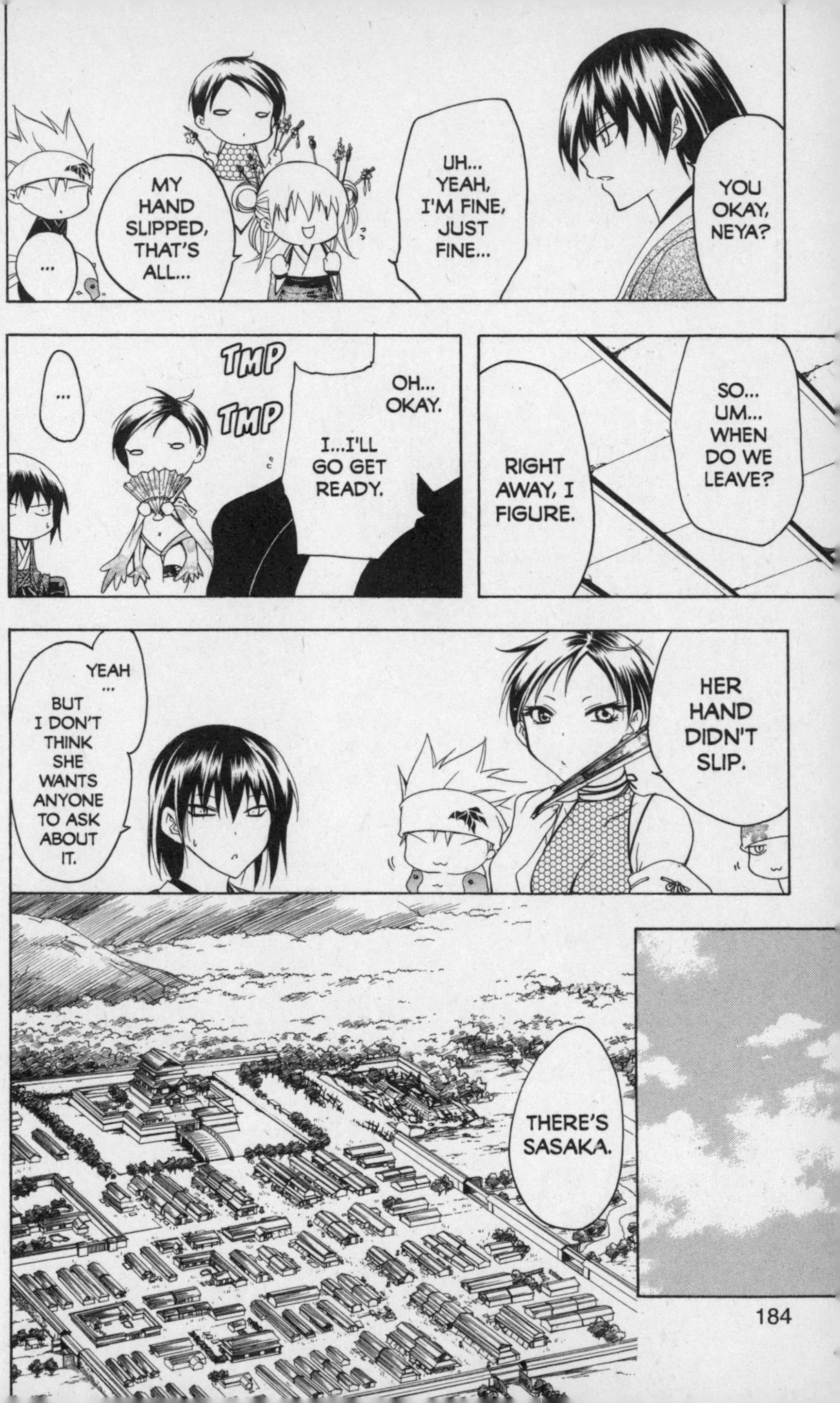

YOU OKAY, NEYA?
UH... YEAH, I'M FINE, JUST FINE...
MY HAND SLIPPED, THAT'S ALL...
...
SO... UM... WHEN DO WE LEAVE?
RIGHT AWAY, I FIGURE.
OH... OKAY.
I...I'LL GO GET READY.
TMP
TMP
...
HER HAND DIDN'T SLIP.
YEAH... BUT I DON'T THINK SHE WANTS ANYONE TO ASK ABOUT IT.
THERE'S SASAKA.

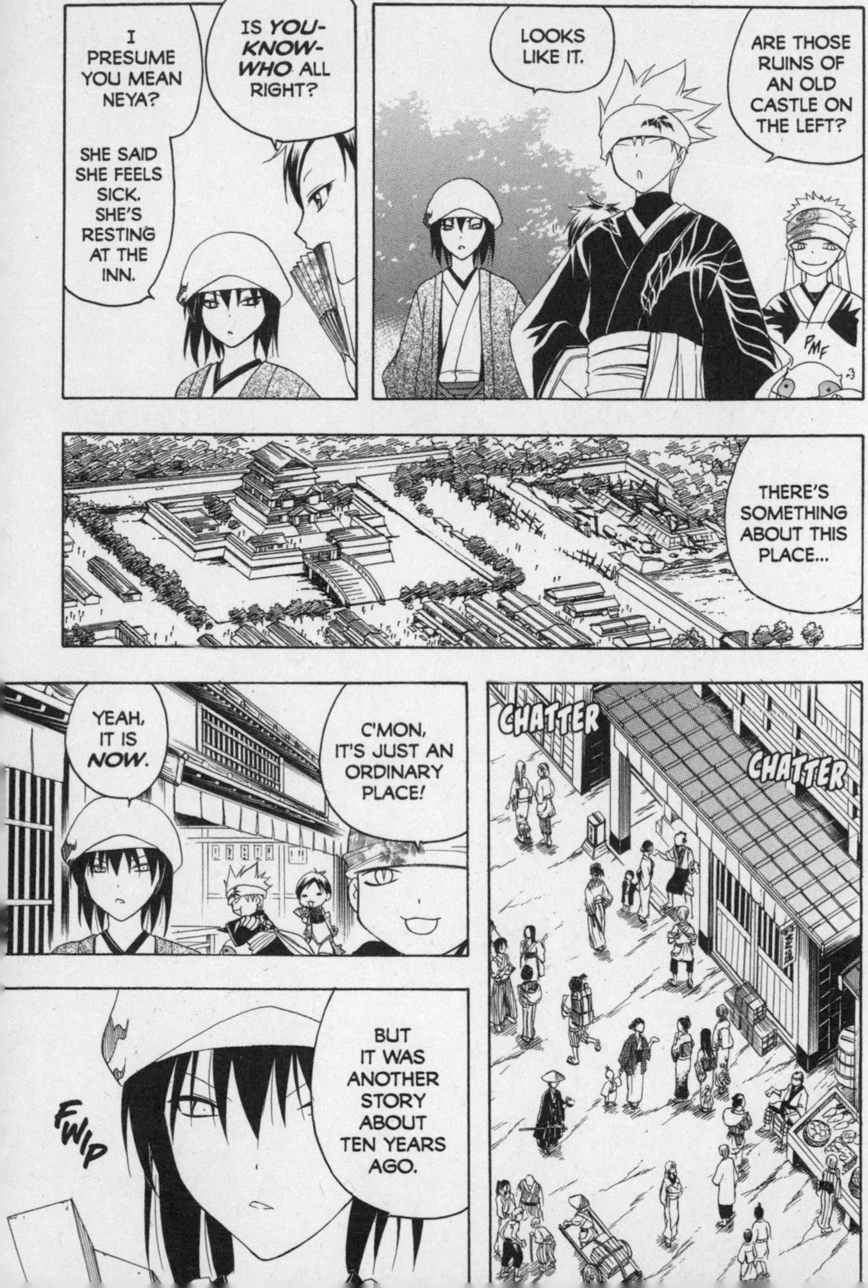
ARE THOSE RUINS OF AN OLD CASTLE ON THE LEFT?
LOOKS LIKE IT.
PMF
IS YOU-KNOW-WHO ALL RIGHT?
I PRESUME YOU MEAN NEYA?
SHE SAID SHE FEELS SICK. SHE'S RESTING AT THE INN.
THERE'S SOMETHING ABOUT THIS PLACE...
CHATTER
CHATTER
C'MON, IT'S JUST AN ORDINARY PLACE!
YEAH, IT IS NOW.
BUT IT WAS ANOTHER STORY ABOUT TEN YEARS AGO.
FWIP

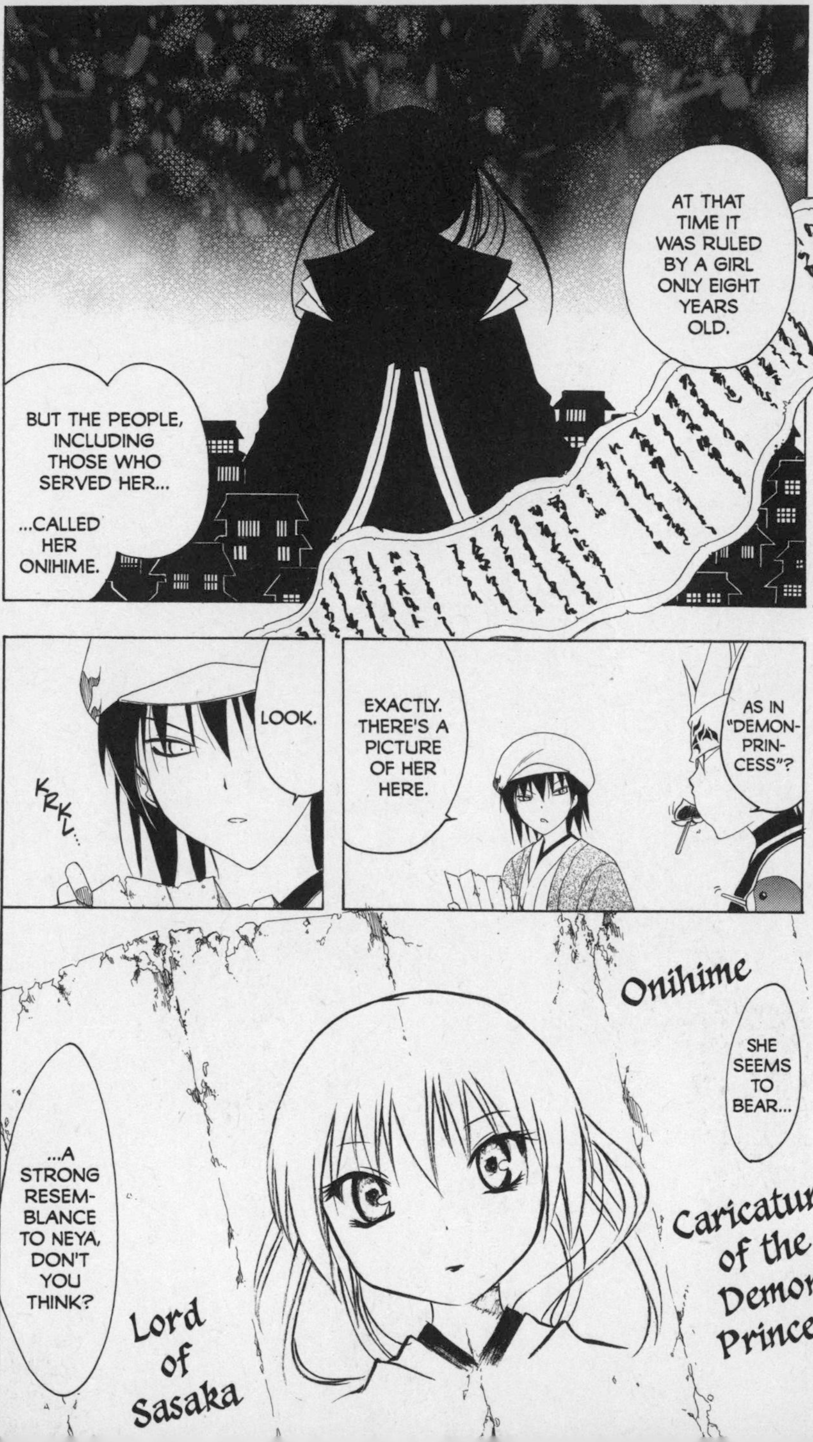
AT THAT TIME IT WAS RULED BY A GIRL ONLY EIGHT YEARS OLD.
BUT THE PEOPLE, INCLUDING THOSE WHO SERVED HER...
...CALLED HER ONIHIME.
AS IN "DEMON-PRIN-CESS"?
EXACTLY. THERE'S A PICTURE OF HER HERE.
LOOK.
KRKL...
Onihime
SHE SEEMS TO BEAR...
Caricature of the Demon Princess
...A STRONG RESEM-BLANCE TO NEYA, DON'T YOU THINK?
Lord of Sasaka

◆ Bonus Manga ◆

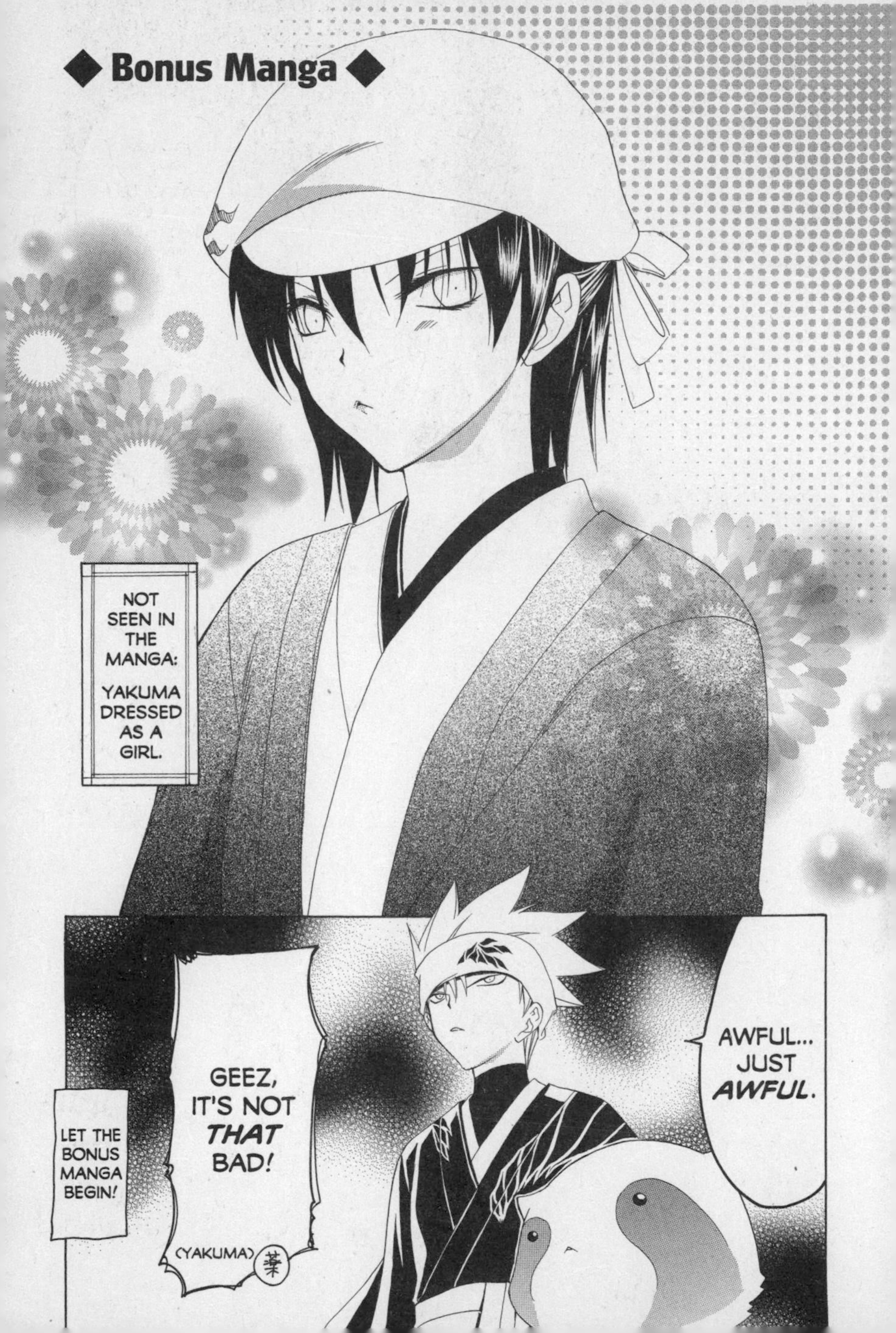

NOT SEEN IN THE MANGA: YAKUMA DRESSED AS A GIRL.
AWFUL... JUST *AWFUL*.
GEEZ, IT'S NOT *THAT* BAD!
(YAKUMA)
LET THE BONUS MANGA BEGIN!

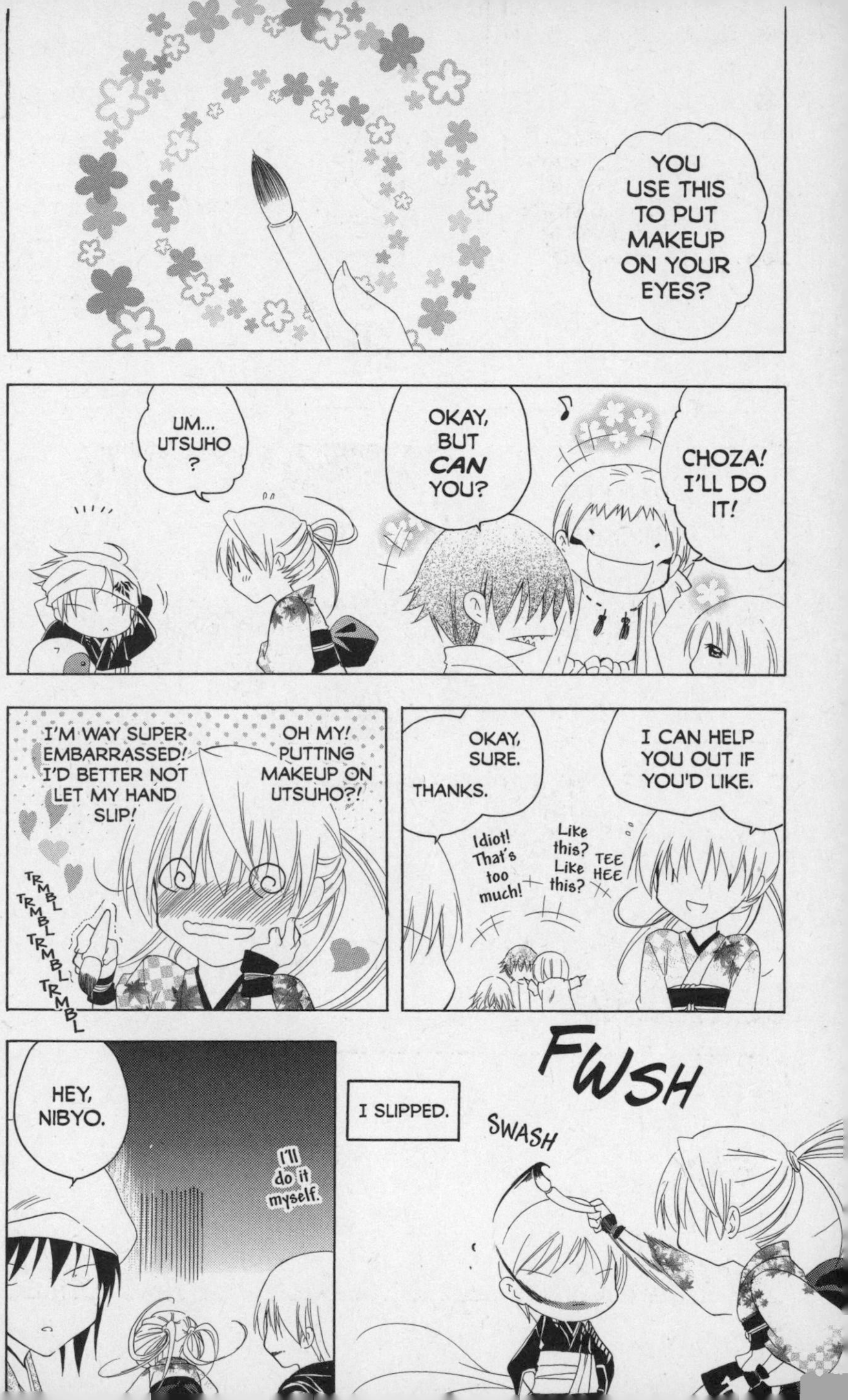
YOU USE THIS TO PUT MAKEUP ON YOUR EYES?
CHOZA! I'LL DO IT!
OKAY, BUT CAN YOU?
UM... UTSUHO?
I CAN HELP YOU OUT IF YOU'D LIKE.
OKAY, SURE.
THANKS.
TEE HEE
Like this? Like this?
Idiot! That's too much!
OH MY! PUTTING MAKEUP ON UTSUHO?!
I'M WAY SUPER EMBARRASSED! I'D BETTER NOT LET MY HAND SLIP!
TRMBL TRMBL TRMBL TRMBL
FWSH
SWASH
I SLIPPED.
HEY, NIBYO.
I'll do it myself.

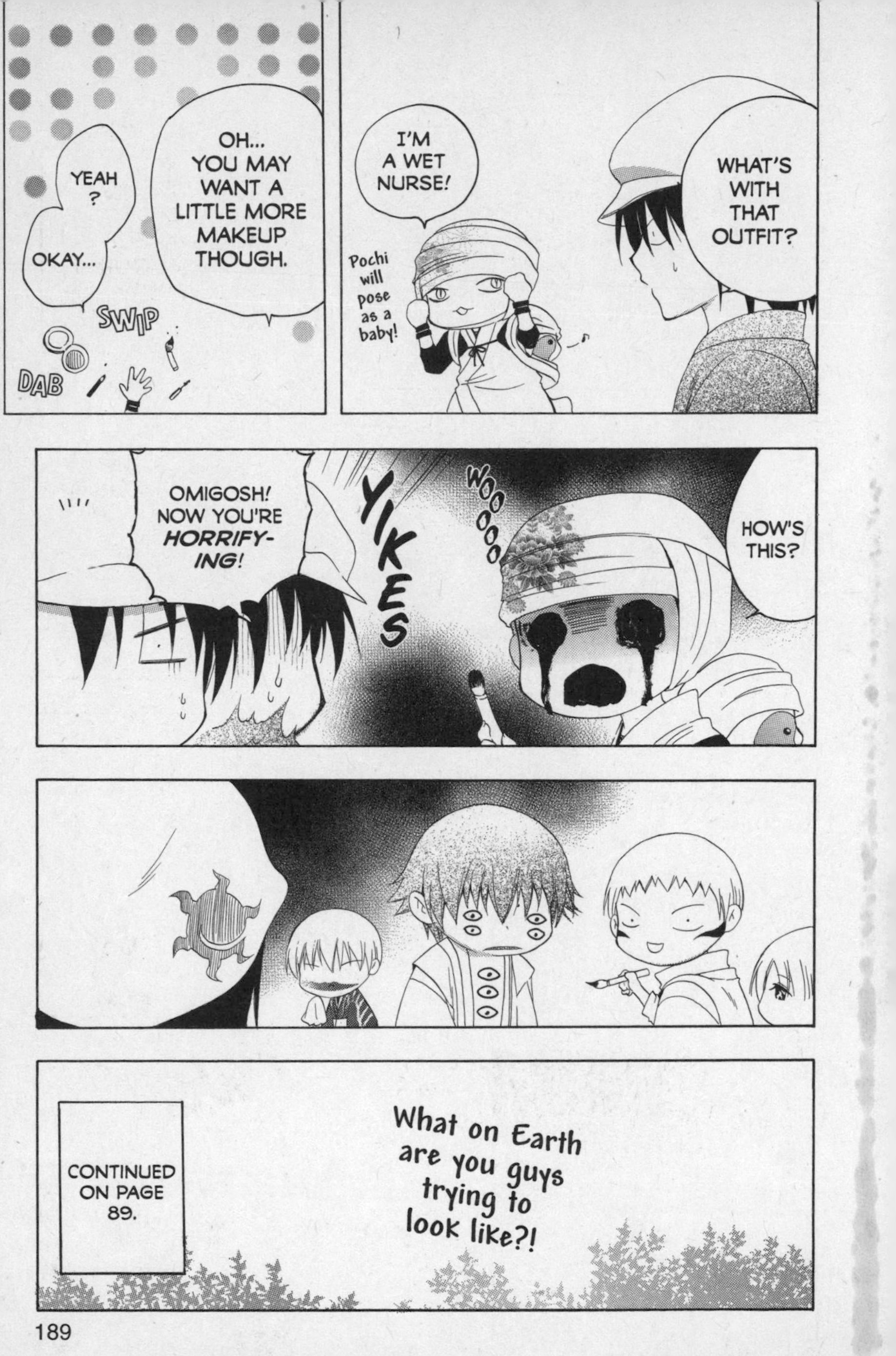
WHAT'S WITH THAT OUTFIT?
I'M A WET NURSE!
Pochi will pose as a baby!
OH... YOU MAY WANT A LITTLE MORE MAKEUP THOUGH.
YEAH? OKAY...
SWIP
DAB
HOW'S THIS?
WOOOOOO
YIKES
OMIGOSH! NOW YOU'RE *HORRIFYING!*
What on Earth are you guys trying to look like?!
CONTINUED ON PAGE 89.

ITSUWARIBITO

Volume 9
Shonen Sunday Edition

Story and Art by
YUUKI IINUMA

ITSUWARIBITO ◆UTSUHO◆ Vol. 9
by Yuuki IINUMA

Original Japanese edition published by SHOGAKUKAN.
English translation rights in the United States of America and Canada arranged with SHOGAKUKAN.

Translation/John Werry
Touch-up Art & Lettering/Susan Daigle-Leach
Design/Matt Hinrichs
Editor/Gary Leach

Printed in Canada

Published by VIZ Media, LLC
P.O. Box 77010
San Francisco, CA 94107

10 9 8 7 6 5 4 3 2 1
First printing, August 2013

www.viz.com

WWW.SHONENSUNDAY.COM

PARENTAL ADVISORY
ITSUWARIBITO is rated T+ for Older Teen and is recommended for ages 16 and up.
FOR OLDER TEEN
ratings.viz.com

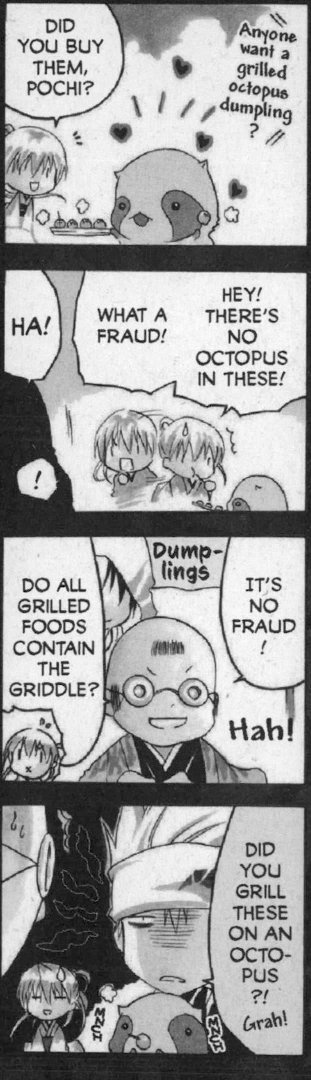
Anyone want a grilled octopus dumpling?
DID YOU BUY THEM, POCHI?
HEY! THERE'S NO OCTOPUS IN THESE!
WHAT A FRAUD!
HA!
!
Dump-lings
IT'S NO FRAUD!
Hah!
DO ALL GRILLED FOODS CONTAIN THE GRIDDLE?
DID YOU GRILL THESE ON AN OCTO-PUS?!
Grah!
MNCH
MNCH

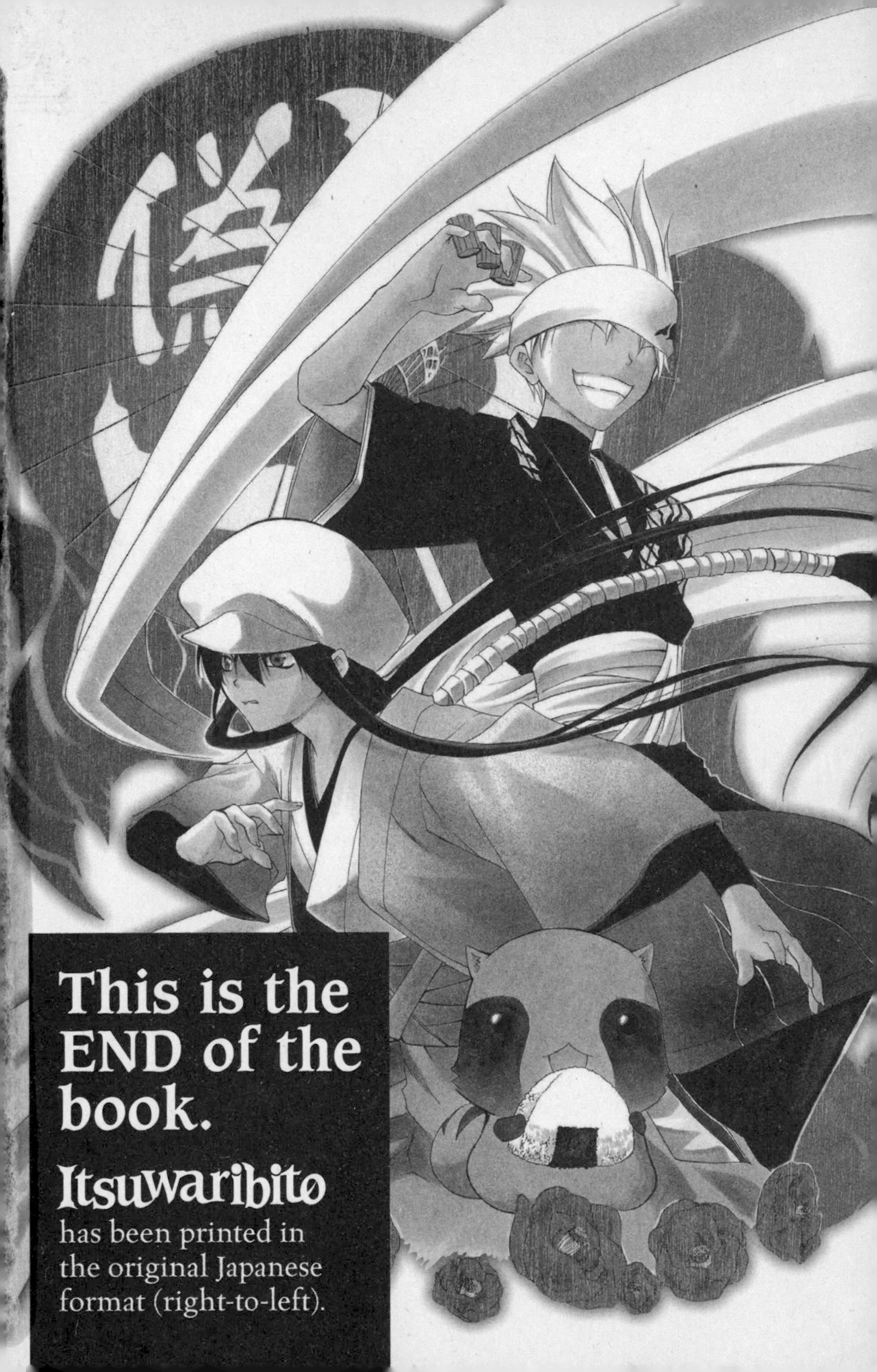

This is the END of the book.

Itsuwaribito has been printed in the original Japanese format (right-to-left).